GERSONIDES

JUDAISM WITHIN THE LIMITS OF REASON

T0313434

THE LITTMAN LIBRARY OF JEWISH CIVILIZATION

Dedicated to the memory of
LOUIS THOMAS SIDNEY LITTMAN
who founded the Littman Library for the love of God
and as an act of charity in memory of his father

JOSEPH AARON LITTMAN
and to the memory of
ROBERT JOSEPH LITTMAN
who continued what his father Louis had begun

יהא זכרם ברוך

'Get wisdom, get understanding:
Forsake her not and she shall preserve thee'

PROV. 4: 5

GERSONIDES

Judaism within the Limits of Reason

SEYMOUR FELDMAN

The Littman Library of Jewish Civilization
in association with Liverpool University Press

The Littman Library of Jewish Civilization
in association with Liverpool University Press
4 Cambridge Street, Liverpool L69 7ZU, UK

www.liverpooluniversitypress.co.uk/littman

Managing Editor: Connie Webber

Distributed in North America by
Oxford University Press Inc., 198 Madison Avenue,
New York, NY 10016, USA

First published in hardback 2010
First published in paperback 2015

Catalogue records for this book are available from the
British Library and the Library of Congress

ISBN 978–1–906764–78–4

Publishing co-ordinator: Janet Moth
Copy-editing: Mark Newby
Index: Seymour Feldman
Design: Pete Russell, Faringdon, Oxon.
Typeset by John Saunders Design & Production

Printed in Great Britain by
CPI Group (UK) Ltd., Croydon, CR0 4YY

To my beloved grandchildren

ANNA, DEAN, NATASHA, AND REESE

Acknowledgements

I WOULD like to express my appreciation of those scholars from whom I have learned much while writing this book: Herbert Davidson, Gad Freudenthal, Ruth Glasner, Alfred Ivry, Menahem Kellner, Sarah Klein-Braslavy, Howard Kreisel, Charles Manekin, and Tamar Rudavsky. All of us are deeply indebted to the master of and pioneer in Gersonides studies, the late Charles Touati.

I want also to thank the editorial staff of the Littman Library for their most helpful advice and assistance in preparing this book: Ludo Craddock, Janet Moth, Mark Newby, and Connie Webber.

Finally, I owe much to my wife Debby, who has for many years encouraged and supported me in my work in Gersonidean scholarship. Her patience with and faith in this project have been invaluable.

Contents

Note on Transliteration   ix

Note on Sources   xi

1. Introduction: Life and Works   1
    Life   1
    Works   3
    Philosophical Environment   7
    Motives and Methods   14

2. The Story of Creation   28
    Gersonides' Cosmological Conundrums   28
    The World Is Not Eternal: It Was Created   31
    The World Is Indestructible   44
    Creation *Ex Nihilo* Is False   48
    Philosophical Cosmology and Biblical Exegesis   55

3. God and his Attributes   59
    How Can the Existence of God Be Proved?   59
    How Can We Speak about God?   69

4. Divine Omniscience   81
    Rabbi Akiva's Dilemma   81
    Gersonides' Solution to Rabbi Akiva's Dilemma   82

5. Divine Providence   104
    The Case for Individual Providence   104
    Why Do the Innocent Suffer?   115
    The People of Israel and Divine Providence   124

6. Divine Omnipotence   131
    'Is Anything Impossible for the Lord?'   131
    Gersonides' Theory of Miracles   134

7. Prophecy   145

What Does Philosophy Have To Do with Prophecy?   145

Gersonides' Theory of Prophecy   147

Moses, the 'Super-Prophet'   159

Are Prophets Infallible?   166

8. Humanity and its Destiny   172

Philosophical and Religious Background   172

Gersonides' Theory of the Intellect   180

The Immortality of the Intellect   185

Gersonides' Critique of Immortality as Conjunction with the
Agent Intellect   189

9. The Torah   198

Do We Need the Torah?   198

How Should We Read the Bible?   208

The Commandments   216

Is the Torah Immutable?   221

10. Conclusion   224

Bibliography   237

Works by Gersonides   237

Primary Sources   238

Secondary Sources   241

Index   251

Note on Transliteration

THE transliteration of Hebrew in this book reflects consideration of the type of book it is, in terms of its content, purpose, and readership. The system adopted therefore reflects a broad approach to transcription, rather than the narrower approaches found in the *Encyclopaedia Judaica* or other systems developed for text-based or linguistic studies. The aim has been to reflect the pronunciation prescribed for modern Hebrew, rather than the spelling or Hebrew word structure, and to do so using conventions that are generally familiar to the English-speaking reader.

In accordance with this approach, no attempt is made to indicate the distinctions between *alef* and *ayin*, *tet* and *taf*, *kaf* and *kuf*, *sin* and *samekh*, since these are not relevant to pronunciation; likewise, the *dagesh* is not indicated except where it affects pronunciation. Following the principle of using conventions familiar to the majority of readers, however, transcriptions that are well established have been retained even when they are not fully consistent with the transliteration system adopted. On similar grounds, the *tsadi* is rendered by 'tz' in such familiar words as barmitzvah. Likewise, the distinction between *ḥet* and *khaf* has been retained, using *ḥ* for the former and *kh* for the latter; the associated forms are generally familiar to readers, even if the distinction is not actually borne out in pronunciation, and for the same reason the final *heh* is indicated too. As in Hebrew, no capital letters are used, except that an initial capital has been retained in transliterating titles of published works (for example, *Shulḥan arukh*).

Since no distinction is made between *alef* and *ayin*, they are indicated by an apostrophe only in intervocalic positions where a failure to do so could lead an English-speaking reader to pronounce the vowel-cluster as a diphthong—as, for example, in *ha'ir*—or otherwise mispronounce the word.

The *sheva na* is indicated by an *e*—*perikat ol*, *reshut*—except, again, when established convention dictates otherwise.

The *yod* is represented by *i* when it occurs as a vowel (*bereshit*), by *y* when it occurs as a consonant (*yesodot*), and by *yi* when it occurs as both (*yisra'el*).

Names have generally been left in their familiar forms, even when this is inconsistent with the overall system.

Note on Sources

REFERENCES to Gersonides' *The Wars of the Lord* (*Milḥamot hashem*) are given in the form *Wars*, 2.4 (ii. 45), where the first two elements refer to book and chapter number of the standard Hebrew edition (Leipzig, 1866) and the parenthetical elements give volume and page number of my own three-volume translation (Philadelphia, 1984, 1988, 1999). In addition, Books 5 and 6 of *Wars* are divided into parts, the numbers for which are given between those for book and chapter (*Wars*, 6.1.6 (iii. 240)).

References to Gersonides' *Commentary on the Torah* (*Perush haralbag al hatorah*) are given in the form *CT*, Num., 'Balak', 197*c* (iv. 132), where the first number refers to the folio of the 1547 Venice edition, and the numbers in parentheses give volume and page number of the Jerusalem edition (1992, 1994, 1997, 1998, 2000). The five volumes of the Jerusalem edition correspond to the five books of the Torah.

Classical sources are all available in the Loeb Classical Library (Harvard University Press) and are cited according to their standard divisions.

ONE

Introduction: Life and Works

Life

SOME PHILOSOPHERS' LIVES are interesting or significant for their philosophies; others have lives without any particular relevance to their thought. Socrates and Spinoza would be examples of the former; Hume and Kant of the latter. Levi ben Gershom, or Gersonides (in Latin), was a member of the latter group. Unlike Socrates he was not brought to trial and executed for his views; nor like Spinoza was he excommunicated from the Jewish community. Nor did he exemplify a third model of a philosopher: a thinker so deeply involved in the life of his community that he becomes its leader in some capacity. Maimonides, his illustrious predecessor, who functioned as a judge for his Jewish community in Egypt, was a prime example of a philosopher engaged in communal affairs. Not so Gersonides: there is no evidence that he had any official position in any of the Jewish communities in Provence where he lived. It may be the case that he had some kind of informal school where he taught philosophy, as some scholars have suggested,[1] but if this is so, such a school was at best private and peripheral to the prevalent pedagogical system characteristic of medieval Judaism. Gersonides was a philosopher, scientist, and biblical exegete whose life was his intellectual activities and the works he composed. Whatever we know about him, and this is not very much, indicates that he spent his entire life in scholarly activities, many of which he pursued as a private, perhaps isolated, individual. Here and there he makes some reference to his family and to a few events that happened in his lifetime: but they are quite sparse. Nevertheless, some facts about Gersonides' life have been established.[2]

He was born in 1288 in the county of Orange in Provence, perhaps in the town of Bagnols, apparently into a family of considerable learning. In his commentaries Gersonides acknowledges his debt to his father (most likely

---

[1] Glasner, 'Levi ben Gershom and the Study of ibn Rushd'.

[2] Touati, *La Pensée philosophique de Gersonide*, 33–48; Shatzmiller, 'Gersonide et la société juive'; Feldman, introduction to *The Wars of the Lord*, i. 3–8.

the talmudist Gershom ben Solomon of Beziers) and his maternal grand-father (Levi Hakohen) for interpretations of several biblical passages.[3] His biblical commentaries clearly testify to a deep knowledge of classical rabbinic literature, which he probably acquired, at least in part, from his father. It is not known who were his teachers of the secular sciences, yet the philo-sophical and scientific culture of Provencal Jewry was considerable, and Gersonides was able to profit from it.[4] He had at least one brother, Solomon, and seems to have married a cousin. However, we have no information about any children from this marriage. We also have no solid information on how he made a living. Although his brother was a well-known physician, it is not certain that Gersonides also practised this profession. It has been suggested by Joseph Shatzmiller that he was a moneylender; after all, this economic activity has at least one advantage, especially for a scholar: there is plenty of time to stay home and study.[5] However he was able to support himself, Gersonides managed to lead a life of relative tranquillity, remaining in Provence all his life, apparently without experiencing any great personal trau-mas, unlike Maimonides, who was forced to leave Spain and live in Morocco and the Holy Land before taking up permanent residence in Egypt. It is not, then, surprising that Gersonides was able to produce an enormous number of philosophical, scientific, and exegetical works.

If there is one fact about his life that is worthy of note, perhaps even remarkable, it is that he had contact with several Christian notables and scholars. This has led some recent scholars to claim that Gersonides was sig-nificantly influenced in his philosophy by Christian scholasticism. This is a matter of some controversy, which will be discussed later. In this context, however, it is important to note that the available evidence only shows that he discussed mathematical and astronomical matters with Christians. Nevertheless, these encounters were productive of several works, some of which he composed at the behest of these Christian contacts.[6]

Gersonides died on 20 April 1344. Although we do not know anything about his progeny, or indeed whether he had any children at all, he bequeathed to us a library of philosophical, scientific, and exegetical works that testify not only to the range of his intellectual concerns but also to his attempt to forge a

    [3] Touati, *La Pensée philosophique de Gersonide*, 34–5 nn. 16–17.

    [4] Freudenthal, 'Les Sciences dans les communautés juives'; Touati, *La Pensée philosophique de Gersonide*, 15–32.

    [5] Shatzmiller, 'Gersonides and the Jewish Community of Orange', 113–15, 120.

    [6] Pines, 'Scholasticism after Thomas Aquinas'; Sirat, Klein-Braslavy, and Weijers (eds.), *Les Méthodes de travail de Gersonide*.

philosophical–scientific synthesis between these secular sciences and Judaism. Unlike many modern scientists or philosophers who either scorn religion or compartmentalize it, he did not see any fundamental discrepancy between the pursuit of truth via reason and its attainment through divine revelation. There is only one truth, with which both reason and revelation must agree. As a philosopher, scientist, and biblical exegete, Gersonides sought to make this agreement evident and firm. Before I illustrate this thesis, let me first say something about his intellectual preoccupations.

Works

As already noted, Gersonides was mostly engaged in philosophical, scientific, and exegetical activities. Although an accomplished talmudist, as his biblical commentaries show, he wrote relatively little on legal matters, and some of his writings on these topics have not survived. In this respect he differs most strikingly from Maimonides, whose legal writings were to him and to many today his most important compositions. In getting a comprehensive picture of Gersonides' literary output we can conveniently categorize it according to the following groups: philosophy, science, and biblical exegesis.[7]

Philosophy

Gersonides' philosophical works can be divided into two sub-groups: independent philosophical treatises and commentaries upon Averroes' commentaries upon Aristotle.

It would appear that his first philosophical writing was a draft of a monograph on the problem of the creation of the world, most likely begun in 1317, which eventually became Book 6 of his most important work, *The Wars of the Lord* (*Milḥamot hashem*). However, this magnum opus would require almost twelve years to complete, for it is an entire philosophical and astronomical encyclopedia and system, consisting of six books, several of which have multiple parts. Within each book Gersonides often ranges over a lot of philosophical and theological territory. For example, in his treatment of divine cognition in Book 3 he takes up Maimonides' theory of divine attributes, criticizing it and offering an alternative account. As a supplement to his discussion of creation he considers the problem of miracles. The work is quite long: the standard printed edition (Leipzig, 1866) consists of nearly 500 closely printed pages; my own recent English translation comprises three

[7] For detailed descriptions of Gersonides' works see Touati, *La Pensée philosophique de Gersonide*, 49–81 and Feldman, introduction to *The Wars of the Lord*, i. 8–30.

volumes. Another independent work, composed in 1319, is his *Treatise on the Correct Syllogism*.[8] Gersonides was deeply interested in logic, and this work shows both his solid familiarity with Aristotelian logic and his willingness to recognize and correct its deficiencies.

In 1321 Gersonides began his project of composing supercommentaries on Averroes' commentaries on Aristotle. By the late thirteenth century Averroes' commentaries had become the major philosophical text alongside the works of Aristotle himself. Averroes wrote three types of commentary: the short (or epitome), the middle, and the long. The first is not a commentary in the literal sense: it is more of a summary and synthesis of Aristotle's work as understood by Averroes. The middle and long commentaries include Aristotle's texts, and in the long commentaries virtually the entire text of Aristotle is reproduced. So a reader of Averroes' middle and long commentaries was actually able to read Aristotle in Hebrew or Latin translations, which were for the most part quite accurate. Moreover, Averroes was quite generous in his quotations from earlier commentators, both Greek and Muslim. In reading Averroes one gains a familiarity with the commentaries of the late Greek commentators, such as Alexander of Aphrodisias, Themistius, and John Philoponus, and the commentaries of the great Muslim philosophers, Al-Farabi and Avicenna. Gersonides' knowledge of philosophy was for the most part acquired from his study of Averroes' commentaries, most of which had become available to him in Hebrew translation. It is not certain that he could read Arabic, and he shows no direct knowledge of any Arabic philosophical work that was not translated into Hebrew.[9]

As far as we know, Gersonides only wrote supercommentaries on Averroes' epitomes and middle commentaries, and the Aristotelian texts that he wrote about were those in logic, natural sciences, and metaphysics. Aristotle's ethics and the Arabic commentaries thereon did not interest him greatly, and he hardly ever refers to them. Nevertheless, one could get some sense of his ethical views from his biblical commentaries, especially from the moral lessons that he extracts and discusses in his exposition of each biblical chapter.[10] The last supercommentary Gersonides wrote was on Averroes' *Middle Commentary on Aristotle's Metaphysics*, about fifteen years before his death. Unfortunately, it is lost. Nevertheless, citations from Averroes' commentary are found in *Wars* and are critically commented upon at length.[11]

---

[8] Manekin, *The Logic of Gersonides*.

[9] Touati, *La Pensée philosophique de Gersonide*, 39; Glasner, 'Knowledge of Arabic among Jewish Scholars'.   [10] Touati, 'Théorie et praxis'.

[11] Touati (*La Pensée philosophique de Gersonide*, 75) believed this to be a supercom-

It is important to note that medieval commentators were not slavish reporters or summarizers of the texts they commented upon. Many of them took upon themselves the responsibility of informing their readers of the problems inherent in the text. Gersonides was one such commentator. Thus, his supercommentaries are important resources for the understanding of his philosophical and scientific thought. As much as he admired both Aristotle and Averroes, he was not reluctant to point out the defects in their works.

Science

Gersonides' scientific writings were primarily devoted to astronomy and mathematics. Since these subjects are not directly relevant to this book, I shall not have much to say about them. Fortunately, they have been studied by competent scholars who have indicated both the originality and significance of his contributions to these fields. As an astronomer Gersonides is noteworthy for his emphasis upon observation and his use of astronomical instruments of his own invention for making these observations. He was prepared to criticize Ptolemy and some of the medieval Arab astronomers for errors in their observations as well as for their theoretical speculations. He rejected, for example, the widely held view, which originated with Ptolemy, that some of the planetary motions should be represented as epicyclical. Nor did he accept the medieval attempt to resurrect the Aristotelian theory of homocentric planetary motions. His adoption of the Ptolemaic theory of eccentric motions was, he believed, more sound, both empirically and mathematically.[12] Part 1 of Book 5 of *Wars* is devoted entirely to astronomy, containing virtually a whole treatise on trigonometry. Because of its length and technical nature it was not included in any of the manuscripts and printed editions of the complete text of *The Wars*.[13] In addition , Gersonides wrote several independent mathematical works, including a partial commentary on

---

mentary on Averroes' *Middle Commentary on Aristotle's Metaphysics*. However, Glasner ('Gersonides' Lost Commentary') has argued that it is a supercommentary on Averroes' *Long Commentary on Aristotle's Metaphysics*.

[12] Freudenthal, 'Human Felicity and Astronomy'; Glasner, 'Gersonides' Theory of Natural Motion'; B. Goldstein, 'Preliminary Remarks'; id., 'The Physical Astronomy of Levi ben Gerson'; Mancha, 'Gersonides' Astronomical Work'.

[13] B. Goldstein, *The Astronomy of Levi ben Gerson*. As far as we know, this part of Book 5 was included in just one complete manuscript of *Wars*, the Turin manuscript, which was destroyed in the fire that devastated the Turin National University Library in 1904 (*Wars*, trans.Touati as *Les Guerres du Seigneur*, 34).

Euclid's *Elements*. Some of these writings were translated into Latin, either in his lifetime or shortly thereafter.[14]

Biblical Exegesis

While composing *Wars*, Gersonides began his project of commenting on the whole Bible, which unfortunately he did not complete. As he was working on Book 4 of *Wars*, 'On Divine Providence', he quite understandably consulted the biblical book that takes up this venerable and controversial issue —the book of Job. Eventually he wrote a complete commentary on Job. Not long afterwards he composed a commentary upon the Song of Songs, which in his interpretation deals with the question of human immortality and thus complements Book 1 of *Wars*. Shortly before he completed *Wars* he wrote a commentary on the book of Ecclesiastes; and after completing *Wars* in 1329 he almost immediately undertook to comment on the remaining books of the Bible. However, there is no evidence that he ever got to commenting upon the Latter Prophets, except for Isaiah. This work has not come down to us, although Gersonides refers to it in his commentaries on Numbers and Deuteronomy.[15]

The most prominent feature of his biblical exegesis is his belief that the Bible teaches philosophy, and that this philosophy is identical with the conclusions reached in his own philosophical works. Nor did he believe, as did Maimonides and others, that the philosophical meaning of the Bible is hidden, indeed intentionally hidden, from the masses. In his biblical commentaries Gersonides frequently discloses the results of his philosophical investigations, even when these conclusions are not commonly held, as for example in his treatment of the Binding of Isaac (Gen. 22). Even in his *Commentary on the Song of Songs*, which, contrary to his usual method of biblical interpretation, treats the biblical book as an allegory, he departs from the traditional understanding of it as a dialogue between God and the people of Israel. Rather, for him it is to be read as a treatise on epistemology with implications for human immortality. Unlike Averroes and Maimonides, Gersonides did not believe that the true, that is, philosophical, meaning of the biblical text had to be restricted to an intellectual elite, rigorously trained in philosophy and the sciences. The reader of Gersonides' biblical commentaries can acquire from them an accurate, if simplified, version of his general

---

[14] Levy, 'Gersonide commentateur d'Euclide'.

[15] *CT*, Num., 'Balak', 197*c* (iv. 132); Deut., 'Shofetim', 227*b* (v. 178); Touati, *La Pensée philosophique de Gersonide*, 63–70.

philosophical position on most topics related to Judaism. In fact, on several subjects, the commentaries are essential complements to *Wars*. In the latter work Gersonides makes no mention of the messiah or the resurrection of the dead, two fundamental principles of Judaism. Nevertheless, he does discuss these issues when he comments on Deuteronomy. For a fuller treatment of his theory of prophecy, especially Mosaic prophecy, one again has to turn to his discussion of these topics in the biblical commentaries.

Philosophical Environment

Very few, if any, philosophers begin or pursue their philosophical enquiries in a vacuum. Before entering any philosophical discussion one has to be familiar with the agenda and language of that particular debate. Both the problems and the terminology used to formulate and solve them are usually set by a canon of philosophical texts transmitted from age to age. For the medieval philosopher this canon was dominated by the works of Aristotle, which had been translated from Greek into Arabic and then into Hebrew and Latin. By Gersonides' time most of Aristotle's writings had been translated into Hebrew, usually as part of Averroes' commentaries. However, the medievals did not read just Aristotle: their Aristotle was transmitted to the Arabs via the Greek commentators, most notably Alexander of Aphrodisias, Themistius, John Philoponus, and Simplicius. Some of these commentators, especially the last, were deeply influenced by the Neoplatonic philosophy of Plotinus and Proclus. Thus, the Aristotle that was studied in the Middle Ages was not a pure Aristotle.

If Aristotle was the dominant philosopher in the Middle Ages, Averroes was his chief commentator. Ironically, his impact upon Jewish and Christian philosophy was greater than his importance for Islamic philosophy. As soon as his commentaries were translated into Hebrew and Latin they became authoritative and gave rise to Hebrew and Latin commentaries on Aristotle and supercommentaries on Averroes. However, there were at least two philosophical topics where Averroes' interpretations and strong defence of Aristotle came into direct conflict not only with Islam but also with Judaism and Christianity: the question of whether the world was created or had existed from eternity and the issue of personal immortality. Averroes' allegiance to Aristotle committed him to defend Aristotle's position on the world's eternity; his interpretation of Aristotle's psychology led him to develop a theory of immortality that deviated substantially from the traditional belief in the individual survival of the whole soul after death. To those medieval philosophers and theologians who were respectful of Aristotle's authority and at the same time committed to a traditional religious understanding of these two doctrines, Averroes' reading and defence of Aristotle could not go unanswered. There were some thinkers, both Jewish and Christian, who were prepared to follow Averroes wherever he led and who sided with him on these two issues, despite the fact that his positions were not orthodox, including Moses Narboni and the so-called 'Latin Averroists'. Gersonides and Thomas Aquinas, however, could not follow Averroes on these and other issues, and proceeded to offer counter-arguments and alternative theories.

Although there was some philosophical activity amongst Jewish thinkers prior to Maimonides, one would not know this from reading Gersonides. His Jewish philosophical library was exceedingly small and almost entirely limited to Maimonides. In his biblical commentaries he mentions Sa'adiah Gaon and Abraham ibn Ezra; he also refers to the latter in chapter 6 of Book 3 of *Wars*. All these references concern biblical exegesis.[16] There is no mention of Sa'adiah's philosophical–theological treatise *The Book of Beliefs and Opinions* or of any of Ibn Ezra's philosophical writings. For Gersonides the only Jewish philosopher of note or value was Maimonides. Nor does he mention any Jewish thinker after Maimonides; in particular, the 'Jewish Averroists', such as Samuel ibn Tibbon, whose translation of Maimonides' *Guide* was used by Gersonides, are never referred to. Nor is there any evidence that would suggest that he was familiar with the more moderate followers of Maimonides in Italy, dubbed the 'Jewish Thomists' by Joseph Sermoneta.[17] Aristotle, Averroes, and Maimonides set his philosophical agenda and the conceptual framework of his discussions.

In recent years there has been an attempt to find some scholastic influence upon Gersonides. In his monograph 'Scholasticism after Thomas Aquinas and the Teachings of Hasdai Crescas and his Predecessors', Shlomo Pines claimed that Gersonides was not untouched by philosophical developments in the Christian world. More recently, an entire book has appeared in support of Pines' thesis.[18] Although an evaluation of this claim can be properly made only after a close investigation of Gersonides' philosophy, it will be useful to make a few observations in the present context.

---

[16] Reference to Sa'adiah Gaon: *CT*, Gen., 'Vayetse', 37*c* (i. 182). References to Abraham ibn Ezra: *CT*, Gen., 'Bereshit', 13*d* (i. 51), 'Vayishlaḥ', 40*d* (i. 101); Exod., 'Va'era', 58*d* (ii. 33), 'Beshalaḥ', 71*b* (ii. 119); Num., 'Balak', 196*b* (iv. 124).

[17] Sermonetta, 'La dottrina dell'intelletto'.

[18] Sirat, Klein-Braslavy, and Weijers (eds.), *Les Méthodes de travail de Gersonide*.

It is most important to note, first, that there is no evidence at all that Gersonides had any knowledge of Latin, the language of philosophical discourse, both oral and written, in the scholastic domain. A recent study devoted to Gersonides' knowledge of languages by Ruth Glasner supports this thesis.[19] It is certainly possible that he could have become familiar with some ideas propounded by the scholastic thinkers from discussions with his Christian contacts, but this knowledge would have been at best second-hand and superficial. It is more likely that he would have avoided such discussions, since philosophy in the Middle Ages was so closely related to theology that a Jew would be reluctant to engage in such encounters with Christians. Indeed, those Christians who were most knowledgeable about philosophy were for the most part theologians as well, and in many instances were located in the universities, to which Jews generally had no access. Moreover, in the Middle Ages theological discussions between Jews and Christians were far from irenic and constructive. It was one thing to talk about some mathematical or astronomical problem, but quite another to discuss a matter of religious import.

Secondly, the period from the late thirteenth century to the fourteenth was a time of striking and significant changes and advances in scholastic thought, especially in logic and natural philosophy, areas in which Gersonides had a deep interest. In logic, the nominalists, especially William of Ockham, developed a *logica moderna* that supplemented the traditional Aristotelian logic with sophisticated semantic theories about meaning and reference.[20] Hardly any of these new ideas can be found in Gersonides' logical writings. In natural philosophy this period saw even more novel ideas, perhaps as an unintended result of an edict issued by the bishop of Paris, Etienne Tempier, in 1277 that listed a large number of heretical philosophical and scientific ideas that henceforth were not to be taught in the universities.[21] Many of these proscribed doctrines were standard Aristotelian or Averroist ideas, especially those in physics and psychology. Their 'indexed' status may have opened the minds of some medieval thinkers to the possibility of plural universes, or that our universe could be infinite, or that matter might be atomic, or that nature could allow for a vacuum, all such ideas being contrary to the basic principles of Aristotelian physics.[22]

[19] Glasner, 'Knowledge of Arabic among Jewish Scholars'; Touati, *La Pensée philosophique de Gersonide*, 38; Feldman, introduction to *The Wars of the Lord*, i. 5–6.

[20] Moody, *The Logic of William of Ockham*, chs. 5–7; Grant, *God and Reason*, 115–47.

[21] Tempier, *Condemnation of 219 Propositions*.

[22] Duhem, *Medieval Cosmology*, 180–2, and see the index for additional references.

Although Gersonides does discuss some of these issues, his treatment is entirely rooted in classical Aristotelian physics, from which he rarely departs. Gersonides took the Aristotelian principles of the absurdity of a vacuum and of an infinite universe for granted and in no way challenged them. Although at times he did deviate from Aristotle, these departures were still within the traditional framework.[23]

What did Gersonides learn from Aristotle? Like every medieval thinker he adopted axiomatically Aristotle's 'two sphere' cosmology, according to which the heavenly and the earthly domains are radically distinct in their chemistry and physics. Whereas the former is immutable and at least ever-lasting, if not eternal, the latter is subject to change and corruption. The two spheres are, however, not totally divorced from each other; rather, the heavenly bodies are important causal agents in the various natural processes that take place on Earth. But these bodies are themselves subject to a different kind of causal relationship: their movers are the 'unmoved movers' of Aristotle's astrophysics that are directly responsible for the motions of the heavenly bodies and indirectly efficacious for terrestrial motion and change. Although Aristotle himself did not arrange this system of unmoved movers in a specific hierarchical scheme, his medieval interpreters did. Perhaps under the influence of Plotinus and his followers, the unmoved movers were now understood as 'separate intellects', incorporeal intermediary agents, which emanate according to a fixed order from some ultimate cause that is absolutely transcendent. The distance between God and the physical universe in Aristotle's cosmology is bridged by the Neoplatonic doctrine of emanation, whereby all reality is tied together and unified by its common descent from the ultimate source, God, or the One.[24]

As we shall see, this apparently tidy scheme raised several vexing questions for medieval thinkers. If Aristotle and Plotinus were right in claiming that the universe is eternal, without beginning or end, how can a medieval thinker, committed to some divinely revealed text which teaches that the world was created, accept Aristotle's cosmology? Something has to give. Maimonides presents this issue in the form of a sharp existential choice: Aristotle or Moses.[25] Moreover, if belief in the concept of creation is oblig-atory for the religious individual, what sort of creation: creation *ex nihilo* or creation from some kind of matter, as Plato suggested according to

[23] Gersonides' deviations will be noted in my treatment of the relevant topics.

[24] Proclus, *The Elements of Theology*; Al-Farabi, *On the Perfect State*; Leaman, *Intro-duction to Classical Islamic Philosophy*, 17–18, 51–4.

[25] Maimonides, *Guide of the Perplexed*, ii. 13 (trans. Pines, 281–2).

Aristotle's reading of the *Timaeus*?[26] In the Middle Ages creation *ex nihilo* was a dogma of all the monotheistic religions. Maimonides himself clearly states that it was what Moses taught.[27] But creation *ex nihilo* seems to contradict the view widely held by philosophers that nothing can come from nothing. Again, medieval thinkers were faced with a cosmological dilemma, this time between Moses and Plato. This dilemma would be quite formidable for Gersonides, who saw himself as a faithful follower of Moses, yet just as loyal to the dictates of sound philosophy. And the latter, he would argue, cannot tolerate the making of something out of nothing.[28]

Moreover, suppose the revealed texts tell us that at some time in the future the dead will return and enjoy a new life. How can this belief be reconciled with the philosophical commitment to the rule of natural law and the impossibility of miracles? If the traditional idea of divine omnipotence is understood in a robust manner, it would not seem to be far-fetched to conceive of God's resurrecting all the dead or even just the righteous among them. However, the very concept of God adopted by the philosophers would seem to preclude the possibility of him giving life to what is already dead. The God of the philosophers is not in the business of violating laws of nature. But this conception of God is quite removed from a deity who is believed to be omnipotent, omniscient, and omnibenevolent. The God of the philosophers seems to be a know-nothing deity with no concern for the sublunar domain. As the medieval Jewish poet and theologian Judah Halevi was to ask, what does the God of the philosophers have in common with the God of Abraham, Isaac, and Jacob?[29] It seemed that the medieval philosophers purchased philosophical sophistication at a very high, perhaps prohibitively high, price. For the medieval thinkers, divine omnipotence and providence, especially the idea that God can intervene in nature and history to bring about wondrous things, were fundamental to their belief system. Yet they had to be understood within some kind of philosophical framework. Can God really do everything? Are miracles possible for a God who is supposed to be immutable? Confronted with the philosophical demand to preserve the natural order and the religious requirement to believe in miracles, Gersonides strove to forge a consistent theory of divine omnipotence and providence that would do justice to both the philosophical and the religious constraints.

The Greek philosophical legacy not only offered a cosmological framework; it also provided a theory of human nature and a picture of human life

---

[26] Plato, *Timaeus*, 49–52; Aristotle, *On the Heavens*, 1.10.280*a*8–9, 3.2.300*b*19; *Physics*, 4.2.209*b*11.   [27] Maimonides, *Guide*, ii. 13 (trans. Pines, 281–2).

[28] *Wars*, 6.1.17 (iii. 322–31).   [29] Halevi, *Kuzari*, iv. 16–17.

that described humanity's place within this cosmic scheme and what an individual should do to achieve fulfilment and happiness. Greek philosophy was not just theoretical; it was also practical. Indeed, one could legitimately characterize ancient philosophy as a praxis, almost a religion, whereby the philosopher attains the goal of salvation by his own means through a rigorous discipline of moral and intellectual growth.[30] If this is so, why do we need revealed religion? What does the latter give us that philosophy does not? Why do we need prophets as well as philosophers? Indeed, what is prophecy in the first place, and if we do have prophets, why bother with philosophy at all? Because of their commitment to both prophecy and philosophy, medieval philosophers were confronted with the pressing question: what are the limits, if any, of reason with respect to revelation? If philosophy is to be allowed, what place and role would it have? Would it just be theology's 'handmaiden'? Or could it be independent of, yet identical with, theology in substance but differ only in language or format?[31]

Even in the Greek philosophical world humanity has a special place, if only because humans are rational animals. Since for many of the philosophers human happiness is conditional upon the attainment of wisdom, the intellect plays the paramount role in the philosophical life. But is the intellectual life by itself sufficient? Is there something else to be gained by its pursuit other than itself? In a few passages in his *On the Soul*, Aristotle raises the question whether or not the soul or some part of it is immortal, as Plato had maintained.[32] Unfortunately, Aristotle did not pursue this question, except in chapter 5 of Book 3 of *On the Soul*, where he suggests that some part or aspect of the intellect is immortal. His language is obscure, and subsequent commentators have spent a great deal of time and energy in trying to decipher it. This was especially true for the medievals, who inherited from their religious traditions the doctrine of the immortality of the entire human soul and its individual reward or punishment in some eternal realm. How could this idea be reconciled with Aristotle's apparent restriction of immortality to the intellect alone and his indifference to the whole notion of reward and punishment in an afterlife?

Some of the later Greek commentators on Aristotle, most notably Alexander of Aphrodisias and Themistius, tried to clarify Aristotle's obscure remarks and bequeathed to the medievals divergent interpretations of Aristotle's language. Muslim philosophers developed these ideas in various

[30] Hadot, *What Is Ancient Philosophy?*

[31] Aquinas, *Summa Theologiae*, I q. 1 arts. 1, 5; Averroes, *The Decisive Treatise*.

[32] Aristotle, *On the Soul*, 1.4.498*b*18–19, 2.1.413*a*6, 2.2.413*b*25–6; Plato, *Phaedo*.

ways, culminating in the highly complex theory of the human intellect and its immortality propounded by Averroes in several of his commentaries and treatises.[33] On this issue Maimonides is, like Aristotle, tantalizingly unclear. Although in his legal works he does argue for an intellectualized version of immortality, in contrast to certain traditional Jewish notions that were to him vulgar and crass, he does not go as far as some of the Muslim thinkers who denied individual immortality.[34] In the *Guide*, however, his treatment of this topic is scattered and sparse, and some commentators have argued that he denied individual immortality.[35] Although Gersonides does not mention Maimonides at all in his extended discussion of immortality, it is quite clear that he too shares the latter's intellectualized version of immortality. His problem will be whether this thesis implies Averroes' doctrine of impersonal immortality.

All these topics are examples of what Thomas Aquinas called 'preambles of faith', that is, issues which both philosophers and theologians can discuss using reason alone without recourse to revealed religion. Indeed, in some cases revealed religion and philosophy reach the same conclusions. But for medieval religious thinkers there were subjects that were peculiar to their belief systems, some of which seemed either to defy or transcend rational belief. For the Jewish thinker, beliefs such as the unique status of the Torah and of Israel would be examples of doctrines for which it would seem no philosophical justification is available. For Christian theologians, such as Aquinas, beliefs of this kind are 'articles of faith', or 'mysteries', which are not accessible to rational argument or analysis.[36] However, for a thinker not especially disposed to embrace the mysterious, like Gersonides, this appeal to the 'asylum of ignorance' was a route to be avoided or adopted only as a last resort. What, then, was Gersonides to do with such beliefs? How could he make them reasonable?

This task became more urgent for those whose compatibilism was so pronounced that they virtually identified revealed religion with philosophy. Averroes, in Islam, was an example of this approach. To demonstrate this compatibility, he justified philosophy by showing that the Quran not only permits its study but mandates it. He does this by a very free exegesis of

---

[33] Davidson, *Alfarabi, Avicenna and Averroes on Intellect*.

[34] Maimonides, *Commentary on the Mishnah, San.* 10; *Mishneh torah*, 'Laws of Repentance', 9.

[35] Maimonides, *Guide*, i. 74, seventh argument (trans. Pines, 221); Altmann, 'Maimonides on the Intellect', 85–91; Ivry, 'Conjunction in and of Maimonides and Averroes', 241–7.　　　　[36] Aquinas, *Summa Theologiae*, I q. 1 arts. 1–2.

several verses from the Quran that convinced very few.[37] Maimonides had to adopt a different approach because his compatibilism was not as thorough-going as that of Averroes. For Maimonides there are questions that cannot be resolved to the satisfaction of the philosopher or the theologian. Some of these questions are religiously defining, or basic, such that to deny them is to exclude oneself from that faith community. If they are incompatible with philosophy, then philosophy has to withdraw and recognize its limitations. In this respect Maimonides and Aquinas were alike. For both thinkers, the creation of the world at the beginning of time is an example of a doctrine that is admittedly rejected by the philosophers, yet taught by the Bible. It cannot be absolutely shown to be true by philosophical means, but nor can it be shown to be false by such means. The honest philosopher or theologian has to admit here the incompetence of reason. Gersonides, however, was not in such a rush to throw away his thinking cap and recite 'I believe with perfect faith' concerning this and many other theological beliefs of Judaism.[38] Although he differed from Averroes on several fundamental issues, as we shall see, he is closer to the Muslim philosopher than he is to Maimonides, who in his eyes is more a theologian in the service of faith than a philosopher pursuing the truth, no matter where it leads him.

Motives and Methods

Gersonides' philosophical and religious aims are expressed most manifestly in his two major works, *The Wars of the Lord* and the *Commentary on the Torah*, supplemented by several of his commentaries on the Prophets and Wisdom writings. To get a good sense of what he was trying to accomplish one could profitably begin by looking at the invocations and introductions to these works. It was quite common for medieval authors, especially in the Muslim and Jewish traditions, to preface their books with some kind of liturgical poem praising and thanking God, no matter what the subject of the book.[39] Gersonides continued this practice, and he begins *Wars* with a poem that reveals much about his philosophical programme. Like many such

---

[37] Averroes, *The Decisive Treatise*, 297–8.

[38] In his commentary to the Mishnah, *San.* 10, Maimonides lays down thirteen theological principles that in his opinion define Judaism. In several forms this creed was included in synagogue worship. One such version prefaces each principle with the formula 'I believe with perfect faith . . .'. In modern times this version has been set to music.

[39] Sa'adiah Gaon, *The Book of Beliefs and Opinions*, introductory treatise, ch. 1 (trans. Rosenblatt, 3); Maimonides, *Guide*, 'Introduction to the First Part' (trans. Pines, 5).

Hebrew liturgical poems, it is a composite of many biblical verses woven together but unified according to several key motifs. These themes announce what will be his main concerns in the treatise.

The poem begins with Psalm 33: 6: 'By the word of God the heavens were made.' Several sentences later, Gersonides tells us what this 'word' really means: 'Through His will the heavens were made beautiful.' Following an exegetical tradition that is at least as old as Sa'adiah Gaon, Gersonides identifies the divine word with God's will.[40] In short, the heavens and in general the whole world is the creative act of God's free will, not the eternal and necessary outcome of either the laws of nature or the essence of the deity, as was maintained by some of the Greek and Muslim philosophers. But he hastens to add that although created, 'it [the heavenly domain] is so firmly established that it will not change'. Here Gersonides foreshadows his theses that nature is subject to a fixed order such that miracles really do not violate its laws and that the world as a whole will not perish. For how can something made wisely and beautifully by a perfect craftsman be subject to change and destruction?[41]

Gersonides next takes parts of verses from Ezekiel and Job and combines them: 'All the bright lights of the heavens [Ezek. 32: 8] He brings forth for loving kindness to do whatever He commands them [Job 37: 12–13].' The key word here is 'loving kindness' (*ḥesed*). Gersonides uses it to link the segments from Ezekiel and Job to express his firm belief that God's creation of the world was an act of love and care for his creatures. This love is perpetual, as are the heavenly bodies, whose continuous activities benefit the terrestrial world. This theme is seconded in the opening invocation to his *Commentary on the Torah*, where Gersonides praises God for having brought the world into existence through grace and his desire to benefit his creatures according to a definite providential plan that never ceases to be operative.[42] Herein Gersonides lays the groundwork for his discussion of divine providence in Book 4 of *Wars*, a theme that resounds throughout his biblical commentaries as well.

The next motif in the invocation to *Wars* is the creation of man. 'God chose for Himself a rational creature ... Man alone shines ... by virtue of the excellency of dignity that God has given him through knowledge and understanding in his heart.'[43] In the invocation to the *Commentary on the Torah*

---

[40] *Wars*, 'Invocation' (i. 87).

[41] On miracles: *Wars*, 6.2.9–12 (iii. 470–97). On the indestructibility of the world: *Wars*, 6.1.16 (iii. 318–20). [42] *CT*, 'Invocation', 2*a* (i. 1).

[43] *Wars*, 'Invocation' (i. 88–9).

this theme is repeated: 'Since God has provided man in such a marvelous manner with the proper limbs and organs to preserve his existence, it is not impossible that he endow him with the means whereby he will proceed to his true perfection, which is the acme of what it is to be a man.'[44] This instrument for the attainment of human perfection is reason. Indeed, the creative scheme as depicted in the Genesis story concludes with the creation of humanity, which, Gersonides believes, implies that humanity is the crown of creation. For in humanity divine wisdom is especially mirrored, albeit partially. Departing from Maimonides' rejection of anthropocentrism,[45] Gersonides has no compunction about elevating humanity and glorifying its position in the scheme of things. For unlike any other of God's creatures humans have free will, just as God has. As we shall see, in Book 3 of *Wars*, this shared feature will enable humans to do something that neither the angels nor the heavenly bodies can do: humans alone can freely deviate from the general natural order, whose laws would normally dictate a course of behaviour but which can be subverted by humanity's free will.

God's free will and love are also manifest in his choosing a particular family and its descendants to be his people: 'From mankind God has chosen for Himself a kingdom of priests and a holy nation.'[46] Although this election of Israel is hardly mentioned in *Wars*, Gersonides gives it his full attention throughout his biblical commentaries. What makes Israel special is the Torah; for it 'gives them access among the angels and through it the soul becomes wise'.[47] This wisdom, the *Commentary on the Torah* adds, is our happiness, for 'those who live by it perfectly attain true felicity'.[48] Here Gersonides intimates that our access to the angelic domain, that is, our immortality, is contingent upon our attainment of intellectual perfection, which after all is what makes us unique amongst terrestrial creatures. This is the topic of Book 1 of *Wars*.

The invocation to *Wars* ends with a song of praise consisting of various biblical verses highlighting several of God's attributes, although God is 'above all blessing and praise' (Neh. 9: 5). Through his benevolence we are the recipients of all kinds of goods, most notably knowledge (Prov. 2: 6–10). Indeed, existence itself is the manifestation of God's favour and pleasure. Yet God's being and essence are so great that no one can withstand them (Joel 2: 11), that is, no one can comprehend them. It is best to praise God in silence by knowing him to the best of our ability, fully aware that our knowledge will

---

[44] *CT*, 'Invocation', 2*a* (i. 1).   [45] Maimonides, *Guide*, iii. 13 (trans. Pines, 451–2).
[46] *Wars*, 'Invocation' (i. 89).   [47] Ibid.   [48] *CT*, 'Invocation', 2*a* (i. 1).

always fall short of the mark. In Book 3 and in part 3 of Book 5 of *Wars* Gersonides discusses the topic of divine attributes and offers an alternative to Maimonides' extreme version of negative theology, which in Gersonides' eyes completely closes the door to understanding God and thus prevents our attaining human happiness. If, as Maimonides says, one of the main commandments is to know and love God, then there must be some way of fulfilling this commandment without remaining entirely mute and empty-headed.

In his introduction to *Wars* Gersonides explicitly states why he wrote the treatise. His philosophical predecessors, Greek, Muslim, and Jewish, did not adequately solve some of the most important problems in philosophy, especially those that impinge upon religion. Their solutions were either false, insufficiently defended, unclearly formulated, or incomplete. Since these problems are so fundamental to our achievement of human happiness, their proper solution is imperative. Indeed, the errors committed by these philosophers and theologians have been so grievous that they can be considered 'wars against God'; and the correction of these errors can be regarded as 'wars on behalf of God'. The title, *The Wars of the Lord*, is therefore most appropriate.[49]

The problems picked out for special treatment are seemingly quite specific: the immortality of the soul (Book 1), dreams, divination, and prophecy (Book 2), divine cognition (Book 3), divine providence (Book 4), the heavenly domain (Book 5), and the creation of the world (Book 6). Two subsidiary theological issues are also considered important enough for special discussion: miracles and 'testing the prophet'. The former is intimately connected with the creation of the world: the latter is obviously related to the subject of prophecy. Gersonides devoted a separate book of *Wars* to each of the six major problems and ended the treatise with his discussion of the two minor topics.

Nevertheless, Gersonides' philosophical agenda is not so narrowly conceived or executed. In his treatment of these issues he ranges over considerable philosophical and theological territory. In discussing immortality, for example, he devotes one long chapter to a detailed analysis of the philosophical problem of universals, which prima facie does not seem to have anything to do with our survival after death. Similarly, in Book 3, on divine cognition, Gersonides addresses the general issue of divine attributes, not just the attribute of knowledge, and Book 6, on the creation of the world, is replete with

---

[49] *Wars*, 'Introductory Remarks' (i. 98).

discussions of some of the fundamental topics in Aristotelian natural philosophy, such as time, motion, and infinity. To read and absorb the entire work is to have achieved not only an almost complete picture of Gersonides' general philosophy but of his specific philosophical understanding of Judaism as well. This undertaking, however, needs to be supplemented by the biblical commentaries, which take up themes that are specific to Judaism as a religion but which in Gersonides' hands become philosophical proof-texts for philosophical ideas.

Underlying Gersonides' philosophical project is a basic assumption, which he shared with several medieval philosophers, that human happiness is the perfection of what it is to be human, namely, the perfection of the intellect. If this is what makes us different from the rest of terrestrial life, then this is what constitutes our essence and our *telos*, or natural goal. It is the *ad quem* of our human journey. For Gersonides this programme is to be achieved not just by the mastery of one discipline, say biblical exegesis or rabbinic jurisprudence, but by competence at least in all the relevant intellectual disciplines, especially those that Aristotle called the 'theoretical sciences': mathematics, the natural sciences, and metaphysics, or 'first philosophy'. It is then not accidental that Gersonides chose to become more than just proficient in all these secular disciplines as well as the specifically Jewish areas of Bible study and rabbinics. All these studies contribute towards the achievement of intellectual perfection and human felicity.

Thus when Gersonides includes astronomy in what purports to be a philosophical book, or when he devotes several sections of the treatise to biblical exegesis, he is not padding his book with superfluous material. One may well wonder why the correct astronomical theory is necessary in fighting 'the wars of the Lord'. But the Bible tells us 'the heavens declare the handiwork of God' (Ps. 19: 1). To know all we can about the heavenly domain is to know a great deal about God's creation, and in particular the wisdom exemplified in this creation. Knowledge about the motions of the planets, for example, will include knowing something about what makes them move, and this in turn will lead us to get some idea of how the movers of these bodies are related to God. So astronomy is part of the story that needs to be told. Analogously, when in Book 4 of *Wars* Gersonides takes up the question of divine providence, he brings into the discussion the book of Job, which he considers to be a philosophical dialogue between Job and his friends. At first sight this seems to be an intrusion into a book that hitherto has been almost entirely philosophical. Yet for Gersonides the Torah and philosophy are not alien to each other. Each supplements and complements the other.

Indeed, in the introduction to his *Commentary on the Torah* he tells his readers that the aim of the Torah is to teach us the path to human perfection, and that this instruction will involve the revelation of important 'secrets of existence', that is, the laws of nature and the principles of metaphysics, beginning of course with the story of creation. For example, right at the outset of this story the Torah explicitly states that the universe did not come about through chance but is the product of an 'agent cause' who acts intentionally and voluntarily.[50] Throughout his biblical commentaries Gersonides is quite generous in revealing these 'secrets', many of which are developed and explicated fully in his philosophical treatise. His intellectual programme is therefore an integrated whole, not to be separated into isolated compartments. Indeed, the fruit of this integrated intellectual quest is the attainment of human immortality. It is, then, quite understandable why Gersonides begins his 'war for the Lord' with this topic. The reader is told at the outset where he is going and what the reward will be for the effort he will have to expend in following Gersonides on this road.

In the introduction to his *Guide*, Maimonides not only stated the motives that led to his writing the book but also laid down several methodological rules for its proper study. Since the main goal of the treatise is to elucidate some fundamental words and parables found in the Bible, many of which deal with the 'secrets of creation' (that is, the natural sciences) and the 'secrets of the divine chariot' (that is, metaphysics), Maimonides had already limited his audience to an intellectual elite capable of understanding and appreciating these secrets. Following the rabbinic dictum that these subjects should be revealed only to a select few and then only orally, Maimonides stipulated the requirements that single out this select group and excused himself for having divulged these secrets in writing. Moreover, even in explaining these difficult passages Maimonides confessed that at times he too would have to resort to using metaphorical language and parables. So the book turns out to be, at least in several subjects, a meta-parable, requiring further elucidation. It is no wonder that ever since its composition commentaries have been written on it.

Maimonides further warned his readers that the insights gained by his analysis of the biblical text are not easily grasped even by those who are qualified to understand them. For the truths that are to be revealed are difficult and often escape our understanding almost immediately after we grasp them. In this respect philosophers are no different from anyone else; for unlike the

[50] *CT*, Gen., 'Bereshit', 9*a*–*b* (i. 20–1).

prophets their intellects are subject to confusion, doubt, and error. Human intellect is essentially imperfect and fallible. It is not surprising, then, that Maimonides insisted that his readers study his book with special care, noting the sequence of chapters, while at the same time expecting the clarification of one chapter by statements in another chapter. He complicated matters further by informing us that his ideas are scattered throughout the work, thus warning the reader not to expect a systematic and organized treatment of every subject. Moreover, he closed the introduction with an additional caveat: take note of any contradictions that are found in the book. This is most surprising. Most authors would be embarrassed to be found to be contradicting themselves. But Maimonides explicitly tells us that he has done so intentionally, and indeed clarifies that his contradictions are of two types, one of which is purposely designed to conceal the truth as much as to reveal it. This last point has occasioned considerable controversy and discussion amongst both medieval and modern commentators, resulting in two radically diverse schools of interpretation. Those who look for intentional contradictions in the *Guide* maintain that there is an exoteric teaching, addressed to a philosophically educated but not expert reader, and an esoteric, or real, meaning, directed at the more advanced philosophical student. It turns out, the 'esotericists' claim, that this concealed meaning is the doctrine of Aristotle. Those who read the book as it is written and seek no hidden secrets see no fundamental disagreement between the *Guide* and Maimonides' earlier and less philosophical writings. For them, his work displays a basic ideological unity. Thus, even as one begins to plunge into the 'great sea' of *The Guide of the Perplexed*, perplexities immediately surface. Readers of the vast Maimonidean literature are aware of the almost endless stream of commentary on this particular point.[51]

Gersonides would have nothing of this! The introduction to *Wars* is almost a direct refutation of Maimonides' methodology. Although Gersonides was perfectly aware of the difficulties involved in the subjects of his investigation and the need to have acquired the appropriate prerequisites for the task at hand, he does not scare or insult the reader. To be sure, not everyone will be interested in a philosophical examination of the basic doctrines of Judaism or qualified to engage in such an enquiry. That is one reason why we have and need the Torah. Nevertheless, those who are interested and

---

[51] The classic modern formulation of this approach is given by Leo Strauss, especially in his *Persecution and the Art of Writing*, ch. 3. Recent critics of the 'esotericist' thesis are Herbert Davidson (*Moses Maimonides*) and Kenneth Seeskin (*Maimonides on the Origin of the World*).

qualified need not worry that they will be continually faced with opaque and metaphorical language, intentional contradictions, or, most of all, frequent warnings on how limited their understanding is. Although the topics under investigation do require technical language for their exposition and analysis, they are the standard vocabulary of medieval philosophy. Gersonides' prose, if not exactly elegant, is straightforward. Rarely does he resort to metaphor or parable. If there are any contradictions in his work, they are not intentional, and he would certainly be embarrassed by them. Nor are there any subversive teachings that have to be concealed by the use of contradictions. If there are any secrets, Gersonides wants to reveal them. Unlike Maimonides' *Guide*, Gersonides' *Wars* and biblical commentaries are 'open' books: there is no esoteric level of meaning intended only for the elite few. Gersonides says what he means and means what he says.[52] Finally, if we are irremediably afflicted with cognitive disabilities, as Maimonides tells us, why bother to pursue philosophy and the sciences? If we have to admit at the outset of our enquiries that we will necessarily fall short, why begin at all? If we fail, let that be the result of our efforts, not the expression of initial pessimism.[53]

In this context there is one issue that especially vexes Gersonides: Maimonides' conclusion that the question of the world's creation cannot be decided such that no doubts remain. At best, Gersonides claims, all that Maimonides has shown is that *he* was not able to offer a demonstrative argument, or decisive proof, for the world's creation *de novo*. But why close the door to further attempts to resolve the question? And even if subsequent investigators do not succeed in coming up with a decisive proof, they may nevertheless provide additional insight or elucidation that will enable later thinkers to discover the desired demonstration. Not only is science an accumulative and progressive pursuit, so is philosophy. Aristotle made several important advances in both science and philosophy over Plato, and there is no reason to deny that Aristotle can be improved upon. Moreover, Maimonides failed to offer an argument why this particular problem is undecidable. The human intellect may have limits; but why do these limitations surface exactly with this issue? To be convinced that no proof on this question is possible, we need a meta-proof showing its undecidability, which Maimonides did not give.[54]

---

[52] *Wars*, 'Introductory Remarks' (i. 100–1). The one biblical book that requires an 'esoteric' interpretation is the Song of Songs (*Commentary on the Song of Songs*, trans. Kellner, pp. xv–xxxi, 'Translator's Introduction').

[53] *Wars*, 'Introductory Remarks' (i. 94).   [54] Ibid., 'Introductory Remarks' (i. 98).

Nor do we have to rush to revelation to gain certainty on this issue, as Maimonides intimates. Yes, the Torah does teach that the world was created at the beginning of time, and this is important in guiding us, especially those who do not undertake the pursuit of this enquiry. But this does not mean that philosophy is impotent. There is no reason to think at the outset that philosophy by itself is unable to reach the truth on this question. Since the truth is one, what philosophy teaches will be identical with what the Torah teaches, provided that we properly understand Scripture. Moreover, although the Torah does serve as a guide in our investigations, philosophy is an independent discipline with its own agenda and methods. Unlike the theologian for whom the truth has been determined *ab initio* through revelation, the philosopher starts out somewhat naked and has to acquire the truth through his own efforts. Gersonides is thus quite confident that the truth that he will discover through philosophy will turn out to be the same truth revealed by the Torah. This will be the case not only for the question of creation but for other controversial or difficult issues as well.

Recent scholarship on Gersonides has paid considerable attention to his methodology, especially his 'diaporematic', or dialectical, method.[55] This method involves first marshalling the various views on the disputed question and then analysing the supporting arguments. This analysis will eventually lead to the evaluation of the diverse positions and ultimately the correct doctrine will emerge. In the introduction to his *Commentary on Ecclesiastes*, Gersonides interprets the Hebrew title of the book, *Kohelet*, as 'gathering'; for in this book King Solomon gathered various views about human affairs and values and then adjudicated among them.[56] It has been maintained by some scholars that this procedure bears close similarities to Latin scholastic methodology.[57] However, Maimonides also presented the different views on a given question and then analysed their arguments before developing his own opinion.[58] Indeed, this is what Aristotle does throughout his investigations. Whatever his source, Gersonides' adoption of this method allows him to cover a vast territory of philosophical debate and doctrine, affording the reader a virtual textbook on the history of ancient and medieval philosophy.

A first-class logician himself, Gersonides was aware of the relative strengths of different kinds of argumentation and cautions us to employ and recognize

[55] Klein-Braslavy, 'Les Méthodes diaporematiques de Gersonides'.

[56] Gersonides, *Commentary on the Five Scrolls*, Eccles., 25d–26a.

[57] Sirat, 'Le Problème posé par les rapports entre Gersonide et le milieu ambiant'.

[58] Maimonides, *Guide*, ii. 14 (trans. Pines, 285–9), iii. 16 (trans. Pines, 461–4), iii. 17 (trans. Pines, 464–74).

the appropriate proof applicable to the question at hand. In his comments on the Song of Songs, he carefully distinguishes amongst the kinds of proof employed in the three theoretical sciences: mathematics, natural sciences, and metaphysics. The most rigorous argument is the mathematical proof, characteristic of Euclid's *Elements*. Here there is no doubt whatsoever: the conclusion is absolutely necessary given the premises, which are taken to be self-evidently true. Mathematics is able to achieve this certainty because it is highly abstract, divorced from the particular perceptual features of bodies, although studying some of their essential properties, such as shape, size, and number. It is in this domain that we have apodictic demonstrations. In his *Commentary on Proverbs* (1: 1) Gersonides calls this a 'proof by means of its cause', which in the Latin tradition was called the a priori, or *propter quid*, proof. Here the inference goes from cause to effect, and thus provides the explanation for the effect. A less rigorous, but by no means feeble, kind of argument is found in the natural sciences. Here the scientist focuses upon many of the physical properties of bodies, such as motion. Employing perceptual experience and in some cases mathematics as well, the scientist, especially the astronomer, can reach conclusions that are virtually indubitable. However, here doubt is possible, for the typical method of proof in the sciences is from effect to cause, or a posteriori. Empirical evidence has to be first gathered and analysed before the explanatory causes are inferred. Indeed, Gersonides himself was not reluctant to criticize some basic teachings of Aristotle's physics, although his general scientific outlook was essentially Aristotelian.[59] He was not happy, however, with Maimonides' scepticism concerning the possibility of attaining a reliable and adequate theory of astronomy and cosmology.[60] True, natural scientists do not achieve the kind of certainty enjoyed by mathematicians, and they are required to 'get their hands dirty' in the laboratory or observatory. Nonetheless, the results attained by the proper employment of the empirical method do yield conclusions that warrant firm belief.[61]

What is problematic is metaphysics, or, as the medievals called it, the 'divine science'. This subject is notorious for its diverse and contrary theories, and there does not seem to be any hope of arriving at a correct doctrine that would command the adherence of most competent philosophers. The

---

[59] Gersonides criticizes Aristotle's account of time in *Wars*, 6.1.10 (iii. 270–8); he criticizes his theory of motion in *Wars*, 5.3.6 (iii. 138–52).

[60] Maimonides, *Guide*, ii. 24 (trans. Pines, 322–7).

[61] Gersonides, *Commentary on the Five Scrolls*, S. of S., 2c–d, 3c–d (*Commentary on the Song of Songs*, trans. Kellner, 9–10).

difficulty here stems from the fact that unlike mathematical proofs, whose premises are self-evident, or scientific proofs, whose data are empirically based, metaphysical arguments have as their premises commonly held opinions. Although it may be that some of these opinions are true, the metaphysician is liable to take them for granted without further examination. But the *consensus gentium* is not always reliable. Nevertheless, Gersonides was optimistic. He was perfectly aware of the relative weakness of metaphysical arguments, compared with those of mathematics and physics. But, as Aristotle taught, it is the sign of intelligence to know what kinds of argument are relevant to a specific discipline.[62] What especially complicates matters in metaphysics is its complete abstraction from perceptual experience, for here we are concerned with the domain of incorporeal beings that transcend our senses. Although science may be of some help here, and is thus a prerequisite for studying metaphysics,[63] at some point in the latter discipline we must literally 'leave our senses' and rely upon a logical analysis of the competing doctrines to determine the validity of their supporting arguments and their compatibility with well-supported scientific principles. If, for example, we are convinced by perception and sound science that the universe is orderly, then the metaphysical doctrine of absolute randomness advocated by the Epicureans should be rejected.

What is particularly vexing about metaphysics is the inverse proportion that obtains between its results and our desire to engage in it. This is ironic, perhaps tragic, for this is the subject that promises much; indeed, it deals with our ultimate perfection and goal. But since it is liable to error and confusion, we can easily be misled and fall further away from what we want most. Here a small error can have big consequences. In this respect Gersonides echoed Maimonides' lament that it is precisely in those questions that we want answers the most that we do not have them.[64] Yet again Gersonides was not so pessimistic. In the first place, reason is a divine gift, and as such cannot be radically insufficient or impotent. Secondly, philosophy has achieved some sound results in metaphysics, such as the belief in the unity of the deity. For on this point the Greek philosophers Plato and Aristotle were in agreement, despite their divergences on other issues. And most philosophers, except the Epicureans again, agree that there is some kind of divine providence,

---

[62] Aristotle, *Nicomachean Ethics*, 1.3.1094*b*12–27; *Wars*, 'Introductory Remarks' (i. 93).

[63] Gersonides, *Commentary on the Five Scrolls*, S. of S., 3*c–d* (*Commentary on the Song of Songs*, trans. Kellner, 10).

[64] Maimonides, *Guide*, i. 31 (trans. Pines, 66); *Wars*, 'Introductory Remarks' (i. 96–7).

although they did disagree over what exactly this providence encompasses. So the metaphysical quest is not as hopeless as it may seem.

For the most part, then, Gersonides is a 'reader-friendly' author. Despite the difficulties inherent in the topics under investigation, he took pains to instruct the reader of *Wars* on how to study his treatise, especially with respect to the order of presentation of the subjects it discusses. He first distinguishes two different ordering principles: (1) cases where one subject is *necessarily* prior to another; (2) cases where the priority of one subject over another is not necessary, but nevertheless *preferable*. In both instances, the choice of which ordering principle is to be used depends upon what the subject or the reader requires. For example, in some cases P is necessarily prior to Q because to know Q one needs to know P (for example, the priority of physics to metaphysics). Here the priority of P to Q arises both from the perspective of the subject under consideration and from the perspective of the student. Yet there are situations where even though P is by nature prior to Q, it is necessary to teach Q first, since it is easier for the student to understand Q. In a formal exposition of geometry the axioms are logically prior to the theorems. But it may be necessary in a given case to begin with a discussion of the theorem, since it is more obvious or accessible to the student. Since Gersonides critically discussed contrasting views on a given topic, it was a matter of concern to determine the appropriate strategy to persuade the reader of the correct doctrine. To do so, Gersonides states that he will begin his analysis by presenting relatively mild criticisms and then proceed gradually with his examination until the true view emerges in such a way that the reader will think that it is the only possible answer. This is especially appropriate, if not mandatory, where, if presented too quickly and dogmatically, the truth would alienate the reader because of his background and prejudices. Gersonides compared the reader to a diseased person for whom the physician applies first a mild therapy and then gradually steps up the treatment as he builds up the patient's confidence and health. It may have been the case that the more logically telling criticisms were given later in the analysis; yet from the perspective of the reader it was more appropriate to begin with the criticisms that he could handle.[65]

This concern for the reader is also present in his biblical commentaries. In his *Commentary on the Torah*, Gersonides adopted the following method: first, he explained the more difficult words in the chapter; then he provided a running commentary on the verses; finally he presented a summary of the

[65] *Wars*, 'Introductory Remarks' (i. 102).

section in the form of 'useful lessons'. The latter in turn are divided into three types: (1) philosophical or theological doctrines, (2) moral teachings, and (3) the commandments. Although he did not adhere to this schema in all of his commentaries, most of them do include the useful lessons, thus affording the reader a comprehensive picture of the biblical material. Moreover, these lessons, especially those of type 1, often restate the views of *Wars* in plainer language, no matter how unorthodox Gersonides' interpretation of the doctrine may have seemed. There is here no dualism between the philosophical author of *Wars* and the exegete of the biblical commentaries. Since the former contains a lot of science as well as philosophy, the mutual cross-referencing with the biblical commentaries reveals that for Gersonides philosophy, science, and Scripture constitute a unified system, whose teachings all contribute to our attainment of human perfection and happiness.

As noted earlier, one of the most salient and novel features of Gersonides' astronomical contributions was his insistence upon close observation and accurate measurement. This adherence to and employment of empirical methods, however, is not just found in Gersonides' astronomical work; it is also present in several discussions in his purely philosophical investigations. Book 2 of *Wars* is devoted to an examination of dreams, divination, and prophecy. Now, there is no disagreement over whether or not dreams exist, although their reliability as a cognitive or predictive technique may be questioned. Divination, however, is another matter: here doubts abound. Prophecy, though, is an empirical phenomenon that all the medievals accepted without question; its nature and causal conditions, however, were subjects of controversy. In several places Gersonides resorts to empirical facts to illustrate or confirm his conclusions on these topics. At the very beginning of the book he justifies investigating these phenomena by appealing to the facts: they occur with sufficient regularity and universality that we can consider them to be worthy of study. Moreover, Aristotle's explanation of these phenomena was inadequate, perhaps because his understanding of prophecy was deficient. So a new approach is warranted. Gersonides states quite explicitly that dreams do give us information, not only about the future but also about practical and theoretical matters. He gives an example of 'a man in my own lifetime' who learned the cure of an illness via a dream, and relates that this is something that many doctors have experienced.[66] In fact, Gersonides himself reports that he received theoretical information in his dreams.[67] This is also the case even in divination, or precognition, a more controversial

---

[66] *Wars*, 2.4 (ii. 42, 46).   [67] Ibid. 2.4 (ii. 45).

phenomenon. Yet, again, Gersonides appeals to his own experience: he tells us that he received premonitions that turned out to be veridical. One concerned himself, the other his brother.[68]

In his discussion of divine providence in Book 4 of *Wars*, Gersonides also employs empirical data to eliminate fallacious accounts of providence. Aristotle's doctrine of divine providence maintained that providence extends only over species, not individuals. This thesis is refuted, Gersonides claims, by the facts: individual people do receive through dreams, divination, and prophecy information that has beneficial consequences, and their reception of such information is ultimately traceable to God. The direct opposite of Aristotle's view is also empirically false. It maintains that divine providence extends over all individual humans, the righteous and the sinners. This view is also refuted by the facts, as the parents of any seriously impaired child know all too well. An adequate theory of providence, Gersonides insists, must be compatible with the facts, as well as with correct philosophy and the Torah.[69] Gersonides' empiricism is nicely summarized in his commentary on Proverbs 2: 13: ' "Those who leave the right paths to walk in the ways of darkness": … these are people who deny the evidence of their senses … and eventually deny the existence of an agent cause [that is, God].' Armed with the weapons of logic, mathematics, empirical facts, and the legacy of revealed traditions Gersonides believed that he was able and qualified to undertake 'the wars of the Lord'. It will not be an easy or short campaign, as the difficulties and length of the treatise amply show. Nevertheless, it must be attempted with confidence and commitment. After all, reason is a divine gift, not to be lightly abandoned, belittled, or despised.

---

[68] Altmann, 'Gersonides' Commentary on Averroes' Epitome of *Parva Naturalia*', 13, 20. [69] *Wars*, 4.3 (ii. 166, 171–2).

TWO

The Story of Creation

Gersonides' Cosmological Conundrums

THE EARLIEST DRAFT OF *Wars* was a monograph devoted to the single problem of the creation of the world. We have already noted that Gersonides held that this question, so important not only to philosophy but to Judaism as well, had not been adequately treated by Maimonides. (Although he does not mention Averroes at all in his discussion of this problem, Gersonides would not have been happy with the latter's views, which echoed Aristotle's doctrine of an eternal universe.) According to Gersonides, Maimonides' theory of creation was deficient because of its hasty scepticism about the decidability of the question, but it was also erroneous in its uncritical adoption of the *ex nihilo* account of creation and in foisting this theory on Scripture. Against Maimonides, Gersonides argued that (1) the creation of the world is provable and (2) the world was not created *ex nihilo*. Now, in his case for creation Gersonides answers Maimonides by presenting a battery of arguments that he believes prove that the world is not eternal.[1] But this undertaking involves him in an extended debate with Aristotle, who believed that he had proved the eternity of the world. Aristotle's arguments for this thesis are various and detailed, and Gersonides' refutations of them are correspondingly many and lengthy. Thus, most of part 1 of Book 6 of *Wars* is an indirect criticism of Maimonides' cosmological scepticism by means of a direct refutation of Aristotle's cosmological dogmatism.

Since in the final version of *Wars* the subject of creation takes up twenty-nine chapters, by far the longest section of the book, the reader might wonder why this particular topic warrants such an extensive and detailed

---

[1] Henceforth, I shall distinguish between the terms 'eternal' and 'everlasting'. The former connotes infinite duration *a parte ante* and *a parte post*. The latter connotes infinite duration only *a parte post*. Aristotle affirmed the eternity of the world (*On the Heavens*, 9–12). Plato and Maimonides, according to one common interpretation, maintained just the everlastingness of the world (*Timaeus*, 41*a*; *Guide*, ii. 27–8 (trans. Pines, 332–6)). Although Gersonides rejects Aristotle's thesis that the world is eternal, he accepts and attempts to prove the Platonic claim that the physical universe is everlasting.

treatment. After all, Maimonides too recognized the importance of the question, and he devoted just eighteen chapters to it, some of them modest in size. In the first place, like Maimonides, Gersonides considered the creation of the world to be one of the central dogmas of Judaism, especially because it highlights the volitional and providential character of divine activity and thus allows room for miracles. A world that is eternal is a necessary effect of divine causation, regardless of whether we interpret God as the first unmoved mover, as Aristotle did, or as the first eternal agent from whom the world eternally derives or emanates, as Plotinus and the medieval Muslim philosophers maintained. In such a world providence is pale, restricted to the general order of the universe but not extending over individuals. And in a world bound by necessity there is no room for miracles. The question of creation is then not just a mere scientific curiosity that can be left to the physicists; it has capital importance for metaphysics and religion.

There is a second reason why creation is so important for Gersonides. Unlike Maimonides, Gersonides believed that if the world had a beginning, the natural question is 'How did it start?' In asking this question we have already gone from physics to metaphysics, or theology, and have introduced God into the discussion. Maimonides, however, wanted to establish his theology, in particular his proofs for the existence, unity, and incorporeality of God, independently of the question of creation. Indeed, he is quite critical of those who tie the two questions together. Since he believed that the createdness of the world is not philosophically decidable, he did not want the questions about God to depend upon an unresolvable issue. For Gersonides, however, the decidability question is still open. If the world can be shown to have had a beginning, its beginning came about because something 'began' it; in short, it was created, and the creator is God. Accordingly, for Gersonides, the beginning of the world implies its creation by God. In this respect the correct physics entails a fundamental metaphysical, or theological, principle. And a created world exhibits properties that are absent in a world that is eternal.

Gersonides' second dilemma concerns his rejection of the traditional belief in creation *ex nihilo*. Again, he confronts Maimonides, who maintained that this is the teaching of the Torah. Not only does Gersonides have to provide a philosophical case for rejecting this doctrine; he has to show that it is not the teaching of the Torah, and this means that he has to engage in biblical exegesis in a book that is for the most part non-exegetical and, with the exception of a few chapters in Book 4, sparse in its citation of biblical material. Nor can he avoid a confrontation with Aristotle. The alternative creation theory proposed by Gersonides is a version of the doctrine attributed by both Aristotle and Maimonides to Plato: creation from some formless eternal matter. Aristotle rejected this theory on philosophical–scientific grounds, and Maimonides rejected it as not being philosophically proved and therefore not necessarily the teaching of the Torah. Thus, Gersonides has to show that Aristotle was wrong in his critique of Plato and that Maimonides was wrong in his reading of Genesis.[2]

A third dilemma has to do with the end of the world. According to Aristotle, anything that has a beginning has an end, and vice versa.[3] This theorem entails that if the world was created, as Gersonides firmly believed, it must have an end. But on this last point the Torah is not explicit, and, as Maimonides had shown, there are passages that can be read as implying the everlastingness of the world.[4] On this latter point Gersonides agreed with Maimonides. So now he has to argue against Aristotle's theorem: it is not the case that everything that has a beginning has an end. And this is the case with the world: it had a beginning but no end. But unlike Maimonides, Gersonides' defence of this thesis does not rely upon biblical citations; indeed, he does not quote any biblical passages at all. His argumentation is wholly philosophical.

Finally, the Torah begins with an account of creation, the interpretation of which is so difficult that for the rabbis it constituted a secret doctrine, to be transmitted only to a select few. As we have seen Gersonides was not an elitist or esoteric philosopher, and he had no compunctions about divulging these secrets to a wide public, and this is what he does in his biblical commentaries, and specifically in his commentary on Genesis 1. But how does one apply the results of a detailed and difficult philosophical treatment of the problem of creation to a text that presents the story of creation in relatively plain language? Maimonides too had this problem, which he addressed in chapter 30 of the second book of the *Guide*, after he had completed his philosophical treatment of creation. For Gersonides, however, this was an especially urgent problem, since his rejection of creation *ex nihilo* went against the traditional understanding of the biblical text, which Maimonides had adopted. Accordingly, he had to provide a commentary on the opening chapter of Genesis that was not only consistent with the results of his philosophical argument on behalf of creation, but also compatible with a plausible reading of the biblical story. The importance of this philosophical–exegetical

---

[2] Aristotle, *On the Heavens*, 3.8.306*b*17–20; Maimonides, *Guide*, ii. 13 (trans. Pines, 281–2), ii. 15 (trans. Pines, 289–90), ii. 25 (trans. Pines, 328–9).

[3] Aristotle, *On the Heavens*, 1.12.

[4] Maimonides, *Guide*, ii. 27–8 (trans. Pines, 332–6).

task is evidenced by the fact that he undertakes to offer this interpretation in both his *Commentary on the Torah* and *Wars*, 6.2.1–8.

The World Is Not Eternal: It Was Created

Gersonides' first task was to prove that the universe as a whole was created. For Gersonides this means that the world had a temporal beginning such that time is finite in the past. By virtue of this, we can date the origin of the world and assign it a 'birthday'. In the Latin of the scholastic thinkers, the world was created *de novo*.[5] Of the twenty-nine chapters in part 1 of Book 6 of *The Wars*, twenty-three are devoted to this task. Aristotle himself admitted the difficulty of this question and his defence of the eternity of the world is based upon a variety of distinct factors, each requiring separate evaluation. Since Gersonides wanted to leave his readers with no doubt in their minds that he had definitively solved the problem, we may forgive him for the prolixity of his discussion. On a somewhat apologetic and cautionary note he began part 1 of Book 6 by mentioning several difficulties that make a successful outcome problematic. First, there is considerable diversity of opinion on the topic, and a thorough examination of these divergent views will not be easy. Second, many of the arguments adduced to support these views rely on aspects of the physical world. This is especially the case with Aristotle's defence of the eternity of the world, which involves arguments, for example, from motion, time, and the heavenly bodies. So we need to know a lot of natural science, and this is no easy matter. Third, what is especially difficult about this question is that we are prevented from proving creation *a parte Dei*. Since we do not know much about God, we cannot begin our investigation by introducing the deity. Success here will be achieved by more mundane means, by first looking at the world as it is and asking ourselves if there are any facts about it that indicate that it was created.

There are about fifteen arguments that Gersonides marshals to prove his thesis. Seven of them are direct proofs, showing that the world is created; eight of them are arguments showing that Aristotle's arguments for eternity are fallacious. However, some of the latter duplicate or just expand upon some of the former, so thankfully there will be no need to discuss each and every one. Consistent with his general method of beginning his discussion with a collation of the diverse doctrines and their respective arguments, Gersonides first disposes of some of the more easily refuted arguments. Here he is quite impartial: he lists the various arguments for the different doctrines

[5] Aquinas, *Summa Theologiae*, I q. 46 art. 2.

and then shows their flaws. Not one escapes unscathed. This preliminary 'deconstruction' clears the stage for his development of his own position. It is interesting to note that at the outset Gersonides manifests his intellectual independence: he is equally generous in his criticisms of all the standard authorities: Plato, Aristotle, medieval Islamic theology (Kalam), and Maimonides. Gersonides makes it quite clear, however, that his debate is with Aristotle; for it is the latter who rejects the very idea of creation, no matter how this concept is interpreted. And it is this question that is decisive. For, as Maimonides had maintained, if the world is eternal in the way that Aristotle argues, many significant consequences ensue, such as the impossi-bility of miracles. Gersonides agrees with Maimonides' concern to show the inadequacy of Aristotle's arguments for the eternity theory. Indeed, he even goes further: he will prove that this theory is untenable. His strategy is to confront Aristotle on his own turf. He will adopt Aristotle's philosophy of nature and show that it really is incompatible with a theory of an eternal world. To this end Gersonides singles out Aristotle's paradigm examples of eternal entities—the heavenly bodies, time, and motion—and demonstrates that these 'continuous' things are not eternal but generated. If he succeeds, he will have proved that the whole universe is generated, since these continua constitute the cosmological framework and matrix of the world. His argu-ment rests upon three principles, all of which are based upon Aristotle's physics: (1) if anything manifests a telic property (T), it is the product of an agent that has generated, or created, it; (2) if anything exhibits a non-essential property (N), it is generated; and (3) if anything has a property that is 'for the sake of something else' (S), it is generated.[6]

Since the first and third criteria both deal with teleological factors, or Aristotle's 'final cause', we shall consider them together. Aristotle's concep-tion of nature is manifestly teleological, and he explicitly reproaches those physicists who think that the world is purely random or determined by mech-anistic laws. Aristotle's nature is more a work of art than a system running according to blind chance or necessity. Making this analogy Aristotle is led to posit a framework within which natural things exhibit ends, or goals, towards which they move and progress. So, for him, a caterpillar does not just grow into a butterfly nor an acorn into an oak tree. The end-states of these two natural living things are goals that nature 'intends'. For 'nature does not do anything in vain'.[7]

---

[6] *Wars*, 6.1.6 (iii. 239–42).

[7] Aristotle, *Physics*, 2.8; *On the Heavens*, 1.4.271*a*34, 3.2.301*a*11.

The second criterion of a generated thing (N) is also based upon Aristotle's philosophy. Along with the telic, or final, cause of a thing is its form, its inherent nature or essence, what it is for that thing to be what it is and not another thing. This is a doctrine of natural kinds, or species, which is nicely illustrated by Aristotle's own biology. A natural kind is defined by a relatively small set of defining properties that differentiate the members of that kind from members of any other natural kind. So however we define the nature of a dog, it will not be the definition of the nature of a cat. This is what underlies the language of general nouns. Yet there are, of course, properties other than those that define a species. Cats are different colours and sizes, but this does not affect the definition of the species. So for Aristotle there are 'accidental' properties that individuate members of one and the same species: such properties may change, be acquired, or be lost, yet the cat remains a cat.

Gersonides claims that any of these three criteria indicates that the possessor is a generated thing, even and especially in the cases of the 'eternal' continua. The first thing to note here is that Aristotle himself emphatically excludes chance from the celestial domain. Although chance does enter the terrestrial world, it has no place in the heavenly world. For the latter is the perfect paradigm of order and immutability, whereas the former obviously exhibits occasional disorder and much change.[8] This absence of chance in the celestial domain is extremely important for Gersonides' argument, since if chance is precluded and telic properties are exhibited, this would imply that these bodies are generated by an agent. Telic properties (T) are for the most part goal-directed in the sense that the property in question is directed towards a specific activity that the body performs or exhibits. This activity, as we shall see, will itself be directed for the sake of terrestrial phenomena, and thus satisfy the third criterion (S) set down by Gersonides. In this context Gersonides avails himself of another fundamental Aristotelian principle: forms are determined by functions. If the eye is for seeing, then the biological structure and chemical composition of the eye will have those properties that enable this organ to see.[9] Gersonides now contends that the heavenly bodies have such properties, and since chance has been *ab initio* excluded, they are demonstrative indicators that they have been generated by an agent.

However, before he proceeds to point to these teleological properties Gersonides limits the application of this criterion. Let us assume that something produces another thing according to some goal or purpose. If the relationship between the cause and its effect is such that the effect necessarily

---

[8] Aristotle, *On the Heavens*, 2.5.   [9] Aristotle, *Parts of Animals*, 1.1.

follows from its cause, then if the cause is eternal, so will be the effect. But if the causal relationship is such that the cause can exist without the effect, then if the cause is eternal, the effect need not be eternal. Gersonides illustrates the latter case with the example of a builder and a house that he has built. The house can be destroyed without affecting the builder at all, since that particular house was not made by the builder necessarily, but only contingently. And of course, the builder existed before he actually built the house. In the case of the heavenly bodies and their continuous properties, such as motion, if their motions necessarily follow from the natures of their movers, as the Aristotelians had maintained, then since the heavenly movers are eternal, so are the heavenly bodies and their motions. But the hypothesis upon which this argument is based is precisely the thesis to be proved. More generally, where the causal relationship is such that the cause and its effect are not necessarily bound to each other, the effect need not be eternal even if its cause is.[10]

The Wars of the Lord contains many examples of these two types of telic properties.[11] Throughout his discussions Gersonides is not reluctant to manifest his terrestrial orientation. In a sense, he argues backwards: since the heavenly bodies have observable and consistent activities that influence earthly phenomena, they must have properties that enable them to have such effects. Thus, the property and the activity, or function, are teleologically ordered. Accordingly, the distances, sizes, shapes, level of radiation, motions, and so on are all ordered in such a way that they maximize the efficacy of the activities emanating from them, such that the earthly domain is optimally benefited. If any of these properties were different from what they in fact are, the earthly domain would be considerably worse off: 'Everything in the substance of the heavenly domain is of the maximum perfection possible for the perfection of these existents [that is, sublunar phenomena], such that if any irregularity in the order of the heavens were to occur, these existents would be destroyed.'[12] Suppose, for example, the roles and the natures of the sun and moon were reversed but their orbits and motions remain the same (keeping in mind that we are in a pre-Copernican world): the sun would be responsible for the change in tides and the moon would give off light and heat. Most of us would then be unable to do much swimming or fishing while the sun is on the horizon, nor would we be able to have a refreshing sleep while the moon is shining on us. If it is maintained that our bodies

---

[10] *Wars*, 6.1.6 (iii. 240); Touati, *La Pensée philosophique de Gersonide*, 171–2.

[11] *Wars*, 5.2.3 (iii. 39–42), 6.1.7 (iii. 243–51), 6.1.9 (iii. 258–69).

[12] Ibid. 6.1.7 (iii. 243).

would on this scheme have the structure that would correspond to the changed roles of the sun and the moon, Gersonides could claim that since our bodies are what they are, the heavenly bodies must be appropriately structured, not the other way around.

Perhaps this view is for us just a quaint specimen of an archaic anthropomorphism and anthropocentrism. But for some ancient, and most medieval, thinkers, as well as for the general populace, it was a common, indeed natural, way of looking at the universe. This perspective persisted well into the early modern age, despite the efforts of Spinoza to eliminate it from enlightened and mature thought.[13] Even the great Isaac Newton was not immune to this way of thinking. Some of the same examples used by Gersonides are mentioned by Newton as signs that the heavenly bodies are not the effects of 'any natural cause alone, but were impressed by an intelligent agent . . . [they] must have been the effect of counsel'.[14] If, as Aristotle himself stated, chance is not a factor, then the door is open to bring in a supernatural cause to account for the origin of the teleological order exhibited by the heavenly domain.

Nevertheless, Gersonides still faces a challenge from those medieval philosophers, particularly the Muslim *falasifa*, who accepted a teleological picture of the universe yet attempted to harmonize it with their commitment to Aristotle's theory of eternity. This is the doctrine of eternal emanation, or eternal creation. Maimonides believed that this undertaking was wrongheaded from the start: it is a coupling of two fundamentally incompatible points of view. For Maimonides the fatal flaw in this theory is its attempt to foist a teleological framework upon a thoroughly deterministic world governed by necessary laws. In Maimonides' eyes, Aristotle was more consistent than his medieval followers: his conception of an eternal universe ruled by fixed laws exhibiting no purpose or design is a logically tenable hypothesis; the view that attempts to marry design with necessity is, however, intrinsically incoherent.[15] Underlying this misconception is the metaphysical theory of Al-Farabi and Avicenna according to which the world is inherently contingent, but necessary by virtue of its cause, which in this case is God, who is necessary per se.[16] Accordingly, the world is necessary and exhibits design in so far as it derives from a voluntary and wise agent. Gersonides

---

[13] Spinoza, *Ethics*, appendix to part i.

[14] Isaac Newton, letter to Bentley, 10 Dec. 1692, in *Correspondence of Isaac Newton*, iii. 235.   [15] Maimonides, *Guide*, ii. 20–1 (trans. Pines, 312–17).

[16] Fackenheim, 'The Possibility of the Universe'; Davidson, *Proofs for Eternity, Creation and the Existence of God*, 331–5.

rejects this theory, but his argument differs from that of Maimonides. As Charles Touati has demonstrated, Gersonides' exposition and critique of the emanation theory is concerned with and directed towards the doctrine of *continuous creation* (*hoveh tamid*) favoured by many of the Muslim theologians.[17] The question now is whether or not something that is possible, or contingent, per se can also be eternally and continuously emanating. Gersonides claims that such a hypothesis is false, indeed absurd.

The thesis underlying Gersonides' argument is that such a doctrine commits one to a notion of discrete time and motion, such that, at each moment, time, motion, and the heavenly bodies themselves are re-created. Thus, that which was assumed at the outset, that is, the Aristotelian theory of the continuity of time, motion, and the heavenly bodies, has been abandoned. Suppose, for example, that Mars is continuously generated at each moment of time *ad infinitum*. This would mean that Mars is only a possible, or contingent, entity, and thus is potentially a non-being. There seem to be then just two possible situations. Either Mars exists at the moment of its generation but is non-existent at the next moment, only to be re-created at the succeeding moment or Mars is both existent and non-existent at the same instant. Now, the latter case is obviously false. Nor is the former case any more plausible. For, if Mars comes to be, vanishes, and comes to be again in successive moments, its continuity has disappeared. Indeed, time and motion themselves would no longer be continuous magnitudes, as Aristotle had argued, but discrete quantities that come into being without any intrinsic connection with what has preceded them. In such a conception, God would be endowing the heavenly bodies not only with their motions and duration but with their very existence, but not continuously, since we are no longer dealing with continuous magnitudes. The idea of many medieval philosophers of a deity that is not only a creating but also a sustaining cause has given way to the idea of a God who creates everything anew at each moment, including the moment itself. If the hypothesis of continuous re-creation has been shown to have unacceptable consequences, especially the rejection of the very premises of Aristotle's own argument for the eternity of the world, it is not then a legitimate party to the present debate. This debate is now just between Aristotle himself and Gersonides.

Having shown previously that the heavenly bodies exhibit teleological properties and hence are generated by an agent, Gersonides strengthens this argument with the second of his criteria for generation: anything having a

---

[17] *Wars*, 6.1.7 (iii. 246–9); Touati, *La Pensée philosophique de Gersonide*, 177–8.

non-essential property (N) is generated. Remember that such a property is accidental to its possessor: the latter may or may not have it. The property itself can be augmented or diminished, strengthened or weakened. Moreover, in acquiring these various properties the possessor changes. Gersonides contends that the heavenly bodies exhibit such properties and hence are generated. Throughout his argument he assumes Aristotle's principles that the heavenly bodies consist of only one element, which is radically distinct from the earthly elements, and that these bodies change only with respect to place.[18] Now, from these principles it ought to follow that the heavenly bodies do not exhibit non-essential properties at all, since they all have the same chemical constitution. But the truth of the matter is that they do manifest different properties that do not follow from this unique nature. There must be, then, some external cause that accounts for one planet having a property that another planet does not.

Gersonides now proceeds to adduce numerous examples of diverse non-essential properties that can be observed in the heavenly domain. Consider the various sizes of the different planets: Mercury is quite small relative to Jupiter. In terrestrial bodies variation in size results from the different proportions in the mixtures of the elements constituting the organism. Although ants never attain the size of an elephant, they do differ among themselves. But in the case of the planets and stars there is no way to individuate their different sizes since they have the same chemical structure. Given their chemical nature they ought to be the same size; but they are not. Or consider the different colours of their radiation: Mars emits a reddish colour, Venus a bluish colour. Again, this ought not to be the case since both planets have the same chemistry: 'But since the heavenly bodies exhibit no [internal] diversity at all by virtue of their uniform nature, this nature cannot account for the differences in the colours [of their illumination].'[19] There is no need for us to multiply examples, as Gersonides so generously does. The point is clear: where the bodies are homogeneous and uniform, as the heavenly bodies are, they should not exhibit non-essential properties. But they do. Hence, they are generated.

Here, Gersonides' uses a version of the Kalam argument known as the 'particularization argument', which was also used by Maimonides in his defence of the notion of creation. Nevertheless, Gersonides' understanding and employment of it differs from the Kalam's in several respects. First, the Kalam understanding of properties is crucially different from the Aristotelian one.

---

[18] Aristotle, *On the Heavens*, 1.2.   [19] *Wars*, 6.1.8 (iii. 255).

According to the Kalam, every property possessed by a body is an accident. To infer generation, or creation, the Kalam had to introduce another principle, the doctrine of 'possibility': where two contrary or contradictory conditions are equally imaginable and hence possible, the occurrence of one and not the other is brought about by some external determining cause that 'particularizes' the effect with the exhibited property.[20] This would mean that since there is no reason why Mars must be bigger than Venus, it is equally possible for the latter to be larger than the former. That one is the larger and not the other is due to a 'particularizing agent'. Gersonides does not accept the Kalam doctrine of properties nor its theory of possibility. For him, as for Aristotle, there are essential and non-essential properties of things. Moreover, not everything imaginable is possible. Second, for the Kalam the presence of an accident that is generable and variable implies that the bearer of that accident is itself generated.[21] Gersonides does not accept this principle either. As I have already noted (see pp. 33–4 above), for Gersonides, it is possible for an eternal substance to exhibit a generable property if the latter necessarily emanates from it. In general, the Kalam arguments to prove that the world was created, especially the particularization argument, presuppose its atomistic and occasionalist physics, whereby time, motion, and bodies have discrete natures and there is no natural causality. God is called upon, then, to create everything anew. This is creation *ex nihilo et de novo* with a vengeance. Although Gersonides' argument from non-essential properties is related to the Kalam particularization argument, its different scientific framework requires that we treat it independently of the Kalam.

So far Gersonides has been primarily concerned to provide proofs for creation. But consistent with his stated goal to remove all doubts regarding this most controversial question, he proceeds to address Aristotle's own arguments in favour of the eternity of the world. He will argue that not one of them is valid. The most important of these arguments are those from time and motion. His general thesis is that since time and motion are eternal, so are the heavenly bodies, and hence the universe as a whole is eternal. In this discussion Aristotle singles out Plato as someone who holds that time and motion had a beginning, and hence are finite in duration *a parte ante*. This is of course the view of Gersonides. Aristotle's argument against this thesis is in the form of a *reductio ad absurdum*: the thesis of creation, or absolute

---

[20] Maimonides, *Guide*, ii. 19 (trans. Pines, 308–12).

[21] Sa'adiah Gaon, *The Book of Beliefs and Opinions*, treatise 1, ch. 1, third proof (trans. Rosenblatt, 43–4); Maimonides, *Guide*, i. 73, sixth and ninth premises (trans. Pines, 200–3, 205).

generation, asserts that there is a first 'now' or moment of time and a first motion; but this is absurd, and hence the thesis of the absolute generation of the universe is false. Aristotle argues for the impossibility of a first moment as follows. The now is defined as a point that marks off both sides of a present moment, the past and the future. So for Aristotle each now is preceded by a segment of past time and succeeded by a segment of future time. If there were a first now, this would mean that there would be no time preceding it, which is inconsistent with the definition of the now. Hence, there is no first moment or now. Time, then, is infinite *a parte ante*.[22]

The argument against a first motion appeals to a different principle. Assume, as do the creationists, that there was a first motion. This motion represents a change; after all, there was *ex hypothesi* no motion prior to the first motion. But the bringing about of this first motion is itself an alteration that needs to be accounted for; there was a change from non-motion to motion. In other words, the first motion had to be effected by a change that was itself a motion. So the former was not the first after all. If I move the book from my desk to the book-case, not only does the book move but my arm as well. I have to lift my arm, grab the book, and place it on the shelf. All these actions are movements that result in changes; indeed, they are themselves changes. Now, if there were a first movement, or motion, its generation had to be the result of a change or antecedent motion. The notion, then, of an absolutely first motion is an absurdity. Motion, like time, is infinite *a parte ante*.[23]

A variant of this argument was formulated by some Neoplatonists who also argued for the eternity of the world. This version of the argument focuses upon the alleged generator of time, motion, and the world. What induced this generator to generate if *ab aeterno* it was not generating? Something must have changed its mind and caused it to generate. The problem here is twofold: first, since it is usually assumed that the generator is an immutable deity, we have to account for the apparent change in its behaviour; secondly, since the latter change must be explained, we ultimately wind up in an infinite regress. So let us block the regress by rejecting what led to it in the first place: the generation of the world.[24]

Although Gersonides generally works within the general conceptions of time and motion set forth by Aristotle, he does not believe that these doctrines entail the eternity of time and motion. Consider first the argument from the impossibility of a first moment or instant. True, in general a

---

[22] Aristotle, *Physics*, 8.1.251*b*10–27.   [23] Ibid. 8.1.250*b*11–251*b*9.
[24] Maimonides, *Guide*, ii. 14, fifth and sixth methods (trans. Pines, 287–9); Sorabji, *Time, Creation and the Continuum*, chs. 15, 17.

moment does function as a mid-point between the past and the future. However, in the case of the putative first moment, this rule does not apply. For the first moment is by definition unique: it is the now that has no past time before it. Here the now is not a marker within a time sequence, but rather the absolute beginning of the sequence. In a 100-metre race, the beginning of the race is the moment when the starter says 'Go'. Prior to that moment there is no race. The time of the race is measured by the number of moments, or nows, that it takes the winner to complete the 100 metres. In this sense the now is a limit, the *terminus a quo* of time itself, not a place in or portion of an already flowing segment of time. Time itself begins with a particular moment that is literally unique.[25]

Against Aristotle's argument for the impossibility of a first motion Gersonides advances an alternative theory of generation, which is based in part on Aristotle's own theory of change and generation. In chapter 1 of Book 5 of his *Physics* Aristotle puts forth a general theory of change that recognizes a kind of change wherein the change is from not-being to being. This kind of change he calls 'genesis', where a new 'subject' that has not previously existed comes into being.[26] In this case the change is between contradictory states, not contraries, as is the case with qualitative changes, such as the change in colour of a leaf from green to brown. In the latter there are intermediary states, that is, the leaf turns first to red and then to yellow before it becomes brown. But in the former case there are no intermediary states between non-being and being. And since there are no such intermediary states, the change is instantaneous, not requiring time, as is the case with the change of colours in the leaf. Now if this is so, Gersonides contends, the generation of the world is the paradigm case of genesis, of change from non-being to being, involving no time at all.[27] Indeed, in this kind of change there is no motion, since motion implies time.

No doubt Aristotle would resist this inference, especially from his very own principles of change, by appealing to another theorem of his physics: if anything is changed, its potentiality for change existed before its actual change. Now, if there were an absolute generation, the potentiality for the world's being generable would have to be actualized, and this would involve a change; but this change would have to be brought about by an antecedent change, and so on ad infinitum. So there is no such thing as a first change.[28]

It is quite true, Gersonides admits, that in the case of natural, or partial,

[25] *Wars*, 6.1.11 (iii. 279–98), 6.1.20–1 (iii. 351–64).

[26] Aristotle, *Physics*, 5.1.225*a*12–13.   [27] *Wars*, 6.1.20 (iii. 351–7).

[28] Aristotle, *Physics*, 8.1; Maimonides, *Guide*, ii. 14, fifth method (trans. Pines, 287–8).

generation, such as the making of a chair or a caterpillar's turning into a butterfly, the effect is the outcome of a series of previous motions and changes that actualized the potentiality of the wood's becoming a chair and the caterpillar's becoming a butterfly. But in our present case—the generation of the world—we are concerned with the instantaneous and simultaneous coming about of a whole system. Here the generation is not natural but voluntary; nor does it involve a series of antecedent changes and motions. In the case of voluntary generation the action of the generator is not fixed or determined by anything. The shoemaker can make the shoe out of leather, plastic, or some other material at any time or place. Nor does he have to make it for a particular customer or any customer at all. In natural generation, however, the act of generation is determined or limited by certain conditions; moreover, the outcome is fixed according to the laws of nature. Caterpillars, after all, do not become birds. But God's making the world is his choice, and this choice is not bound by any set of determinate conditions, and in particular not by any particular moment, since time itself is generated by God.[29]

Throughout this debate Gersonides challenges and rejects the principle that to generate something requires some antecedent change and a temporal matrix. Whatever may be the case with ordinary generation in nature and the arts, the generation of the entire universe is a different matter altogether. Not only are we dealing here with the creation of the whole system within which ordinary natural and artistic generations take place, but the generator in this case is not one that is limited by time or other conditions. A wholly voluntary agent can make what it wants at any time and from no particular, or specific, motive:

Possibility in choice . . . differs from the other kinds of possibility in that it is uniformly related to all moments of time, since its actualization is not the consequence of a change at all; rather it is consequent upon the will of an agent. Hence, there is no one moment that is more propitious than another for the actualization of a particular possibility.[30]

In the case of the creation of the world, the creator was not limited by any particular moment of time, since time itself is part of what was created in the first place. Nor was it the case that some specific stimulus induced the creator to create such that one might say that a change occurred. A change would have been involved had the generation consisted in an act that required a period of time during which certain potential states were actualized resulting in something being made. Aristotle's arguments assume this notion of

---

[29] *Wars*, 6.1.24 (iii. 368–80).   [30] Ibid. 6.1.24 (iii. 372–3).

change. But in the case of creation we do not have a period of time within which the end-state, or product, emerges out of a preceding series of states. On the contrary, here the first state is the completion of the act: the generation of the world is instantaneous. It did not take any time at all for God to create the world, not even seven days. He made it in one moment, the first moment of time. And this moment was itself the beginning of all change without requiring a change to bring it about.

So far Gersonides has attempted to prove that the universe had a beginning both directly and by undermining Aristotle's main arguments against this thesis. There is, in addition, another argument in his armoury that if valid would further undermine Aristotle's entire case for the eternity of the world. He now claims that Aristotle's own physics entails the beginning of the universe. If this physics is true, and Gersonides believes so, then Aristotle too should have maintained that the world had a beginning. This internal critique of Aristotle's eternity thesis makes use of an argument whose seeds lie in some ancient Greek thinkers, but which was developed and employed by the late Greek Christian philosopher John Philoponus, or John the Grammarian (*c.*490–570).[31] The central idea in this argument is based upon the Aristotelian principle of the impossibility of an actual infinite. An actual infinite is a magnitude all of whose infinite parts or members co-exist. If the magnitude in question is spatial, this would mean that there could not be an infinitely large body or an infinite set of coexisting finite bodies. In this sense Aristotle's physics is a finitistic physics. Nevertheless, there can be successive or serial infinites: these are potential infinites in the sense that the infinite members of such magnitudes do not coexist but are generated successively, one after the other. Accordingly, for Aristotle there could be, indeed there is, a series of human beings coming into being and passing out of being ad infinitum. But at any given time the number of human beings is finite.[32]

Gersonides argued that the impossibility of an actual infinite precludes the possibility of an eternal world. Consider, for example, time itself. If, as Aristotle contends, time is infinite in the past, it will turn out that the notion of past infinite time entails the existence of an actual infinite. Hence, the Aristotelian cosmological hypothesis is incompatible with his physical principle of the impossibility of an actual infinite. Before he demonstrates this

[31] Philoponus, *On the Eternity of the World*, 9–11; Sorabji, *Time, Creation and the Continuum*, ch. 14; Davidson, *Proofs for Eternity, Creation and the Existence of God*, 86–9.   [32] Aristotle, *Physics*, 3.4–8.

incompatibility Gersonides considers the nature of time itself. One of the points about time that is especially relevant here is the essential difference between past and future. Aristotle maintained that in a sense the past and the future are alike in that both do not now exist.[33] For Aristotle at least, this is puzzling, since we do not want to say that time itself is unreal. But for Gersonides this apparent puzzle reveals an interesting and indeed crucial difference between the past and the future. For in an important sense the past is real, or actual, whereas the future is utterly potential; that is, the past is full, or closed, whereas the future is empty, or open. We can see this in two ways. Any portion of past time is filled with facts, events that have taken place in a determinate chronological scheme. Some of these events have effects that are even present to us now; for example, the emergence of a mountain at some time in the past or a crater caused by a meteorite hitting the earth thousands of years ago. Speaking Aristotle's language we can say that the potentialities of these events happening have been actualized. Or, we can say that one of the disjuncts of the disjunction 'A meteorite fell on this place 10,000 years ago or it did not fall on this place 10,000 years ago' is true. Accordingly, any interval of past time is 'filled up' with facts and truths. Such an interval is closed in the sense that no new fact or event can enter it or disappear from it. Indeed, this is true for any moment in past time: each such moment consists of a plurality of facts or truths that 'fill up' that moment and close it. In contrast, the future, Gersonides maintains, is open: some events at least are wholly undetermined in the sense that the sentences describing them have now no determinate truth-value. The 'doors to the future' are so to speak wide open. So for Gersonides although the future is potential, the past is actual.[34]

Now suppose the past is, as Aristotle insists, infinite. But since the past is actual, unlike the future, this would mean that we have an actual infinite, something Aristotle's physics does not allow. Remember that the past has already happened, and in this sense all past facts coexist, filling up the past. If the past is infinite, it consists of an infinite collection of facts that are all simultaneously true. Although the events that have transpired are 'all over' and no longer exist, their corresponding facts do now exist as truths recorded in some hypothetical encyclopedia of all the facts of the world. Such a collection would be analogous to an infinite set of coexisting individuals. But this is not something that Aristotle would countenance. Accordingly, past time is not infinite, and the universe is finite in duration *a parte ante*.[35]

---

[33] Ibid. 4.10.217*b*32–218*a*2.

[34] *Wars*, 6.1.10 (iii. 270–8).   [35] Ibid. 6.1.11 (iii. 291–8).

The thesis of infinite past time is even more problematic, for it engenders a series of difficulties, which have been called the 'paradoxes of the infinite'. Before we develop this problem, we need to note that the notion of infinity employed here is pre-Cantorian. Prior to the ground-breaking work of Georg Cantor (1845–1918), the common understanding of infinite magnitudes assumed that no infinite magnitude is larger than another infinite magnitude. Although there is no explicit formulation of this principle in Aristotle, several passages in his writings suggested it to later Greek and medieval philosophers, so that Gersonides assumed it to be genuinely Aristotelian. After all, to compare lengths and to judge that one is longer than another is to measure them and designate them by finite numerical values. But this is impossible if the lengths are both infinite. With this principle in hand Gersonides exposed several absurdities inherent in the notion of infinite past time.

Suppose time is infinite in the past. It is an observable fact that the planets have different velocities as they rotate around the sun. In the Aristotelian system these different velocities are explained in terms of the number of rotations a given planet completes in a finite interval of time. A planet making more rotations than another planet is faster. Accordingly, the velocity of Mercury is greater than the velocity of Saturn, since in a period of 100 years it will make more rotations than Saturn. But if past time is infinite, the number of rotations completed by each planet is the same: infinite. They would then have the same velocity, which is false. Hence, past time is not infinite. Another example is lunar eclipses: if past time is infinite, the amount of time the moon has spent eclipsed is equal to the amount of time it has spent not eclipsed: again infinite. But this too is absurd. Gersonides generously supplies additional examples all showing the absurdity of the Aristotelian thesis of infinite past time. Time and the universe, then, have been generated, or created.[36]

The World Is Indestructible

Things that have beginnings normally have ends. If it is the case that the universe was generated, it should then have an end: that is, at some moment in the future the universe should cease to exist. If this is true, then either there is something about the world itself that eventually leads to its destruction or something about its creator that leads him to destroy the world. This is easily seen in natural phenomena, such as plants and animals. Both have determinate life spans. Even diamonds can be destroyed. It is equally obvious for

---

[36] *Wars*, 6.1.11 (iii. 292–3); Feldman, 'Gersonides' Proofs', 237 n. 57.

artefacts, which can either wear out or be destroyed by some external cause, even by their maker. So what led Gersonides to maintain that although the world had a beginning, it will not, indeed cannot, have an end?

It should be noted at the outset that Gersonides' thesis differs here from the similar doctrine of Plato, who also maintained that the universe has no end, although it was created. Gersonides' thesis is quite strong: the world is *indestructible*, that is, its continuous existence is inevitable. For Plato, however, the unceasing duration of the world is a gift, endowed by the divine craftsman to the heavenly bodies that are essentially corruptible by virtue of their corporeal and created nature. Without this divine cosmological endowment these bodies would perish, just as terrestrial bodies ultimately decay and die. Accordingly, the world's time-line is such that although it is temporally finite *a parte ante*, it is infinite *a parte post*. But this is the result of divine will.[37] Gersonides' thesis is stronger. He claimed that the created universe is indestructible: there is nothing about it or its creator that entails its destruction; indeed, its ceasing to exist is impossible. Now, since Aristotle vigorously criticized Plato on this issue, Gersonides will have to come up with a reply to Aristotle's critique of Plato that preserves the valid points in Aristotle's critique yet will allow him to maintain cosmic indestructibility. As Aristotle did in proving the eternity of the world, Gersonides focuses upon the heavenly bodies to show their indestructibility. If they are indestructible, so is the whole world.

What causes a body, living or inanimate, to decay and decompose? According to Aristotle, bodies will naturally decompose because of their chemical and physical make-up. A body is composed of certain material elements, which in Aristotle's system are contraries in so far as their essences are opposed to each other: fire (hot and dry), water (cold and moist), earth (cold and dry), air (hot and moist). Although contrary to each other the elements in a specific type of body are kept in equilibrium so long as the elements preserve a certain proportion to each other. Since some of the contrary qualities are active, whereas others are passive, so long as the active powers prevail, the body remains intact. If they are overwhelmed by the passive powers, the body decays.[38] However, in the case of the heavenly bodies this law is inapplicable, since the heavenly bodies are of just one element, the unique fifth element, or quintessence, and thus exhibit no chemical contrariety. They do not therefore have any internal cause of corruption and are

---

[37] Plato, *Timaeus*, 37*d*, 41*b*; Maimonides, *Guide*, ii. 27–8 (trans. Pines, 332–6).
[38] Aristotle, *On Generation and Corruption*, 1.7, 2.3–4; id., *On the Heavens*, 1.12.

thus everlasting, albeit not eternal; that is, they are infinite in the future but not in the past.[39]

So far Gersonides agrees with Aristotle, although he will soon need to depart from Aristotle's principle that whatever is generable is corruptible and vice versa (principle C). But before he tackles Aristotle head-on, he has to consider another opponent: Philoponus. In his sustained argument against the 'eternalists', Aristotle and Proclus, Philoponus proposed to show that from Aristotle's principle C and Aristotle's theorem that a finite body has only finite force, or energy (principle F), the universe will self-destruct and hence had a beginning. Although Gersonides agrees that the universe had a beginning, he rejects its destructibility, and in so doing he rejects both principles C and F. In this context both Philoponus and Gersonides assume that the exertion of force is interchangeable with the very duration, or existence, of the body, such that when the body ceases to move or act, it ceases to exist. Loss of energy eventually leads to decomposition and destruction.[40]

Why do moving bodies stop moving? If I kick a ball with a certain amount of force, it will roll along with a proportionate amount of velocity determined by the force transmitted to it by my foot and the presence or absence of friction. Eventually, however, the force will diminish and ultimately be expended, at which point the ball will cease to move. Or, if I throw a ball upward, it will soon fall because its natural motion is downward. Now in the case of the heavenly bodies, the force that moves them is constant; hence, their velocity is invariable. Indeed, their movements do not involve any pushes or physical stimuli at all. Moreover, they have only one kind of motion—circular, which has no contrary.[41] Accordingly, the heavenly bodies do not cease moving and have therefore infinite duration *a parte post*. Philoponus' attempt to prove creation from destruction fails, at least in the case of the heavenly bodies.[42]

Gersonides' argument against Aristotle's principle C takes up one of the

---

[39] Aristotle, *On the Heavens*, 1.2–3; *Wars*, 6.1.16 (iii. 318).

[40] Philoponus, *On the Eternity of the World*, 230, lines 6–22; Sorabji, *Time, Creation and the Continuum*, ch. 14; Davidson, *Proofs for Eternity, Creation and the Existence of God*, 89–91, 409–11; Philoponus, *Against Aristotle*, 142.

[41] Aristotle, *On the Heavens*, 1.3–4, 1.9.

[42] *Wars*, 5.3.6 (iii. 145–52), 6.1.14 (iii. 309–13). In this context it is interesting to note that in his discussion of Kalam arguments for creation, Maimonides does not include this argument of Philoponus, whereas Sa'adiah Gaon does (Maimonides, *Guide*, i. 74 (trans. Pines, 215–22); Sa'adiah Gaon, *The Book of Beliefs and Opinions*, treatise 1, ch. 1, first proof (trans. Rosenblatt, 41–2)).

longest chapters in the entire treatise and is exceedingly complicated. What Gersonides has to do is to show that some generated things need not be destructible, and hence even if the world has been created, it will not necessarily cease to exist. Throughout his arguments against Plato, Aristotle assumes that if a thing is contingent, that is, if it may or may not exist, then it is necessarily corruptible. Since, for Plato, the heavenly bodies are essentially corruptible and continue to exist only by divine fiat, for Aristotle, this means that they contain the possibility of non-existence and that eventually they will cease to exist. For all genuine possibilities are sooner or later actualized. The world's contingent character implies, therefore, its destruction. However, for Aristotle the world's existence is eternal and hence necessary.[43]

Gersonides accuses Aristotle here of failing to distinguish between the contingency of something and its corruptibility. Something may exist and be contingent in so far as it may not exist, say a dog. Now a dog is the kind of thing that because of its chemical nature will sooner or later decompose and die. It is therefore destructible. But it is not its contingent character that leads to its destruction. Its destruction is due to its biochemical nature as a living thing. In the case of inanimate things destruction follows upon their internal chemical contrariety, as we have seen. But the heavenly bodies, although they are contingent in so far as they have been generated, and as such may not exist, are not thereby destructible, since they have no internal contrariety. Their contingent status does not therefore imply corruptibility. Something can be contingent just by being generated. Corruptibility and contingency are then two independent conditions: the former comes about by virtue of the chemical constitution of a thing; the latter is a matter of a thing's not being eternal, or necessary. The heavenly bodies are, for Gersonides, not eternal, or necessary, and hence they are contingent; but their inherent contingency does not imply their corruptibility.[44]

Nevertheless, granted that there are no internal causes for the destruction of the heavenly bodies and, thus, the world, what about the possibility of an external cause, indeed God himself, destroying them? If God is truly omnipotent, it would seem that he could willingly destroy the world, just as he willingly created it. Indeed, since the creation of the world is viewed by both Plato and Moses as a work of art, why can the divine craftsman not destroy the product if he so desires, just as painters or novelists destroy their works if they want?

[43] Aristotle, *On the Heavens*, 1.12.
[44] *Wars*, 6.1.27 (iii. 384–405); Feldman, 'Platonic Themes in Gersonides' Cosmology', 396–402.

Yes, Picasso may wish to destroy a painting he has painted, because for one reason or another it does not meet his demands or satisfy the customer; or the artist may be drunk or angry and destroy the work in a maniacal fit. But none of these conditions is applicable to God. His 'works are perfect' (Deut. 32: 4). What God made he made as perfect as it could be. Is there anything that could thwart or impede God's plan or action? Nor is God subject to any of the psychological conditions that may lead to someone destroying what he makes. Even when God brought about the Flood in the days of Noah, the Earth as a whole was not destroyed. Here Gersonides adopts a version of the 'principle of sufficient reason': a rational agent has a reason for what he does. Since God is the rational agent *par excellence*, he cannot destroy the universe because he has no reason to do so:

It is not proper to attribute to God a reprehensible act that is performed by inferior men who intentionally destroy for the sake of destroying . . . Neither is it possible for God to be angry, since no causes of anger can be attributed to Him . . . Moreover, it is impossible that God will destroy this world in order to make a better one. For if this were possible, I would like to know what prevented Him from making this better world at the outset.[45]

The world's indestructibility does not, however, impair God's omnipotence, since for a perfect rational agent destroying what he has made is not possible. Omnipotence means the ability to do what is doable. For God to destroy what he has made is not doable. Thus, the world has been shown to be indestructible.[46]

Creation *Ex Nihilo* Is False

Throughout classical Jewish, Christian, and Muslim theology the dominant creation theory has been creation *ex nihilo*. It was believed that if God needed some independent matter to create the universe, he would be no better than any human artist. If God is truly omnipotent, then he creates from nothing. In medieval Jewish theology a very vigorous defence of this principle was formulated by Sa'adiah Gaon, and Maimonides claimed that this is the view of the Torah, although the Platonic doctrine of creation from matter is not theologically heretical or philosophically untenable.[47]

---

[45] *Wars*, 6.1.16 (iii. 319).

[46] Ibid. 6.1.16 (iii. 319–21); Feldman, 'Platonic Themes in Gersonides' Cosmology', 397–8; id., 'The End of the Universe', 61.

[47] Sa'adiah Gaon, *The Book of Beliefs and Opinions*, treatise 1, ch. 2 (trans. Rosenblatt, 46–50); Maimonides, *Guide*, ii. 13 (trans. Pines, 281–2), ii. 25 (trans. Pines, 328–9).

Gersonides maintains the direct contrary of this view: the universe has been created from some kind of shapeless, eternal body. In defending this theory, he first modifies Plato's doctrine in order to avoid Aristotle's criticisms of it and then provides a proof for it.

For our purposes let us assume that Plato's theory can be revised in such a way as to meet Aristotle's objections. Gersonides believed that he succeeded in doing this. What he focuses upon is showing that the *ex nihilo* model of creation is false, indeed absurd. If the universe is created, it was created either from nothing or from something. He will prove that it could not have been created from nothing; so it was created from something.

In short, the philosophical principle *ex nihilo nihil fit* is necessarily true, contrary to what Sa'adiah Gaon and Maimonides believed. Gersonides offers us several different arguments showing the absurdity of the traditional dogma: some metaphysical, others physical. His underlying assumption is one shared by most medieval thinkers, including Maimonides: God is pure form, which in God's case means pure intellect. In this respect they are all good Aristotelians. The problem then is how to account for the emergence of matter from what is pure form; or, in the language of the medieval emanationists, how can matter 'emanate' from pure form? From themselves forms can emanate forms. And so it is possible that from God the separate intelligences, or immaterial forms (the biblical angels), can emanate. In this very limited case one could speak of creation *ex nihilo*. But we are now concerned with the creation of the material world. And how is this possible if all that exists prior to its creation is wholly immaterial?

'In general, a form gives something *similar* to itself; thus, it gives the form . . . But would that I knew how a form can give corporeality!'[48] It is important to note that Maimonides himself was aware of this problem and was sceptical of the Muslim Aristotelians' attempt to answer this question.[49] But he could offer no better explanation than just claiming that the principle *ex nihilo nihil fit* is not applicable in the case of the world's generation, which is an act *sui generis*, the product of God's free will. However, this is just begging the question; no philosophical argument has been given. It certainly did not satisfy Gersonides, although he shared Maimonides' belief that the world was created by a voluntary divine act. Since God is pure form and the world is a material system, we have to explain how it came about in a way that is consistent with the laws of metaphysics and physics. Maimonides' answer is just a precipitous rush to the asylum of ignorance.

[48] *Wars*, 6.1.17 (iii. 325), my italics.
[49] Maimonides, *Guide*, ii. 22 (trans. Pines, 318).

In addition to this metaphysical argument Gersonides adduces an argument based upon a fundamental theorem of Aristotle's physics: the impossibility of a vacuum.[50] In Aristotelian language, a vacuum is empty space that can be occupied or filled. The *ex nihilo* model of creation amounts to the following scenario: before the creation of the world there was nothing except God (the temporal language here is to be taken loosely); then a physical system came into existence. Like an empty box into which something could be placed, the empty space was potentially 'fillable'. According to the *ex nihilo* model, the 'nothing' is this empty space into which the world came to be; hence a vacuum existed prior to the creation of the world, just as the box was empty before it was filled. Now, according to Aristotle's physics all bodies are finitely large; and this law applies to the universe as a whole. So if the universe is made to occupy the antecedent empty space, then there will still be some space surrounding it, unless it is assumed that the space was exactly the same size as the universe: an unlikely and arbitrary assumption. There will then be a vacuum even after the world has been created, just as, if the volume of the box is greater than the volume of the item placed in it, there will still be some empty space in the box. But a vacuum is impossible. Finally, since the antecedent space is larger, perhaps infinitely so, than the world, why does the world occupy a certain region of space and not another? Since God has no reason to make the world in one region and not another, empty space being homogeneous, the world should occupy all of space, and hence be infinite. But this too is absurd. Nor could there be any feature of the homogeneous space that would localize the world in one specific region, since *ex hypothesi* there is nothing besides God. If there were anything that determines the region that the world occupies, it would itself be a body, which is *contra hypothesem*. Hence, the *ex nihilo* theory is absurd.[51]

Although Maimonides has no explicit philosophical argument for creation *ex nihilo*, it might be thought that he could avoid the force of the principle *ex nihilo nihil fit* by applying the argument that he used against Aristotle's proofs for the eternity of the universe: the laws of physics are not necessarily true of the first moment of the world's existence, that is, the moment of creation. This would seem to allow us to claim that the universe was created from no antecedent matter. In introducing this argument Maimonides first tells a story of young boy isolated on an island with only his father and other males. The boy matures but is puzzled about how he came about. The father proceeds to tell him the basic laws and facts about sexual reproduction and

---

[50] Aristotle, *Physics*, 4.6–8.
[51] Aristotle, *On the Heavens*, 3.2.302a5–10; *Wars*, 6.1.17 (iii. 325–7).

the development of the foetus inside a female. The son is incredulous, not only since is he ignorant of what a female is but also because he understands eating and breathing from the way he now eats and breathes. His father responds: it is true that a human being outside the mother's womb obtains oxygen by breathing either through its nose or mouth, but this law does not hold when the foetus is in its mother's womb. The same is true for eating: although we now ingest food by putting it in our mouths, in the case of the foetus it acquires nourishment from its mother. From this example Maimonides formulates the general principle that what is now true of something in its developed state may not have been the rule at some past state of that thing.[52] Hence, the law *ex nihilo nihil fit* need not have been true at the very first moment of creation, and creation *ex nihilo* is at least possible.

Gersonides rejects the blanket use of this general principle and its employment to defend creation *ex nihilo*. It may be that some conditions that are true of a developed organism were not true when the organism was initially conceived or born. But there may be some conditions that are necessarily true for the very existence of an organism, no matter the stage of its existence. The foetus does not get its oxygen by breathing through its nose; nevertheless, it gets the needed oxygen from its mother. Oxygen is a necessary condition for the organism at every stage of its existence, including even its very generation. More generally, Gersonides argues, there are certain necessary conditions for the very existence or generation of anything: for example, for the existence or generation of some X, it must be the case that X can exist or be generated; that is, X is not a logically impossible state of affairs. Also, it must not be the case that the generation of X be naturally impossible, and violates some law of nature; for example, if the mother and father are both human, it is naturally impossible for the child to be a horse. The impossibility of the transformation of species was true for the generation of Cain, Abel, and Seth from Adam and Eve as it was true for the generation of Reuben from Jacob and Leah. Accordingly, the philosophical principle *ex nihilo nihil fit* is universally true, even in the case of the generation of the universe. The possibility of creation *ex nihilo* is therefore absurd.[53]

Having rejected the doctrine of creation *ex nihilo* Gersonides offers in its place a version of the Platonic theory of creation from something. He now provides a description of the nature of this something and how the world was actually created from this something. In his astronomical theory Gersonides postulated the existence of a 'body that does not preserve its shape'. This

[52] Maimonides, *Guide*, ii. 17 (trans. Pines, 294–8).
[53] *Wars*, 6.1.17 (iii. 327–8, and see n. 20).

body is introduced to prevent the different planetary motions from interfering with each other:

We have already shown in Book Five of *The Wars* that between each heavenly sphere there is a body that doesn't preserve its shape. This is the reason why the motions of the higher spheres do not interfere with those of the lower [spheres] and conversely. This body is called 'water' [*mayim*] . . . because of water's lack of shape.[54]

Between the planetary spheres there is then this shapeless, fluid-like body that absorbs the motions of the planetary spheres but does not transmit them to the spheres, whose individual motions remain independent of each other. This body is the primordial material cause that is required in order to explain the actual making of the universe. As understood by Aristotle and the medievals, Plato's 'receptacle', or the receiver of the creative act of the divine craftsman, is formless, having no intrinsic form of its own; otherwise it would not be able to receive or embody forms of the elements and their compounds. Nevertheless, Plato describes this matter as undergoing disorderly motions, which are put into order by the divine craftsman, resulting in an ordered cosmos.[55] Both Aristotle and Gersonides rejected this idea of disorderly motion. For Gersonides, this was the reason why Maimonides did not take the Platonic theory more seriously.[56] Gersonides' primordial body is like Plato's receptacle in being formless; but it undergoes no motion or rest, since only formed bodies are subject to motion and rest. In creating the universe God endows some of this body with form, and thus produces our world, which is an ordered system of formed bodies.[57]

   Realizing the difficulties of this theory, as well as its novelty, Gersonides addresses some of the objections that have been or could be raised against it. One of the oldest objections has its roots in the thesis of Plato, Aristotle, and Philo of Alexandria that the matter of the universe is all the matter there is; there is no matter outside the universe.[58] But if the universe embodies all the

[54] *CT*, Gen., 'Bereshit', 9*c* (i. 22); see also *Wars*, 5.2.2 (iii. 36–8); Touati, *La Pensée philosophique de Gersonide*, ch. 8; Freudenthal, 'Cosmogonie et physique chez Gersonide'; Glasner, 'The Early Stages', 22, 35–42; B. Goldstein, 'Levi ben Gerson's Theory of Planetary Distances', 287–8.

[55] Plato, *Timaeus*, 43*b*, 52*e*–53*a*, 69*b*; Vlastos, 'The Disorderly Motion in the *Timaeus*'; id., 'Creation in the *Timaeus*'.

[56] Aristotle, *On the Heavens*, 3.2.3000*b*18–19; *Wars*, 6.1.17 (iii. 322–4).

[57] *Wars*, 5.2.2 (iii. 36–8), 6.1.18 (iii. 340–2).

[58] Plato, *Timaeus*, 32*d*–33*b*; Aristotle, *On the Heavens*, 1.7.275*b*7–12, 2.4.287*a*12–16; Philo, *On the Eternity of the World*, 21; id., *On Providence*, 1; id., *On Planting*, 2.2.

matter there is, is it not strange that the primordial matter was exactly the same size as the universe? Could this be just mere coincidence? Although Plato, Aristotle, and Philo did not acknowledge this difficulty, it was raised by the early Christian theologian Origen. However, unlike Gersonides he used it to conclude that the world was created *ex nihilo*: since it would be unbecoming to make chance a crucial factor in creation and hence impair divine omnipotence, creation was from absolutely nothing by divine fiat. If, however, there were some matter that remains after the creation of the world, what purpose would it have? After all, in nature there is nothing in vain.[59]

Moreover, if this body is eternal, as Plato and Gersonides maintained, there would then be two eternal entities, whose eternal existence places them both on the same ontological level. Indeed, it would imply a kind of dualism that biblical monotheism precludes. Furthermore, how do we determine which of these two eternal entities is the active cause or even if they can enter a causal relation with each other? This objection was raised earlier by Sa'adiah Gaon and was seconded several centuries after Gersonides by Isaac Abravanel.[60]

Finally, can there be a body that has no form whatsoever? Even Plato admitted that this receptacle was a shadowy thing and arrived at only by a 'bastard kind of reasoning'.[61] Moreover, it is a fundamental principle of Aristotelian physics that all bodies are formed and have a determinate nature, and this seems to be confirmed by our everyday experience. Because of their respective forms fire, for example, moves upwards and water downwards.

In attempting to respond to these and other objections, Gersonides admits that his solutions to some of them are not indubitable arguments. Nevertheless, he does not shy away from trying to solve them; he attempts to answer these objections to the best of his ability and with the information at his disposal. In particular, he is not afraid to buck the trend and admit the possibility of surplus matter. In creating the world, God endowed some of the primordial formless and shapeless body with form, both celestial and terrestrial; yet some of it remains unformed, or without any permanent shape. By positing this surplus matter Gersonides can dispose of the questions concerning the quantity of the primordial matter. Since the world

---

[59] Origen, *First Principles*, 2.4.110, cited in Wolfson, 'Plato's Pre-Existent Matter', 180–1.

[60] Sa'adiah Gaon, *The Book of Beliefs and Opinions*, treatise 1, ch. 2 (trans. Rosenblatt, 46–50); Abravanel, *The Deeds of God*, 2.5, 16*b*; Feldman, *Philosophy in a Time of Crisis*, 49.   [61] Plato, *Timaeus*, 52*b*.

exists, the primordial matter had to be sufficient in quantity for the generation of the world. Otherwise, there would not be a world at all. That it was just by chance that the primordial body was of the exact size as that of our world is unlikely, since chance is rare and irregular and thus cannot serve to explain anything, especially something as momentous as the generation of the world. Moreover, by postulating surplus matter, we no longer have to worry about a vacuum. For in creating the world God took this matter and shaped it into a sphere without leaving a vacuum behind. If there were no surplus matter, the shaping of the primordial matter into a sphere without any residue would result in a vacuum. The hypothesis of surplus matter not only then accounts for the quantitative sufficiency of the matter for the creation of the universe without having to admit chance, but also eliminates the worry about a vacuum.[62]

Gersonides' response to the eternity objection is more confident. Just because this body is eternal does not mean that it is divine. In fact, it is most imperfect, since it lacks permanent shape and has no intrinsic form. Indeed, one could consider it to be just one step above sheer nothingness:

It doesn't follow when we posit this body to be eternal that it is on the same level of being as God . . . For God is not divine because He is eternal . . . God is the deity precisely because of His great level [of perfection] . . . The eternal body, however . . . is utterly and essentially deprived of goodness.'[63]

Ever respectful of tradition, Gersonides suggests that this is perhaps what is intended by saying that the world was created from nothing. Being unformed, this body is virtually nothing. There is then no need to worry about its being an object of veneration or worship. If God is the utmost in perfection, this body is the utmost in imperfection. In fact, because of its imperfection, it is the source of all defect and evil. Here Plato's notion of the 'necessity of matter' is relevant. In his cosmological story the primordial stuff is resistant to order, and this explains the various imperfections in the universe.[64] As we shall see, this notion will have an important role to play in Gersonides' theodicy.[65] There is then no need to worry about anyone worshipping it.

But can there be a body without any form whatsoever? And how is it possible that from this amorphous body different levels and types of form can be created? To the first question Gersonides responds that a shapeless or formless body has been shown to be theoretically necessary, at least, to

---

[62] *Wars*, 6.1.18 (iii. 334–7).   [63] Ibid. 6.1.18 (iii. 338).

[64] Plato, *Timaeus*, 48a–51; Maimonides, *Guide*, iii. 10 (trans. Pines, 440).

[65] *Wars*, 4.2 (ii. 162), 4.3 (ii. 168–170).

account for the independent motions of the planetary spheres. Then, using an argument that Maimonides had used to prove the existence of pure forms, Gersonides asks rhetorically, why cannot there be matter without any form at all? If immaterial forms are possible, indeed actual, why not formless matter? If the notion of form as such does not entail that forms be embodied, then why cannot the concept of matter be independent of form?[66]

In answering the second question, Gersonides reverts to a fundamental principle in his cosmology: creation was the result of divine will. Since the primordial matter is utterly formless, it is absolutely amenable and capable of taking on any form or shape that the divine craftsman chooses. Since in this case the craftsman is pure form, its activity is not limited in any way; in particular, its activity is not restricted to a limited part of the matter or to the giving of a specific form. In these respects, at least, the divine craftsman differs from natural agents, such as animals that generate offspring of the same species, and from artisans who in making an artefact use a limited portion of the material to make a particular shape or form: 'This creation [of a world as a totality] is the effect of [God's will], not of nature. Accordingly, it is possible for the one [primordial] matter to be endowed . . . with different characteristics.'[67] Gersonides makes an analogy here between God's creative activity and the governance of Plato's philosopher-king. Just as the latter establishes a perfect state by assigning different kinds of people to different roles, so God sets up a perfect world by endowing some parts of the primordial body with sublunar forms, that is, terrestrial bodies, and other parts with celestial forms, that is, the heavenly bodies, separated from each other by the 'body that does not preserve its shape'. Another analogy is also appropriate: just as a superior artist is not restricted in the kind of work he or she is about to create with respect to genre, material, subject, or style, God is not confined to creating a limited number of forms in a determinate part of matter. His activity is in this sense 'boundless'.

Philosophical Cosmology and Biblical Exegesis

While composing *Wars*, Gersonides was also engaged in biblical exegesis, especially after he completed his philosophical enquiries. Indeed, the last years of his life were devoted to his *Commentary on the Torah*, in which the opening chapter of Genesis offered him ample opportunity to apply his philosophical conclusions to the biblical text. In addition, in part 2 of Book 6

[66] Ibid. 6.1.18 (iii. 339); Maimonides, *Guide*, ii. 1 (trans. Pines, 246–7).
[67] *Wars*, 6.1.18 (iii. 340).

of *Wars* he provides the reader with an exegetical epilogue, in which the preceding results of part 1 are immediately employed to elucidate the opening chapter of the Torah according to the teachings of philosophy. He asserts in the very opening sentence of chapter 1: 'Religious principles do not imply the belief in creation *ex nihilo*.' Since the latter belief has been demonstrated to be false by impeccable philosophical arguments and the Torah does not teach anything false, 'it is necessary that we posit what the Torah teaches in such a way that it is in agreement with philosophical inquiry'.[68] In these remarks we have a fundamental principle of Gersonides' biblical exegesis: nothing in the Torah is inconsistent with the truths of philosophy and science. Moreover, what the latter teach is exactly what the former teaches, *if we know how to read the Torah*. And this is exactly what he undertakes to show in the first eight chapters of part 2 of Book 6.

His first step is to focus upon what Maimonides took to be the deciding criterion for determining which cosmological theory is consistent with the Torah: the possibility of miracles. Since for Maimonides only a creation theory allows for the possibility of miracles, and since Plato's theory has not been proved, he was satisfied to maintain creation *ex nihilo* as the authentic teaching of the Torah.[69] Quite shrewdly Gersonides agrees with Maimonides in taking miracles to be the touchstone of the question; but he proceeds to show that the miracles described in the Torah exemplify his theory of creation from matter, not creation *ex nihilo*. The Torah therefore is not only consistent with his theory, but actually teaches it where it is most relevant to do so. For if we look at many of the miracles recorded in the Torah, we shall see that often the event is brought about by the transformation of some kind of matter into something else. Consider for example, some of the Ten Plagues: the plague of blood comes from water; the plague of flies from dust; Moses' staff becomes a snake. Accordingly, if we just stick to the biblical text, we have evidence of creation from matter, at least in the case of miracles.

Since the aforementioned miracles are obviously cases of only partial or limited generation of one kind of matter from another kind, we need to see if the Torah does indeed teach creation from matter in the case of the creation of the whole universe. At the outset of this investigation it is interesting to note two points. First, unlike Sa'adiah Gaon or Maimonides, Gersonides does not assume or assert that the opening biblical verb *bara* ('created') implies creation from nothing.[70] Indeed, neither in *Wars* nor in

---

[68] *Wars*, 6.2.1 (iii. 428).   [69] Maimonides, *Guide*, ii. 25 (trans. Pines, 328–9).

[70] Sa'adiah Gaon, *The Book of Beliefs and Opinions*, treatise 1, ch. 2 (trans. Rosenblatt, 46–50); Maimonides, *Guide*, ii. 30 (trans. Pines, 358).

his comments on Genesis does Gersonides even comment upon this verb. Here he may have been influenced by Abraham ibn Ezra's interpretation, according to which *bara* means to 'cut' or to 'shape'.[71] Second, in the *Commentary on the Torah*, he begins by positing three principles, one of which is the doctrine of the 'body that does not preserve its shape' that exists between the planetary spheres. Now, as we have seen, Gersonides explicitly identifies this inter-spherical body with the element water mentioned in the biblical account. Already Gersonides has prepared the reader for his theory that water is the primordial matter.[72]

Indeed, even a non-philosophical reading of the opening chapter of the Torah could easily suggest that the water referred to therein is in some sense primordial, for it is never stated that it was created; rather, it was just 'there' (Gen. 1: 2). Moreover, when the heavenly domain is about to be created on the second day, it is related that both this domain and the sublunar world are fashioned out of this primordial water, and that these domains are separated from each other in such a way that some of the shapeless watery body remains as it is in the heavenly domain between the planetary spheres, whereas the sublunar waters are formed into seas and oceans (Gen. 1: 6–7). The act of separation refers to the different natures of the heavenly matter and of the sublunar world. Whereas the sublunar matter is the domain of elemental change and the formation of corporeal compounds, the heavenly matter is formed into bodies that never change, except for their motions, which are themselves invariable. Nevertheless, both originate from the 'body that does not preserve its shape'.[73] Accordingly, the Torah itself teaches the theory, philosophically proved by Gersonides, that the world was created by God from some material substratum.

In undertaking to prove that the world was created Gersonides had a daunting task: on the one hand he had to provide what Maimonides thought was not available and perhaps impossible to obtain—a proof for creation; on the other hand, he had to show that Aristotle's arguments against creation and for the eternity of the world were invalid. But even when he managed to succeed (at least in his eyes) in meeting these challenges, he had the additional task to explain why the traditional theory of creation *ex nihilo* was false, indeed impossible, and why some version of Plato's doctrine of eternal

[71] *CT*, Gen., 'Bereshit', 9*c* (i. 22).

[72] *Wars*, 6.2.8 (iii. 450); *CT*, Gen., 'Bereshit', 10*b*–12*a* (i. 26–31); Touati, *La Pensée philosophique de Gersonide*, 273–8.

[73] *Wars*, 6.2.5 (iii. 438–9), 6.2.8 (iii. 449); *CT*, Gen., 'Bereshit', 9*b*–10*b* (i. 26); *Midrash Psalms*, Ps. 27.

amorphous matter was true. And if that was not enough, he felt obliged to show that his entire theory of creation was not only compatible with the Torah but is actually taught by it. It is no wonder then that Book 6 of the *Wars* is the longest book of the treatise. But it is also the most important; for it contains the seeds for other ideas that will be developed by Gersonides, concepts concerning God, divine providence, humanity, and immortality.

THREE

God and his Attributes

How Can the Existence of God Be Proved?

A CONSIDERABLE AMOUNT of energy has been spent on trying to show that the existence of God is philosophically provable. In reading the medieval philosophers one could reasonably ask why this enterprise was taken up at all, since all the medieval thinkers believed in the existence of a deity. Nevertheless, this was not an idle question for them. Given their deep commitment to philosophy, either as an independent intellectual discipline or as a 'handmaiden' of theology, medieval philosophers and theologians attempted to show that, however the relationship of philosophy to religion was to be defined, on the issue of God's existence there would be no disagreement. Here philosophy and religion were in complete harmony. Indeed, if we go back to Aristotle's understanding of the science that ultimately became known as metaphysics, we see that one of his characterizations of this discipline is the study of the divine,[1] and many of the medievals called metaphysics, 'the divine science'. Moreover, both Plato and Aristotle had a monotheistic conception of the divine. So given this agreement, the medieval preoccupation with this issue is a bit puzzling.

To understand the relevance of this topic to medieval philosophy it will be useful to adopt the terminology of Thomas Aquinas. In attempting to delineate the distinct domain of theology, Aquinas distinguished between the 'preambles of faith' and the 'articles of faith'. Whereas the latter is theology proper, the dogmas of a particular religion, the former is where philosophy and religion intersect. It is here that philosophy and religion have a common language and set of concerns. And it is here that philosophy undertakes to prove some of the fundamental beliefs of religion, such as the existence of God.[2] Equivalent expressions for Aquinas' 'preambles of faith' have been used: 'natural theology', 'philosophical theology', 'natural religion'. The underlying assumption here is that human reason is able to prove and explain

---

[1] Aristotle, *Metaphysics*, 1.2.

[2] Aquinas, *Summa Theologiae*, I q. 1, I q. 46 art. 2.

some of the basic beliefs of monotheistic religion. It is not only the common ground for philosophy and religion, but it is also a place where the monotheistic religions can speak to each other without religiously based assumptions.

In the medieval literature various arguments were adduced to show that God's existence is philosophically provable, and hence an obligatory belief for any rational person. These arguments can be divided into two groups, the first of which has only one member: the so-called 'ontological proof' of Anselm of Canterbury (1033–1109), according to which God's existence follows logically and necessarily from the very concept of 'a being greater than which nothing can be conceived'.[3] The second group consists of various arguments that take as their data some facts about the world and then attempt to show that these facts cannot be explained without positing the existence of God.[4] We can dismiss the Anselmian argument, since it is not found in any medieval Jewish or Islamic philosopher or theologian, and is thus irrelevant in a study of Gersonides.[5] Arguments of the second type, however, are quite diverse; for our purposes we shall concentrate upon the arguments that were used by Gersonides. The first of these arguments is the 'proof from motion', which was originally proposed by Aristotle[6] and then picked up and advocated by Averroes, Maimonides, and Aquinas as the most evident of the proofs for God's existence. The general thesis of this type of argument is that an adequate explanation of motion, especially the motions of the heavenly bodies, requires the existence of immaterial, supernatural, and transcendent causes. These are the notorious 'unmoved movers' that 'move' the heavenly bodies by their being 'objects of desire'.[7]

However, before we examine Gersonides' evaluation of this argument, we need to note an important interpretation of the argument that resulted in a

---

[3] Anselm, *Proslogium*, chs. 1–2. The title 'ontological proof' was introduced by Kant (*Critique of Pure Reason*, B 620–30 (trans Kemp Smith, 500–7)).

[4] It is customary to call the former argument a priori and the latter argument a posteriori. The ontological argument has as its starting point the concept of God and infers from it alone that this concept is instantiated. In this sense the concept of God is the logical, or formal, cause of the existence of God. The a posteriori arguments, however, begin with some empirical fact about or in the world and prove that its cause is God. It is an argument from effects to cause.

[5] Wolfson, 'Notes on the Proofs of the Existence of God', 561, 569–70.

[6] Aristotle, *Physics*, 8.6; id., *Metaphysics*, 12.6–8.

[7] Averroes, *Long Commentary on Aristotle's Metaphysics*, 1588–98 (trans. Genequand, 146–50); Maimonides, *Guide*, ii. 1 (trans. Pines, 245–6); Aquinas, *Summa Theologiae*, I q. 2 arts. 2–3.

different conceptual and terminological transformation of it. Even before the medieval period Aristotle's unmoved movers were identified with 'separate intellects' in post-Aristotelian Greek philosophy. If the unmoved movers are not bodies, what are they? Aristotelian philosophy immediately rules out the option of their being separate Platonic forms, for there are no such things. Since the primary and supreme unmoved mover is God, whom Aristotle characterizes as pure intellect,[8] it was quite understandable that the subordinate unmoved movers should be identified as intellects as well. As early as Plotinus this identification was made explicit,[9] and this is how many of the medievals understood Aristotle's argument from motion: the unmoved movers are incorporeal intellects separate from matter, external to the heavenly bodies they move, and they move their corresponding bodies without themselves undergoing motion.[10] We shall now see, however, that although Gersonides accepts the existence of separate intellects, one of which is God, he does not believe that the Aristotelian argument for their existence is valid. In rejecting this argument he will introduce some novel ideas in the physics of motion.

The argument for the existence of God from motion rests upon several theorems in Aristotle's physics: (1) everything that moves is moved by something else, (2) a finite body has only finite force, or energy, hence (3) motion needs to be conserved as well as caused, and (4) there is no infinite series of movers. Taking as the paradigm case of motion the motion of the heavenly bodies, the Aristotelian theory then concludes from these premises that the only adequate explanation of the continuous motion of the heavenly domain is the existence of unmoved movers that continuously conserve these motions. One of these unmoved movers is primary. This is God. Aristotle and his medieval disciples were not sure how many of these unmoved movers were needed to explain all the diverse movements of the heavenly bodies; Aristotle himself transferred this question to the astronomers.[11]

As is evident, this argument assumes that motion in general, and especially the continuous, perhaps eternal, motion of the heavenly bodies, requires explanation. For Aristotle there are no self-movers. If a body is moving, its motion needs to be accounted for by something external to it. If the body in question is moving eternally, as Aristotle and Averroes believed the heavenly bodies are, their eternal motion must be preserved; so even here something other than themselves is needed to account for their eternal motion. Gersonides rejects the underlying principle of this argument: for him, once

---

[8] Aristotle, *Metaphysics*, 12.9–10. [9] Plotinus, *Enneads*, 5.1.9.
[10] Grant, *Planets, Stars and Orbs*, 523–48. [11] Aristotle, *Metaphysics*, 12.8.

a thing is in motion it does not necessarily require another thing to keep it moving. Under certain conditions it could move by itself indefinitely. If this is so, the Aristotelian argument is invalid, even if it is assumed that the motion of the heavenly bodies is eternal. As we saw in Chapter 2, Gersonides proved that the heavenly bodies are indestructible. Not liable to any internal cause of deceleration or corruption nor exposed to any external impediment, they move continuously without needing to have their motions conserved. This is one of the differentiating features of the celestial realm, as Aristotle had pointed out. Thus, Aristotle's very attempt to exempt the heavenly bodies from all the debilitating factors characteristic of terrestrial bodies turns out to undermine his argument for unmoved movers and separate intellects.

This critique of the argument from motion as a proof for the existence of separate intellects, one of which is God, has several important consequences: (1) the role of the separate intellects in explaining celestial motion will need to be redefined, (2) the conserving cause of celestial motion will no longer be external to the celestial body, and (3) the a posteriori proof for God's existence will have to be reformulated in non-kinetic terms, such that God is not understood primarily as the first cause of motion. In Gersonides' celestial mechanics the immediate cause of the continuous motion of a celestial body is its form, which is internal to it. Concluding his argument against Aristotle, Gersonides claims: 'It does not follow from this [Aristotle's argument] that this mover is separate; but it can be a material form [that is, a form in matter], since the latter does not itself move when it moves [something else].'[12]

Since the relationship of a form to that of which it is the form is invariable,[13] the motions of the heavenly bodies are constant and unceasing without requiring an external cause to keep them moving. Indeed, this form is an intellect, which is 'separate' only in the sense that it operates without the use of a corporeal organ; it is not separate in the sense of being external to the celestial body. It is an embedded form, or intellect.[14] Lest this seem somewhat bizarre, remember that in Aristotelian philosophy every substance, especially a living substance, has a form and that in the case of a living body this form is its soul.[15] For Gersonides, then, the heavenly bodies have

---

[12] *Wars*, 5.3.6 (iii. 152); see also ibid. 6.2.8 (iii. 449); *CT*, Gen., 'Bereshit', 10*a* (i. 26); Glasner, 'Gersonides on Simple and Composite Motions', 564–5, especially the references in n. 101; Staub, *The Creation of the World According to Gersonides*, 299 n. 244.

[13] If the form that accounts for my being human were to change, I would not be human any more; forms are not changeable or corruptible.

[14] Glasner, 'Gersonides on Simple and Composite Motions', 576–7.

[15] Aristotle, *On the Soul*, 2.4.

intellects, or intellectual souls, which, as their forms, move them naturally and continuously. As intellects they are the causes of the motions of the heavenly bodies by conceptualization: each such intellect conceives the emanative plan governing that part of the terrestrial world for which it is responsible: 'This conceptualization is nothing but the fact that from this motion there emanates something to the sublunar world.'[16] Again, the analogy with the artisan is relevant. In so far as a carpenter makes a cabinet according to a plan or design he has conceived, the plan can be said to be the 'mover' that causes the movements of the carpenter resulting in the construction of a cabinet. Analogously, the intellect, qua form that moves the heavenly body, apprehends the emanative scheme for which it is the formal and efficient cause. And just as the plan is internal to the carpenter, so too the separate intellect of the heavenly body is internal to it.[17]

How then can we prove God's existence? There is a sense in which this question has already been answered: since the world has been proved to be created, there is a creator. The proof of creation is at the same time the proof of God's existence. According to Maimonides, this argument was characteristic of Kalam, and for him completely objectionable, since it made the question of God's existence logically dependent upon the validity of the Kalam arguments for creation, which for Maimonides were invalid.[18] Gersonides did not seem to be disturbed by Maimonides' criticism of the Kalam method of proving God's existence from creation. After all, as we have seen, he was quite confident that he had proved that the world was created and that it was created by an agent acting purposefully. Nevertheless, as always he is generous with his arguments, and he does give us an argument for the existence of God that is independent of his proofs of creation.

---

[16] *Wars*, 6.1.17 (iii. 323–4); see also Glasner, 'Gersonides on Simple and Composite Motions', 571–7.

[17] As if recognizing the weakness of this argument Aristotle offers a very different proof, also based on motion, in *Metaphysics*, 12.7: if there are things that move others by themselves moving, and if there are things that are moved without themselves moving anything else, there must also be things that move others without themselves moving. Accordingly, the series of moving things terminates in something(s) that is itself unmoved and separate from sensible, or corporeal, things. These are the unmoved movers. Both Averroes and Maimonides give this argument (Averroes, *Long Commentary on Aristotle's Metaphysics*, 1588–98 (trans. Genequand, 146–50); Maimonides, *Guide*, ii. 1 (trans. Pines, 244–6)). Gersonides, however, rejects it. For it could be, as we have just seen, that the mover is an embedded intellect, or form, which itself does not move while it moves its body (*Wars*, 5.3.6 (iii. 152)).

[18] Maimonides, *Guide*, i. 71 (trans. Pines, 179–82).

The formal structure of this proof is not simple; it consists actually of two stages, or sub-proofs. Nor is it presented as a distinct or main subject of enquiry in any of the six books of *Wars*. It has to be extracted from the more general question of the existence and role of separate intellects, which in the Bible and rabbinic literature are termed 'angels'.[19] This is the general theme of part 3 of Book 5 of *Wars*. Gersonides begins his argument by demonstrating first the existence of a separate intellect that operates in the sublunar world; then he proceeds to show that this intellect is a member of a set of such separate intellects, whose ultimate and prime member is God.

What is especially interesting about Gersonides' argument is that, although an outstanding astronomer, he begins with biology. In the opening chapters of part 3 of Book 5 of *Wars*, Gersonides engages in a prolonged debate with some of the commentators on Aristotle, especially Averroes, on the question of the primary cause of animal reproduction. Aristotle himself wrote a treatise on the generation of animals in which he somewhat cryptically suggested that in the generation of humans the intellect 'supervenes', or enters from the outside. Some of Aristotle's commentators, notably Themistius and Avicenna, although recognizing the unique status of humanity by virtue of its intellect, were prepared to extend the influence and intervention of this outside force to all animal generation. Accordingly, all living things owe their origin and development to a separate intellect, specifically the 'Agent Intellect', that is responsible for their possession of form. This intellect was commonly called the 'giver of forms'.[20] Averroes, however, was prepared to extend the role of the Agent Intellect only to the generation of the human intellect; otherwise, animal generation is a purely natural phenomenon, perfectly explicable in biological terms, requiring no appeal to transcendent causes or separate intellects.[21]

Gersonides' discussion of these views is quite detailed and presupposes the framework of Aristotelian biology. At the outset we need to recall Aristotle's definition of a living thing as a composite of form and matter. Moreover, its

---

[19] Maimonides, *Guide*, ii. 2 (trans. Pines, 252–3), ii. 4 (trans. Pines, 258–9).

[20] Aristotle, *Generation of Animals*, 2.3.736*b*28–9. A good discussion of the views of Themistius and Avicenna is provided by Davidson, *Alfarabi, Avicenna and Averroes on Intellect*, chs. 2, 4. See also *Wars*, 5.3.1–3 (iii. 81–122); H. Goldstein, 'Dator Formarum'.

[21] In his exposition Gersonides finds three distinct views in Averroes' commentaries on Aristotle. The third view is the 'naturalistic' interpretation and receives the most attention from Gersonides. For Averroes' theories, see Touati, 'Les Problèmes de la génération et le rôle de l'intellect agent', and Davidson, 'Averroes on the Acting Intellect as a Cause of Existence'.

form is its soul.[22] In the generation of a dog, for example, the egg (Aristotle's 'female blood') is inseminated by the sperm (Aristotle's 'male seed'), resulting in the foetus. For Aristotle the female factor in generation is the matter, whereas the male factor is the form.[23] Accordingly, the form is in some sense in the male seed.[24] Now the form, or soul, of a living thing is for Aristotle the sum total of its typical activities, that is, those behaviours that characterize the organism and constitute its membership of a definite species. However, as Aristotle himself emphasized, these behavioural patterns are teleological: they not only serve to preserve the individual as a member of a definite species, but enable the organism to function to its maximum ability as well. Living things are then goal-directed, and their behaviour is governed by laws dictated by their forms. What the biologist observes in living things are regulative mechanisms that preserve the species in general and the particular individual of the species. In all living things we can recognize these patterns, which Gersonides now labels, using one of his favourite phrases, 'the law, order, and rightness' inherent in the sublunar domain.[25]

Aristotle's embryology is, then, formulated for the most part in purely biological terms. Although teleological in its orientation, Aristotle's biology posits the goal-directed formal structure of living things within the organisms themselves. Indeed, for him the artisan imitates nature, where teleological processes take place without deliberation but according to a fixed order. His teleology is then immanent rather than transcendent. Other Greek thinkers, most notably Plato, were also teleological in their natural philosophy, but conceived the teleological order as the result of a transcendent force that 'makes', or endows, nature with this structure. On this view, nature imitates the artisan.[26] Accordingly, for these thinkers, the teleological character of the natural world is itself an argument for a transcendent cause of this order. This is the venerable proof of the existence of God known as 'the argument from design', which Kant considered to be the only one worthy of respect.[27] On this point Averroes followed Aristotle; Gersonides, however, was more of a Platonist.

Let us enquire further into Aristotle's question concerning the origin of the soul, or form, in the seed. From a purely physical perspective the seed is just a conglomeration of biochemical elements, that is, a piece of matter. What is formal, or soul-like, in it? In his lengthy and laborious discussion of this issue, Gersonides canvasses a variety of answers that attempt to identify

---

[22] Aristotle, *On the Soul*, 2.4.   [23] Aristotle, *Generation of Animals*, 1.21–2.

[24] Ibid. 2.1.735a5–29, 2.3.736b30–737a34.   [25] *Wars*, 5.3.5 (iii. 137).

[26] Plato, *Timaeus*, 29–31.

[27] Kant, *Critique of Pure Reason*, B 650–8 (trans. Kemp Smith, 519–24).

the form, or soul, in the seed with some kind of physical feature, such as heat. Diverse terms are used to refer to this element: 'elemental heat', 'vital heat', 'measured heat', 'soul-heat', 'soul-power'.[28] Throughout his own discussion of this power, Aristotle connects it with motion, or physical activity. It is a power that moves the foetus in the direction that the particular animal is supposed to develop until it reaches maturity. In Gersonides' report of Averroes' different accounts of generation, he finds this purely physicalist theory of soul in Book 7 of Averroes' *Long Commentary on Aristotle's Metaphysics* and takes this to be Averroes' ultimate understanding of Aristotle's theory. In short, 'material forms generate material forms'; that is, the embodied form, or soul, of an animal is generated by semen, which is itself material.[29]

But, Gersonides asks, how can form, or soul, come from something that is just matter? Semen, according to Aristotle, is just some kind of liquid mixed with hot air.[30] Why would anyone think that boiling water is soul-like? It is true, Gersonides concedes, that heat in the seed is a factor in the reproductive process; but it is only an instrument used by the proper, or real, agent of the process. Gersonides employs an analogy here with the artisan: although the carpenter certainly uses various instruments in making a cabinet, one of which is his own energy, or heat, the real agent is the carpenter, or more precisely the form, or plan, in his mind. None of the instruments, including his energy, endows the cabinet with its structure, or form. The concept in the mind of the carpenter does. The same is true, Gersonides contends, of the generation of animals. If the mature animal embodies a formal structure that determines its typical behaviour, the cause, or generator, of this structure must itself contain this structure in some manner. Here Gersonides quotes Aristotle against Averroes: 'Whatever is potentially something becomes actually that thing by virtue of something actual that is similar to that which is actualized.'[31] The semen as liquid mixed with hot air cannot be the agent of the soul, or form, of the animal. The latter must be produced by something else, and this agent is a 'separate intellect' that endows all living things with their form, or soul. It is the Agent Intellect that is the source, indeed the proximate cause, of the 'law, order, and rightness' embodied in the terrestrial world. Since, in the medieval theory of the separate intellects, the Agent Intellect is the intellect whose influence immediately reaches the terrestrial domain, it is responsible for the course of

---

[28] *Wars*, 5.3.1 (iii. 83–4) and see nn. 9, 14.

[29] Ibid. 5.3.2 (iii. 100); Touati, *La Pensée philosophique de Gersonide*, 325–34.

[30] Aristotle, *Generation of Animals*, 2.2.735a30–735b11.

[31] Aristotle, *Metaphysics*, 7.7.1032a4–25; *Wars*, 5.3.3 (iii. 100–1).

animal generation. As the agent of this order, it contains this law but in a more perfect and unified manner. At this juncture a bit of Platonism insinuates itself into Gersonides' argument. The presence of form in a material thing cannot be accidental; it derives from some cause in which this form is present in a more perfect manner. No matter how successfully the form in the material thing has been instantiated, it still is a copy, an imperfect realization of the paradigm. In Gersonides' Platonism the paradigm for the order in the sublunar world is present in the Agent Intellect, which corresponds to Plato's Demiurge or Plotinus' Nous.[32]

The first stage of Gersonides' proof has been completed: there is an incorporeal intellect that is the agent of animal generation in which the teleological order embodied in living things is represented in a more perfect manner. But we now have to ascend from the sublunar domain to the heavens to reach our ultimate goal, God. Although Gersonides rejected Averroes' purely naturalistic account of animal generation, he did not exclude the heavenly bodies from having a role to play in the world of living things. If the Agent Intellect is the 'giver of forms', the heavenly bodies supply living things with the heat or physical energy needed for growth and nourishment. Aristotle was at least partially right in saying that 'man is generated by man and the sun'.[33] But the heavenly bodies and their intellects are just instruments in this process, analogous to the energy expended by the carpenter in making a cabinet. Nevertheless, since this whole process exhibits a definite integrative order constituting a unified ecological system, there has to be some kind of unifying principle or cause responsible for this order. According to Gersonides, the Agent Intellect works in tandem with the intellects of heavenly bodies by collecting or synthesizing the various particular emanations that derive from each of the heavenly bodies. Whereas each heavenly body emanates according to the plan envisaged by its own intellect, or form, the Agent Intellect incorporates all these partial emanations and represents them as a systematic whole. For this reason it really is superior to the other separate intellects even though its domain is the sublunar world. Here Gersonides departs from several of his predecessors, including Maimonides, who like most of his sources located the Agent Intellect at the lowest level in the rank of the separate intellects.[34]

Now the heavenly domain also exhibits 'law, order, and rightness'. If the regularity and order inherent in the sublunar world emanate from the Agent

---

[32] *Wars*, 5.3.4 (iii. 135); Feldman, 'Platonic Themes in Gersonides' Doctrine of the Agent Intellect'.

[33] Aristotle, *Physics*, 2.2.194*b*13.   [34] Maimonides, *Guide*, ii. 4 (trans. Pines, 257–8).

Intellect, what about the heavenly order? The plan that they embody must also have a cause, and this cause must also be the cause of the order of the entire universe. Gersonides maintains that this order accrues to the heavenly domain because all of these intellects emanate directly from a first intellect that is 'the law, order and rightness of existent things in the absolute sense'.[35] This intellect comprehends the entire order of the universe, whereas the other, or secondary, intellects, including the Agent Intellect, function only as subordinate workers, subject to the overarching plan of the master crafts-man. Explicitly referring to Plato, Gersonides introduces the analogy of a perfect state wherein there is a division of labour planned and supervised by the ruler according to rational principles. The universe, for Gersonides, is like the perfect state: it exhibits an order governed by the division of labour wherein the various subordinate intellects have specific roles to play but are all directed by a primary agent, God.[36] And this is the relationship of God to his universe: the order and lawfulness of the universe exemplifies the plan conceived by God; this plan exists in God in a paradigmatic form. In this way the divine order is both immanent and transcendent.[37]

Gersonides' teleological proof for the existence of God, or his version of the argument from design, integrates both the celestial and terrestrial domains, astronomy and biology. Not only do the heavens manifest the handiwork of the Lord but so do earthly creatures. The law, order, and right-ness exhibited here on earth is partial evidence of a more comprehensive plan governing all existent things. And this universal order is the best proof for the existence of God, the master architect. This is why the study of the empir-ical sciences was so important for Gersonides. Commenting upon Song of Songs 1: 3, Gersonides remarks:

By virtue of the divine wisdom exhibited in existent things recognizable at first sight because of their maximum order, rightness and perfection, men are stimulated to investigate them until they attain the nature of this wisdom . . . For this continuous perfection manifested in existent things provides strong confirmation of Your exis-tence and Perfection. It would be impossible for them to come about by themselves or through chance given their perfection and continuous order.[38]

The study of the natural sciences is indeed fundamental and a prerequisite for the ascent to metaphysics not because the explanation of celestial motion requires the postulation of separate movers, but because the whole of nature, even our own bodies, displays the handiwork of the Lord (Ps. 8: 3).

---

[35] *Wars*, 5.3.5 (iii. 137).   [36] Ibid. 6.1.18 (iii. 340–1).   [37] Ibid. 5.3.13 (iii. 190).

[38] Gersonides, *Commentary on the Five Scrolls*, S. of S., 7c; (*Commentary on the Song of Songs*, trans. Kellner, 24–5).

In concluding this section, we need to note that, in rejecting the classic argument for God's existence from motion, Gersonides also rejects the associated thesis that God is the mover of a celestial sphere, specifically the outermost sphere of fixed stars. This issue was a subject of considerable controversy in medieval Islamic philosophy. Avicenna denied that God is the mover of a particular sphere, whereas Averroes maintained that God is the mover of the outermost one. On this issue Maimonides sided with Avicenna, and, contrary to his usual preference for Averroes over Avicenna, Gersonides agrees here with Maimonides. If God were the mover of a particular sphere, then his activity would be restricted to that sphere alone. But, as we have seen, God is the paradigmatic cause of the whole universe. Since the entire universe derives from God and its order reflects, albeit imperfectly, the order inherent in his mind, his causal efficacy cannot be limited to one part of the universe. Indeed, since the causal efficacy of any of the separate intellects emanates from their intellectual activity and hence is restricted to the domain of their respective influence, if God were the mover of a specific sphere, his knowledge would be limited to that sphere alone. But this is inconsistent with the thesis that God is the 'absolute' cause of the entire universe. His knowledge and supervision are not limited or circumscribed, as is the case with the activities of the subordinate separate intellects. If God's activity were so restricted, he would be like these secondary intellects, which is absurd since he is their cause. Finally, since what establishes God's existence is not motion but the constant telic order inherent in the universe, it would misrepresent God's place and role in the universe to characterize him as a mover of a specific celestial body or sphere.[39]

How Can We Speak about God?

The topic of the divine attributes was one of the central questions in medieval philosophical and theological speculation. If there is a divine being, we want to know what it is like and, in particular, how we can speak about it, since *ex hypothesi* it is very different from us and anything else we are familiar with. There are two closely related questions here: the specific attributes possessed by God and the appropriate language to be used in describing these attributes. Like Maimonides, Gersonides deals with the second question first. However, whereas Maimonides devotes almost the whole of the first part of his *Guide* to these issues, Gersonides discusses them in the context of other

---

[39] *Wars*, 5.3.11 (iii. 168–171); Maimonides, *Guide*, ii. 4 (trans. Pines, 258–9); Aquinas, *Summa Contra Gentiles*, 3.23.

topics, such as the problem of one specific divine attribute—omniscience—and the theory of the separate intellects. In Book 3 of *Wars* he takes up the problem of the proper language to be used in speaking about God in the context of refuting Maimonides' account of divine knowledge, since the latter's theory of this topic hinges upon his doctrine of divine attributes. In the course of criticizing Maimonides' doctrine and developing his own theory, Gersonides lays the groundwork for his later discussion of the specific attributes to be predicated of God in *Wars*, 5.3.12.

As the works of David Kaufmann and Harry Wolfson have demonstrated, the question of divine attributes developed quite early in medieval thought. Theological debates within Christianity and Islam, as well as debates between these two religions concerning the persons of the Trinity and the specific attributes of God, gave rise to an extensive literature on these subjects.[40] Independently of these theological discussions there developed a parallel philosophical problem concerning the applicability of any kind of predicates to God. This problem was introduced by Plotinus' characterization of the ultimate reality, the One, as 'beyond being', as ineffable.[41] Plotinus' doctrine imported into the theological arena the *via negativa* as the most proper mode of discourse about God: we come to know God, to the extent that we can know him, only by negating predicates or properties of him; this is the only legitimate mode of theological discourse. In medieval Jewish philosophy the exemplary proponent of negative theology was Maimonides.

Maimonides' doctrine of divine attributes can be usefully divided into three stages: first, a general theory of religious language; second, the application of this theory to specific terms or phrases used in the Torah to refer to God; and finally, his advocacy of negative theology. Proceeding from his claim that language in general, and religious language in particular, contains three types of non-univocal terms: those that are homonymous (that is, absolutely equivocal), those that are metaphorical, and those that are ambiguous, Maimonides concludes that most, if not all, of the property terms, or attributes predicated of God, are absolutely equivocal.[42] He then constructs a philosophical theory of theological discourse, the upshot of which is that no positive attributes, whether they be essential, accidental, or relational, can be predicated of God. If they were essential attributes defining

---

[40] Kaufmann, *Geschichte der Attributenlehre*. Wolfson wrote several articles on this subject. The most relevant for our enquiry are 'Maimonides on Negative Attributes' and 'Maimonides and Gersonides on Divine Attributes'.

[41] Plotinus, *Enneads*, 5.1.7–8, 5.2.1, 5.3.12, 6.7.32–3, 6.9.3.

[42] Maimonides, *Guide*, i. 'Introduction', 1–49 (trans. Pines, 17–110).

God, they would imply that God is definable, and that would mean that God is 'composable', or analysable into several properties that make up his essence. But God is believed to be indivisible, not composed of distinct properties, or elements, as is, for example, water. If the attributes were accidents, this would imply that God is subject to properties that can be acquired or lost, to which changes accidental properties are prone. But this is impossible, for God is supposed to be immutable. And if relational attributes were admitted to be possible, this would entail that there is some kind of real relation between God and something else. But this is impossible, since this would involve putting God and that to which he is allegedly related into a common genus or species, which is also absurd. As if realizing the radical import of his argument against affirmative attributes, Maimonides then pulls up and allows us, as a kind of concession, to use actional predicates in talking about God, for example, 'God created the world'; for such predications do not assert of God a property belonging to him but merely designate some act performed by him. Moreover, these are attributes sanctioned by the canonical texts of Judaism, and as such have religious authority and tradition behind them.[43]

Underlying this radical rejection of positive attributions, other than actional predications, is Maimonides' worry that affirmative attributes impair divine unity: to assert of God attributes, such as goodness, wisdom, or power, would imply that these various properties are distinct things, different not only from each other but from God's essence as well. And even if they were regarded as essential attributes, as some theologians had maintained,[44] this would not lessen in any way the implied multiplicity in God. Divine unity, for Maimonides, is so fundamental that it forbids our saying or believing anything that would suggest that God is intrinsically plural or composite. In this sense divine unity for Maimonides really is tantamount to divine simplicity: the absence of any kind of internal compositeness or multiplicity. As Maimonides himself explicitly says, the belief in such attributes is no different from the Christian doctrine of the Trinity, which for him is philosophically absurd and religiously heretical.[45]

If, then, language about God is equivocal, and affirmative attributes other than actional predications are not legitimate, what can we say about God when we are not praying but thinking philosophically? Is there some kind of language that is philosophically proper and meaningful that would enable us to speak about God without falling into error or gibberish? It is here that the

---

43 Maimonides, *Guide*, i. 51–7.
44 Wolfson, *The Philosophy of the Kalam*, 217–18.
45 Maimonides, *Guide*, i. 50 (trans. Pines, 111).

via negativa enters the discussion. In general, any property that we deem to be a perfection, such that it would be better to possess it than not, and is thus prima facie thought to be appropriate as a divine attribute, is to be formulated as the absence of its privation or the negation of its opposite imperfection. If to be benevolent is a perfection, then the correct way of attributing this property to God is to say 'God is not malevolent' or 'God is not the kind of being to be malevolent'. In speaking in this manner we are not making any assertions as to what God is but only removing from him properties that we believe to be imperfections. In a way this is a kind of Socratic enquiry in which someone offers a positive account or definition of a moral concept, such as justice, and Socrates then proceeds to show that this definition leads to contradictions or absurdities, and hence has to be rejected. The Socratic dialogue ends on a sceptical, or negative, note in so far as no positive account of the concept in question has survived or emerged from the enquiry. Nevertheless, we do know something: that the ordinary concepts about morality are deficient, and the more we know of their defects the closer we shall get to the truth about them. Analogously with negative attributes: the more we eliminate from our God-talk erroneous concepts by means of negations, the more we cleanse our minds of false notions about God. It is better to know that God is not the kind of entity to lie than to say or think that God is truthful, since in asserting the latter we imply that, like Abraham, God tells the truth but could on occasion tell a lie. In short, affirmative attributes say too much, and the more one says the more one is liable to fall into error.[46]

Gersonides rejected Maimonides' account of divine attributes and proposed an alternative theory that he believed was philosophically more tenable and more consonant with religious practice. Indeed, he challenged Maimonides' equivocation thesis and offered a different account of the semantics of God-talk, one crucial consequence of which is the refutation of the *via negativa*. Remember that for Maimonides some terms in religious discourse are less than completely equivocal; they are 'ambiguous', in so far as there is some common feature that is true of the things to which it applies.[47] For example, the Hebrew word *elohim* denotes God, angels, and judges, all of which are considerably different from each other. Yet they do connote some common property of all of them: authority. This notion of

[46] Maimonides, *Guide*, i. 55, 58–60 (trans. Pines, 134–7); Wolfson, 'Maimonides and Gersonides on Divine Attributes'; Feldman, 'A Scholastic Misinterpretation of Maimonides' Doctrine of Divine Attributes'.

[47] Maimonides, *Guide*, i. 56 (trans. Pines, 130–1).

semantic ambiguity plays a central role in Aristotle, who used it frequently in many areas of his philosophy. A good example is his refutation of Plato's doctrine of the forms, especially the notion of the 'super-form', the Good. Plato assumed that the terms referring to the forms were univocal, connoting one and only one concept. Aristotle rejected this thesis, and in the case of the form Good he argued that the term 'good' is ambiguous. Yet it is not absolutely equivocal either; rather, there is some common feature present in all the things to which the term is predicated, although they exhibit this feature in different ways. Consider the term 'healthy': we apply it to a person, to a diet, to exercise, to vitamins. Even though the term signifies differently in each of these cases, nevertheless, its different connotations are related to each other in some way. The diet, exercise, and vitamins are productive of health in the person, but in different ways. And since the person is the ultimate referent of these diverse yet related predications, we can consider it to be the primary referent. Hence, the term 'healthy' can be said to be primarily predicated of the person, whereas it is predicated of the other items secondarily; that is, the former predication is prior, whereas the other applications of the term are posterior.[48] In this sense the healthy person is the paradigmatic subject of the predicate 'healthy', to which diet and exercise are subordinate. Sometimes Aristotle designates this semantic relationship by the term 'analogy'.[49]

Consider now the fundamental attributes of existence and unity as predicated of God: they are also predicated of many other things. Maimonides claimed that in the former case these terms are completely equivocal, and therefore their connotations have nothing in common with their corresponding application to creatures. Hence, we have to use some kind of negative formulation to apply these terms to God. On the contrary, Gersonides replies, these terms are not so equivocal that we are forced into using an artificial language when we apply them to God. Rather, they are ambiguous terms, words that denote their subjects differently, yet connote something that relates them in some way. In these cases, since God is believed to be the creator of the universe, he exists as cause, whereas everything else exists as an effect of his causal efficacy. Here the term 'exist' is predicated of God in the primary, or prior, sense, whereas it is true of the planet Jupiter in the secondary, or posterior, sense. Both God and Jupiter, however, do exist, that is, it is true to say of both of them that they are members of the set of real entities, although to be sure they exist in different ways.

---

[48] Aristotle, *Nicomachean Ethics*, 1.6; id., *Metaphysics*, 4.2.
[49] Aristotle, *Physics*, 7.4.249a23–4; Aquinas, *Summa Theologiae*, I q. 13 arts. 5–6.

With respect to such terms as 'exists', 'one', 'essence' and the like . . . they are predicated of God primarily and of other things secondarily. For His existence, unity,
and essence belong to Him essentially, whereas the existence, unity and essence of
every [other] existent thing emanate from Him. Now when something is of this
kind, the predicate applies to it in a prior sense, whereas the predicate applies in a
posterior sense to the other things that are called by it insofar as they are given this
property directly by the substance that has this property in the prior sense.[50]

In general, then, certain attributes are assigned to God with the understanding that he is the paradigm case, or instance, of that property, and its application to God is legitimate despite its ambiguity. Although its predication of
both God and some creature is not univocal, the predicate is not completely
equivocal: there is some property that both referents exemplify, albeit not in
the same way or to the same degree. Once this semantic point is appreciated,
there is no need to introduce the artificial and cumbersome linguistic device
of negative predications. Indeed, such a manoeuvre results in several logical
difficulties.

  First, consider the logic of affirmation and negation. It is a basic rule of
logic that in affirming or negating a proposition or property, the terms in the
proposition must not be equivocal; otherwise the fallacy of equivocation
results. If someone says 'Abraham is truthful' and another says 'Abraham is
not truthful', the predicate 'truthful' must not be equivocal. If it were, the
affirmer and the denier would not be speaking to each other. Now if, following Maimonides, I must transpose all affirmative attributions of God into
some kind of negative statement, the predicate must have the same meaning
when it is affirmed as when it is negated of the subject. If not, what would be
the point of the negation? After all, what point would there be in negating
'God is a body' if the term 'body' were equivocal? I have to have some idea
of what the term 'body' means such that my negating it of God has some
definite meaning. If I want to rule out the possibility of God's being a body,
no matter what form my negative translation has, the predicate 'body' must
not be equivocal; otherwise I have not made a legitimate negation of the
inapplicable predicate.

With respect to those attributes concerning which we want to know whether or
not they can be predicated of God, it is evident that such predicates have one
meaning regardless of whether we affirm or deny them. For example, if we want
to know whether God is corporeal or incorporeal, the term 'corporeal' has the
same meaning in some sense in either case. For if the term 'body' has a completely

different connotation in the negation from the meaning it has in the affirmation, these statements would not be considered genuine contradictions.[51]

Second, how do I know which terms to negate of God? If I want to deny that Abraham is mendacious, I have to know what this term means. If it is equivocal, then how can I be sure that in some sense it might apply to Abraham, and thus not be susceptible of negation? The only way we have to even begin to talk about God is to work from the bottom up, that is, to assume that certain predicates that connote certain imperfections in our case are to be negated of God. To do this, however, implies that these predicates are not absolutely equivocal. Otherwise, the door is open for someone to say, 'There is a sense in which God is corporeal; it is just that by the term "corporeal" I do not mean the property of being a magnitude but some other property which can be truly applicable to God.' To shut the door and not allow this kind of argument we need to know at the outset that our language here is not completely equivocal, and thus we are able to set limits to what are acceptable predications about God.[52]

Finally, if our only proofs of the existence, unity, and incorporeality of God are a posteriori, from effects to causes, there has to be some commonality between the effect and the cause. Let us assume, as did Maimonides, that the Aristotelian proof for the existence of God from motion is valid. Its validity, however, requires that in the argument the terms 'motion', 'mover', and 'movable' are not equivocal. Suppose someone thinks that any or all of these terms are equivocal, and hence would say that, although in moving the heavenly bodies God is not moved in the same way as I am moved when I move the keys on the keyboard, nevertheless, he is moved but in a completely different way, and thus is not unmoved; or, in the case of proving divine unity, suppose again someone were to say that God is one but in such a way that there are three divine persons without impairing divine unity, since the term 'one' is equivocal and hence can have this Trinitarian connotation. Certainly Maimonides would not allow this kind of reasoning.

This is the core of Gersonides' theory of divine attributes. Maimonides was right in insisting upon the fact that many religious terms are not univocal in meaning. But he went too far, for some of these terms are not equivocal to the extent that he thought. As we have seen, there is a type of semantic multivalence that is, so to speak, intermediate between univocity and absolute equivocation: paradigmatic analogy, or predication by way of priority and posteriority. This means that the cause of something having a

---

[51] Ibid. 3.3 (ii. 109–10).   [52] Ibid. 3.3 (ii. 110).

specific property has that property in the primary, or more perfect, manner. Gersonides will now apply this principle to specific attributes that he believes are most expressive of the divine nature. Let us consider several examples.

One of the fundamental categories in Aristotle's philosophy is the category of 'substance', that which truly exists or is truly real.[53] God is indeed a substance, but in a paradigmatic, or prior, sense; for God is the cause of substantiality in everything else. In this context, Gersonides conceives of substance as form; for it is the form that constitutes or makes a thing what it is. If to be rational is what makes humans truly human, then rationality is their form, or substance. Now, God is the origin and cause of all form in so far as God contains the law and order of all reality, and according to this plan he created the universe. God is then the ultimate form, or substance, from which every created form, or substance, is derived. In predicating 'substance' or 'form' of God, we do not imply that the attribute is univocal; for, since God is the primary and paradigmatic referent of this attribute, there is some kind of disparity between the attribute's application to God and its application to something else. Yet we do want to affirm that God is indeed a substance, that his being constitutes the formal structure of the universe, and hence is responsible for the substantiality and form in all existent things:

In general, since the intelligible [form] of a thing that is a substance is itself a substance, and since God (may He be blessed) is in some sense the intelligible [form] of all existent things, He is necessarily a substance . . . for all existent things emanate from this intelligible form [that is, God], as artifacts emanate from the intelligible form of that artifact in the soul of the artisan.[54]

Again, the metaphor of the architect and the architectural design of the universe is exemplified in this account of the divine attributes.

Consider next the closely related attribute 'exists'. God certainly exists, as we have seen; but again his existence is paradigmatic. In so far as he is the cause of existence in everything else he exists in the primary or prior sense, whereas everything else exists in the secondary or posterior sense. The difference is expressed by Gersonides as follows: 'For He exists by His very essence and does not acquire His existence from anything else, whereas all other substances acquire their existence from Him.'[55]

Here Gersonides anticipates the fundamental notion in Spinoza's metaphysics that God is *causa sui*, that his existence follows from his essence, or his essence is to exist. All other things acquire their existence; God simply,

---

[53] Aristotle, *Categories*, 5; id., *Metaphysics*, 5.8, 7.1–4.
[54] *Wars*, 5.3.12 (iii. 174).   [55] Ibid. 5.3.12 (iii. 174–5).

and in the literal sense originally, exists.[56] By understanding the way in which the attribute applies differently in the two cases, we grasp the difference between God's existence and our existence, and thus meet Maimonides at least part of the way in recognizing the great distance between God and us. Yet even in conceding this disparity we affirm that on the list of existent things both God and we are members, albeit not on the same level or rank.

Of special significance in his list of divine attributes is his inclusion of an attribute that was largely ignored by his predecessors—divine joy. What is especially interesting about this attribute is the way in which Gersonides derives it from knowledge. According to Aristotle, the pleasure involved in knowing is the greatest pleasure.[57] Since God knows himself and in so doing knows the plan of the entire universe, which he has created, he takes pleasure in this knowledge. As it is said in Genesis (1: 31): 'And God saw all that He made, and it was very good.' Now God's knowledge is unique, since he knows not only the entire law and order of the universe but knows it as a unity and simultaneously. We, however, come to know the world piecemeal, accumulating information as we go along, which accounts for the fragmentary and incomplete character of our knowledge. Nevertheless, we do take pleasure in this knowledge, however imperfect it may be. All the more then does God, whose knowledge is perfect, have greater pleasure in his knowledge. Gersonides nicely and creatively expresses this idea in his exegesis of Genesis 2: 2, where the phrase *vayekhal elohim* is usually rendered as: 'And God completed all the work He had been doing.' Gersonides understands this verb as 'desire', basing his interpretation on a passage in 2 Samuel 13: 39: *vatekhal david*, 'And David desired'.[58] Accordingly, Genesis 2: 2 should be rendered: 'And God desired [that is, took pleasure in] all the work He had been doing.' In short, God's creative act, of which he has complete knowledge, is the experience of supreme pleasure, or joy. It is no wonder then that the sages have said: 'The joy is in His dwelling place.'[59]

Nevertheless, there still remains the worry that obsessed Maimonides: affirmative attributions would imply internal compositeness, or plurality, in God, and this is impossible.[60] Gersonides, however, believes that he is able to dissipate this problem by means of his theory of prior and posterior predication. Let us first consider what conditions account for plurality in a subject of predication. In the logic and metaphysics of Aristotle, such a subject is composite if and only if it satisfies the following two conditions: (1) the matter–form

[56] Spinoza, *Ethics*, 1.7.   [57] Aristotle, *Metaphysics*, 12.7, 12.9.
[58] *Wars*, 6.2.8 (iii. 467).   [59] BT *Ket.* 8a.
[60] Maimonides, *Guide*, i. 52 (trans. Pines, 114–19).

distinction is applicable to it and (2) its definition consists of a combination of generic and specific (differential) properties such that the latter are predicable of the former. For example, human beings are composite subjects because they are constituted by matter and exhibit a definite form that distinguishes them specifically from other animals. Moreover, in defining humanity we predicate of it the generic property 'animal' and the specific, or differential, property 'rational', where the two properties are distinct from each other and the latter is predicated of the former. In this case, the genus, or generic property, animal is, in Gersonides' terminology, a 'real subject'.[61] Now, in contrast a simple, or non-composite, subject does not satisfy these two conditions: it not analysable into the form–matter distinction, nor is it definable in terms of generic and specific properties such that the latter are predicated of the former.

To illustrate this logical point Gersonides gives two examples, one a physical subject, the other an abstract, or non-physical, subject. In the first case we have a red colour: Gersonides claims that here the apparent genus 'colour' is not a real subject of which the specific differential property 'red' is predicated, but just a 'logical', or 'linguistic', subject. This is so because there is no such thing as colour per se which takes on, as it were, a supervenient property, in this case red. We do not have here two distinct properties, one of which particularizes the other, such that one is the real genus of the other. Colours are simples: each colour is in itself a genus, a 'one of its kind'. In saying of a rose that it is reddish in colour, we are not assigning to it two distinct properties 'redness' and 'colour'; for to be red is to be a colour.[62] In the case of a non-physical subject too, such as a separate intellect, we do not have a genus, or generic property and another distinct property that particularizes the former. Gersonides' example is not easy for us to understand, since it is embedded in his doctrine of the separate intellects and their particular roles in astronomy. According to this theory, each heavenly sphere is moved by a distinct intellect that is differentiated from the intellects that move other spheres by knowing the plan governing the movements of that particular sphere. Since for the Aristotelian the knower and the object of knowledge are identical, especially where the knower is incorporeal,[63] that which defines

[61] *Wars*, 3.3 (ii. 112–14), and see n. 12; Wolfson, 'Maimonides and Gersonides on Divine Attributes'; Touati, *La Pensée philosophique de Gersonide*, 108–28.

[62] *Wars*, 3.3 (ii. 112–13). In early modern philosophy colours were favourite examples of simple subjects or concepts (Locke, *An Essay On Human Understanding*, 2.2–3; Hume, *A Treatise on Human Nature*, 1.1.1).

[63] Aristotle, *On the Soul*, 3.5; id., *Metaphysics*, 12.7, 12.9.

or distinguishes one such intellect from another is really identical with the intellect. We do not have here the form–matter distinction nor the distinction between generic and specific properties; indeed, the genus is the species: 'For these intellects differ from each other *essentially* without having anything [that is, the genus] in common. If they had anything in common, they would be composite, not simple entities.'[64]

Now if this is true of the subordinate intellects, how much more is it the case with the supreme intellect, God? Divine simplicity is not therefore impaired by positing essential attributes. For God is not a genus, or real subject, and the properties that we attribute to him are not distinct from his essence but are identical with it. Yet we do not fall into the error, of which Maimonides warned us, of thinking that these attributes are univocal, since they are predicated of God primarily and of creatures secondarily. If they were univocal they would import plurality, or compositeness, in their subject, since they would constitute a real definition of the subject, placing it within a genus–species framework involving plural attributes and substantial similarities with other entities in the same genus or species. Predications of priority and posteriority, however, do not have such weighty ontological implications. They are descriptive statements that say enough about the subject but not too much. In the case of God, such attributions tell us something about God, but not enough either to define him or to equate him with us. Predications of priority and posteriority inform us that God is the paradigmatic subject of any attribute we believe is a perfection, yet at the same time indicate that there is no strict parity between creator and creature.

Gersonides' theology can be seen as an attempt to bridge the ontological gap between God and humanity. Having rejected the astrophysical approach to proving the existence of God favoured by Aristotle, Averroes, and Maimonides, he focuses upon seeing God in our very generation and development as living creatures. God is not so much the mover of the heavenly bodies as the force in and behind our birth and growth. In a literal sense Gersonides' proof for the existence of God is a philosophical and scientific explanation of Job 19: 26: 'and from my flesh I see God'. God is closer to us than Maimonides thought. Biology, not astronomy or physics, provides the best evidence for the existence and activity of God. Gersonides' treatment of the divine attributes also reduces the distance between God and his creatures. Unlike Maimonides, who goes out of his way to maximize this gap, Gersonides wants to make God 'human-friendly'. There is no need to

[64] *Wars*, 3.3. (ii. 113–14).

manufacture an artificial language to speak about God nor to wonder if any language whatsoever is legitimate as a vehicle for humans to speak about or to God. By rejecting the *via negativa*, Gersonides gives us a philosophical justification for using ordinary language in theological discourse, removing the fears of anthropomorphism and absolute equivocation yet preserving the necessary ontological differences between God and his creatures.

FOUR

Divine Omniscience

Rabbi Akiva's Dilemma

IT WOULD SEEM THAT there should be no problem concerning whether or not God has knowledge of everything. After all, the Bible and the Quran depict God as speaking to, caring for, and rewarding or punishing specific individuals. Moreover, if God created the world, he should have knowledge of what he has created. Why then did one of the most important teachers of the Mishnah, Rabbi Akiva, bother to utter the apparent dilemma: 'All is fore-seen; yet freedom is given'?[1] The first clause would have been obvious to his audience. The second clause seems to be an emphatic response to the objec-tion that if God knows everything, how is human choice possible? Rabbi Akiba explicitly asserts that there is no problem in believing in both divine omniscience and the possibility of choice. The dilemma is indeed only appar-ent. In the latter clause Rabbi Akiva removes this doubt and affirms that although God knows everything, we still have choice.

Rabbi Akiva's dictum is puzzling and intriguing: puzzling because rabbinic literature is almost silent on this issue; intriguing since it stimulates us to ask what motivated Rabbi Akiva to enunciate this apparent dilemma. Was the saintly rabbi bothered by a theological conundrum? Was he respond-ing to some question raised by an anonymous doubter? Rabbinic literature contains examples of rabbis responding to questions raised by non-Jews, some of whom are introduced as philosophers.[2] It is therefore not idle to speculate what is behind his categorical affirmation of both divine omnis-cience and human freedom.

Some scholars have argued that the mishnaic teachers were not isolated intellectually from the Graeco-Roman world, that one can detect in their say-ings echoes at least of themes in Greek and Roman philosophy.[3] Without com-menting here upon the alleged influence of the latter upon rabbinic thought,

---

[1] Mishnah *Avot* 3: 5.
[2] *Mekhilta derabi yishma'el*, Bahodesh 6; Mishnah *AZ* 3:4.
[3] Fischel, *Rabbinic Literature and Greco-Roman Philosophy.*

we can definitely say that the apparent dilemma between divine omniscience and human freedom was well known and discussed in ancient philosophy. Indeed, Aristotle laid the philosophical foundations for virtually all subsequent philosophical and theological treatments of the subject in chapter 9 of his treatise *On Interpretation*. Now, it is important to realize at the outset that Aristotle was not concerned at all with the specific issue of divine omniscience; in fact, the term 'god' does not appear at all in this chapter. Aristotle was concerned with a logical question that arose out of his earlier discussion of a basic principle of his logic, the 'law of the excluded middle': a proposition is either true or false.[4] If this principle is true, does it apply universally, including statements about the future, especially those that we consider to be contingent, that is, statements that may or may not be true? Aristotle proceeds to show that if this principle does apply to such statements, their contingency would be annulled and there would be no such thing as choice and deliberation. Every future event would have a determinate truth-value *now*; the future would be as fixed as the past. These consequences worried Aristotle and he attempted to resolve them. Although scholars have not agreed on the precise nature of Aristotle's solution, subsequent ancient philosophers admitted the force of the dilemma and opted for one or other of its horns. The Epicureans wanted to preserve human freedom at all costs, and thus were prepared to deny the law of the excluded middle. Other thinkers believed in this logical principle without reservation and denied contingency completely.[5] Not long after Rabbi Akiva, the Greek philosopher and commentator on Aristotle, Alexander of Aphrodisias (*fl.* 198–211 CE), wrote a treatise *On Fate*, in which he explicitly defended the genuine contingency of some future events, and thus denied divine omniscience and affirmed human freedom.[6] These discussions, as we shall now see, spawned a voluminous literature throughout the whole history of philosophy and philosophical theology.

Gersonides' Solution to Rabbi Akiva's Dilemma

Although we cannot say definitively that Rabbi Akiva was influenced or stimulated by these philosophical discussions, it is clear that his dictum is an

[4] Aristotle, *On Interpretation*, 4.17*a*3–4, 9.18*a*27.

[5] Cicero's *On Fate* is a good source for the views of the Epicureans, who rejected determinism and defended an indeterministic philosophy of nature, and of the Stoics, who defended determinism.

[6] Alexander of Aphrodisias, *On Fate*, 30. Cicero too rejected divine foreknowledge: see *On Divination*.

attempt to dissipate the force of the dilemma by the dogmatic assertion of the truth of both divine omniscience and human choice in spite of their apparent logical incompatibility. To assent to the validity of the dilemma and then to be forced to choose between omniscience and free will was not an option for anyone who believed in the Bible or the Quran. Accordingly, we find quite early in Christian and Muslim theology various attempts to dissolve the dilemma and to provide what Rabbi Akiva did not, a solution that would justify belief in both divine omniscience and human freedom. Augustine and Boethius, in Christian thought, and the Muslim Kalam provide good examples of this undertaking.[7] Virtually all the major medieval thinkers followed suit.[8]

The medievals, however, broadened the scope of the issue. For them it was not only the question of future contingency and choice but the precise domain of divine knowledge in general. What does God really know? Again, Aristotle is not too far in the background. In chapters 7 to 10 of Book 12 of *Metaphysics*, he suggests that there are things that it is better for God not to know, in particular, changeable things, that is, the terrestrial domain, including human affairs.[9] Some of the Muslim Aristotelians, notably Avicenna, developed this theme further and concluded that God's knowledge does not encompass singular deeds and events; his knowledge is restricted to the universal. Accordingly, future contingencies, a subset of the domain of individual events, do not fall within the extent of divine cognition. Indeed, again following Aristotle, some of these thinkers maintained that God knows only himself.[10]

As is often the case, Gersonides' treatment of this issue grew out of his debate with Maimonides. The latter had maintained the validity of Rabbi Akiva's dictum, but in addition provided an answer as to how the apparent incompatibility between omniscience and freedom can be removed. For Maimonides, the problem arises only if we believe that divine knowledge and human knowledge are sufficiently alike such that what is true of the latter must be true of the former. In short, the dilemma disappears if we apply the *via negativa* analysis to the nature of divine cognition. God's way of knowing

---

[7] Augustine of Hippo, *On the Free Choice of the Will*, 3.2–4; Boethius, *The Consolation of Philosophy*, Book 5; Wolfson, *The Philosophy of the Kalam*, ch. 8.

[8] A good treatment of the medieval Christian literature on this topic can be found in Craig, *The Problem of Divine Foreknowledge*.

[9] Aristotle, *Metaphysics*, 12.9.1074*b*25–34.

[10] Ibid. 12.9.1074*b*33–4. For Al-Farabi and Avicenna, see Leaman, *Introduction to Classical Islamic Philosophy*, ch. 3, and Marmura, 'Some Aspects of Avicenna's Theory of God's Foreknowledge of Particulars'.

things is radically different from our mode of cognition, so there is no point in applying the rules of human epistemic logic to his knowledge of the future. If we could know how God knows everything, especially future contingencies, we would be God.[11] Like Rabbi Akiva we must confess our ignorance and dogmatically accept the truth of both divine omniscience in the strongest sense and human freedom.[12]

Gersonides devotes all of Book 3 of *Wars* to the question of divine cognition; in addition, his biblical commentaries contain extensive discussions of this topic, such as his interpretation of the Binding of Isaac (Gen. 22). As was his practice, I shall present the philosophical treatment first, and then examine the application of his philosophical conclusions to the biblical text. Gersonides begins by presenting a debate between the philosophers and the followers of the Torah, most notably Maimonides. It is interesting to note here that, as in his treatment of creation, Gersonides saw Maimonides more as a theologian than as a philosopher, one whose primary task was to defend traditional theological beliefs rather than to discover the real truth of the matter. Using Maimonides as his main source, Gersonides presents the main arguments of the philosophers and of Maimonides, although he adds some arguments on behalf of the philosophers that do not appear in Maimonides. After a close analysis of both sides of the issue he arrives at the conclusion that they have both reached some of the truth but not all of it, a typical expression of his attempt to appear faithful to tradition while really going beyond it. The philosophers are right in realizing that there are insurmountable difficulties in maintaining omniscience in the strong sense that includes knowledge of individual events, including future contingencies; but they go too far in concluding or suggesting that God has no knowledge of any kind pertaining to human affairs. The theologians, however, are more in error; for in asserting both strong omniscience and human freedom they fail to appreciate the real logical difficulties of this position. Moreover, Maimonides' attempt to defend this position by means of the *via negativa* has turned out to be a dead end, as we have seen. What is required here is a more refined

---

[11] Maimonides, *Guide*, iii. 16–21 (trans. Pines, 461–85).

[12] Despite this expression of loyalty to tradition, in one passage Maimonides asserts that to hold both omniscience and human freedom is to commit a logical howler. In this passage he is criticizing Mutazilite Kalam, of which Sa'adiah Gaon was a Jewish representative, for maintaining Rabbi Akiva's dictum (*Guide*, iii. 17 (trans. Pines, 468)). Is this one of the notorious intentional contradictions of the *Guide*? Hardly any of the commentators, medieval or modern, have noted this apparent inconsistency. The only exception I know of is the late medieval exegete Profiat Duran, also known as Efodi.

notion of omniscience that satisfies the rules of logic and is compatible with religion. Gersonides believed that he had succeeded in achieving this goal.

Consistent with his method, Gersonides begins his discussion with a summary of the arguments of the philosophers and of the theologians. He reproduces Maimonides' list of the philosophical arguments against divine knowledge of particulars, explaining them at greater length than his predecessor. Like Maimonides he sees that one of the arguments against divine omniscience is the argument from evil: there is so much injustice in the world, especially the suffering of the righteous and the prosperity of the wicked, that God cannot be omniscient if he is just and omnipotent. Hence, omniscience must be abandoned.[13] Gersonides dealt with the question of divine providence in Book 4 of *Wars*, and I will consider it in the next chapter.

Several of the philosophical arguments against strong omniscience concern the question: 'What does it mean to know a particular?' Since in this context we are focusing upon space–time particulars, events that occur within a spatial–temporal framework, we need to know how such particulars are known. According to the philosophers, we know them through our sensory organs, which are themselves rooted in a space–time framework, and hence can apprehend what is spatially and temporally located. In short, in order to know a space–time particular I must be able to pick out this particular by specifying its spatial and temporal place within the world of space–time events. This is not a problem for us, since we have the appropriate sensory apparatus to accomplish this task. But what about someone who does not have such an apparatus? As Kant argued, the world of space–time is knowable only to those who are themselves endowed with the sensory equipment to grasp it. If there are beings that do not have this apparatus, the world of space–time is not an object of knowledge for them.[14] The philosophers then conclude that since God is *ex hypothesi* incorporeal and transcendent, God does not have the cognitive apparatus that would enable him to have knowledge of space–time particulars. Being outside space–time, God does not know what is in space–time.[15]

The cognitive disparity between God and the world of particulars is further highlighted by the fact that particulars may be infinite in number, especially if the world is infinite in duration, either in the past or in the future, and are subject to continual change. Since, the philosophers argue, to know

[13] Maimonides, *Guide*, iii. 16 (trans. Pines, 461–2).

[14] Kant, *Critique of Pure Reason*, B 70–2 (trans. Kemp Smith, 89–90).

[15] Maimonides, *Guide*, iii. 16 (trans. Pines, 463); *Wars*, 3.2, first and second arguments (ii. 92).

something is literally to grasp and limit it within specific boundary conditions, the infinite by its very limitlessness is unknowable.[16] Moreover, since the domain of particulars is a world of continually changing objects, each cognition of them constitutes a change in the knower, whose knowledge is then not only accumulative but multiple and diverse as well. Whereas in our case this is normal and indeed constitutes our cognitive perfection, in a being that is supposed to be immutable and simple, this is an intolerable result. Indeed, from these impossibilities it follows that God knows only himself, as Aristotle had maintained.[17]

As we have indicated at the outset, the problem of divine omniscience becomes most acute when it is applied to the question of future contingency and human choice. On this score the philosophers mount two arguments that focus on the unknowability of the future. In the first place, a future event is by definition something that does not yet exist. As a space–time event it is knowable only through sensory perception. But if there is now nothing to perceive, how can we know it? Or, as Gersonides puts it, 'knowledge is necessarily [the cognition] of an existent, apprehended thing'.[18] An epistemic claim about some future event makes a reference to something that does not exist and has therefore, in Maimonides' language, nothing to 'attach to'.[19] Secondly, as Aristotle had argued in chapter 9 of *On Interpretation*, if I know that a sea-battle will take place tomorrow off the shore of Cyprus, then the statement 'there will be a sea-battle off the shore of Cyprus tomorrow' is true. But if it is true, then the battle's occurring tomorrow is a determinate and fixed event, whose non-occurrence is impossible. If God knows these events, then his knowledge of them robs them of their contingency. It would then follow that whenever we seem to be faced with a choice between two courses of action, we do not really have any real choice: what we shall do is already written down in God's personal library. So we are back to Rabbi Akiva's dilemma. But whereas he was content to accept both horns of the dilemma, the philosophers must obey logic and sacrifice strong omniscience in favour of human freedom.[20]

---

[16] Aristotle, *Physics*, 3.6.207a25; id. *Posterior Analytics*, 1.24.86a5.

[17] Aristotle, *Metaphysics*, 12.9; *Wars*, 3.2, fourth and fifth arguments (ii. 93).

[18] *Wars*, 3.2, sixth argument (ii. 93–4).

[19] Maimonides, *Guide*, iii. 16 (trans. Pines, 463).

[20] *Wars*, 3.2 (ii. 93–4). Gersonides completes his exposition of the philosophical arguments against divine omniscience by citing an eighth argument, whose mathematical technicalities, although quite interesting in themselves, are not relevant to our present purpose. In brief, the argument concerns the physical theory of atomism and the math-

In his exposition of the view of the sages of the Torah, Gersonides again relies upon Maimonides, this time on the latter's defence of the traditional doctrine of strong omniscience: God knows absolutely everything, including future contingencies. To deny this doctrine would be to impute to God an imperfection; after all, ignorance is one the most serious imperfections one could ascribe to anyone, all the more so to God. Moreover, if God is the creator of the universe, he must have knowledge of what he has created. Any artisan knows what he has made. However, in one very important respect divine cognition is radically different: whereas the carpenter's knowledge is cumulative and multiple, consisting of successively acquired information, God knows what he has made simultaneously and completely in such a way that all the facts are known by him as one unified cognition. Whatever objections the philosophers raise against this doctrine can be obviated, Maimonides goes on to claim, by the application of the *via negativa*. Using this method, Gersonides reports, Maimonides responded to the various arguments of the philosophers and believed that he had refuted them. In short, the philosophers had a faulty conception of God if they thought that the epistemological factors and criteria relevant to human cognition pertain to divine cognition.[21]

Since Gersonides has rejected the *via negativa* as a general theory of divine attributes, does this mean that the philosophers are right, that God does not know particulars at all? Are we then obliged to accept on faith Rabbi Akiva's dictum and confess our inability to explain how his thesis is true? To do so would seem to contradict Maimonides' own claim that proper belief involves conception and affirmation based upon evidence.[22] What is required now is a nuanced assessment of exactly what the yield is of the philosophical arguments against strong omniscience. What do they really prove? It turns out that although these arguments do provide us with some important information

ematical and philosophical problems it raises. If God knows everything, he would know every part of a divided magnitude. But if a magnitude is divisible *ad infinitum*, as the Aristotelians maintain, this would imply that God knows the infinite, which has already been ruled out. If God does know this divided magnitude, he knows it only because its parts are not infinitely divisible, but terminate in indivisible elements, or atoms, which the Aristotelians reject. Hence, since divine omniscience in the strong sense implies atomism, it is false (*Wars*, 3.2 (ii. 95–6)). This argument has been recently discussed by Rudavsky (*Time Matters*, 83–8) and Glasner ('On the Question of Gersonides' Acqaintance with Scholastic Philosophy', 281–4).

[21] Maimonides, *Guide*, iii. 16 (trans. Pines, 19–21); *Wars*, 3.2 (ii. 96–106).
[22] Maimonides, *Guide*, i. 50 (trans. Pines, 111–12).

about the nature of divine cognition and what is required to know a space–time particular, they prove too much, or their conclusions are stronger than is justified by their premises. Perhaps here, as elsewhere, we have an instance of one of Gersonides' favourite philosophical tactics whereby he attributes to a doctrine some of the truth, but not all of it.

Now, when we consider these arguments that have been brought forth in favor of divine knowledge of particulars and the arguments adduced by the philosophers against this thesis, there is no alternative but to say that God knows particulars in one respect but does not know them in another respect.[23]

It is clear from Gersonides' exposition of the philosophical arguments against strong omniscience and his rejection of Maimonides' attempt to defend this doctrine by means of negative theology that his sympathies lie with the philosophers, whose logic convinces him that if Rabbi Akiva's dictum is to be accepted it must be understood differently. Gersonides' task now is to determine in what sense God does not know particulars, as the philosophers had claimed, and the sense in which he does know them, as Rabbi Akiva and the sages of the Torah had believed. It will turn out that in answering this question he will have formulated a different and perhaps novel theory of divine omniscience.

But before we enter into his detailed exposition of this theory in *Wars*, it will be pertinent to look at two other texts where he discusses the nature of the future, which for many of the participants in this debate is the crucial issue. The first is in chapter 9 of his *Supercommentary on Averroes' Commentary on Aristotle's On Interpretation*. In interpreting this passage Gersonides follows what has been called the 'traditional' interpretation of Aristotle's position; in order to preserve future contingency and the genuineness of human choice, the law of the excluded middle needs to be restricted or understood more precisely. Unlike statements about the past or present whose truth-values are determinate or definite, statements about future contingencies do not have truth-values when they are uttered or asserted, although they acquire such values when the events to which they correspond occur:

With respect to future contingencies [*hadevarim ha'efshariyim ha'atidim*], e.g., 'Reuben will go tomorrow' or 'Reuben will not go tomorrow', such statements do not divide the true and the false determinately [*al hashelemut*] . . . for in these propositions one or the other of them will be true but it is not determinately

---

[23] *Wars*, 3.4 (ii. 117).

known now which of them is true . . . But when the time arrives one of them is true and the other is false.[24]

The key term in this passage is 'determinately'. In statements about the past or present one or other of the contradictory disjuncts has a specific truth-value, whether or not it is known. For example, in 'On 7 December 1941 the Japanese bombed Pearl Harbor or they did not', either the affirmation or the negation is true. It is true because the event referred to in this proposition has occurred. In this case there is no uncertainty or indeterminacy: the event's occurrence fixes forever the truth-value of the corresponding affirmation or negation. However, Aristotle, as most of the medievals interpreted him, argued that statements about future contingencies cannot have such truth-values; if they did, there would not be any genuine contingency. Accordingly, in cases of statements about future contingencies, the law of the excluded middle has to be understood as claiming that although such statements do not have a truth-value now, they will have one when the event in question becomes 'history'.[25]

Just as Aristotle did not introduce God into his logical discussion, neither does Gersonides in his supercommentary. However, as we have seen, some of the post-Aristotelian philosophers did, and Gersonides did so in *Wars*. Although Aristotle's restriction of the law of the excluded middle is not explicitly epistemological, his analysis can easily be applied to the question of whether or not God knows future contingencies. The philosophers, as Gersonides reports, denied that God has such knowledge; for in so far as contingent statements about the future have no determinate truth-value, they cannot be known. Their inherent uncertainty precludes our having knowledge of them. Gersonides agrees. Only statements having definite truth-values can be objects of knowledge. I cannot know now which team will win the World Cup in the year 3000, since that event has not yet occurred, and the statement asserting that one team or another has won it has no present truth-value. This holds in God's case too. If he had such knowledge, he would know the non-existent; but the non-existent has no truth-value. Moreover, such knowledge would fix the truth-value of the statement, and

[24] Gersonides, *Supercommentary on Averroes' Commentary on Aristotle's On Interpretation*, 9 (my trans.). Gersonides' supercommentary was translated into Latin and reprinted in the Venice complete Latin translation of Aristotle's works with Averroes' commentaries between 1562 and 1574 (vol. i, pt. 1, pp. 82*b*–83*a*). This was reprinted in Frankfurt am Main in 1962 by Minerva.

[25] Kneale and Kneale, *The Development of Logic*, 46–54; Prior, *Formal Logic*, 240–9; Craig, *The Problem of Divine Foreknowledge*, ch. 1.

then its contingency evaporates. The ontological and logical indeterminacy of future contingencies prevents anyone from having any knowledge of them, even God.[26]

The indeterminate nature of the future is evident in Gersonides' discussion of the nature of time itself. As we saw in Chapter 2, in arguing against Aristotle's thesis that past time is infinite, Gersonides affirmed a sharp distinction between past and future time. If we now focus upon future time, we see that it is for the most part potential, or 'open', whereas the past has been already actualized, or 'closed', by the way things have turned out. The past is over. Nothing can happen now or in the future to undo what has already taken place. For every pair of contradictory disjuncts, one of them is not only true but forever true. Not so the future. Its openness means that it is still indeterminate as to which of two contradictory disjuncts will be true. One can wager on the outcome of the 400-metre race in the 2020 Olympic Games; to make a bet on the winner of the event in 2000 makes no sense at all. The future is precisely what it is because of its contingency. And, as we have seen, statements about future contingencies have no determinate truth-value, and hence cannot be known, even by God.[27]

The overall thrust of these passages, as well as the exposition of the arguments of the philosophers in Book 3 of *Wars*, suggests that for Gersonides the philosophers were more right than wrong. They were right in concluding that there are events that are not knowable by God: particular events as such, events in all their particularity, are not knowable by a knower who transcends the spatial–temporal order. Indeed, future contingent events are not knowable by anyone, since to know them is to rob them of their contingency. If the traditionalist theologian or believer angrily retorts that these conclusions imply that God is not omniscient, that he is ignorant of human affairs, and that this is heresy, Gersonides has an answer that he believes is sufficient to preserve divine omniscience without sacrificing human choice, which he maintains is as much a basic belief of Judaism as is omniscience.

As we have already mentioned, Gersonides believes that the philosophers concluded too hastily that God does not know particulars at all. We know now that their arguments show only that God does not know them in their intrinsic individuality. Nevertheless, Gersonides claims, there is a sense in which he does know them. Particular events do exhibit order; they are governed by the laws of nature.[28] This orderliness allows us to predict the future

---

[26] *Wars*, 3.4 (ii. 122).   [27] Ibid. 6.1.10 (iii. 270–8).

[28] Ibid. 3.4 (ii. 117–18). It should be noted that the laws of nature that Gersonides refers to here are primarily astronomical and astrological laws, the latter having special

with reasonable accuracy. In this sense the future, even in its contingent domain, is knowable. The laws of nature are genuine pieces of knowledge; they are propositions having a determinate truth-value, and thus God knows them. Accordingly, divine omniscience must be understood in the following way: God is omniscient in the sense that he knows all the laws of nature. These laws are, however, general hypothetical statements of the form: if x is A, then x is B; that is, if events of a certain type A occur, then events of type B will occur. Particular instances, or tokens, of these types, however, are not known by God. In the case of statements about human actions where choice is involved, they are knowable only as types. We know that people generally behave in a specific way under certain types of conditions. But whether or not a particular individual will behave in that way in the particular circumstances in which he or she finds him- or herself is not knowable, if choice is to be preserved. In creating humans with intellect God knew they would have free will, and that being endowed with free will they could act contrary to the laws of nature and hence contrary to any law-like knowledge or prediction about their behaviour. 'God does know from this aspect [from the fact that humans have choice] that these events may not occur because of the choice, which He has given man.'[29] In short, humans can subvert the laws of nature governing their behaviour by virtue of free will. And this possibility renders knowledge of future contingencies impossible. Predictions can be made, but they can turn out to be false.

In this context, however, we need to keep in mind Plato's distinction between knowledge and belief. Knowledge in the strict sense, and that is what we are talking about, implies certainty and infallibility; belief does not. Speaking about predictions concerning future contingencies, Gersonides says:

When we say that we *know* that one particular possibility of two contradictory possibilities will occur, we thereby imply that it is impossible that it will not occur, whereas if we *think* [or believe] that it cannot occur, we call this 'opinion', not 'knowledge'.[30]

significance since they are concerned with human affairs. Nevertheless, we need not be put off by Gersonides' commitment to astrology. His argument can easily be applied to any true law-like generalization, especially those concerned with human behaviour. Those events governed by such laws are knowable to the extent that they are covered by these laws, and hence predictable. In his language, they are 'ordered' by these laws. However, these events are not knowable as 'particulars'; they are knowable only in so far as they instantiate or satisfy some law. In a sense, what is really known is not the event as an individual but the event as a member of a class of events falling under a law.

[29] *Wars*, 3.4 (ii. 118).   [30] Ibid. 3.2 (ii. 103).

So if we are to attribute knowledge to God, it cannot be of events that do not possess the certainty and determinacy that knowledge implies. What God knows are the laws of nature; these are universally true propositions about types, not individuals. The concept of divine omniscience implies that God is never in error: God's beliefs do not contain any statement that is or could be false. On this score Rabbi Akiva was right. But his dictum has to be understood as follows: everything, that is, all the laws of nature, including those of human nature, are known; nevertheless, choice, which is a divinely given human faculty, allows humanity to act contrary to these laws. Humanity has, then, what some modern philosophers have called, 'contra-causal freedom'; that is, although human nature is law-like and hence predictable, humans are free to act contrary to these laws; whether or not any given individual will do so, however, is not predictable.[31]

Gersonides' denial of knowledge of future contingencies has appeared to some interpreters as an example of 'weak or limited omniscience',[32] as opposed to the traditional notion of omniscience, which has generally been more robust than just knowing the laws of nature. But what does a limitation mean in this context? I am limited in my not being able to high-jump seven feet; yet some humans can do this. In this case, my inability is a genuine limitation. If, however, I were asked to jump in such a way that I move up and down at the same time, my inability to accomplish this is in no way a limitation or defect; for I have been asked to do the impossible. Even if I failed to do something that looks less impossible, such as high-jumping a hundred feet, it would still be stretching the notion of possibility to accuse me of weakness or impotence. According to what we know about the biological structure of the human body, this is naturally impossible. The capacity to do something requires that we know either the logical possibility or the natural possibility of performing the stipulated task. If the task is logically impossible, as in the case of simultaneously jumping up and down, or physically impossible, as in the case of jumping a hundred feet, then someone's inability to perform the deed is not a genuine instance of limitation. If future contingencies are logically unknowable, as the philosophers and Gersonides maintain, then even if God is the knower in question, his not knowing these events is no real cognitive limitation. Not to know future contingencies is analogous to not knowing the precise number of the infinite set of natural

---

[31] Lucas, *The Freedom of the Will*, ch. 14; Swinburne, *The Coherence of Theism*, ch. 10.

[32] For an excellent critical discussion of this interpretation see Manekin, 'On the Limited-Omniscience Interpretation of Gersonides' Theory of Divine Knowledge'.

numbers. Since there is no such number, not to know it is not ignorance. And this is the case with future contingencies: they cannot be known; so there is no point in bemoaning this fact, or in thinking that since God cannot know such facts we have 'weakened' or 'limited' his knowledge. Divine omniscience is then to be understood as *God's knowing all that is knowable.*

For the most part our discussion has focused upon divine knowledge of future contingencies, the possibility of which vexed both the ancient philosophers and Rabbi Akiva. But as we have seen from Gersonides' analysis, the question is broader than just whether or not God knows the winner of the World Cup in 3000. The philosophers argued that God cannot know any space–time particular, and Gersonides accepted their arguments at least in the sense that God cannot know these particulars in their individual particularity. This would then imply that God cannot know even present particular events occurring in the spatial–temporal domain. This seems bizarre as well as theologically heterodox. If God cannot know that I am now writing this sentence, he would really be ignorant. After all, if I am now writing, then there is no possibility that I am now not writing. As Aristotle so neatly put it: 'Now that which is must needs be when it is and that which is not must needs not be when it is not.'[33] So in the case of present particular events there is no indeterminacy that would render cognition of them impossible. Even worse, Gersonides has denied of God what we apparently have knowledge of, for, as spatial–temporal beings, we have the cognitive apparatus that enables us to have knowledge of space–time particulars. We then seem to be in a better epistemic state than God with respect to spatial–temporal events: whereas God can know only universal laws, we can know particular facts as well as general facts.

To help Gersonides escape from this predicament let us again appeal to Aristotle. In his *Posterior Analytics* he developed a theory of knowledge that construes the term 'knowledge' in a very strict sense. Formulated in the context of his proof theory, wherein a strict, or scientific, proof is one that is based upon necessarily true premises, thus yielding an apodictic, or necessarily true, conclusion, this theory implies that scientific cognition is knowledge of necessary truths.[34] Thinking here of mathematics, especially geometry, Aristotle conceives a science to be a deductive body of necessary truths arranged in axiomatic form. Anything less than this is not science in the strict sense. Indeed, Aristotle goes on to claim that non-necessary facts

---

[33] Aristotle, *On Interpretation*, 9.19a22–3.
[34] Aristotle, *Posterior Analytics*, 1.6.22, 1.6.24.

or truths really do not constitute a science by the mere fact that they are not demonstrated or scientifically proved: 'But objects so far as they are an indeterminate manifold are unintelligible; so far as they are determinate, intelligible: they are therefore intelligible rather in so far as they are universal than in so far as they are particular.'[35] Elsewhere Aristotle formulates this principle in terms of the notion of accidents: accidental, or chance, events are not knowable in the strict sense; hence, there cannot be a science of them.[36] If, then, a particular truth about some contingent event is not really a scientific truth or a constituent part of a genuine science, not knowing such a proposition is not an epistemic defect or sign of ignorance. That which is not a science is not knowledge in the strict sense. Just as we do not convict someone of ignorance because he cannot give the size of the last part of an infinitely divisible magnitude, so we should not think God is ignorant because he cannot know particulars as particulars. They are just unknowable.[37]

That Gersonides' doctrine of divine cognition deceived hardly any of his medieval successors is evidenced by the stream of criticism from such thinkers as Hasdai Crescas (*c*.1340–1412), Isaac Arama (*c*.1420–94), and Isaac Abravanel (1437–1509).[38] They had no reservations about the truth of Rabbi Akiva's principle construed in the strong sense and had no use for Gersonides' version, which they understood as a 'limited' interpretation of this principle. With prescience, a phenomenon that Gersonides confidently accepted and believed he had himself experienced, Gersonides anticipated their dissatisfaction and responded to objections to his theory in chapter 6 of Book 3 of *Wars*, 'The Identity of Our View with the Doctrine of the Torah'. It would seem that his intellectual integrity compelled him to consider an insurmountable challenge: the Torah is replete with passages in which God speaks to particular individuals, such as Abraham and Moses, and foresees future events, such as the Egyptian exile and Israelite backsliding. How then can Gersonides escape the charge of deviating from the plain

---

[35] Aristotle, *Posterior Analytics*, 1.24.86*a*5–8; id., *Rhetoric*, 1.2.1356*b*32–3.

[36] Aristotle, *Metaphysics*, 6.2.1026*b*3–4; id., *Posterior Analytics*, 1.31.87*b*27–8.

[37] In addition to Touati's discussions of this general topic in *Les Guerres du Seigneur* and *La Pensée philosophique de Gersonide*, see Klein-Braslavy, 'Gersonides' on Determinism, Possibility, Choice, and Foreknowledge' (Heb.); Manekin, 'Conservative Tendencies in Gersonides' Religious Philosophy', 320–32; Rudavsky, 'Divine Omniscience and Future Contingencies in Gersonides'; Samuelson, 'Gersonides' Account of God's Knowledge of Particulars'.

[38] Crescas, *Or adonai*, 2.1.4; Arama, *The Binding of Isaac*, Gen., gate 21; Abravanel, *Commentary on the Torah*, Gen., 'Vayera'.

meaning of the Torah? Moreover, it is not just a matter of accepting what the Torah obviously says; it involves understanding the religious and theological implications of these passages. What would Judaism, or for that matter any revealed religion, be if it did not teach that God knows and cares for individuals as individuals? What would be the point of praying to a God devoid of such knowledge? Gersonides' commitment to sound philosophy seems to have subverted his fidelity to Judaism.

Gersonides is fully aware of his situation, and formulates a general hermeneutical principle that serves as his guideline for meeting such challenges to his religious loyalty. Since there is only one truth, there cannot be any real discrepancy between the correct philosophical teaching and the Torah *properly understood*:

In short, there is nothing in the words of the Prophets . . . that implies anything incompatible with the theory that we have developed by means of philosophy. Hence, it is incumbent to follow philosophy in this matter. For, when the Torah, interpreted literally, seems to conflict with doctrines that have been proved by reason, it is proper to interpret these passages according to philosophical understanding, so long as none of the fundamental principles of the Torah are destroyed. Maimonides . . . too followed this practice in many cases . . . It is even more proper that we not disagree with philosophy when the Torah itself does not disagree with it.[39]

So it is a question of exegesis: what is the most reasonable way of reading a biblical passage or doctrine in the light of what correct philosophy has taught? In cases where there is an apparent conflict it is the obligation of the exegete to find a plausible reading of the biblical passage that agrees with correct philosophy.

Moreover, it is important to understand exactly what Scripture requires us to believe with respect to a given issue. In this particular matter Scripture explicitly says: 'I am the Lord—I have not changed' (Mal. 3: 6). Accordingly, Scripture itself precludes God's knowing particular things cumulatively, or successively. Whatever he knows he knows simultaneously, or, better, eternally, in one unified, comprehensive vision. Nevertheless, Scripture explicitly teaches that there are contingent states of affairs, especially pertaining to human actions; otherwise there would be no human choice, and there would be no point to God's giving us commandments and rewarding or punishing us. With respect then to the second horn of Rabbi Akiva's dilemma Scripture is quite clear: we are free agents. Hence, any theory of divine omniscience

[39] *Wars*, 3.6 (ii. 136).

must allow for choice. But what about the former principle concerning the nature of God's cognition? This horn of the dilemma, especially Rabbi Akiva's use of the term 'everything', would seem to be a real problem for Gersonides. In its plain meaning it seems to imply that God knows all particular events, including those of the future. And this has been the traditional understanding of Rabbi Akiva's dictum.

Gersonides avoids this implication by taking a close look at 'everything' (*hakol*). The key component of this term is the word 'every', or 'all' (*kol*). Gersonides cites Psalm 33: 15, where *kol* appears in a cognitive context: 'He who fashions the hearts of them *all*, who discerns *all* their doings' (emphasis added). Understood literally, the verse seems to imply that God, omniscient in the strong sense, knows absolutely everything, including all particular things and events in the world, especially human beings and their actions. Not so, Gersonides maintains. He reads the passage as follows:

That is, God created the hearts and thoughts of men *at the same time* in so far as He endowed the heavenly bodies with those patterns from which [these thoughts] are in their entirety derived. In this way God considers *all* [*kol*] their deeds, i.e., simultaneously, not in the sense that His knowledge refers to the particular as particular. This shows that [according to the Torah] God understands all human affairs in a *general* way.[40]

Consistent with the epistemological principles he inherited from Aristotle, Gersonides claims that this passage confirms his understanding of the nature of knowledge in general and divine knowledge in particular. To know something is to grasp it as falling under or instantiating some general law or pattern. Human nature and behaviour exemplify general laws. Knowledge of these laws enables someone to know what humans in general will do in specific circumstances. This is how God knows what we are up to. And this is what Rabbi Akiva meant when he said 'Everything is foreseen'; that is, God knows all the laws that govern human action. But this does not imply that he knows if and when a given individual instantiates any of these laws. Scientific knowledge, that is, knowledge of universal laws, constitutes God's omniscience, and anyone who has some of this knowledge has to that extent something in common with God. Of course, God is in a higher position than we are, since he knows all the laws, whereas we know only some. Thus, in his comments on Job 37: 16, Gersonides interprets the adjectival phrase 'perfect knowledge' (*temim de'im*), attributed to God, as 'God is perfect knowledge,

---

[40] *Wars*, 3.6 (ii. 135–6).

i.e., He knows all the objects of knowledge.'[41] As we have just seen, however, the objects of knowledge are universal truths. Omniscience then is the comprehension of all the laws of reality, that is, all that which is genuinely knowable.

Realizing that he has gone out on a limb, Gersonides appeals to the important biblical exegete Abraham ibn Ezra. In discussing the story of Sodom and Gomorrah, Ibn Ezra interprets the verse 'I must go down and see whether their deeds warrant the outcry which has reached me. I am resolved to know the truth' (Gen. 18: 21) as follows: 'the truth is that He knows every particular generally, but not as a particular'.[42] Both Ibn Ezra and Gersonides find this passage troublesome: does God need to conduct a survey in order to verify his beliefs? Is his knowledge so much like ours that he needs evidence acquired by observation and testing? The literal meaning of the biblical text suggests that God assumes that the people of Sodom and Gomorrah are wicked and that the outcry reflects their wickedness. Nevertheless, he is not quite sure, and so he goes to see for himself. Neither Ibn Ezra nor Gersonides can accept this understanding of the story, as it undermines any notion of divine omniscience. So we have to understand the passage differently. Instead of God's attempting to find out something he did not already know or was not sure of, we are to understand the text in terms of the theory of omniscience advocated by Ibn Ezra and Gersonides: divine omniscience means that God knows all the laws pertaining to the human species; but these laws can be contravened by individuals, who act not according to their biological constitution or social customs but by virtue of their choice, freely exercised:

Now, human choice rules over the pattern ordered for them by the heavenly bodies. Therefore, it is possible that what men do can be different from what God knew of the pattern [governing] their actions. For He knows their actions to the extent that they are knowable, and this is in so far as they are ordered and determinate. However, in so far as they are contingent [*efshariyim*] there is no knowledge of them. For if we were to allege that they are knowable, they would not be contingent.[43]

---

[41] Gersonides, *Commentary on Job*, 37: 16 (trans. Lassen, 222–7). In explaining the Hebrew phrase in this verse, *temim de'im*, Gersonides uses the technical epistemological term *muskalot*, which literally means 'objects of knowledge'. Since for Gersonides the objects of knowledge are laws, or universal truths, omniscience amounts to knowing general facts, not particular events.

[42] Ibn Ezra, *Commentary on the Torah*, Gen. 18: 21.

[43] *CT*, Gen., 'Vayera', 28*d* (i. 137).

As I have noted, Gersonides firmly believes that God has endowed humanity with free will, a necessary component of human reason. Unlike other animals we can choose what we shall do; unlike the angels, or separate intellects, our choices may be right or wrong. That is what it is to be human.[44]

In the very same paragraph in which he cites Ibn Ezra in support of his own position, Gersonides also mentions Maimonides as holding the same view. This is most puzzling, since previously he presented Maimonides as the defender of the traditional Torah doctrine, which he criticized and rejected. Gersonides quotes Maimonides in Ibn Tibbon's Hebrew translation, which differs from Pines's translation from the Arabic and contains a phrase that is crucial for Gersonides' understanding of the passage: 'Some thinkers have been inclined to say that [God's] knowledge refers to the species and uniformly encompasses all members of the species. This is the view of any believer in a revealed religion who is guided by the necessity of reason.'[45]

Maimonides' language, as is often the case, is cryptic. To whom is he referring? Moreover, and more importantly, this passage raises a doubt not only about Maimonides' critique of the philosophical doctrine of divine knowledge but also Gersonides' initial understanding of Maimonides' position. Was Maimonides one of those thinkers who adopted this doctrine of divine knowledge? It would seem so from the second sentence of this passage. How then are we to construe his strong criticisms of those philosophers who deny divine knowledge of particulars as particulars? Finally, what did he mean by the term 'uniformly'?

Consciously or not Gersonides answers these questions by glossing Maimonides' phrase as follows: the individuals comprising a species are comprehended within the species without distinction, that is, not as particulars. To know that a dog has certain typical features is not to know that a particular dog, Lassie, has these features qua individual dog. Dogs in general bark, and thus I can safely assert that Lassie barks; but knowing this does not imply that I have heard Lassie bark or that I even know Lassie. And this is true in God's case as well. Accordingly, on this interpretation Maimonides, at least in this

---

[44] *CT*, Gen., 'Vayera', 16*b* (i. 65), emphasis added; Feldman, appendix to *The Wars of the Lord*, ii. 226–30.

[45] Maimonides, *Guide*, iii. 20, cited in *Wars*, 3.6 (ii. 136–7). Samuel ibn Tibbon, the son of Judah ibn Tibbon, the 'father of translators', translated the *Guide* into Hebrew in 1204, shortly before Maimonides' death. Although there is another medieval Hebrew translation by Judah Harizi, Ibn Tibbon's translation became the 'canonical' text of the *Guide*. All the medieval Jewish commentaries of the *Guide* were based upon the Ibn Tibbon translation.

passage, agreed with Gersonides, who believed that this is the authentic view of the Torah. Perhaps this is an example of one of those intentional contradictions that Maimonides inserted in the *Guide* to conceal his real beliefs from some of his readers while revealing them to others. At any rate, Gersonides' deep respect for Maimonides led him to include Maimonides, along with Ibn Ezra, as having the right idea on this issue, at least some of the time.

Medieval Jewish thinkers almost unanimously rejected Gersonides' doctrine of divine omniscience. We may be inclined to respond to them by simply regarding their views as expressing an obsolete medieval theological outlook. Nevertheless, a similar reaction has been voiced by several non-partisan modern historians of medieval Jewish philosophy. In his classic survey *A History of Medieval Jewish Philosophy*, Isaac Husik characterized Gersonides' theory as a 'theological monstrosity'.[46] More recently Colette Sirat has stressed the inherent incompatibility between Gersonides' doctrine and biblical religion:

Gersonides' theory of divine knowledge radically destroys the whole history as told in the Bible, and that all his biblical exegesis cannot mitigate the fundamental impossibility of harmonizing the two conceptions of God: God knowing the world in its order and law . . . or, God knowing man in his [particular] body and soul.[47]

Underlying this negative reaction seems to be a genuine worry that such a doctrine undermines the fundamental belief of any monotheistic religion that God is so involved in and concerned with human affairs that not only does he know human events in all their particularity but in addition exercises individual providence over them. As we have seen, Maimonides closely linked the question of omniscience to the issue of divine providence. This linkage is also evident in Gersonides, as we shall see in the next chapter. After all, if God does not know what a particular person is about to do or has done, how can reward or punishment be justly meted out? Gersonides' theory goes against the theological grain in a radical way, and it is not easy to see how it can be accepted as a legitimate interpretation of either the Bible or Rabbi Akiva's dictum.

However, one could plausibly say on his behalf that his theory is philosophically true or at least is the most adequate philosophical account of divine knowledge. If we adopt Gersonides' methodological principle of first finding the correct philosophical or scientific account of the matter under

---

[46] Husik, *A History of Medieval Jewish Philosophy*, 346.
[47] Sirat, *A History of Jewish Philosophy*, 296.

investigation, then if philosophy concludes that knowledge of particulars as particulars, especially of future contingencies, is impossible, this conclusion must serve as the touchstone for all subsequent theological and exegetical discussions. Furthermore, if the principle of human free will is so fundamental to morality and religion, as Gersonides firmly insisted, then it cannot be weakened or surrendered merely because of a widely entrenched theological belief that philosophy has demonstrated to be false. Human freedom cannot be sacrificed on the altar of a false belief about divine knowledge. With respect to the principle of omniscience, Gersonides sincerely believed that he had preserved the core meaning of this dogma by offering a more precise notion of what this belief entails. The simple formula—God knows everything—is now understood to mean: *God knows everything that is knowable*. What remains to be determined is the specification of the class of knowables. Since philosophy has shown that certain types of propositions are either not knowable at all (for example, statements about future contingencies) or, even if well confirmed, do not count as genuine items of knowledge (for example, statements about space–time accidental events), such propositions are not members of the class of knowables. Hence, someone's not knowing them does not imply a cognitive deficiency. Unlike us, God is omniscient because he knows the entire set of knowable propositions. And so 'everything is foreseen', that is, all the *universal truths* are known by God; and 'choice is given', that is, humans have the power to act contrary to these truths by virtue of their free will, and God knows that some humans exercise this power. For Gersonides this notion of omniscience is not only philosophically true but theologically adequate as well: it gives God his due and grants humans what they require in order to be morally responsible agents.[48]

---

[48] The topic of divine foreknowledge still stimulates philosophical and theological interest, and there is a sizeable corpus of contemporary literature devoted to many of the issues that vexed the medievals. The logician Arthur Prior, for example, argued that future contingent propositions are neither true nor false, and hence not knowable, and suggested the employment of a three-value truth logic. He also maintained that the future is essentially open, whereas the past is 'over', and hence closed (*Past, Present and Future*, ch. 7). Other philosophers, for example Nelson Pike, have concentrated upon the compatibility problem and have reached the conclusion that knowledge of future contingencies is logically incompatible with human freedom ('Divine Omniscience and Voluntary Action'). Still others have claimed that the notion of an eternal, timeless deity's knowing temporal particulars is fraught with difficulties (Kenny, 'Divine Foreknowledge and Human Freedom'; Pike, *God and Timelessness*). It turns out, then, that Gersonides' theory would find favour amongst many modern philosophers.

The theological conservative, armed with the language of the Torah, would most likely baulk at the seemingly subservient position that Gersonides has assigned to the biblical text. Yet Gersonides' stance does not appear to be so radical or novel. Quite early in the exegesis of the Bible, diversity of interpretation has been the norm. As Maimonides neatly put it, 'the gates of interpretation are not locked'.[49] In this particular context Maimonides was concerned to free the biblical text from over-zealous literalists who would force us to take seriously the many anthropomorphic descriptions of God and thus oblige us to believe in a corporeal deity. With complete justification, Maimonides appealed to the attempt by the Aramaic translations of the Bible to tone down these anthropomorphisms, and if he had known the Septuagint and Philo he could have referred to their 'purifications' of the original texts. Rabbinic exegesis also took liberties. So why not Gersonides? If there is such a thing as Jewish fundamentalism, and there may not be, it is not the attempt to preserve the literal meaning of the Torah at all costs. This has never been the primary concern of Jewish biblical exegesis. Gersonides' reading of the Torah concerning divine knowledge is, therefore, rooted in a tradition of interpretative liberty. As long as the reading conforms to the basic belief structure of Judaism, exegetical freedom is permitted. As we have indicated, Gersonides believed that Judaism requires a conception of God that preserves his immutability and a notion of humanity that presupposes a robust concept of choice. Divine omniscience must then be consistent with these two fundamental dogmas. He sincerely believed that his theory of divine cognition satisfied these two criteria and that his reading of the Torah was justified, just as most Jews read the text according to a non-anthropomorphic conception of God despite the literal language of the text.

Before I conclude my discussion of this topic it may be useful to note, if only briefly, a recent trend in Gersonides scholarship, stimulated in large part by Shlomo Pines, to show the influence of Christian scholasticism upon Gersonides.[50] Since this is a large topic requiring separate treatment, I shall have to limit my discussion to the question of omniscience, a topic specifically discussed by Pines. It is important to appreciate, first, that virtually all the scholastic theories are 'compatibilistic': they aim to show that both divine omniscience in the strong sense and human freedom are logically compatible. Although various thinkers proposed different solutions to the

---

[49] Maimonides, *Guide*, ii. 25 (trans. Pines, 327).

[50] Pines, 'Scholasticism after Thomas Aquinas'; Sirat, Klein-Braslavy, and Weijers (eds.), *Les Méthodes de travail de Gersonide*.

apparent dilemma, they all subscribed to a robust principle of divine omnipotence.[51] Although Gersonides believed that he too was a compatibilist, his compatibilism would have been regarded by the scholastics as limited and weak, just as his medieval Jewish critics judged. In particular, his denial of God's knowing particular, especially contingent, events as particulars is utterly alien to the scholastic mentality and would have been rejected by them as heretical as well as false.

It is not only for this reason that I find the thesis of scholastic influence unconvincing. If we look closely at Gersonides' argument we see virtually no echoes of any of the dominant scholastic theories of omniscience that were prevalent in his day. For the sake of brevity, let us consider just one such theory, that of Thomas Aquinas. In comparing the two thinkers I do not detect in Gersonides any awareness of Aquinas' idea of a God who simultaneously sees all events in his eternal, that is, timeless, present such that even contingent events *must* turn out as God knows them, although they preserve their logical status of contingent propositions. In Aquinas' terminology the necessary truth of God's knowing the outcome of a logically contingent event is only *de dictu*, that is, only of the proposition 'God knows that I shall go to the opera tomorrow evening'; or, in the language of Boethius, this proposition is necessary only 'conditionally'. The necessity here is only hypothetical, and hence harmless, since God could have known otherwise. For example, if God eternally knows that the winner of the World Cup in 3000 is Israel, then the proposition 'Israel wins the World Cup in 3000' is true; indeed necessarily true given what God knows. However, since God could know that the USA wins the World Cup in 3000, an outcome certainly within the scope of logical possibility, the latter is equally true given this alternative hypothesis. In the latter case, there is the same necessity, but it is just as harmless as in the former case.[52] Gersonides' acceptance of the logical force of Aristotle's argument in chapter 9 of *On Interpretation*, however, precludes any such notion. If there were knowledge of a contingent event, it would cease to be contingent, and that is the end of the matter. In Gersonides' entire discussion of this issue Aquinas' distinction between *de dictu* and *de re* necessities is not mentioned. Comparisons with the views of

---

[51] Craig, *The Problem of Divine Foreknowledge*.

[52] Aquinas, *Summa Theologiae*, I q. 14; id., *Summa Contra Gentiles*, 1.64–9. Pines refers to Aquinas in 'Scholasticism after Thomas Aquinas', 95–6. Aquinas' theory is based upon the doctrine developed by Boethius in his *Consolation of Philosophy*, 5. Aquinas, however, usually employs the technical logical terminology of *de dicto/de re* necessities to express Boethius' language of conditional and absolute, or simple, necessities.

John Duns Scotus and William of Ockham would reveal the same result. Although they were strong advocates of contingency, especially in human choice, they defended an equally strong conception of divine omniscience that entailed God's having foreknowledge of these contingent events, a conclusion that Gersonides rejected.[53]

Nevertheless, recent research by Chris Schabel on Peter Auriol, a French Christian contemporary of Gersonides, has raised the possibility that there may be some significant relationship between the two medieval thinkers on this issue.[54] The specific point on which there is some common ground is one of general logical interest: the question of a multi-value logic. Both Gersonides and Auriol accepted the force of Aristotle's argument in chapter 9 of *On Interpretation* and concluded that statements about future contingents have no determinate truth-value, and thus they cannot be known in their future contingent particularity. Thus, from a purely logical point of view, they have no definite truth-value, and as such cannot be known; for only that which is true can be known. Some modern logicians have inferred from this argument that statements referring to future contingents have 'neuter truth-value'.[55]

But when the theological question of omniscience is introduced into the debate, there is a parting of the ways between Auriol and Gersonides. As Chris Schabel admits, when we come to their final conclusions, 'Auriol and Gersonides differ greatly'.[56] For the former, like most of the scholastics, wants to eat his proverbial cake and keep it too. Like most scholastic thinkers, he too ultimately believes in divine knowledge of contingent events in a way that impairs neither their contingency nor divine immutability. However, to understand this affirmation of omniscience 'is in a way incomprehensible to us and ineffable'.[57] As Schabel correctly comments, Auriol is closer to Maimonides here than he is to Gersonides, who generally abhors the flight to the asylum of ignorance. In sum then, it is best to work with the simpler hypothesis that on this topic, and perhaps on most, Gersonides was free of any significant influence from scholastic philosophy.[58]

---

[53] Craig's discussion of their views in *The Problem of Divine Foreknowledge*.
[54] Schabel, 'Philosophy and Theology across Cultures'.
[55] Prior, *Formal Logic*, 240–50.
[56] Schabel, 'Philosophy and Theology across Cultures', 1108.   [57] Ibid.
[58] Freudenthal, 'Gersonide, génie solitaire'.

FIVE

Divine Providence

The Case for Individual Providence

DOES GOD CARE FOR CREATURES? Is this care universal or limited to certain kinds of creatures? Can this care reach individuals as particulars, or does it emanate only to species, or kinds, of individuals? And if there is divine care, or providence, for individuals, why does it seem to be arbitrarily distributed such that the righteous or the innocent suffer, whereas the wicked prosper? These are some of the questions about divine providence that have puzzled and perplexed not only philosophers and theologians but also the ordinary religious person throughout the ages. The general topic of providence is also another one of those questions where Greek philosophy and biblical religion come into contact, and in some cases confront each other with divergent points of view. In fact, it is an issue that is explicitly discussed in detail in one specific biblical book, the book of Job, which may be considered to be the most philosophical book of the Bible.

Many of the major Greek philosophers addressed this issue. In his *Laws*, Plato confronts an anonymous denier of divine providence and attempts to answer the latter's doubts by appealing to the perfection of the universe and the benevolence and omniscience of the gods.[1] In the Hellenistic period the question of divine providence was a major bone of contention between the Epicureans and the Stoics, the former rejecting divine providence, the latter affirming it. For the Epicureans the world was characterized more by chance and randomness than by order, and they thought the gods were too busy enjoying their own serenity and happiness to concern themselves with us. The Stoics, however, were firm believers in a natural providential order that manifests divine wisdom and beneficence.[2] The later Platonists too were concerned with this issue. Plotinus dealt with it in two books of his *Enneads*, Proclus devotes several treatises to the subject,[3] and in his philosophical

---

[1] Plato, *Laws*, 10.899*d*–907*b*.
[2] See Cicero, *On the Nature of the Gods*, 1 (on the Epicureans), 2 (on the Stoics).
[3] Plotinus, *Enneads*, 3.2–3; Proclus, *Ten Doubts Against Providence*.

treatise *The Consolation of Philosophy*, written shortly before his execution, the Christian Platonist Boethius discussed this topic in detail.[4]

But what about Aristotle? Was he oblivious to these questions? Here we are faced with a problem of distinguishing between what Aristotle actually says and how he was understood by medieval philosophers, especially Gersonides. Aristotle himself may actually have held a theory of divine providence; but for the medievals this theory was so limited that it amounted in their eyes virtually to a denial of it. In fact, Aristotle's brief and infrequent pronouncements on this topic do not constitute a consistent doctrine. In chapter 9 of Book 12 of his *Metaphysics*, he claims that God thinks only of himself, for 'there are even some things which it is better not to see than to see'.[5] Yet in the very next chapter Aristotle maintains that the universe contains the highest good and that all the things in it are 'ordered to one end'.[6] To complicate matters even further, he enunciates an idea in the concluding book of his *Nicomachean Ethics* which suggests that divine providence extends to those individuals who live the life of reason and have reached the highest level of intellectual perfection attainable by humanity.[7] Nevertheless, in spite of this latter text, Maimonides, Gersonides, and others held the view that Aristotle's doctrine of divine providence was, at most, a theory of general providence, the claim that the various natural species have the means whereby the species is preserved qua species, although individuals within the species are, as Maimonides puts it, subject to chance.[8]

Whether or not the book of Job was in any way influenced by Greek philosophy is questionable. But Jewish responses to the issues concerning providence are to be found in Philo of Alexandria and in some of the early rabbinic literature. In his treatise *On the Creation of the World*, Philo, following Plato, links divine providence to God's creation of the world. For how could a benevolent creator not care for what he has created?[9] Philo is also traditionally regarded as the author of a treatise *On Providence*, presumably addressed to his apostate nephew Tiberius Alexander, in which he explicitly defends a theory of divine providence along Stoic lines.[10] These discussions are, however, not so surprising from a philosophically educated Alexandrian

---

[4] Boethius, *The Consolation of Philosophy*, 4–5.

[5] Aristotle, *Metaphysics*, 12.9.1074*b*21–34.

[6] Ibid. 12.10.1075*a*12–19.   [7] Aristotle, *Nicomachean Ethics*, 10.8.

[8] Maimonides, *Guide*, iii. 17, second opinion (trans. Pines, 464–5). See Pines' discussion of this topic in the introduction to his translation, pp. lxv–lxvii. See also *Wars*, 4.1. (ii. 157–8).   [9] Philo, *On the Creation of the World*, 2; Plato, *Timaeus*, 30*b*.

[10] Philo, *On Providence*, 2.

Jew. What is especially interesting are the echoes of this debate in some rabbinic texts.

In the famous story of the four sages who enter Paradise, one of them, the notorious Elisha ben Abuya, or Aher, leaves Paradise as an 'Epicuros' (*apikoros* in Hebrew).[11] It is worth considering the etymology of this term. In rabbinic Hebrew the word is not a proper name denoting the philosopher Epicurus; rather, it describes a person who shares some of the beliefs of the Greek philosopher, in particular the denial of the doctrine of divine providence. In several stories about Elisha it is reported that he denied divine providence because of the suffering experienced by the innocent. Accordingly, 'there is no justice nor judge'.[12] The one sage who returned from Paradise 'whole', our old friend Rabbi Akiva, however, was not so troubled by the apparent injustices occurring in this world. For in the very passage in which he enunciates his belief in both divine foreknowledge and human freedom he proclaims: 'The world is judged by goodness and everything is reckoned according to the multitude of the deed.'[13] Here, as in the case of divine omniscience, faith in divine goodness trumps any doubts concerning divine providence.

However, this faith became more difficult to maintain in the face of the philosophical onslaught beginning in the tenth century, especially with the victory of Aristotle's philosophy not long afterwards. By this time the terms of the debate had changed: although the existence of divine providence was not doubted, questions were raised concerning its precise domain and distribution. In particular, does providence extend over individuals as such, or is it manifest only over species? And if the latter is the case, are all species recipients of providence? Moreover, as I indicated in the last chapter, a close connection was made by the philosophers between the question of providence and divine omniscience. It is not surprising, then, to see that Maimonides discusses these two questions together in chapters 16 to 24 of the third book of the *Guide*, and that Gersonides treats the question of providence immediately after his discussion of divine knowledge. Indeed, for Gersonides the problem of providence was especially urgent, since his doctrine of divine omniscience seems to rule out any kind of individual providence. Hence, to forestall this impression, Gersonides presents a theory of providence that he believes is consistent not only with his doctrine of divine knowledge but with the Torah as well. Moreover, it is not far-fetched to

[11] BT *Ḥag.* 14*b*.
[12] Fischel, *Rabbinic Literature and Greco-Roman Philosophy*, pt. 2.
[13] Mishnah *Avot* 3: 15.

suggest that Gersonides was almost obsessed with this issue; for his earliest biblical commentary is the *Commentary on Job*, to which he frequently refers in Book 4 of *Wars*. In chapter 2 of Book 4 of *Wars* Gersonides discusses in detail the book of Job, which is unusual, since, with the exception of part 2 of Book 6, there are few biblical references in *Wars*. In his later *Commentary on the Torah* references to divine providence abound. Although it will turn out that his doctrine of providence is less daring and unorthodox than his theory of divine omniscience, he seems to have been quite apprehensive about the possible implications of the latter for the former.[14]

The two principal questions that Gersonides attempts to answer are: 'Is there individual providence?' and 'Why do the righteous and innocent suffer and the wicked prosper?' The philosophical groundwork for his discussion was established by Maimonides in his own debate with the Aristotelians, on the one hand, and the Kalam on the other. Against the former Maimonides defended individual providence; against the latter he restricted individual providence not to the human species as a whole but only to a subset within that species, to individuals whose moral and intellectual achievements warrant it. His main philosophical argument against Aristotle presupposes a theory of species-concepts that he attributes to the philosophers, but uses instead to criticize their theory of general providence: species as such do not exist in reality; our species-concepts are really just convenient devices for speaking about individuals that the human mind arranges into groups. Accordingly, the kind of natural providence admitted by Aristotle has to be understood as really extending over individuals; for that is all that exists. The Kalam doctrines that admit individual providence, on the other hand, make the mistake of believing that it extends over *all* individuals in *all* animal species. In maintaining this belief they fall prey to a variety of problems, the most serious of which is the problem of the apparently unfair distribution of this providence. Maimonides ultimately adopts a theory of selective, or restricted, individual providence: individual providence is a function of the intellect. The more one perfects the intellect, the more one is eligible to receive individual providence. Since humanity is the only earthly species possessing intellect, this means that only certain individuals within the species receive providence.[15]

Although Gersonides' theory of providence works within the general parameters set forth by Maimonides, there are some important differences.

[14] On Gersonides' theory of providence see Touati, *La Pensée philosophique de Gersonide*, pt. 5, ch. 4; Kellner, 'Gersonides, Providence and the Rabbinic Tradition'; Eisen, *Gersonides on Providence*; Leaman, *Evil and Suffering in Jewish Philosophy*, ch. 5.

[15] Maimonides, *Guide*, iii. 17–18 (trans. Pines, 471–6).

Not only does his argumentation differ from that of Maimonides, but his exposition, especially of the distribution problem, is more detailed. It is interesting to note at the outset that he does not mention Maimonides' argument against Aristotle, most likely because he does not share Maimonides' view about species-concepts.[16] Instead, he mounts an attack against Aristotle that employs an empirical argument and a critique of the philosophical argument that God's not having foreknowledge of contingent affairs precludes individual providence. Nor does he argue directly against Kalam theories of individual providence. Instead, he examines a general theory of individual providence according to which God distributes rewards or punishments to individuals directly and according to a strict principle of measure for measure; he attributes this doctrine to 'most of the followers of the Torah'.[17] As we shall see, Gersonides rejected this theory. Finally, unlike Maimonides, Gersonides considers certain types of phenomena to be providential that Maimonides tended to disparage and whose explanation, in some cases at least, involved astrology, a subject that was strongly criticized by Maimonides. Gersonides' attitude towards astrology was generally positive: although he recognized the imperfections of the discipline, he believed that it did have at least some scientific basis and explanatory power. Since his account of individual providence appeals to astrology, I need to say something about this discipline, especially as it was understood by medieval thinkers.

Two important distinctions should be noted at the outset. First, as early as Ptolemy a distinction was made between astronomy proper and astrology. Whereas the former was the study of the behaviour of the heavenly bodies, primarily relative to each other, using observations and mathematics, the latter was concerned with the relationships of the heavenly bodies to the earth and their effect upon it. Even though the former is more certain than the latter, Ptolemy insisted that the latter is a legitimate and important subject of enquiry. Indeed, he composed a special treatise devoted to it, the

---

[16] Gersonides' theory of universals, or species-concepts, is more 'realist'. He maintains that species-concepts designate real patterns, or forms, exemplified in nature. These patterns are perfectly instantiated in the Agent Intellect, the separate intellect responsible for human cognition according to the interpretation of Aristotle's *On the Soul*, 3.5, as developed by Alexander of Aphrodisias and accepted by several medieval Muslim and Jewish philosophers. Gersonides frequently refers to these patterns as the 'law and order' or 'the intelligible order' of the physical world (*Wars*, 1.10 (i. 195–6, 205–6), 3.4 (ii. 83–4); see also Touati, *La Pensée philosophique de Gersonide*, pt. 6, ch. 2; Guttmann, 'Levi ben Gerson's Theory of the Concept' (Heb.)).   [17] *Wars*, 4.1 (ii. 155).

Tetrabiblos.[18] Second, astrology is subdivided by Ptolemy into two parts: one focuses upon the purely physical and general effects of celestial bodies upon terrestrial phenomena, such as the warmth of the sun and the moon's effect upon the tides; the other concerns the effects of the heavenly bodies upon human individuals. Ptolemy called the former 'universal', the latter 'genethlialogical' or particular, having to do with nativities and horoscopes.[19] Eventually, the universal aspect of astrology became known as 'natural astrology', whereas the particular aspect became known as 'judicial astrology'.[20]

We have already seen how Gersonides made use of natural astrology in his theory of creation: the providential effects of the heavenly bodies provide him with indubitable evidence that the world was created. But those effects are general and for the most part concerned with the production of certain terrestrial physical properties. Aristotle, too, recognized the importance of the heavenly domain in the generation and conservation of living things.[21] Natural astrology in fact accomplishes a goal that perhaps eluded Aristotle: cosmic unity. Since Aristotle's astrophysics is essentially dualistic in so far as the heavenly domain has a different chemistry and kinetics from those of the earth, there is a hiatus between the two spheres that renders difficult a unified picture of the physical universe. Natural astrology attempts to provide a bridge between the two realms and create a unified cosmology.[22] For us there would be relatively little reluctance to consider natural astrology as a science in its own right or at least as a part of astronomy. Our problem is with judicial astrology. But we should remember that some of the greatest figures in the history of astronomy, from Ptolemy to Newton, believed in judicial astrology. In his critique of the Aristotelian position on individual providence, Gersonides appealed to different types of phenomena experienced by humans, which he takes to be examples of individual providence. To explain these phenomena, Gersonides employed Ptolemy's genethlialogical, or particular, astrology to refute the Aristotelian claims that God cannot exercise providence over individuals because he does not know individuals, and that humankind is beneath God's notice.

Gersonides maintained that some individuals receive communications, or have types of cognitive experience, that enable them to avoid a danger or obtain a benefit. This providential information is supranatural in the sense that it cannot be adequately accounted for by ordinary biological or psychological

---

[18] Ptolemy, *Tetrabiblos*, 1.1–2; Tester, *A History of Western Astrology*, ch. 4.

[19] Ptolemy, *Tetrabiblos*, 2.1, 3.1.   [20] Tester, *A History of Western Astrology*, 178.

[21] Aristotle, *On Generation and Corruption*, 2.10–11; Sambursky, *The Physical World of the Greeks*, chs. 4, 6, 7, 9.   [22] Langermann, 'Gersonides and Astrology'.

mechanisms. As his discussion of this subject shows, what Gersonides has in mind are psychological phenomena that today we call parapsychological or extrasensory. These are perceptual phenomena that some people experience but whose objects or causes are not ordinary or normal. Gersonides devotes Book 2 of *Wars* to these phenomena; its title is 'Dreams , Divination and Prophecy'. Now, we all dream, but most dreams lack providential import. Nevertheless, Gersonides is interested in those that do benefit the individual dreamer. Divination, however, is quite problematic. Many people deny that there is such a thing. Not so Gersonides: he called this general type of perception *kesem*, a biblical term used to refer to various extraordinary forms of cognition, some of which are prohibited, such as witchcraft. The underlying idea here is that, in addition to our five senses, some people enjoy a sixth sense whereby they are able to perceive phenomena, usually having to do with the future, that our normal senses cannot. To divine is then to perceive something beyond our usual powers of cognition. In the ancient world almost all cultures believed in some form of divination. The ancient Greeks and Romans were firm believers in omens and oracles, which transmitted information to special individuals, usually about the future. Gersonides was a believer in this kind of communication, the prime example of which is prophecy. But dreams and divination also are genuine kinds of extrasensory perception, whereby the individual receives extraordinary information that enables him or her to have providential precognition, or clairvoyance.

Let us begin with dreams. What is especially significant for Gersonides is that some people learn things from their dreams that have providential value. For Gersonides such experiences are too common and widespread to be attributed to mere chance. Indeed, they are possible only because the world is an orderly system manifesting sufficient regularity that accurate prediction and forecasting become feasible. This is true not only for the natural scientist but for the ordinary person as well.[23] Gersonides gives several examples of dream communications resulting in individual providence, among which is one that he himself had. Once he dreamed that he saw a man, whom he had never seen before, about to strike him. The next day he saw that same person, whom he recognized from his dream, but avoided him, and was thus delivered from harm.[24] In short, some dreams are verificatory and pertain to some future event the outcome of which has some benefit to the dreamer. Another kind of providential dream is one in which medical information is conveyed

---

[23] *Wars*, 2.1 (ii. 27–9), 2.5 (ii. 48).

[24] Altmann, 'Gersonides' Commentary on Averroes' Epitome of the *Parva Naturalia*', 13; Klein-Braslavy, 'Gersonides on the Mode of Communicating Knowledge'.

that turns out to have therapeutic value to the dreamer. Gersonides gives an example of someone having a dream in which he is commanded to take a specific drug for a medical condition. When he awakes he takes the drug and is cured.[25]

More extraordinary are waking experiences in which the individual has some kind of precognition. Here we are not dealing with oracles or any other kind of professional visionary, but with ordinary people having extrasensory perceptions about the future with providential import. Again Gersonides gives some personal examples of this kind of experience. Once he was sitting in his study when he had a vision of his younger brother sitting on a table in another room and then falling. He immediately ran to the other room and saw him on the floor. Another example of his precognitive experiences is the time when he 'saw' that he would soon meet a man who would strike him with a sword but only slightly. Soon thereafter this event occurred.[26] These cases of precognition are, for Gersonides, signs of individual providence, no matter how they are to be explained.

We now turn to Gersonides' explanatory theory, which makes heavy use of judicial astrology. In these cases of providential communication, whether transmitted via dreams or daytime premonitions, the beneficiary receives the relevant information because of the *type* of individual he or she is. That is, this individual was born under a certain astrological configuration governing a specific group of like individuals. In this sense, the individual has a 'lucky star'. Ptolemy devoted a good portion of his *Tetrabiblos* to a discussion of nativities and the specific influences of different stellar configurations upon individuals' characters and behaviour. Indeed, there was a special term for that part of judicial astrology dealing with medicine—*iatromathematica*, literally 'medical mathematics'; but since astronomy was often considered a branch of mathematics in the ancient and medieval curriculum, the term can be understood as 'astrological medicine'. Specific planets have unique effects, both positive and negative, upon certain parts of the body, and hence someone born under a certain astral pattern is likely to be affected by that particular configuration. The cures too are affected by these patterns: specific herbs are assigned to particular planets. Cinquefoil, a creeping plant, for example, is 'Mercury's plant', and can be used to cure diseases that are governed by Mercury.[27]

---

[25] *Wars*, 2.4 (ii. 46).

[26] Altmann, 'Gersonides' Commentary on Averroes' Epitome of the *Parva Naturalia*', 20.   [27] Tester, *A History of Western Astrology*, 60–4.

But for Gersonides the heavenly bodies alone are not a sufficient condition for these types of communication; indeed, they are just an instrumental cause for the operations of the primary agent, the Agent Intellect. The Agent Intellect plays an extremely important role in Gersonides' general philosophy, and thus we need to say something about it before we see how it works in transmitting providential communications to individuals. In Aristotle's psychology, especially his theory of cognition, there has to be an active cause of our coming to know something, just as there is such a cause in our perceiving some sense object. In the latter case it is some type of sensory medium, such as light or air. In intellectual cognition it is some power, or faculty, that stimulates our cognitive capacity in such a way that we come to know actually what we can potentially know.[28] The ancient and medieval commentators were excusably perplexed by Aristotle's brief and enigmatic remarks on this subject; their explanations were as various as they were complex.[29] For our purposes, however, we shall adopt the interpretation favoured by many medieval philosophers, including Maimonides and Gersonides, that this Agent, or Active, Intellect is an eternal, incorporeal, and transcendent intellect, one of several such intellects that constitute intermediary forces between God and the earthly domain. According to some of these interpreters, such as Maimonides, the Agent Intellect is the lowest or nearest to the earth of these intellects and has a special role to play in prophecy as well as in human cognition.[30]

Although Gersonides' theory of the Agent Intellect is developed within this general framework, it differs from it in several important respects, one of which is crucial to his doctrine of providence, and in particular his explanation of extrasensory perception. Gersonides agrees that the Agent Intellect is the lowest of the transcendent intellects, yet its proximity to the earth does not have for him the pejorative connotations that the term 'lowest' may suggest. Just the contrary: for him the Agent Intellect is the most important transcendent intellect after God himself.[31] As we have seen in his theory of celestial motion, most of these intellects, except God, are the movers of specific heavenly spheres; as such they know their respective kinetic activities and the terrestrial effects emanating from these activities. But their knowledge is restricted to their own specific functions. The intellectual

---

[28] Aristotle, *On the Soul*, 3.5.

[29] See Hicks's notes to his edition of Aristotle's *De anima*, 498–510.

[30] Maimonides, *Guide*, ii. 4 (trans. Pines, 257–8), ii. 11 (trans. Pines, 275); Davidson, *Alfarabi, Avicenna, and Averroes on Intellect*.

[31] *Wars*, 5.3.4 (iii. 134–6), 5.3.13 (iii. 185–91).

movers of the moon, for example, know only lunar motions and influences.[32] In order, however, for all these disparate effects to constitute a harmonious system they have to be co-ordinated and unified by one intellect, and this is where the Agent Intellect comes into the picture. The Agent Intellect represents all the patterns that the other celestial intellects represent individually; it 'embodies' them in one unified order governing the terrestrial domain. In this capacity it resembles Philo's Logos and Plotinus' Nous: it is, in Gersonides' language, 'the law and order' of the earthly domain. Accordingly, whatever influences the celestial bodies have upon terrestrial individuals and affairs are filtered through or ordered by the Agent Intellect, which serves as the ideal paradigm for the earth. In Platonic language, this means that terrestrial corporeal forms participate in their transcendent counterparts in the Agent Intellect, in which these forms exist more perfectly.[33] Thus, for Gersonides, the Agent Intellect is the primary efficient and formal cause of all kinds of cognition, including the precognitive powers that some people enjoy in dreams and clairvoyance.[34]

But human beings are not entirely passive in this kind of communication and cognition. The recipient of verificatory dreams and precognitive perceptions has to be prepared to receive them. A vivid imagination and a deep concern for specific affairs in the receiver's circumstances are required. In therapeutic dreams, for example, the dreamer needs to be concerned about the disease and its cure. In precognition the person should be concerned about the circumstances and individuals in his or her immediate environment, as well as those of his or her own situation. If these conditions are satisfied, it is not impossible that a person would be *providentially* affected by the Agent Intellect and the influence of his or her astrological pattern. The individual's psychological and cognitive capacities *particularize* what is general in the content communicated by the Agent Intellect via the astral configurations. Although the message is universal, the reception and application of the message are particularized by the individual recipient. That the knowledge of God and of the Agent Intellect is universal and law-like is then not an obstacle to a particular person's receiving providential communication relating to his or her individual circumstances. Herein Aristotle's objection from the universal character of divine knowledge is refuted.[35]

Since it is the imagination alone that is the receptive capacity involved in dreams and divination, it is not surprising that people who are not

---

[32] Ibid. 5.3.7 (iii. 153–5), 5.3.8 (iii. 161), 5.3.9 (iii. 164).
[33] Feldman, 'Platonic Themes in Gersonides' Doctrine of the Agent Intellect'.
[34] *Wars*, 2.3 (ii. 38–41). [35] Ibid. 2.6 (ii. 50–1).

remarkable for their intellectual abilities receive such communications.[36] However, the imagination is not the only cognitive faculty; humans have intellect as well, and just as the more perfectly developed and isolated imagination is eligible to receive extrasensory cognitions, so too the more developed intellect can receive theoretical knowledge in dreams and in prophecy, as well as in normal, or ordinary, intellectual enquiry. In these cases, the agent of communication is the Agent Intellect alone, dispensing with the celestial bodies. This type of communication is purely intellectual: the human intellect alone is the receiving faculty.[37] Later we shall see that this intellectual connection between the human intellect and the Agent Intellect has for Gersonides several important implications, especially in his theory of prophecy and in his doctrine of human immortality. In his account of individual providence, too, the intellect and its level of perfection constitute a type of individual providence, whereby those who have highly developed intellects enjoy a level of individual providence not experienced by those who have not attained this state of intellectual perfection:

It is evident that what is more noble and closer to the perfection of the Agent Intellect receives the divine providence to a greater degree . . . Since man exhibits different levels of proximity to and remoteness from the Agent Intellect by virtue of his individual character, those that are more strongly attached to it receive divine providence individually . . . Accordingly, divine providence operates individually in some men [and] in varying degrees and in others it does not appear at all.[38]

At the highest level of this nexus between a particular human intellect and the Agent Intellect is the prophet; just below this level are the sages whose intellectual attainments result in a close cognitive relationship with the Agent Intellect, and thus are able to capitalize on the practical implications of their knowledge. In this sense, knowledge is power: knowing how nature works enables someone to benefit from the natural course of events, whereas those who are not as intellectually eminent may miss out on such benefits. It is reported that the pre-Socratic philosopher Thales made a lot of money by buying olive presses because of his knowledge of astronomy and meteorology, and was thus able to predict a good season for olive-growing.[39] But it must be remembered that all forms of individual providence are particularized by the individual receiving them. Spurning natural science, Socrates would not have thought of purchasing olive presses, and thus remained poor all his life.

---

[36] *Wars*, 2.6 (ii. 59–63), 2.7 (ii. 66–8).   [37] Ibid. 2.6 (ii. 59–63), 4.5 (ii. 178).
[38] Ibid. 4.4 (ii. 174).   [39] As reported by Aristotle, *Politics*, 1.11.1259a6–22.

Whatever the merits of Gersonides' attempt to explain the sources of individual providence and how it is transmitted to and particularized by individual recipients, it is clear that he believed, from his own personal experience, as well as from experiences of others whom he knew, that providential communications are received by all kinds of people. In this respect both Aristotle and Maimonides were wrong: the former in his rejection of individual providence altogether, even for the human species, the latter in his limiting it only to the intellectually deserving. The facts refute their theories. God does not care only for intellectuals.

Why Do the Innocent Suffer?

Much of Book 4 of *Wars* is devoted to the ancient problem that still vexes not only philosophers and theologians but ordinary people as well—why do the righteous suffer while the wicked prosper? This is the problem of *theodicy*: justifying God in the face of counter-evidence to his omnipotence, omniscience, and omnibenevolence. If God is all-powerful, all-knowing, and supremely good, how can he allow the righteous or innocent to suffer all types of evils and the wicked to enjoy all kinds of benefits? Our focus here is not so much on the type of communication received and the agent of communication but upon the apparent arbitrariness of its dissemination and distribution. Why should some get it and others not, *ceteris paribus*? Take any two persons whose intellectual and moral virtues are identical: one prospers, the other suffers; or, what is more grievous, take two individuals of unequal intellectual and moral virtues: the inferior one prospers, the superior suffers.

As did Maimonides and Gersonides, let us look at the book of Job. The main character, Job, is a righteous man; yet he suffers horrendous evils. He reaches a point in his meditations where he rejects the belief that God is just and merciful. In short, he is or becomes an Aristotelian. In his misery his friends come to console him. But instead of consolations they give him reproof. God is truly just and merciful; Job has it all wrong. There is individual providence, and it is distributed justly. These friends represent for Maimonides common beliefs held by both Jewish and Muslim theologians; for Gersonides they are widely held views in the Jewish community. Like Maimonides, Gersonides holds that both Job and his friends are wrong, albeit for different reasons. Whereas Job erred in following Aristotle, his friends naively believed in the distribution of individual providence to all individuals, perhaps even to non-human animals. Since we have already shown how Gersonides refutes the Aristotelian position, accepted by Job at the outset of his protests against God, we now have to consider how he addresses the criticisms of Job's friends and their defence of the belief in a just and universal individual providence.

The traditional belief assumes at the outset that God is not only omniscient in the strong sense, such that he knows individuals as individuals, but that, being perfectly just and good, all his actions are just and good. Accordingly, whatever the distribution of goods and evils may be, what is the case is just and good. We have already seen that Gersonides rejected the traditional account of divine omniscience, so the traditional theodicies offered by the theologians and Job's friends are philosophically unsound.[40] In this respect Job is closer to the truth than they are. But Gersonides is willing to grant for the sake of argument their more generous account of divine knowledge; he gives more attention here to their conviction that Job's rejection of individual divine providence is totally unjustified and indeed sinful. As always Gersonides marshals all their arguments and makes the appropriate distinctions relevant to the various versions of their general thesis. In his staging of the debate between Job and his friends, Gersonides identifies each of the friends with a specific version of the traditional belief in divine providence as perfectly and justly extending to all.

The first friend who speaks is Eliphaz the Temanite, who maintains that all of God's acts are perfect and just, yet asserts that the apparent unjust distribution of goods and evils is not to be attributed to God. If an individual pursues some inappropriate goal or uses some inappropriate means to attain an acceptable goal but suffers some evil, he or she should not blame God but his or her own vanity and stupidity. God has given humanity intellect and free will; humanity has to use these faculties properly to enjoy divine providence.[41] The second friend, Bildad the Shuhite, claims that the sufferings of the righteous are not what they seem. From a wiser and wider perspective these events can be seen to have some benefit or useful purpose. A momentary evil may very well be the best means to the attainment of a real good. If we knew the whole picture, as God does, we would see that the suffering was really a good.[42] Finally, Job's friend Zophar the Naamathite offers the suggestion that our judgements concerning the unfair distribution of benefits are based on inadequate knowledge either of what is genuinely a true benefit or of the real moral character of the recipient. If we really know what is truly a good and what the moral status of the recipient truly is, we would see that the distribution of benefits is just.[43]

[40] *Wars*, 4.3 (ii. 166–7).   [41] Ibid. 4.3 (ii. 159–61).
[42] Ibid. 4.3 (ii. 159, 161, 164–5).   [43] Ibid. 4.3 (ii. 159, 161, 163–4).

After presenting these views Gersonides proceeds to refute them one by one, mainly on the grounds that they do not fit the facts. Nevertheless, he is somewhat sympathetic to Eliphaz's claim that if anyone suffers some evil, it is not to be attributed to God. For, as the sages insist, 'nothing evil descends from above'.[44] If someone suffers from a genuine evil, this fact has to be attributed to some other cause. Eliphaz attributes the evil to the sufferer's own shortcomings. But this answer does not account for the fact that evils occur to people who do not exhibit the relevant moral or intellectual defects.[45] This is after all Job's complaint. Gersonides recognizes another factor at play here: the 'necessity of matter'. Human beings are material entities; as such they are necessarily subject to the various defects of matter or the side effects of being a physical being. The most obvious and indeed inevitable such defect is the eventual decomposition of our bodies. But this is a fact of nature and as such is not something to complain about. Sometimes nature short-changes us: some people are born with three fingers or no toes. Here we need to recall Gersonides' theory of the primordial shapeless body from which our world was created. Its inherent imperfection is in a sense hereditary, resulting in what Aristotle called 'natural monstrosities'.[46] Indeed, people often attribute these evils to chance, sometimes even suggesting that chance is some kind of independent force or power. This apparent randomness, however, is to be understood in the context of the 'necessity of matter'. Earthquakes necessarily occur because of certain natural laws that govern the behaviour of the earth. There is nothing chancy about earthquakes. What is a matter of chance is that a particular house is damaged or a particular person is killed by one. We cannot say with Eliphaz that it was the foolishness of the victims to have chosen that place to live: earthquakes and other natural disasters can occur anywhere and at any time. This does not impair the overall orderliness and beneficence of nature; it is just the inevitable result of what a physical, or material, system is like. In these cases neither God nor man is to blame. More generally, human affairs exhibit a certain indeterminacy such that even when we choose a reasonable goal and the appropriate means to achieve that goal, we fail. Not everything works out as we had planned. All kinds of obstacles can

---

[44] *Genesis Rabbah* 51: 3. In his *Commentary on Job*, Gersonides says that Eliphaz's position is closer to the truth than the views of Bildad and Zophar, for unlike the latter Eliphaz recognizes that God cannot be the cause of evil and he is more aware of the empirical facts of human suffering (*Commentary on Job*, 11 (trans. Lassen, 87)).

[45] *Wars*, 4.3 (ii. 170–1).

[46] Plato, *Timaeus*, 48–51; Aristotle, *On the Generation of Animals*, 4.4.770b2–27.

intervene to frustrate us. And so the innocent do suffer, contrary to the theodicy advanced by Eliphaz.[47]

Neither Bildad nor Zophar is any more successful. They too fail to consider all the facts. Yes, sometimes a wider or more informed perspective helps us see that some apparent evil suffered by an innocent person may be 'for the best' or 'for a reason', as Bildad argued. But is this always so? Gersonides is not convinced: 'We observe that many of the evils that are experienced by the righteous do not contribute toward their benefit; rather, the righteous still suffer. The same is true of the goods received by the sinners [that is, the good is not a trap for them].'[48] Yes, we need to have a sounder awareness of what is a real good or a real evil, as Zophar argued. We also need to know the moral capacities, characters, and motivations of people before we blame their sufferings and successes on God. But even then we see that it does not always turn out that the righteous never suffer real evils; nor is it always the case that the goods received by the wicked are not genuine goods. Moreover, is it true that the morally perfect always enjoy the level of individual providence appropriate for them and the morally imperfect always receive their due? Real saints suffer from cancer, and real criminals escape punishment.[49] Eliphaz, Bildad, and Zophar need to recognize reality for what it truly is.

Consistent with his general tendency to find some merit in positions that he does not wholly accept, Gersonides now constructs his own theory of providence that will incorporate some of what his opponents have claimed. We have already seen how he accepted the philosophers' thesis that God does not know particulars as particulars. Nevertheless, he claims that this thesis does not entail that there is no individual providence. Providence, as it emanates from God via the Agent Intellect and the heavenly bodies, is universal, or general; it is, however, particularized by individuals by means of their character, circumstances, and capacities. As we have just seen, he also accepts the view, advanced by Eliphaz and others, that God is not the cause of evils. But unlike these traditionalists he does not always shift the blame onto humanity. The 'necessity of matter', on the one hand, and the indeterminacy of human affairs, on the other, do not always work to our benefit, no matter what we choose or do. Sometimes one and the same person will prosper and at another time, though in similar circumstances, suffer. In this respect Job was right: it at least seems that 'there is no justice nor judge'.[50]

[47] *Wars*, 4.3 (ii. 169–71).   [48] Ibid. 4.3 (ii. 172).   [49] Ibid.
[50] Fischel, *Rabbinic Literature and Greco-Roman Philosophy*, 35.

Although Gersonides has apparently taken Job's side in refusing to accept the answers of Job's friends as adequate responses to his complaints, he does not concede the debate to Job either. Zophar had a point when he argued that our judgements as to what is good or evil or who is righteous or wicked are not always correct. But his argument still worked within the common understanding of these concepts. The goods and evils are understood in materialistic terms; the righteous and the wicked are judged according to conventional moral categories. Gersonides' critique of Zophar's view has shown, however, that if we remain within this framework it will not blunt the force of Job's complaints. To provide an adequate answer to Job we shall need to have a different conception of what a genuine good is, and of who a really righteous person might be. Gersonides now undertakes to provide this new framework and to show that there is justice and a judge.

Like Maimonides, and indeed the author of the book of Job, Gersonides makes Elihu the advocate of the true theory of divine providence. Elihu makes his appearance quite late in the book, appearing for the first time in chapter 32, after Job's friends have presented their responses and Job has refuted them. Despite his youth, Elihu does not refrain from criticizing all of them and accuses them all of betraying God. But it is questionable whether he really offers a genuine theodicy. His answer to Job is more a rebuke for his impertinence, and he insults the intelligence of Job's friends. Although Gersonides claims that his theory is the doctrine expounded by Elihu, it is clearly a novel theodicy.

There is a kind of asymmetry to the problem of theodicy: it is not so much the prosperity of the wicked that disturbs us as the suffering of the innocent. In fact, the former is relatively easy to explain. The general providential order produced by the heavenly domain and the Agent Intellect provides for all. Even the wicked enjoy sunlight and beautiful sunsets. Some of the wicked are smart enough to obtain material benefits from natural processes, such as looking for diamonds in river beds and planting olive trees at the right time. Others enjoy material goods simply by having been born under a beneficent astral pattern.[51] Since God created of the world as an act of love and beneficence, we should not be surprised if the wicked benefit from the wisdom inherent in this creation. But these are all instances of general, natural providence. However, in some cases the wicked may in fact enjoy benefits by virtue of the fact that they are the offspring of righteous parents who have themselves received individual providence. This is the traditional rabbinic

---

[51] *Wars*, 4.6 (ii. 184–5).

doctrine of the 'merit of the fathers'.[52] But these benefits are just the indirect result of individual providence received by others.

What really needs explaining is the suffering of the innocent, especially if we hold, as did Gersonides, that 'no evil descends from above'. We have already learned that some evils do not come from God at all but from the 'necessity of matter' and chance. However, even in these cases, human reason, which God has given to all individuals, can often help us avoid or mitigate the undesirable consequences of materiality or the indeterminacy in human affairs. An intelligent person may choose not to live in a place where earthquakes are frequent or where certain diseases are prevalent; moreover, one can prepare for the uncertainties of life. Finally, natural evils, especially those deriving from maleficent astral configurations, are relatively infrequent and of short duration. And compared to the overall beneficent effects of general providence they can be considered accidental. In this sense, Bildad was right: in the long run and from a wider perspective things are not so bad, especially for the virtuous whose intellectual accomplishments enable them to come out on top even in unfavourable circumstances.[53]

But we are still working within the framework set by Job's friends, the spokespersons of the ordinary, traditional religious perspective, whose moral judgements in this context are defined in material terms. On this score Zophar was right: we often operate with mistaken notions of good or evil. Nevertheless, according to Gersonides, he too conceived good and evil in material terms. What we need here is a different paradigm altogether, one that takes us out of the realm of matter and leads us into a very different sphere of activity and reflection. The truly righteous literally live in a different world, one defined and reflected in their pursuit of intellectual and moral perfection. To the extent that their lives are devoted to this pursuit they enjoy a special relationship with the Agent Intellect and with God. The stronger the link between them and the Agent Intellect, the greater their individual providence. Genuine happiness, or prosperity, is the life of the spirit.[54] In support of this claim Gersonides quotes at length an extraordinary passage from Maimonides' *Guide*, where the latter, in the form of a passing remark, claims that those who are completely devoted to the 'intellectual love of God' enjoy unremitting divine providence such that no material evil occurs to them. For such people the only thing that matters is the link between them and God, and this link is established and preserved by the intellect. But when

---

[52] *CT*, Exod., 'Ki tisa', 115*a* (ii. 436–7).
[53] *Wars*, 4.6 (ii. 184–5); *CT*, Exod., 'Yitro', 76*a–b* (ii. 150–1).
[54] *Wars*, 4.6 (ii. 192).

this link is broken, even momentarily, anything can happen; at that point, they are exposed to the 'sea of chance'.[55] Nevertheless, even though they may suffer from some material evil, no matter how severe, they know that such suffering is irrelevant to their ultimate goal. For them it is not a real evil; the only real evil is that the link has been broken. For Gersonides this idea enables him to defend and employ a rabbinic doctrine that Maimonides had rejected. If the righteous suffer some material evil when this link has been severed, the pain reminds them of their failure to preserve the link and stirs them to re-establish it. In this sense, the material evil leads to a spiritual good, which is another expression of individual divine providence. This last point is suggestive of the rabbinic concept of the 'chastisements of love', whereby the righteous are 'punished' in such a way that by virtue of their suffering they realize their deviation from the right path and thus return to the 'pathways of the righteous'. Maimonides, however, believed that these chastisements would be inconsistent with the doctrine of absolute justice: 'In the discourse of the sages, there occurs something additional over and above what is found in the text of the Torah, namely, the dictum of some of them regarding the *sufferings of love* . . . But there is no text in the Torah expressing this notion.'[56] According to Gersonides the 'chastisements of love' are of two kinds: those that save the righteous from greater evils that follow from the astral order and those that save the righteous from committing a greater sin, that is, a spiritual evil. Both manifest individual providence, since the righteous make use of reason to rectify their moral lapses, and reason is a divine gift.[57]

To support his theory of individual providence, and in particular his claim that the sufferings of the righteous do not impugn divine justice, Gersonides appeals to some rabbinic sayings. In the face of the various Roman persecutions the sages were well aware that the innocent do suffer. But they tried to alleviate this suffering with their doctrine that genuine reward for the observance of the commandments is not earthly: 'The reward for a commandment is not in this world.'[58] Although we shall discuss in detail Gersonides' doctrine of immortality in a later chapter, it is sufficient to note here that, like Maimonides and other medieval Jewish and Islamic philosophers, Gersonides conceived of immortality in intellectual terms. Immortality is the attainment of a state of intellectual perfection.[59] Here Gersonides refers to

---

[55] Ibid. 4.7 (ii. 206–7); Maimonides, *Guide*, iii. 51 (trans. Pines, 625).
[56] Maimonides, *Guide*, iii. 17 (trans. Pines, 470–1), citing BT *Ber.* 5a.
[57] *Wars*, 4.6 (ii. 188).   [58] BT *Kid.* 39b; *Wars*, 4.6 (ii. 197).
[59] *Wars*, 1.11 (i. 212–17), 1.13 (i. 223–5).

and discusses an important rabbinic text that deals with the question of divine providence. In attempting to explain how such a learned sage as Elisha ben Abuya could become an *apikoros,* some sages suggested that he saw a boy fall from a roof in an attempt to fulfil his father's commandment to catch a bird yet obey the divine injunction not to take the bird in the presence of its mother. Where is the reward of obeying a commandment of the Torah?, asked Elisha ben Abuya. In response to his sceptical question, the sages pointed out that the real reward is in the world to come, 'on the day that is wholly good'.[60] Unlike Job's friends who, according to Gersonides, did not face the facts, the sages were only too aware of what life has in store for us. And so they deferred genuine reward to the hereafter, which they defined in spiritual terms. Maimonides quotes the following talmudic passage: 'In the world to come there is no eating, drinking . . . or sexual intercourse; but the righteous sit with their crowns on their heads enjoying the radiance of the Divine Presence.'[61] Maimonides goes on to describe this 'enjoyment' in intellectualistic terms: the greatest enjoyment is knowledge, in particular our knowledge of God in so far as it is attainable by humans; it is this that survives death. Gersonides supports this conception of the world to come by citing a passage from the Talmud: '[the length of life], children and sustenance do not depend upon merit but [rather on] the stars'. Here, however, he uses it to show that whereas corporeal benefits or the lack thereof result from natural causes, real, or spiritual, benefits are fully realized only in the hereafter.[62]

But the righteous, that is, the intellectually perfect, do not have to wait until they die. Even in this life they can enjoy the perpetual rewards of the hereafter, if only temporarily. The intellectual link between them and the Agent Intellect is a kind of 'appetizer', or foreshadowing, of what they will experience in the future. The cognitive link is an earthly equivalent of the spiritual life to be enjoyed on the 'day that is wholly good'. As long as this link is firm, nothing else matters. Although Gersonides does not refer to the following passage from Aristotle's *Nicomachean Ethics,* his theory comes very close to the spirit of it:

Now he who exercises his intellect and cultivates it seems to be in the best state and most dear to the gods. For if the gods have any care for human affairs, as they are thought to have, it would be most reasonable both that they should delight in that

---

[60] BT *Ḥul.* 142*a*; *Wars,* 4.6 (ii. 197).
[61] BT *Ber.* 17*a*; Maimonides, *Commentary on the Mishnah, San.* 10.
[62] BT *MK* 28*a*; *Wars,* 4.6 (ii. 198).

which was best and most akin to them [that is, intellect] and that they should reward those who love and honour this most . . . The wise man . . . is therefore the dearest to the gods. And he who is that will presumably be the happiest.[63]

In short, Job was not enough of an Aristotelian. He failed to realize that our true goal is not material happiness. True happiness is the life of the intellect, and this is what makes us 'like the divine'. This is genuine individual providence.[64]

Let us now recapitulate the results of Gersonides' theodicy. The traditional difficulties raised against divine justice rest upon a mistaken principle: goods and evils are material and temporal. Once we appreciate that genuine happiness is spiritual or intellectual, we understand that (1) the material prosperity of the wicked is due to general, or natural, providence, the effect of the heavenly bodies and the expression of divine beneficence to all of creation; (2) some of the material evils that occur happen as the inevitable 'side effects' of the 'necessity of matter'; (3) the wicked truly suffer in so far as they are wicked and the righteous truly prosper precisely because they are righteous; (4) the true reward of the righteous is deferred to the world to come and the true punishment of the wicked is their exclusion from the world to come; and (5) there are different types and degrees of individual providence. Point 1 explains why there are wicked billionaires; point 2 accounts for the occurrence of earthquakes, diseases, and physical deformities; point 3 informs us what our true happiness is; point 4 tells us where and when this reward or punishment will ultimately be dispensed; and point 5 explains why and how those who are either intellectually deficient or employ their imagination alone do receive a kind of individual providence, which, however, is inferior to the type received by those who are intellectually perfect. There are, then, no grounds for complaint: 'All of God's ways are just' (Deut. 32: 4) and 'The eyes of the Lord are on the righteous' (Ps. 34: 16).

Before we leave this topic, let us note an interesting link between Gersonides' theory of divine providence and his doctrine of creation. In rejecting creation *ex nihilo* in favour of creation from some primordial shapeless matter Gersonides maintained that this matter was eternal and in this sense ontologically independent of God. Yet its very shapelessness, or formlessness, is an imperfection, and thus although eternal it is not on the same level as God. In so far as it is imperfect, it is no wonder that, no matter how perfect God's creative activity is, various kinds of material shortcomings arise from it and from it alone. In this respect, at least, Gersonides' theory has an

---

[63] Aristotle, *Nicomachean Ethics*, 10.8.1179a22–30.   [64] *Wars*, 4.4 (ii. 175).

advantage over those theorists, such as Maimonides, who believed in creation *ex nihilo* and accounted for material evils by appealing to the 'necessity of matter'. For against these theorists one could object: 'If God created matter, why did he not create it in such a way that these material evils would not occur?' But if matter is uncreated, as it is in Gersonides' cosmology, this objection cannot arise. Accordingly, we cannot blame God for earthquakes and diseases. Insurance companies, therefore, have it wrong when they attribute earthquakes and floods to 'acts of God'.

The People of Israel and Divine Providence

Gersonides' 'double providence theory' seems to be incongruent with a basic doctrine of traditional Judaism, the *election* of Israel, a teaching that is repeated many times and in many ways in the Bible. The Jews are to be a 'holy nation' (Exod. 19: 6); they are a 'special nation' (Exod. 19: 5); they are God's servants and have been chosen by God (Isa. 41: 8): they are 'God's witnesses' (Isa. 43: 10) and a 'light unto the nations' (Isa. 49: 6). As the Bible makes clear, this prerogative stems from a covenant established between God and the patriarchs, especially Abraham (Gen. 15). This covenant is transmitted biologically and sealed through the rite of male circumcision. Moreover, whatever happens to the Jewish people, even in their most catastrophic suffering, this covenant is eternal (Jer. 30–1). By means of this covenant a providential relationship is entered into between God and Israel that involves, amongst other things, a special concern and action on God's part for Israel. The appearance of prophets, the performance of miracles, and the giving of the Torah are all expressions and manifestations of this special kind of providence.[65]

Now what kind of providence is this? Since we are here dealing with a people, a collectivity, it is not individual providence. God's selection of Abraham may be an instance of individual providence; but the covenant between God and Abraham's 'seed' is not strictly a case of individual providence, nor does it fit Gersonides' doctrine of general providence. The latter, as we have learned, is governed and implemented through natural means, especially the celestial bodies and their movers. Here God is only the remote cause of providence. God's unilateral and voluntary creation of the universe is the sole sufficient condition for his providing for the world. But God's special concern for Israel is too particular to be considered a type of general providence even though it is

---

[65] See Eisen, *Gersonides on Providence*, for a thorough and insightful discussion of these topics.

not strictly a form of individual providence. The Jewish people is a group of individuals singled out by God as a subject of special concern and care. As a group they seem to have something like general providence; but as a particular people there is something individual about this providence. Is then the chosenness of Israel a combination of general and individual providences, a special type of individual providence or a form of providence *sui generis*? Finally, whatever this kind of providence turns out to be, we shall have to see how, if at all, it is compatible with Gersonides' theory of divine knowledge.

As I have already noted, the special status of Israel began with the covenant with Abraham. Let us take a closer look at this covenant and what it implies. In the genealogical list in Genesis 11, Abraham is mentioned for the first time as the son of Terah. Without further ado he is commanded by God to leave his home and family and go to a land that God will show him (Gen. 12: 1–3). There he and his offspring will become a great nation. Abraham trusts God and immediately sets out on his historic journey. The Bible tells us nothing about Abraham's background or why he was chosen by God to be the father of a great people. Perhaps some of the subsequent chapters reporting Abraham's sense of justice for the righteous of Sodom and Gomorrah and his willingness to sacrifice Isaac answer the latter question. At any rate, Abraham as an individual and his progeny as a whole are singled out. Note here the tight connection between Abraham's future family and the Promised Land: both the people and the land are chosen and intimately linked together. For Gersonides this relationship is the paradigmatic case of 'inherited providence', where the providential link between God and the recipient of providence is not only transmitted throughout generations but is also tied to the eternal possession and inheritance of a piece of land. This is the core of the covenant between God and Abraham: 'On that day God established a covenant with Abram to give his seed all the land of the peoples of Canaan' (Gen. 15: 18). Indeed, possession of the land is itself a sign of the special covenant between God and Israel.

Someone might ask, 'Why the land of Canaan?' What was so special about this piece of earth? Although the Bible itself suggests in several places that the Canaanites had forfeited their rights to the land by virtue of their immoral behaviour (Lev. 18), a point repeated by Gersonides, he is more interested in another factor: 'And thus God commanded him to go to the land of Canaan because it is more eligible and fit [to receive] the conjunction of the divine emanation.'[66] This is a rabbinic theme that Gersonides makes

[66] *CT*, Gen., 'Lekh lekha', 22*b–c* (i. 101–2); see also *CT*, Gen., 'Bereshit', 17*c* (i. 72).

his own and repeats often: there is something special about this land that makes it 'chosen', just as the seed of Abraham is chosen. The sages believed that the very air of the land of Israel makes one wise.[67] Gersonides reformulates this dictum according to his own technical language: 'The air of the land of Israel is ready to receive the divine emanation.'[68] What could this mean? How can climate affect intellectual activity and perfection?

At this juncture we need to consider some aspects of medieval geography, in particular the theory of climatic zones.[69] It was a commonplace of both ancient and medieval geography that the earth can be divided into seven specific climatic regions having different physical, socio-economic, and cultural effects upon their inhabitants. In some versions of this general theory astrological notions were incorporated, such as the dominance of certain planets in specific terrestrial regions. The fourth, or middle, region, in which the land of Israel is located, was considered to be the most moderate, or 'mixed', and hence most conducive to advanced civilization. After all, it is not surprising that people living near the North Pole have not produced great artists, musicians, or philosophers. They have enough on their hands just to survive. So it is reasonable to assume that some regions are more favourable for certain pursuits and the development of certain talents than others. But again what is so special about the land of Israel that distinguishes it from all the other lands in the middle climatic region?

There is another factor in this covenantal link among God, the Israelites, and the land of Israel. It is not only that a particular people and land are singled out as special; the people and land are also the recipients of and the locus for an extraordinary phenomenon: prophecy. It is as if in promising Abraham that the land of Israel will be the land of his offspring, God had other things in mind that would be particularly tied to this land. This seems to be implied when God is about to reveal to Abraham his plan for Sodom and Gomorrah:

Abraham will surely be a great nation and all the nations of the earth shall be blessed because of him. For I have singled him out so that he will command his sons and house after him, and they shall observe the way of the Lord, to do righteousness and justice, so that the Lord will bring about all that he has said to him. (Gen. 18: 19; my translation)

In this sense the covenant is conditional upon the Israelites living according to the mandates of God. The possession of the land is not absolute; it is conditional upon a certain way of life: 'The covenant derives from God's love for

[67] BT *BB* 158*b*.   [68] Gersonides, *Commentary on the Former Prophets*, 1 Kgs 18: 42.
[69] Melamed, 'The Land of Israel' (Heb.).

a person deserving it.'[70] Here Gersonides links the covenant with the Israelites, and the land of Israel with the notion of Israel's compliance with God's commands, the fulfilment and implementation of which involve the possession of and residence in the land of Israel. Failure to comply with this regimen results in punishment, and in the extreme case, exile. But this regimen is the result of prophecy. Hence, it is prophecy that makes the land special.

Nevertheless, one could still ask, 'Why this particular land?' There seems to be an element of caprice in God's picking out a particular piece of land among all the 'middle' regions as worthy of receiving the divine emanation and prophecy. It makes sense to say that a particular person or people is worthy of some reward or gift. Does it make sense to say this about a piece of land, especially one so small and bereft of natural resources? In some cases, such as agricultural fertility, it is reasonable to characterize a particular region as having 'rich soil'. But are there analogous properties of land, especially the land of Israel, that make it the special locus of prophecy?

Here Gersonides seems to be a firm believer in a tradition in Jewish thought, advanced by Judah Halevi and Abraham ibn Ezra, that the land of Israel is uniquely endowed as the privileged place for prophetic revelation.[71] Lest this belief be attributed to Jewish particularism, we should note that for a medieval Christian or Muslim too the land of Israel was special, indeed holy. After all, why did Jesus appear there and not in Athens? Why did Muhammad, according to Muslim tradition, make a miraculous trip to Jerusalem?[72] Whether the special character of the land of Israel be accounted for mainly in terms of the theory of climates or by the covenantal link between God and Abraham, the belief in the uniqueness of the land of Israel was a commonplace of medieval thought. Without explicitly referring to any rabbinic traditions in this context, Gersonides appears to have in mind those that ascribe to God, in his initial revelation to Abraham, the plan to have the Holy Temple built in Jerusalem and thus to make the land of Israel the centre of prophecy.[73] The singular character of both the people of Israel and the

[70] Gersonides, *Commentary on the Former Prophets*, 1 Kgs 8: 23, twenty-seventh lesson.

[71] Halevi, *Kuzari*, i. 115, ii. 14; Ibn Ezra, *Commentary on the Torah*, Exod. 25: 40. Maimonides, however, did not emphasize the privileged character of the land of Israel or even the 'chosenness' of Israel; see Kreisel, 'The Land of Israel and Prophecy in Medieval Jewish Philosophy' (Heb.); Twersky, 'The Land of Israel and Exile in the Teaching of Maimonides' (Heb.); Kellner, *Maimonides on Judaism*.

[72] Quran, Sura 17; Peters, *Jerusalem*, 182–5.

[73] *CT*, Gen., 'Bereshit', 17*c* (i. 72), 'Vayetse', 36*d*, (i. 178); Exod., 'Beshalaḥ', 70*b* (i. 118).

land of Israel is intimately linked with the divine presence as manifested in prophecy and in the Temple. It turns out that what particularizes the land of Israel is not a natural property, such as agricultural fertility or oil, but some non-natural, supranatural if you will, features, which along with the original covenant with Abraham render this land, and no other, holy. Or we might say that, even though Gersonides believes, as we shall see, that prophecy is a natural phenomenon, a human potentiality, it becomes actual only under certain specific conditions, one of which is the fitness of the recipient and another the proper location. Thus, along with the two passages quoted above wherein Gersonides insists upon the fitness of the individual to be a covenantal partner with God, we need to add the notion of the fitness of the land: 'Now He commanded Abraham to go to the Land of Canaan because it is more eligible and fit, such that the divine presence be conjoined with it.'[74] We might say, then, that there is a kind of covenant with the land of Israel, as well as with the people of Israel.

Earlier we raised the question of how Gersonides' doctrine of divine providence upon Israel falls within his distinction between general and individual providence. Although sometimes he speaks of it as a manifestation of individual providence,[75] there is a passage where he indicates that it shares some features of general providence:

There is something similar to general providence in particular providence. That is, just as there accrues to a person something from general providence such that he and his progeny benefit from it for a long time, this is also the case with particular providence when it is perfect. Thus you find that because of the divine [particular] providence over the Patriarchs their progeny continually benefited from it . . . And because of this [particular providence over the Patriarchs] God was provident over the [whole] people of Israel in Egypt, redeeming them with marvelous miracles, in order to bring them to His service so that they would be worthy to inherit the land. For this purpose He gave them the perfect Torah.[76]

Certain kinds of individual providence are therefore inherited. Where the originating individual was the recipient of beneficial providence, this continues to be present in his descendants if they merit it. This is the case with the providence enjoyed by Israel throughout the generations. Nevertheless, it could work the other way: non-beneficial individual providence, or suffering, can also be passed down, especially if, as Gersonides points out, the progeny

---

[74] *CT*, Gen., 'Bereshit', 22*b* (i. 100); see also *CT*, Gen., 'Vayetse', 36*d* (i. 178).

[75] Gersonides, *Commentary on the Former Prophets*, 1 Kgs 11: 27.

[76] *CT*, Deut., 'Va'et ḥanan', 210*c*, eighteenth lesson (v. 31).

have persisted in the evil ways of their ancestors.[77] Certain kinds of providence are, then, genetic.

Nevertheless, we still have to ask the question concerning this form of individual yet general providence that Gersonides himself raised about his general theory of divine providence: is this doctrine compatible with his theory of divine cognition? The latter theory asserts that God does not know particulars as such; hence, particular providence of any kind cannot be construed as a case of God's selectively picking out a definite individual or group as the beneficiary of his special care. We need to recall here what Gersonides means by individual providence. Unlike the case of someone singling out one, and only one, of their descendants as their heir, divine individual providence is conditional and in this sense really general: if *anyone* satisfies certain general conditions, they will receive benefits, such as prophecy or redemption, which those who do not satisfy these conditions will not. To the individuals who satisfy these conditions the benefit appears as an instance of individual providence, such that they see themselves as the recipient of special care or concern on God's part. Yet in reality they have not been singled out by God, who does not know them as individuals; it just so happens that they satisfied the conditions of the 'laws of individual providence'. Just as a person receives prophecy, a form of individual providence, by fulfilling the conditions of prophetic reception, so too in the case of individual providence. In neither case is there any direct selection by God of the particular individual. Anyone who fits the job description gets the job. The same is true for a people: a group can be chosen in the sense that it, like an individual person, satisfies certain stipulated conditions that qualify it for special benefits. In principle it is logically possible that some other group could be eligible for these benefits. But in fact only one nation satisfied the specified conditions. This is the import of the rabbinic *midrash* in which all the nations are first asked by God to accept the Torah but refuse; only Israel accepts it. In theory these nations could have received the Torah but did not want to. One, and only one, nation did.[78]

At the beginning of Deuteronomy 4, Moses speaks to the whole of Israel and ties together these themes nicely. He tells them that the inheritance and possession of the land and their special place in the divine plan for human history is indeed based upon the original covenant established by Abraham; but it is conditional upon their acceptance and performance of the commandments of the Torah: the second covenant established at Sinai. On this passage Gersonides comments: 'What [disposed] God to choose to give to Israel the

---

[77] *Wars*, 4.6 (ii. 186–7, 201), Gersonides cites BT *Ber.* 7*a*.

[78] *Exodus Rabbah* 27: 9; Ginzberg, *Legends of the Jews*, iii. 81–2, 205, 341, 454.

Land [of Canaan] was because this land was especially prepared for the attainment of human perfection.'[79] As we shall see in Chapters 8 and 9, human perfection is open to all, Jew and non-Jew alike. It is attainable through the proper exercise of both the moral and intellectual virtues, as Aristotle had indicated.[80] Yet, by virtue of God's covenant with Abraham, whose faithfulness and righteousness justified his election, Abraham's progeny, the people of Israel, were chosen to perpetuate Abraham's legacy and were given the Torah to enable them to achieve human perfection, not only individually but as a group. This achievement will be realized in a particular place that was initially selected by God as especially appropriate for this purpose, the land of Israel.

[79] *CT*, Gen., 'Lekh lekha', 22*c*, fourth lesson (i. 102).
[80] Aristotle, *Nicomachean Ethics*, 1.

SIX

Divine Omnipotence

'Is Anything Impossible for the Lord?'

THE VERY FIRST SENTENCE of the Bible seems to give a definitive answer to this question: God created the entire universe. What could count as greater proof of his omnipotence? Indeed, the Bible records many divine acts that explicitly testify to his overwhelming power, especially to alter the natural behaviour of things. In short, every miracle is proof of divine power, as well as of divine providence. Indeed, the very occurrence of miracles could have been used by Gersonides as evidence of individual providence. Besides the specific descriptions of particular miraculous events, the Bible enunciates two statements that formulate the general principle of divine omnipotence. In Genesis 18: 14, in the context of Sarah's doubt that she will ever give birth to a child, God rhetorically asks Abraham, 'Is anything impossible for the Lord?'[1] Sarah's menopausal state is no impediment to God's ability to cause her to give birth. In Job 42: 2, Job finally realizes his impertinence and confesses his ignorance in the face of God's power: 'I [now] know that you can do everything, and that nothing is beyond your purpose.' Both Christianity and Islam would agree. It is not surprising, then, that the late medieval Jewish theologian Hasdai Crescas makes belief in divine omnipotence one of the six dogmas of any revealed religion.[2]

But once Judaism made contact with Greek philosophy the belief in divine omnipotence, and in particular in miracles, became problematic. Whether because of their conviction that nature was a system of fixed laws or because of their belief in an indifferent deity, the Greek philosophers did not admit miracles into their belief systems. Indeed, in some of the early recorded encounters of pagan philosophers with Judaism or Christianity, the belief in miracles is singled out for ridicule.[3] Philo of Alexandria seems to have been aware of this philosophical challenge, for he is not reluctant to discuss and

---

[1] From the Hebrew word translated here as 'impossible', *yipale*, we get two biblical terms for 'miracle', *pele* and *niflaot*.   [2] Crescas, *Or adonai*, 2.3.

[3] Galen, as reported by Maimonides in his *Medical Aphorisms*, 25; Celsus, *On the True Doctrine*, 86–7, 98.

defend divine omnipotence and miracles. In his treatise *On the Creation of the World*, he argues against those thinkers who attribute the terrestrial seasons and changes to the actions of the heavenly bodies by reminding them that earthly things were created and generated before the heavenly bodies were created. God did not need them to assist him in getting things started on earth, 'for all things are possible to God'.[4] Nor is Philo embarrassed to discuss particular miracles: he is especially lavish in his descriptions of the miracles performed by Aaron and Moses in Egypt. In connection with Aaron's rod, which turned into a serpent and devoured the serpents produced by Pharaoh's magicians, Philo repeats the biblical principle, 'to the divine power all things are easy'.[5] When the Egyptians are afflicted by the Ten Plagues, Philo comments that 'the whole world that belongs to God, and all its parts, obey their master . . . And if anyone disbelieves these facts [that is, the plagues], he neither knows God nor has he ever sought to know Him.'[6] Yet in the very same passage Philo becomes a bit uneasy and evinces an awareness that philosophically educated readers might find his faith in divine omnipotence naive. To remove their doubts, and perhaps his own, he provided an explanation of these events, and in so doing initiated a tradition of rationalizing miracles that would be continued by many religious philosophers throughout the ages. Consider the example of the piece of wood that Moses used to sweeten the bitter waters (Exod. 15: 22–5). Philo attempts to naturalize this miracle as follows: 'a piece of wood . . . which indeed had been made by nature with such a power for that purpose, and which perhaps had a quality which was previously unknown, or perhaps was then first endowed with it for the purpose of effecting the service which it was then about to perform'. In these various alternative explanations Philo is trying to make miracles believable by minimizing or removing altogether the supranatural factor—God—or by making God employ nature as his assistant.[7]

The sages certainly believed in God's ability to perform miracles, and like Philo they relished magnifying them. Nevertheless, in at least one passage of the Mishnah they seems to have some reservations about how far divine power extends. In Mishnah *Berakhot* 9, a certain type of prayer is prohibited: prayers in which God is asked to change what has already taken place. Two such prayers are singled out: a prayer requesting that a catastrophe be undone, and a prayer requesting the newly born child be a son. These are vain prayers because the person is asking God to change the past, to make some fact a non-fact, as if it never happened. Although there is no evidence

---

[4] Philo, *On the Creation of the World*, 45–6.   [5] Philo, *The Life of Moses*, 1.93–5.
[6] Ibid. 1.201, 1.212.   [7] Ibid. 1.185.

that the sages had read Aristotle, their view is similar to his saying, quoting another Greek author: 'For even from God this power is kept, this power alone: to make it true that what's been done had never been done.'[8] As the sixteenth-century commentator on the Mishnah, Obadiah of Bertinoro, put it: 'What's past is past!'[9]

The pointlessness of requesting God to change the past is used by Sa'adiah Gaon as an example of a logical absurdity in terms of which the notion of divine omnipotence can be defined:

It will furthermore laud and praise Him justly and uprightly, not by attributing to Him exaggerations and absurdities . . . It will not therefore praise Him for being able to cause five to be more than ten without adding anything to the former . . . nor for being able to bring back the day gone by in its original condition. For all these things are absurd.[10]

The domain of logical possibility is therefore defined by the laws of logic. This conception of omnipotence is repeated later by Maimonides: the impossible has 'a stable nature' such that 'it is impossible to change it in any way'.[11] Maimonides believed, therefore, that the notion of logical impossibility is fixed by the laws of logic and that omnipotence is to be understood as the power to do what is logically doable.

Maimonides addresses the problem of miracles, as particular manifestations of divine power, in several of his legal writings and in one chapter of the *Guide*. His discussions focus upon two rabbinic passages suggesting that miracles were pre-programmed at the creation of the world.[12] What is significant for Maimonides about this idea is that it removes a serious philosophical objection to the notion of a miracle. As in the case of the creation of the world, it could be objected that the performance of a miracle represents a change in God's will; it is a *novum* that cannot be allowed in a being that is supposed to be immutable. If, however, all miracles have been pre-established at creation, there is no genuine change in God when these events occur. They are literally 'prescribed'.

It will be useful to discuss here another passage from Maimonides concerning miracles, especially since Gersonides' own account of miracles is in

---

[8] Aristotle, *Nicomachean Ethics*, 6.2.1139b8–11.

[9] Obadiah of Bertinoro, *Commentary on the Mishnah*, ad loc.

[10] Sa'adiah Gaon, *The Book of Beliefs and Opinions*, treatise 2, ch. 13 (trans. Rosenblatt, 134). [11] Maimonides, *Guide*, iii. 15 (trans. Pines, 459).

[12] Mishnah *Avot* 5: 6; *Genesis Rabbah* 5: 5; Maimonides, *Commentary on the Mishnah*, Avot 5:6; id., *Eight Chapters*, 8; id., *Guide*, ii. 29 (trans. Pines, 345).

part a critique of Maimonides' theory. It occurs in perhaps his latest writing, the *Treatise on Resurrection*, wherein he defends his inclusion of resurrection of the dead as one of the dogmas of Judaism. In the course of this defence Maimonides differentiates this dogma from the belief in immortality, or in the world to come, on epistemological grounds: whereas the latter principle is philosophically provable, the former is not; indeed, it is a miracle, and like all other miracles it must be believed on faith, based upon reliable tradition.[13] Referring to the *Guide*, Maimonides bolsters this belief by reminding his readers that in the latter work he had shown that miracles are possible once one believes in the creation of the world. For the latter principle implies that the laws of nature are not necessarily and universally true; hence, there is some logical space for divine intervention and miracles.[14] In the course of this argument, Maimonides makes use of two terms that are crucial to this issue: 'what is impossible according to nature' and 'what is impossible according to reason'. Some things are impossible 'naturally speaking', whereas others are just simply impossible, for they are incompatible with the laws of logic. All miracles, including resurrection of the dead, Maimonides maintains, fall within 'logical space', despite their unnaturalness. They are indeed ruled out by the laws of nature, but not by the rules of logic. Hence, under special circumstances they could occur.[15]

Imagine a large circle, the domain of the logically possible (L). Within this circle there are two smaller, non-concentric, circles: the domain of the naturally possible (N), governed by the laws of nature; and an even smaller domain—the domain of miracles (M), which is outside N but within L. Thus, miracles are logically possible, albeit naturally impossible. For Maimonides, the belief in creation, perhaps the greatest miracle of all, proves the logical possibility of miracles. Every other miracle 'inherits' this possibility. Divine omnipotence is therefore to be understood in terms of the domain L: any state of affairs within L is a possibility over which God has potency. Miracles, then, pose no logical problem for God.

Gersonides' Theory of Miracles

In part 2 of Book 6 of *Wars*, chapters 9 to 12 are devoted to the topic of miracles. That these chapters are included in the concluding part of the treatise entitled 'Religious Questions' is significant. It suggests that in one sense

[13] Maimonides, *Treatise on Resurrection*, 224–5.
[14] Maimonides, *Guide*, ii. 25 (trans. Pines, 328).
[15] Maimonides, *Treatise on Resurrection*, 228.

the issue here is not strictly speaking philosophical, yet in another sense it is philosophically germane if only because it requires some kind of philosophical justification. These four chapters come immediately after his attempt to show that his philosophical theory of creation is actually taught by the opening chapters of Genesis and before his discussion of the testing of prophets. The location of these chapters is not accidental. Since, for Gersonides, the creation of the world is not only a fact but a philosophically proven fact, showing that the world's production is the effect of a voluntary and beneficent act of God, miracles, as particular manifestations of God's benevolence, are not only possible but even likely. Moreover, since Scripture reports miracles almost always in the context of the activities of prophets, the connection between prophecy and miracles needs to be examined. Indeed, for Gersonides there is an intimate relationship between the performance of miracles and the presence and role of the prophet. But is the performance of a miracle a necessary condition for someone to be a prophet? Indeed, is the performance of a miracle through a prophet sufficient proof of his genuine status as a prophet? Moreover, even if there is a close connection between prophecy and miracles, is the prophet the actual agent of miracles?

There is an interesting epistemological connection between the phenomenon of miracles and prophecy. Miracles are empirical phenomena: they occur in space–time and can be observed, indeed need to be observed, by witnesses: otherwise, their function as proofs of divine power and providence would be pointless. But the miracles that interest the religious believer are those that are mentioned in Scripture, and we were not there to witness them. So why do we believe them, especially if similar events do not seem to occur now? This question provided the eighteenth-century philosopher David Hume with a weapon to attack the whole concept of miracles. In order to believe in the occurrence of miracles that we ourselves have not seen, we have to rely upon reports and the testimony of witnesses. But are these witnesses and their reports and traditions reliable? Hume maintained for various reasons that they are not.[16]

Gersonides recognized this problem. But, unlike Hume, he knew that a similar problem surfaces in the sciences, especially astronomy, where experiments cannot always be performed or observations repeated. Astronomical tables are drawn up recording astronomical events that have taken place many millennia ago. That these events have taken place and that the details pertaining to these events are accurate is accepted on the basis of documents

[16] Hume, *An Inquiry Concerning Human Understanding*, §10.

reporting the observations of earlier astronomers whose competence we accept. There is then in the sciences a 'faith in reliable tradition', just as there is in religion. It is therefore legitimate to have confidence in the latter, especially if the reporters of these miracles have been accepted by millions throughout the ages as reliable.[17] Writing in the Middle Ages, when the Bible was accepted in the West as a trustworthy record of Israelite history, Gersonides could appeal to this well-accepted argument, confident that his audience would be as trusting as he was. However, for Gersonides the veracity of reports of miracles was not at issue; of greater importance for him were the two questions: 'What kinds of things or events can be considered miraculous?' and 'How are miracles brought about, or who is the "agent of miracles"?'[18]

Like Sa'adiah Gaon and Maimonides, Gersonides rules out states of affairs that violate the laws of logic. Hence, divine omnipotence is not diminished because God cannot make the interior angles of a triangle total more than 180° or change the past. Miracles have to be logically possible. Nor can miracles occur for no purpose or last so long that they result in an essential change in nature. By its very nature a miracle is an accidental event, and accidents do not endure forever.[19] But Gersonides adds another restriction that neither Sa'adiah nor Maimonides mentions: for Gersonides there cannot be miraculous events in the heavenly domain. This apparent limitation will become very important in his explanation of one of the great miracles reported in the Bible, as we shall see. Why is the heavenly domain so special? Why could a star or planet not be miraculously destroyed or significantly altered? Terrestrial changes are temporally and spatially localized. An earthquake occurring in Iran, for example, might have some immediate impact upon Iraq or Afghanistan for a limited time, but it would not affect Peru or Japan. A celestial change, however, would have cosmic effects that would impinge upon everything in the universe. If the moon, for example, were destroyed or changed in a major way, the whole earth could be flooded. Since miracles are basically providential in purpose, what would be the point in introducing a miracle in the heavens, when such an event would have disastrous consequences? Moreover, it was a well-accepted principle of ancient and medieval science and philosophy that the heavenly domain is paradig-

[17] *Wars*, 6.2.9 (iii. 477–8).

[18] I have reversed the order of Gersonides' exposition. He treats the problem of the agent of miracles before he discusses the domain of miracles. On Gersonides' general theory of miracles, see Touati, *La Pensée philosophique de Gersonide*, 469–77; Kellner, 'Gersonides on Miracles'; Kreisel, 'Miracles in Medieval Jewish Philosophy', 122–6; Klein-Braslavy, 'Gersonides' Use of the *Meteorology*'.   [19] *Wars*, 6.2.12 (iii. 489).

matic of order and perfection. Any change in this order would suggest something was lacking or incomplete and hence needed to be repaired. A miracle in the heavenly world would imply divine impotence rather than divine omnipotence.[20]

At this point the traditional believer in the reliability of the Bible will immediately cry out: 'What about the miracle performed for Joshua? Didn't God cause the sun to stop moving?' (Josh. 10). Gersonides' discussion of this question is quite extensive and ingenious, showing his astronomical expertise and hermeneutical originality. He claims that indeed there was a miracle on that day, but the miracle took place on earth, not in the heavens. For, as we have seen, any such miracle would have had cosmic effects throughout the entire world, and hence would have been reported by other nations. But this was not the case. Moreover, what would stopping the sun actually accomplish? How would that have helped Joshua's military efforts? If anything, it would have had disastrous effects upon the Israelites as well. Such an event would then be lacking providential value. So what exactly was the miracle? The miracle was the rapidity of Joshua's defeat of his enemies. It took only about an hour, the time when the sun is at its highest point in the horizon, which is from about half an hour before noon to about half an hour after. The sun moves so slowly at this time that it seems to stand still. But this happens every day, and hence is not a miracle. To the astronomically uninformed the temporarily idling sun may appear to really cease to move, but this does not fool the astronomer. It is just what is to be expected. What was not expected was the quickness of Joshua's victory.[21] Finally, if the miracle had actually taken place in the heavens, it would have been a greater miracle than any of those performed for or through Moses. But the Bible explicitly says in Deuteronomy 34: 11 that the miracles of Moses were greater than any of those of the other prophets. Miracles, then, are earth-bound.

Even if we restrict miracles to the terrestrial domain, there seem to be several serious problems with them. First, in what sense are they deviations from the natural order, which supposedly was created by God, and hence perfect? Second, if they are real deviations from what is naturally possible, as Maimonides had maintained, how deviant are they? Finally, if miracles are in some sense pre-programmed, are they inevitable?

In answering the first question, Gersonides rejects Maimonides' distinction between what is naturally possible and what is naturally impossible, such

[20] *Wars*, 6.2.12 (iii. 491).
[21] Ibid. 6.2.12 (iii. 491–3). See also Gersonides, *Commentary on the Former Prophets*, Josh. 10; Feldman, ' "Sun Stand Still" '.

that the miracle falls within the latter definition but is still logically possible. According to Gersonides, a miracle is *naturally possible*. The force of this claim is nicely expressed by a principle, frequently asserted in his accounts of biblical miracles, that in the occurrence of a miracle the most natural means are employed so as to minimize their strangeness. For example, the Flood was brought about when great amounts of water were produced by subterranean springs and by atmospheric moisture; the Flood ended when it was dried up by a strong wind (Gen. 7: 11, 8: 1):

The Torah teaches in this story that when God brings about miracles He accomplishes them with the most fitting causes according to the natural order . . . This is contrary to what the foolish believe, even amongst the followers of the Torah, who try to explain miracles by exaggerating the strangeness, and in this way they think they are magnifying God.[22]

Gersonides' frequent repetition of this principle amounts to placing miracles within nature, rather than outside it, since natural means are used to bring them about. Indeed, according to Gersonides, there is a certain economy, even frugality, about miracles that also minimizes their contravention of the natural order: 'Although God is able to do whatever He wishes . . . He seeks the causes that are the most fitting and does not create a miracle unless it is necessary; for He does not hate nature, since He created it. Therefore, He doesn't deviate from it except when necessary and infrequently.'[23] Echoing the rabbinic dictum that one should not rely upon miracles, Gersonides tells us not to overdo entreating God for a miracle even if we are genuinely worthy of having a miracle done for us.[24]

However, if a miracle is naturally possible and brought about by natural means, what is so special about it that it would cause people to wonder and believe in the authority of the agent who produced it? In short, what makes a miracle a miracle? In reply to this question Gersonides emphasizes the point that the event itself is not only logically possible but natural in the sense that what is miraculously produced is itself a natural possibility: there is nothing unnatural about an earthquake or snake. In the cases of Korah and his company being swallowed up by an opening in the earth or of Moses' staff becoming a snake, what was unusual was that these phenomena did not come about as part of the natural course of events, which would have taken a very long time:

[22] *CT*, Gen., 'Noaḥ', 20*d* (i. 91), see also *CT*, Exod., 'Shemot', 56*c* (ii. 20), 'Beshalaḥ', 68*b* (ii. 107).   [23] *CT*, Deut., 'Ekev', 215*d* (v. 76).
[24] *CT*, Gen., 'Toledot', 35*b* (i. 170); BT *Kid.* 39*b*; *Pes.* 64*b*.

An opening in the earth . . . can occur *naturally*. The novelty in this occurrence [that is, the opening of the earth and its swallowing up of Korah and his company] consisted in the rapidity of this event; for according to the natural course of events this occurrence would occur only after a long time. This event is like other such miracles: the transformation, [for example] of the staff into a snake would in the regular course of nature require a very long interval of time [during which] the [matter of the staff] would acquire and lose various forms until it became transformed into a snake.[25]

Miracles of this type are, then, short cuts whereby the natural course of events is bypassed or accelerated.[26]

By reducing the unnaturalness of miracles and placing them within the realm of natural possibility, Gersonides has in fact introduced into the scheme of creation what some commentators have called a 'law of miracles', which, like the ordinary laws of nature, have been pre-established at the very creation of the world.[27] The domain of natural possibility comprises two sub-domains: normal nature and miracles. The former are governed by the regular laws of nature, the latter by their own ordering principles. But it needs to be noted that Gersonides' account of this law of miracles is not identical with the previously mentioned view of the sages and Maimonides. For, according to Gersonides, that theory would imply that the miracle occurs necessarily, since it has been pre-programmed into the initial scheme of creation. This implication is intolerable to Gersonides, for it would mean that the miracle would occur no matter what anyone did or did not do. For example, if the earth's opening up had to occur necessarily, then Korah was not a free agent when he rebelled against Moses, and hence not culpable. The notion that miracles are pre-programmed must not imply their unconditional actualization. Some contingency has to be involved in order to preserve human choice and responsibility. The law of miracles has to be understood hypothetically: if Korah chooses to rebel against Moses, then the earth will open up and swallow him and his company. In this way, God's immutable will can be preserved without sacrificing human free will. The novelty in a miracle is thus not that at some specific moment something totally new is brought about by a

[25] *Wars*, 6.2.12 (iii. 496).

[26] Touati, *La Pensée philosophique de Gersonide*, 474; Kellner, 'Gersonides on Miracles', 27–8. This explanation of transformational miracles was suggested by the medieval Muslim theologian Al-Ghazali (*The Incoherence of the Philosophers*, 'Concerning the Natural Sciences', first question (trans. Hyman, 287)).

[27] Guttmann, *Philosophies of Judaism*, 248; Touati, *La Pensée philosophique de Gersonide*, 472; Kellner, 'Gersonides on Miracles', 28; *Wars*, 6.2.10 (iii. 491).

supernatural agent, but that some human being freely acts in such a way as to trigger a particular pre-arranged outcome.[28]

But the problem that really vexes Gersonides is the identity of the agent of miracles. And it is perhaps here that his originality and audaciousness are most evident. By 'agent' Gersonides means the immediate efficient cause of the miraculous event. He considers three possible answers to this question: (1) God, (2) the Agent Intellect, and finally (3) humans, especially prophets. At this point his discussion displays his usual penchant for detailing all the arguments for each thesis and the arguments against them before he reaches his own conclusion. Now, it would seem that God is the agent. Indeed, most, if not all, the miracles reported in the Bible have God as their cause. So why look elsewhere? Throughout most religious literature God is depicted as the miracle-maker; it is he to whom people pray to perform a miracle, especially since prophets are no longer to be found. Moreover, to claim that anyone else is the agent would seem to impugn God's omnipotence. After all, God freely created the entire universe and laid down all the laws of nature. Does this not imply that as the maker of the world and its laws he can freely break them? Just as the act of creation is proof of God's omnipotent will and providence, so is every particular miracle a sign of his voluntary providential intervention in human affairs.[29]

Nevertheless, Gersonides rejects this traditional belief. God is not the direct cause of miracles. Let us first consider the close connection between the occurrence of miracles and prophecy. As we have already noted, for Gersonides the former almost always takes place in the presence of a prophet, who frequently announces the imminence of the miracle. It was a widely held belief among medieval Jewish and Islamic philosophers that the prophetic experience was mediated and transmitted to the prophet by the Agent Intellect. Indeed, the ordinary religious believer believed that an angel was the immediate transmitter of prophecy. So even if we grant that God is the ultimate cause of prophecy, he is not the proximate cause. The same is true for miracles. Since miracles are concerned with human affairs and involve transformations and changes in terrestrial matters, the proximate cause of miracles has to be an agent directly concerned with the world of humanity, and this is the Agent Intellect. Indeed, we have seen that in his theory of providence Gersonides allots to the Agent Intellect an essential role in the emanation of providence, especially to the prophet and the sage. Accordingly, in Gersonides' cosmological scheme the spiritual force, or 'separate intellect',

---

[28] *Wars*, 6.2.10 (iii. 486).   [29] Ibid. 6.2.10 (iii. 482).

generally responsible for the administration of earthly matters is the direct
agent of miracles, as well as prophecy and providence. Just as God represents
the 'law, order, and rightness' of the whole universe, the Agent Intellect
represents this same law on a smaller scale: it is the nomological paradigm for
the terrestrial domain. The laws of nature, then, are exemplifications of the
law in the Agent Intellect. If there are to be exceptions to these laws, such
deviations have to be ordered and controlled in some way by the Agent
Intellect.[30] In support of this argument Gersonides concludes by citing a
rabbinic saying: 'God does nothing without first consulting his divine minis-
ters.'[31] Gersonides interprets this passage as implying that the performance
of miracles is accomplished by the Agent Intellect, the minister in charge of
the earthly domain.[32]

But what about the prophets? Gersonides has already affirmed the crucial
role the prophets play in the occurrence of miracles. Why does he not make the
prophets the proximate cause of miracles? Indeed, many passages in the Bible
seem to support this hypothesis, especially Deuteronomy 34: 10–12, which
asserts the superiority of Moses over the other prophets because of the miracles
that he performed. Moreover, since miracles express and manifest individual
divine providence, and the prophets are most eligible for and deserving of
obtaining this providence by virtue of their intellectual and moral perfection,
it would seem that through attaining this level of perfection the prophets
should be able to perform miracles. It is thus not surprising that the Bible is
replete with reports of prophets performing miracles. This view has recently
been called the 'anthropological theory of miracles', one of whose advocates
in medieval Jewish philosophy was Abraham ibn Ezra, the exegete whom
Gersonides admired most.[33] Nevertheless, Gersonides rejects this view, despite
his insistence upon the role of the prophet in the occurrence of miracles.

In his critique of this view Gersonides makes a subtle distinction between
someone being the 'agent' of something and someone being the 'through
whom' of something.[34] In Greek philosophical terms, the former would be
the direct, or effective, cause, the latter an accessory, or auxiliary, cause.[35]

---

[30] Ibid. 6.2.10 (iii. 483–6, 489–91). The fact, proved in *Wars*, 5.3.13 (iii. 188), that the
Agent Intellect emanates from all the separate intellects that move the heavenly spheres
also shows that the latter cannot be changed in any way, for the Agent Intellect has no
causal efficacy in the heavenly domain.

[31] BT *San.* 38*b*. Maimonides also uses this passage in his discussion of angels in *Guide*,
ii. 6 (trans. Pines, 262–3).   [32] *Wars*, 6.2.10 (iii. 493).

[33] Ravitsky, 'The Anthropological Theory of Miracles' (Heb.); *Wars*, 6.2.10 (iii. 484–5).

   [34] *Wars*, 6.2.11 (iii. 495).   [35] Frede, 'The Original Notion of Cause'.

Although the Agent Intellect is the primary cause of a miracle, the miracle itself is accomplished through the efforts of the prophet, who is its announcer and interpreter. Nevertheless, the prophet is not the proximate, or effective, agent of the miracle. First, if the prophet were the agent, there would be no need for him to receive a communication or announcement from God or the Agent Intellect that a miracle is immediately forthcoming, as the Bible frequently reports. He would just do it himself without the attendant fanfare. Second, since a miracle is in some sense a departure from the natural order, the agent of the miracle would have to possess complete knowledge of this order so that it could change the order. But no human, including the greatest of the prophets, has such complete knowledge. Finally, if the prophet had such a power, he could transform himself into another species, as in the case of the rod becoming a snake. For he should have this power to change himself if he has it to change anything else. But this is absurd.[36] Accordingly, although the presence of the prophet in the performance of miracles may be a necessary condition for their occurrence, the prophet is not the actual agent.

So far Gersonides has claimed that, contrary to the commonly held beliefs that either God or the prophet himself are the direct, effective agents of miracles, it is the Agent Intellect, along with the prophet as an auxiliary cause, that is the proper agent of miracles. It is now incumbent upon him to show how the miracle itself is brought about by the joint activity of the Agent Intellect and the prophet, and in particular to delineate the precise role of the prophet in miracle-making. But let us note at the outset that the Agent Intellect, no less than God, is immutable. To say that the Agent Intellect performs a miracle is not to imply that it suddenly wills something and brings it about, akin to our deciding to go to the refrigerator to get a drink. Whatever the Agent Intellect does, it does according to an unchangeable law without itself undergoing any internal change. In this respect it is like God. If this is so, how then does the miraculous event occur in a specific place at a particular time for the sake of a certain person or group of people?

It is here that the prophet becomes crucial. And it is not just his role as the announcer of the miracle that is important. The prophet is the earth-bound stimulus that occasions the implementation of the law governing the occurrence of miracles. In many instances the prophet actualizes the miracle through prayer: 'God performs the miracles through the prophet by means of prayer . . . This shows that the miracles were not determined at the beginning

---

[36] *Wars*, 6.2.10 (iii. 487–8).

of the creation of the world to occur when they in fact occurred.'[37] Although in this passage Gersonides attributes the production of the miracle to God, we must remember, Gersonides tells us, that Scripture frequently refers to God as the cause of everything, often skipping over the proximate causes.[38] It is also not without interest to note that in his various discussions of miracles in his biblical commentaries Gersonides rarely refers to the Agent Intellect.[39] These commentaries are popular, addressed to non-philosophically educated readers, who might have been puzzled or even offended by the claim that God is not the proximate agent of miracles. In the passage cited above from his comments on I Kings, what is important is the role of prophetic prayer in triggering the miracle. The miracle is a particular member of a subclass of events that are comprised in and governed by the Agent Intellect. Under certain specific conditions, including prayer, the miracle is instantiated.

The miracles that took place through Elijah are for Gersonides good examples of the role of the prophet. Elijah prays for the recovery of the mortally ill boy, and the boy returns to life (1 Kgs 17: 17–24). Similarly, Elisha, the disciple of Elijah, prays for the recovery of another boy who was believed to have died (2 Kgs 4). In these cases the prophet is not the real agent of the miracle but the external stimulus that puts into play the miracle that is included in the law of miracles contained in the Agent Intellect. Had the prophet not been present, or if he had not prayed, or if the mother of the boy had not been good to the prophet, perhaps the boy would not have recovered. This is the contingent, or hypothetical, feature inherent in all miracles. Although in some sense the miracle is there, waiting to occur, certain conditions have to be present in order for it to be manifested. Thus the prophet is more than just an auxiliary factor in miracles; the prophet is virtually a necessary condition for the occurrence of a miracle.[40] Indeed, since one of the functions of a miracle is to strengthen belief in God and his prophets, it is not surprising that the connection between prophecy and miracles is so intimate. Finally, as we shall see in the next chapter, the prophet attains prophecy through the mediation of the Agent Intellect. It is therefore not accidental that in the production of miracles the Agent Intellect and the prophet work together, the former the active cause, the latter the almost necessary instrument.

[37] Gersonides, *Commentary on the Former Prophets*, 1 Kgs 22, twenty-fourth lesson.

[38] *Wars*, 6.2.10 (iii. 490).

[39] *CT*, Gen., 'Yayeḥi', 50c (i. 255). This is the only passage in his commentary that I have found in which he refers to the Agent Intellect in the context of miracles.

[40] Gersonides does not rule out the possibility of miracles in the absence of prophets, but they would be rare (*Wars*, 6.2.12 (iii. 495–6)).

Gersonides' doctrine of miracles is novel, indeed audacious, in its tendency to bring miracles 'down to earth' and to relegate God to the background. In doing this Gersonides was not betraying his faith in God or the Torah. On the contrary, he believed he was being faithful to several fundamental principles of sound philosophical theology: (1) the immutability of God, (2) the perfect order of nature, and (3) the contingent character of human affairs. The naive view of miracles that sees them as sudden divine interventions 'violating' nature does not do justice to these principles. The universe, created by God, is a perfect, law-governed natural system; even the exceptions to its ordinary workings are law-governed, albeit not completely determined. Nor does the more sophisticated view, suggested by some of the sages and Maimonides, that miracles are pre-established events, do justice to the role of human free action. Finally, although no human being is the agent of miracles, certain individuals play a crucial role in their production. We might say that Gersonides humanizes miracles at the same time as he naturalizes them.[41]

[41] Gersonides' account of miracles was sharply criticized by two fifteenth-century Spanish Jewish thinkers: Isaac Arama and Isaac Abravanel (Kellner, 'Gersonides and his Cultured Despisers').

SEVEN

Prophecy

What Does Philosophy Have To Do with Prophecy?

WE HAVE ALREADY SEEN that in Gersonides' theories of providence and of miracles the prophet plays an important role. As the recipient of the highest level of individual providence the prophet receives information that is not only of benefit to himself but is also providential for the community to which he is sent. And as a crucial factor in the occurrence of miracles, albeit not their real efficient cause, the prophet appears to have a special role in those moments in human history when the normal routine seems to be annulled and something strange but providential occurs. Prophecy is, then, an essential element in biblical religion; indeed, it is the very medium through which the Bible itself is revealed. Prophetic utterances and messages in the Bible are not just forecasts; they transmit an entire legal and religious system. It is therefore no wonder that in his theological creed Maimonides lists prophecy as one of the Thirteen Principles of Faith.[1]

However, unlike the problems of creation, divine foreknowledge, and providence, prophecy was of little interest to the Hellenic philosophers. In their minds it was virtually indistinguishable from divination and oracles, which had no epistemic validity or value. In his *Timaeus*, Plato locates the power of divination in the liver, where raw biology reigns. This is the locus and source of premonitions and forecasts, especially those in dreams:

That divination is the gift of heaven to human unwisdom . . . in that no man in his normal senses deals in true and inspired divination, but only when the power of understanding is fettered in sleep or he is distraught by some disorder or, it may be, by divine possession . . . When a man has fallen into frenzy and is still in that condition, it is not for him to determine the meaning of his own visions and utterances.[2]

Although there are some passages in Plato where the notion of prophecy as divine madness is expressed in apparently positive language,[3] that it is a form

---

[1] Maimonides, *Commentary on the Mishnah*, San. 10.

[2] Plato, *Timaeus*, 71*d*–72*b*.   [3] Plato, *Phaedrus*, 244*b–d*.

of madness is more indicative of Plato's real view. Indeed, shortly after he praises it, he demotes it to the fifth level of the types of soul, below the soul of the physician and above the soul of the poet and painter.[4] For Plato the true 'knower' is the philosopher, whose intellectual expertise is expressed through dialectical argument and activity. The philosopher, unlike the prophet, acquires and attains the truth by virtue of his own efforts; he is not the passive recipient of some message transmitted by a transcendent agent.

Nor was Aristotle any more sympathetic to prophecy. In his short treatise *On Prophecy in Sleep*, he begins on a sceptical note: 'As for prophecy which takes place in sleep and which is said to proceed from dreams, it is not an easy matter either to despise it or to believe in it.'[5] Although Aristotle is open to the idea that there may be verificatory dreams, he is definitely opposed to the claim that such dreams, or prophecies, are sent by God; for any sort of person can have such dreams, not just the wise and the virtuous. As we shall see, this intellectualist prejudice will be important for Gersonides' own theory. That Aristotle shows little interest in prophecy is revealed in the remainder of the treatise, which is devoted entirely to the phenomenon of ordinary dreaming; prophecy per se has vanished from the discussion. It is not surprising, then, to find Gersonides' beginning his discussion of dreams, divination, and prophecy by saying: 'We have not relied upon what is mentioned in Aristotle's *On Sense and Sensible Objects*. For it does not provide an adequate account of these phenomena, and many of the things it does say are indeed false.'[6] The notion of a supernaturally gifted and inspired human bringing a divine message of major importance to humans was not an idea that fitted nicely with the Platonic and Aristotelian emphasis upon the role of man's natural intellectual endowments and purposes.

Prophecy thus presented a serious challenge to the medieval philosopher, especially to those firmly rooted in the Platonic–Aristotelian tradition. As someone committed to a religious community, the medieval philosopher had to make sense of prophecy, as it was presented in the Bible or Quran, in philosophical terms. As philosophers, Al-Farabi or Maimonides could not just retreat and say that prophecy was a mystery or miracle, not amenable to rational analysis or discussion. In short, a philosophical theory needed to be formulated that would make prophecy philosophically comprehensible. Eventually a theory was advanced that placed prophecy within a philosophical framework that incorporated Platonic political theory along with

---

[4] Plato, *Phaedrus*, 248d–e.   [5] Aristotle, *On Prophecy in Sleep*, 462b12–14.

[6] *Wars*, 2.1 (ii. 27).

Aristotelian cosmology and psychology. From Plato this theory borrowed the notion of the philosopher-king but transformed this role to make the philosopher-king a prophet as well. Al-Farabi is an excellent example of this approach. Muhammad was for him Plato's hoped-for philosopher-king, the leader of a religious community based upon philosophical truths formulated in the language of religion.[7] Similarly, Maimonides saw Moses as a philosopher leading the Jewish nation and giving it a law revealed to him by God.

The Aristotelian component of this theory is its transformation of the scriptural tradition that prophecy is mediated through an angel into the philosophical doctrine of the role of the Agent Intellect. The prophet—like the philosopher, or, better, the prophet-philosopher—is the person who has attained some kind of intellectual union or conjunction with the Agent Intellect, the immediate source, or cause, of prophetic revelation.[8] Aristotle's 'separate, eternal intellect' in chapter 5 of Book 3 of *On the Soul* has assumed an angelic guise to make the biblical prophet both philosophically comprehensible and religiously acceptable; or, we may say, prophecy has become 'naturalized'. The route to becoming a prophet is not much different from that of the philosopher: intellectual and moral perfection, which results in some kind of cognitive contact with the Agent Intellect. Whether or not satisfaction of these conditions necessarily results in the reception of prophecy becomes a problem for some of the medieval thinkers, most notably Maimonides, as we shall see.

Gersonides' Theory of Prophecy

Gersonides discusses prophecy in *Wars* in two quite disparate contexts. In Book 2, it is treated as one element in a more general account of extrasensory perception. He is more concerned here with distinguishing prophecy from dreams and divination than with discussing in detail the nature of prophecy. At the end of Book 6, one of the two concluding religious issues discussed is the question of tests to determine if a prophet is genuine. On the question of Moses' prophecy, which for Maimonides was a major theme requiring special analysis, Gersonides' discussion in *Wars* is brief and incomplete. The

---

[7] Al-Farabi, *The Political Regime* (in Lerner and Mahdi (eds.), *Medieval Political Philosophy*, 36–7). id., *The Attainment of Happiness* (ibid. 77–80).

[8] Maimonides, *Guide*, ii. 36 (trans. Pines, 369–70); Averroes, *Tahafut al-tahafut*, 'About the Natural Sciences', first discussion (trans. Van den Bergh, i. 316).

reader of *Wars* would not know whether or not another prophet like Moses is a possibility, and if it was, how such a prophet would differ from Moses. Gersonides' more detailed treatment of this subject is to be found in his biblical commentaries.

Book 2 of *Wars* is in fact a very un-Maimonidean book. It is full of astrology, a subject that Maimonides vigorously opposed, and other topics that he had little interest in and usually dismissed as possessing little, if any, genuine intellectual value. Maimonides is mentioned only once in Book 2, and the citation has to do with his reference to Galen on the transmission of medical information in dreams.[9] If neither Aristotle nor Maimonides provided an explicit or immediate intellectual stimulus for Gersonides' theory of prophecy, who or what did? In chapter 7 Gersonides refers to his own *Supercommentary on Averroes' Epitome of the Parva Naturalia*, and it appears that his earlier encounter with Averroes was the original stimulus for his discussion of these phenomena.[10] Indeed, it was Averroes' treatment of dreams, divination, and prophecy as different manifestations of abnormal, or extrasensory, perceptions[11] in chapter 3 of the *Epitome* that provided the context for Gersonides' discussion of these topics. It will be useful therefore to begin with the main points in Averroes' account that were important for Gersonides, and then see how Gersonides commented upon them.[12]

At the very outset of his *Epitome*, Averroes accepts the existence of verificatory dreams, dreams that communicate to the dreamer information about the future that may have providential value. He also links such dreams with divination and prophecy. Indeed, he believes that all these things belong to the same category of psychological phenomena in which the perception is not of an extra-mental object present to the perceiver but, rather, of some kind of 'image' of it. Nevertheless, Averroes goes on to report a theory, which he attributes to the 'opinions of people', that attempts to differentiate

---

[9] *Wars*, 2.4 (ii. 44).

[10] Altmann, 'Gersonides Commentary on Averroes' Epitome of the *Parva Naturalia*'; Averroes, *Epitome of the Parva Naturalia*.

[11] Averroes' term for these phenomena is 'things that are not perceived by sensation'.

[12] In addition to Touati, *La Pensée philosophique de Gersonide*, 451–68, and Feldman, 'Synopsis of Book 2', in *The Wars of the Lord*, ii. 5–23, the following should be consulted: Kellner, 'Maimonides and Gersonides on Mosaic Prophecy'; Klein-Braslavy, 'Prophecy, Clairvoyance and Dreams' (Heb.); Kreisel, 'Verificatory Dreams and Prophecy in Gersonides' (Heb.); id., *Prophecy*, 316–424; Silverman, 'Some Remarks of Gersonides Concerning Prophecy'; Sirat, *Les Théories des visions surnaturelles*, 166–74; Eisen, *Gersonides on Providence*.

these types of extrasensory perception in terms of their respective causes. On this popular view, dreams are caused by angels, divination by demons, and prophecy by God, either directly or mediately. Moreover, on the popular view, prophecy differs from true dreams in that through it we receive information concerning theoretical matters that are essential to our happiness. Averroes' subsequent discussion, however, reveals that his own accounts of both verificatory dreams and prophecy differ considerably from the popular theory.

In the first place, he make use of the philosophical theory of the Agent Intellect, which acts as the proximate cause of both dreams and prophecy. Since both of these belong to the same genus of psychological phenomena and dreams are produced by the imagination, the Agent Intellect in both cases acts directly upon the imagination to produce true dreams and prophecy. The imagination, then, is the receiving faculty of both dreams and prophecy and the efficient cause is the Agent Intellect.[13] On an issue that will be of considerable importance to Gersonides, Averroes candidly admits that there is an epistemological problem in this theory: since the knowledge exemplified paradigmatically in and transmitted by the Agent Intellect consists of only general truths, yet dreams and prophecy concern contingent and individual facts, how are the former translated into information that humans can understand and apply to their particular concerns? This is the function of the imagination. The imagination receives the general information communicated by the Agent Intellect in a particular way, since the imagination is by its very nature a corporeal faculty, closely connected to sense perception, and hence is particular in its mode of receptivity.[14] In this way the communications can be applied to ordinary human affairs, which are by nature concerned with particular events and matters. Like verificatory dreams, prophecy is primarily predictive; it differs from dreams, however, in communicating information that bears upon our true happiness rather than our mundane concerns. Prophecy is not, Averroes insists, an alternative mode of receiving theoretical knowledge. That is the business of philosophy and the sciences. Only rarely does the prophet receive such information, and if he does, it is not superior in any way to the knowledge obtained by purely rational means.[15] Finally, it should be noted

---

[13] Averroes, *Epitome of the Parva Naturalia* (trans. Blumberg, 40, 42). In *Tahafut al-tahafut*, Averroes states that the Agent Intellect is the mediating agent of prophecy, ('About the Natural Sciences', first discussion (trans. Van den Bergh, i. 316)).

[14] Averroes, *Epitome of the Parva Naturalia* (trans. Blumberg, 46–7); Davidson, *Alfarabi, Avicenna and Averroes on Intellect*, 346–7; Kreisel, *Prophecy*, 333–5.

[15] Averroes, *Epitome of the Parva Naturalia* (trans. Blumberg, 51–2).

that in some of his other writings Averroes emphasized the legal and political aspects of prophecy. Thinking of Moses and Muhammad as law-givers and political leaders, Averroes claims that divine revelation is primarily juridical in nature, concerned with the giving of a law that is the divine constitution for the entire community of believers. Prophecy is, therefore, primarily practical rather than theoretical.[16]

In both his *Supercommentary on Averroes' Epitome* and Book 2 of *Wars* Gersonides accepts Averroes' approach in treating prophecy in the context of dreams and divination, as phenomena which have to do with precognition and prediction. He attacks the commonly held view about the causes of dreams and divination reported by Averroes. Dreams, he claims, are not caused by angels; they have ordinary natural causes. Some of these causes are our own psychological faculties, which, as Maimonides had pointed out, can be considered figuratively as 'angels'; the other causes are the heavenly bodies and their forms.[17] If, however, the dream is prophetic, then the cause is the Agent Intellect, but most dreams are not prophetic.[18] Divination is definitely not caused by demons; for demons do not exist.[19] Here again Gersonides manifests his intellectual independence, for the belief in demons was a widely held one in antiquity and the Middle Ages. Although in his *Supercommentary on Averroes' Epitome* Gersonides does not proceed to give an alternative account of the causes of divination, he does so in Book 2 of *Wars*, where, as we have seen in our discussion of divine providence, he invokes his astrological theory to explain divination.[20]

Since, in the *Epitome*, Averroes does not say much about prophecy itself, Gersonides is also relatively silent on this topic in his *Supercommentary on Averroes' Epitome*. He agrees with Averroes in making the Agent Intellect the immediate efficient cause of prophecy and emphasizing the predictive

---

[16] Averroes, *Epitome* (trans. Blumberg, 52). In *Tahafut al-tahafut* Averroes seems to suggest that prophecy does supplement philosophy by teaching theoretical truths to the masses in a language comprehensible to them ('About the Natural Sciences', fourth discussion (trans. Van den Bergh, i. 360–2)). On this topic see Davidson, *Alfarabi, Avicenna and Averroes on Intellect*, 350–1; Rosenthal, *Averroes' Commentary on Plato's Republic*, 155, 185; id., *Political Thought in Medieval Islam*, 183; id., 'The Place of Politics in the Philosophy of ibn Rushd'.

[17] Maimonides, *Guide*, ii. 6 (trans. Pines, 262–5); Altmann, 'Gersonides' Commentary on Averroes' Epitome of the *Parva Naturalia*', 10; *Wars*, 2.6 (ii. 63–5).

[18] Altmann, 'Gersonides' Commentary on Averroes' Epitome of the *Parva Naturalia*', 10.

[19] Ibid.; Averroes, *Tahafut al-tahafut* ('About the Natural Sciences' (trans. Van den Bergh, i. 312)).   [20] *Wars*, 2.6 (ii. 63–5).

role of the prophet. He is, however, a little more open to the possibility of a prophet's receiving theoretical information, although he admits that it is not too frequent and not the primary role of the prophet.[21] The exception is of course Moses, as we shall see in the next section. Yet, even if a prophet receives such truths, they have no greater epistemic weight because of their prophetic transmission than if they are taught by a philosopher, especially if the latter can prove them by means of demonstrative arguments.[22] Here again he agrees with Averroes that philosophy is competent to arrive at the truths necessary for our happiness.

Gersonides' major criticisms of Averroes' account of prophecy stem from his rejection of Averroes' assumption that dreams and prophecy belong to the same genus. He contends, on the contrary, that although both are concerned with prediction, each involves different receptive capacities and different causes. According to Gersonides, 'the receptive faculty in divination and dreams . . . cannot be the material [human] intellect . . . Thus, the capacity that receives this emanation in dreams and divination is the imagination, whereas the capacity that is receptive in prophecy is the intellect.'[23] Gersonides makes a sharp distinction between these types of extrasensory perception in terms of the psychological faculties that are involved in the reception of these phenomena. In his epistemology there is no direct contact between the Agent Intellect and the imagination: 'It is evident that the Agent Intellect does not work upon the imaginative form at all . . . Rather, the Agent Intellect works upon the material intellect and enables it to become cognitive in actuality after having been cognitive only potentially.'[24] The imagination serves as the repository of images derived from sense perception. Like the latter, the imaginative capacity is part of the corporeal structure of a person, and as such it inherits the particularistic character of sensation. We see particular dogs, resulting in images of those individual dogs. Neither sensation nor imagination is capable of generalization, or conceptualization. This is the function of intellect. Now, since the Agent Intellect consists only of general knowledge, it has no affinity with the imagination, and hence has no direct epistemic relationship with it: 'For it is in so far as two things have something in common that the one of them is supposed to act and the other to be acted upon.'[25]

Thus, it is not, contrary to Averroes, the imagination that receives the prophetic emanation from the Agent Intellect but the human intellect, which

---

[21] Ibid. 2.4 (ii. 44–6).   [22] Ibid., 'Introductory Remarks' (i. 94–5).

[23] Ibid. 2.6 (ii. 62–3).   [24] Ibid. 1.10 (i. 204–5).

[25] Aristotle, *On the Soul*, 3.4.429*b*26–7.

as intellect has the capacity to enter into a cognitive relationship with the Agent Intellect.[26] It is not without interest to note that in his sole reference to the role of a 'separate, eternal intellect' in chapter 5 of Book 3 of *On the Soul*, Aristotle makes no mention of the imagination. In that chapter the epistemic relation is solely between active and passive intellects. On this point Gersonides was closer to Aristotle than was Averroes.

Now, if the receptive capacities differ, so too do the immediate causes of these types of phenomena. Although the Agent Intellect, as Averroes pointed out, has a role in bringing about verificatory dreams, for Gersonides its role here is indirect and secondary. The immediate and primary causes of verificatory dreams are the configurations of the heavenly bodies: 'We suggest that the Agent Intellect is the source of this communication [in dreams and divination] in one sense but not the source in another sense. Accordingly, it seems that the Agent Intellect is the source of the communication in divination and dreams through some intermediary, not directly.'[27] In Gersonides' cosmological scheme, the heavenly bodies are themselves endowed with intelligences and souls, and it is through the latter that the Agent Intellect is operative in dreams and divination: 'So . . . the imagination, when it is isolated from the other faculties of the soul, will . . . be prepared to receive the [astrological] pattern inherent in the intellects of the heavenly bodies.'[28] Dreams and divination are thus directly produced by the causal activity of the heavenly bodies and their intellects upon the imagination, with the Agent Intellect acting as a 'remote', or indirect, cause. In prophecy, however, the human intellect receives the communication from the Agent Intellect itself, which is the sole producing cause.[29] Again, Gersonides shows his independence by disagreeing with Averroes, the 'Commentator'.

Gersonides makes no mention of Maimonides' account of prophecy. Nevertheless, since for both thinkers the general subject of prophecy and the special status of Moses play an important role in their thought, it will be useful to compare their treatment of these topics. Let us begin with their points of agreement. They both shared the common medieval philosophical view that the Agent Intellect was the immediate cause of the prophetic experience. They agreed that the would-be prophet has to have attained a very high level of intellectual and moral perfection.[30] Thus, whereas Averroes did not seem to make the intellect an essential factor in prophecy, Maimonides

---

[26] *Wars*, 1.10 (i. 204–5); Davidson, 'Gersonides on the Material and Active Intellects'; Kellner, 'Gersonides on the Role of the Active Intellect'.   [27] *Wars*, 2.6 (ii. 63).

[28] Ibid. 2.6 (ii. 64).   [29] Ibid. 2.6 (ii. 61–5).

[30] Maimonides, *Guide*, ii. 36 (trans. Pines, 369–73); *Wars*, 2.6 (ii. 56, 59).

and Gersonides do. Finally, adhering to Deuteronomy's closing encomium to Moses, they both insist upon the special character of Moses' prophecies.[31] Yet, despite these basic agreements, the differences are considerable.

Right at the outset of their respective accounts of how the prophetic emanation is generated and experienced, there is an important difference regarding the role of the imagination in prophecy. According to Maimonides the prophetic emanation is transmitted to the prophet by the Agent Intellect in two stages: it first illuminates the intellect of the prophet and then reaches his imagination: 'Know that the true reality and quiddity of prophecy consist in its being an overflow overflowing from God . . . through the Active Intellect, toward the rational faculty in the first place and thereafter toward the imaginative faculty.'[32] There are then, according to Maimonides, two receiving faculties in prophecy: the intellect and the imagination, both of which must have attained a very high level of perfection. Although it is not clear from this passage why perfection in both of these mental powers is necessary, in chapter 38 of the second book of the *Guide*, Maimonides supplies us with the answer: 'Know that true prophets indubitably grasp speculative matters'; accordingly, they need to have mastered the theoretical sciences. Since for Maimonides the prophet is, among other things, a disseminator of theoretical truths, he needs to be philosophically and scientifically literate. But what about the imagination? Why is it necessary? The answer is that it is the faculty that, when perfected and then affected by the Agent Intellect, enables the prophet to predict the future. Thus in so far as prophets communicate speculative doctrines to the people they need to be intellectually perfect; to the extent that they are forecasters they need to have a vivid imagination. Yet, as we shall see, there is one exception to this general account: in Moses the imagination plays no role.[33]

There are several problems with Maimonides' account. In the first place, is it the main function of the prophet to teach philosophy and science? Maimonides' emphasis upon the prophet's need to have studied and mastered these subjects gives the impression that the prophet is more a person of the 'theoretical intellect' than one of the 'practical intellect'. But were the prophets primarily teachers of such truths? Secondly, if the primary function of the imagination in prophecy is to foretell the future, but Moses' prophecies are purely intellectual, how is it that Moses on occasion does foretell the

---

[31] *CT*, Deut., 'Va'etḥanan', 209*d*–210*a*, eighth lesson (v. 27–8), 'Vezot haberakhah', 248*a*, fifteenth lesson (v. 350–1).

[32] Maimonides, *Guide*, ii. 36 (trans. Pines, 369).

[33] Ibid. (trans. Pines, 372–3), ii. 45 (trans. Pines, 403).

future? Consider his prophecy that the Israelites will worship idols (Deut. 31: 29). Indeed, in his closing speech to the Israelites before his death, he predicts what will happen to the twelve tribes. Is the imagination then really necessary, if in Moses' predictions it has no role? Moreover, and perhaps most importantly, according to Maimonides, the imagination is often the source of error, both theoretical and practical. Indeed, it is the imagination that prevents us from having a correct conception of what is logically possible and what is logically impossible.[34] In this sense, having a vivid imagination can be a mixed blessing, and the philosopher is fortunate in not having it. In making the imagination a prerequisite for prophecy Maimonides opened the door to the devastating critique of Spinoza, who claimed that it is precisely because prophecy is imaginative that it is philosophically and scientifically irrelevant.[35] Finally, according to Maimonides, a person who fulfils the psychological requirements for prophecy will receive prophecy *unless* God withholds prophecy from him.[36] Such a divine intervention is virtually a miracle. In other words, according to Maimonides, the attainment of prophecy is in principle something that can be achieved through the perfection of one's natural faculties. The only way the would-be prophet who has satisfied all the requirements cannot receive the prophetic emanation is through the miraculous intervention of God. But does this make sense? Why would God withhold prophecy from someone who deserves it? Divine intervention in this case seems to be an arbitrary expression of God's will. But Maimonides is quite insistent that the divine will is not arbitrary.[37]

Whether or not Gersonides consciously developed his theory of prophecy as a modification or critique of Maimonides, it differs in several significant respects from his predecessor's account. In the first place, his psychological-epistemic analysis of the prophetic experience assigns a different function to the imagination. If Averroes erred in ignoring the activity of the human intellect in prophecy, Maimonides mistakenly made the imagination a receptive faculty in prophecy. As we have seen, for Gersonides, the intellect alone is the recipient of the information communicated to the prophet by the Agent Intellect, and this information will include predictions. Thus, in prophetic prediction, the intellect, not the imagination, is the faculty by means of which the prophet, unlike the dreamer or diviner, makes his forecasts. The epistemic worries of Maimonides concerning the imagination's cognitive disabilities

---

[34] Maimonides, *Guide*, iii. 15 (trans. Pines, 459–61); see also ii. 47 (trans. Pines, 409).

[35] Spinoza, *The Theological-Political Treatise*, chs. 1–2.

[36] Maimonides, *Guide*, ii. 32 (trans. Pines, 361–2).

[37] Ibid. iii. 17, third opinion (trans. Pines, 466–7), iii. 25 (trans. Pines, 504).

are therefore not an issue for Gersonides. Nevertheless, the imagination is not without a role to play in prophecy. Like Averroes, Gersonides recognizes that there is a problem in how the general information transmitted by the Agent Intellect becomes applicable to individuals, especially in forecasts concerning their everyday affairs. This is a problem that Maimonides ignored. Whereas Averroes believed that the imagination by itself has the capacity to particularize the general information transmitted by the Agent Intellect, Gersonides maintains that the imagination alone does not have this power. Just because my imagination consists of particular images of individual items of my sensory experience does not mean that it is able by itself to translate the general content of the message transmitted by the Agent Intellect into something that applies to me or to others. So even if we accept Averroes' proposal that the imagination is the receiving power in prophecy, he has not adequately explained *how* the imagination receives and particularizes the information conveyed by the Agent Intellect.[38]

Consider the following example: Jeremiah receives in prophecy the general rule that a tributary nation ought to pay its tribute to the stronger nation to which it is subservient, otherwise it will suffer dire consequences. Now what does Jeremiah do with this general law of political science? In the first place, we must recognize that our mental powers, although different, are not entirely independent of each other. The human mind is a unit, and the imagination is influenced by the intellect, and vice versa.[39] Moreover, the mind in both its intellectual and imaginative functions is rooted in the particular circumstances of the person receiving the information transmitted by the Agent Intellect. In prophecy this means that the prophet takes the general message conveyed and interprets it in the light of the particular situation in which he finds himself: 'The emanation [itself] concerns the general pattern; the reception, [however], is particularized by the existential [conditions of the recipient].'[40] Whether we are dealing with dreams, divination, or prophecy the information transmitted is always general in nature. It is particularized, and thus made relevant to the individual receiving it, by the individual's particular circumstances and his almost single-minded concentration upon these conditions. Here Gersonides' notion of 'isolation' (*hitbodedut*) plays a crucial role. Indeed, the isolation of his mental powers, especially the intellect, is for Gersonides necessary for making the communication relevant to him and his people. But the recipient of the information

[38] Averroes, *Epitome of the Parva Naturalia* (trans. Blumberg, 46–7); *Wars*, 2.6 (ii. 49, 51–2).   [39] *Wars*, 2.6 (ii. 61).   [40] Ibid. 2.6 (ii. 51).

has to make the application; he has to translate the general law to the present circumstances: 'The Agent Intellect imparts to the material intellect the pattern pertaining to a particular man instead of another man because the recipient of this communication has been thinking about this man, not because of any factor in the Agent Intellect itself.'[41] This passage highlights the facts that it is the human intellect that receives the prophetic emanation and that it is the specific situation of the recipient that determines the translation of the general pattern or law: 'The material intellect must attend to the thing about which this knowledge is concerned in order to receive this knowledge . . . Hence, a diviner or prophet gives information about what will befall people whom he has previously thought about in some way.'[42] If Jeremiah had not been deeply concerned for his people, he would not have been able to use or apply the general information transmitted to him. But, loving his people and troubled by their plight, he was able to see the relevance of this information to his and his people's circumstances. He then spoke to the people.[43]

It is in this latter activity that the imagination has an important role. Unlike the philosopher, the prophet is primarily a man of the 'practical intellect': he is sent to the people to inform them of what is necessary for true perfection and what will happen to them if they follow the right path and what will happen if they do not. To fulfil this role, the prophet needs to know how to speak to the people. He must be able to convey to them the essential practical truths and their consequences in understandable language, using stories, metaphors, and parables. But the use of these linguistic forms involves the imagination. A vivid imagination is, then, for Gersonides, an important rhetorical tool for the prophet, not an epistemic condition for receiving prophetic emanations from the Agent Intellect. The language used by the prophet is imaginative; but what is received by the prophet from the Agent Intellect is purely intellectual, and thus is received by the intellect alone. In his comments on the Song of Songs, Gersonides expresses this difference by means of two metaphors: the intellect is male, whereas the imagination is female, the imagination is the 'little sister' of the intellect.[44] Indeed, we might extend this analogy a little further: the imagination is the faculty that gives birth to the linguistic images, whose origin is in the 'seeds' implanted in it by the intellect. The imagination is a reproductive power: its job is to take some general concept and formulate it in linguistic terms in such a way

[41] *Wars*, 2.6 (ii. 54).   [42] Ibid. 2.6 (ii. 53).

[43] Ibid. 2.6 (ii. 52–3), see also n. 6; *CT*, Gen., 'Vayeḥi', 50c, eighth lesson (i. 255).

[44] Gersonides, *Commentary on the Five Scrolls*, S. of S., 4c (*Commentary on the Song of Songs*, trans. Kellner, 13).

as to make it understandable to the people. Since the imagination is the repository of particular images derived from sensation, it is able to produce particular formulations of the universal intellectual content of prophecy. It is in this sense the faculty of representation. Since the imaginative powers vary considerably from individual to individual, there will be variation in the linguistic perfection and style of the prophecies: 'When the imagination of the recipient is perfectly prepared to represent what has been transmitted of the cognition to the material intellect, it will represent the very same pattern received by the intellect. But if it is not perfectly prepared, it will not represent that pattern but something similar to it, and this is the content of the parable.'[45] Here Gersonides highlights the representative function of the imagination and its role in formulating linguistic analogues to the conceptual content received by the intellect. These linguistic formulations may vary in style and specificity, as the sages had already realized. The prophet Nathan's parable of the poor man whose sole lamb is taken from him by the rich man to feed a guest is easy to understand and apply to David's taking of Bathsheba from Uriah. Ezekiel's parables, on the other hand, are to this very day baffling to most.[46] In either case, however, it is the representative function of the imagination that is in play. In this sense, whereas the intellect is the receptive faculty in prophecy in so far as it apprehends and conceptualizes the information transmitted by the Agent Intellect, the imagination represents this information linguistically and thus makes it available to others, either individuals or nations.[47]

Gersonides' theory of prophecy differs from that of Maimonides in another respect. Unlike the latter he is interested in what we can call the 'techniques of prophecy', or the means by which the prophet prepares himself for receiving the prophetic emanation. We are concerned, here, not with the general intellectual and moral prerequisites that both Maimonides and Gersonides demand of the prophet, but the precise mechanisms that the prophet employs to open his mind to the activity of the Agent Intellect once he has fulfilled these general requirements. I have already noted the importance of concentration (*hitbodedut*, 'isolation'), but there are some exterior

---

[45] *Wars*, 2.6. (ii. 56–7).

[46] 2 Sam. 12; Ezek. 1. The sages were sensitive to the difficulties of Ezekiel's parables and developed the doctrine of the 'secrets of the divine chariot', which constituted for them an esoteric teaching. Maimonides identified this teaching with Aristotle's metaphysics and cosmology and provided an interpretation of it in *Guide*, iii, 'Introduction', 1–7 (trans. Pines, 415–30).

[47] *Wars*, 2.6 (ii. 54–7); *CT*, Exod., 'Yitro', 74*b* (ii. 139); Num., 'Beha'alotekha', 184*d* (iv. 42).

rituals that are also instrumental in preparing the individual for prophetic reception, most notably sacrifices.

Unlike Maimonides, who regarded sacrifices as necessary for teaching the proper worship of a single deity at the time of the Exodus but as having no intrinsic religious value,[48] Gersonides believed that the offering of sacrifices has some inherent influence upon the prophet that makes him ready to receive the prophetic emanation. In particular, the act of offering the sacrifice is a means whereby the prophet is able to isolate his intellect. In commenting upon Noah's sacrifice immediately after leaving the ark (Gen. 8: 20), Gersonides remarks:

There is in sacrifices some relevance for the receiving of prophecy . . . It was explained in Book Two of *The Wars* that in prophecy there is need for the isolation [*hitbodedut*] of the intellect from the other faculties of the soul . . . Therefore, it is necessary for the prophet when he wants to prophesy that he stimulate the intellect and subdue [literally, 'put to sleep'] the other faculties . . . Now, you find in sacrifices that they stimulate the intellect and subdue the perceptual faculties.[49]

Gersonides continues by explaining how sacrifices assist in isolating the intellect. While the sacrifice is being performed, the prophet focuses upon the precise laws pertaining to the sacrifice and the resulting destruction of the animal. In so doing he realizes the utter temporality and destructibility of sensible objects and the sensible parts of his soul, including the imagination. Note that in the above passage he says that the intellect 'subdues' the other mental faculties. As we shall see in the next chapter, the only permanent thing about a human being is the incorporeal intellect; the senses and imagination perish along with the rest of the body. Sacrifice brings home this truth in a most visible way. As prophecy is itself an intellectual mode of communication, the isolation of the intellect is brought about by a physical act that reveals to the person offering the sacrifice the separateness and independence of the intellect from the rest of his body.[50]

Music, too, is helpful in this process of isolation and concentration, especially in removing obtruding and impeding emotions from the mind. This is nicely illustrated in the story of Elisha the prophet and King Jehoshaphat, as reported in 2 Kings 3. Facing battle against the king of Moab, Jehoshaphat

---

[48] Maimonides, *Guide*, iii. 32 (trans. Pines, 525–32).

[49] *CT*, Gen., 'Noaḥ', 21*a–b* (i. 92–3).

[50] Ibid.; Gersonides, *Commentary on the Former Prophets*, 1 Kgs 11, second lesson; Feldman, appendix to *The Wars of the Lord*, ii. 245–7; Klein-Braslavy, 'Prophecy, Clairvoyance and Dreams', 48–50; Kreisel, *Prophecy*, 374–6.

asked Elisha for divine guidance. The prophet replied: ' "Fetch me a minstrel", and while he was playing, the power of the Lord came upon Elisha and he said . . .'. In his explanation of this story, Gersonides points out that certain emotions, especially anger, obstruct the prophetic emanation. Appropriate music removes the anger and enables the prophet to receive the emanation. As the sages and Maimonides had already observed, anger is antithetical to prophecy.[51]

The prophet, then, is an individual who merits, by virtue of his intellectual and moral perfection, a cognitive relationship with the Agent Intellect. This relationship affords the prophet information that is for the most part providential in content, but general in form. It is one of the functions of the prophet to provide a translation of this content for an audience. This is achieved through the prophet's concentration upon the immediate circumstances of his social environment or personal situation. The prophet is then able to apply the message to that specific context. In conveying the message he employs the imagination to formulate the information received by his intellect in a language comprehensible to the widest audience. This whole process occurs naturally, in the sense that no sudden divine intervention enters the picture that alters the prophet in any way. His natural endowments warrant the reception of prophecy; they alone account for his contact with the Agent Intellect, whose storehouse of information is always available for communication and dissemination. Maimonides' problem of the withholding of prophecy from a deserving individual does not arise for Gersonides, whose deity is more generous.

Moses, the 'Super-Prophet'

There are several passages in the Torah that explicitly distinguish Moses from all other prophets. In Numbers 12: 1–8, Aaron and Miriam mount a challenge to Moses' authority and uniqueness, claiming that they are his equals with respect to prophetic inspiration. Not waiting for Moses to defend himself, for he was a most humble man, God immediately responds to their challenge by specifying the ways in which Moses is superior to any other prophet: 'If any of your prophets of the Lord [prophesies], I reveal myself to him in a vision; [or] I speak to him in a dream. But not so with Moses, my servant . . . I speak to him mouth to mouth; [not] in a vision nor in a dream.' This passage sharply

---

[51] *CT*, Gen., 'Noaḥ', 21*a* (i. 92); Gersonides, *Commentary on the Former Prophets*, 2 Kgs 3: 15; BT *Shab.* 30*b*; Maimonides, *Guide*, ii. 36 (trans. Pines, 372); Klein-Braslavy, 'Prophecy, Clairvoyance and Dreams', 50–1.

distinguishes Moses' prophecies from those of the other biblical prophets in
eliminating any intermediary factor, whether it be a dream or vision. Moses'
prophecies come to him directly. In Exodus 33: 11, this theme is anticipated
when the people are made to realize that Moses has direct access to God, 'as
one man speaks to another'. Finally, when Moses dies, the closing words of
Deuteronomy emphasize his uniqueness: 'There has never yet risen in Israel
a prophet like Moses, whom the Lord knew face to face: remember all the
signs and portents which the Lord sent him to show in Egypt and to Pharaoh'
(Deut. 34: 10–12). These passages clearly indicate the superior status of Moses'
prophecies, specifying the immediacy of his relationship with God and the
extraordinary nature of the miracles performed on his behalf.

This thesis is the major theme in Maimonides' theory of prophecy. In the
Principles of Faith contained in his *Commentary on the Mishnah, Sanhedrin*
10, the uniqueness of Moses' prophecy is explicitly singled out as the Seventh
Principle: 'We are to believe that he was the chief of all other prophets . . .
He surpassed the normal human condition and attained the angelic . . . All
his powers of sense and fantasy were repressed, and pure reason alone
remained. This is what was meant by saying that he spoke to God without
angelic mediation.' As we can see, for Maimonides the uniqueness of Moses'
prophetic capacity was not just the absence of dreams and visions but the lack
of any angelic mediation. In the case of the other prophets, however, the
Bible often describes their prophetic epiphanies as occurring through or in
the presence of an angel (to Abraham (Gen. 18), to Jacob (Gen. 31: 11), to
Joshua (Josh. 5: 13–15), to Zechariah (Zech. 1: 8–14)). Maimonides concludes
his discussion of this principle by adding two other differentiating features
of Moses' prophecies: (1) Moses did not experience fear and trembling when
he received prophecy, whereas the other prophets did, and (2) he could
prophesy at will, whereas the other prophets had to wait upon God's will.

However, according to Maimonides this notion of angelic transmission
is problematic, especially when we turn to the *Guide*, where he singles out
Moses' prophecies as extraordinary and unique. The question now is: 'What
exactly is the angel that is absent from Moses' prophecies?' Since the general
theory of prophecy held by Maimonides makes the Agent Intellect the
transmitter of prophecy, does Maimonides believe that in Moses' case the
Agent Intellect was not needed at all? Or does he mean by the absence of an
angel the absence of something else? Modern interpreters disagree on this
point: some have argued for the first interpretation, others for the second.[52]

---

[52] For the first interpretation see Wolfson, 'Hallevi and Maimonides on Prophecy',

The first interpretation seems to be confirmed by the account given in the *Commentary on the Mishnah* discussed above. Since Moses attained the angelic state, he was not in need of any mediation from another angel to speak to God. However, in chapters 36 and 45 of the second book of the *Guide*, Maimonides asserts that the absence of an angel in Moses' prophecies means the lack of imagination, or fantasy: 'all prophets hear speech only through the intermediary of an angel, the sole exception being Moses . . . in these cases the intermediary is the imaginative faculty . . . Moses . . . on the other hand, heard Him . . . without action on the part of the imaginative faculty.'[53] Since the imagination is the locus and producer of dreams and visions, and since Moses' prophecies are marked by the absence of the latter, the fact that for Moses there is no intermediary means that in him the imaginative faculty is not in play. It should be noted, however, that advocates of the second interpretation are confronted with another problem: if in Moses the imagination is absent and his prophecies are purely intellectual, how does he differ from the philosophers, who according to Maimonides employ only reason, not imagination?[54] How is Moses different from and superior to Aristotle?

Although Gersonides is as committed as Maimonides to the uniqueness of Moses as a prophet, his account of this uniqueness differs in several respects. We can say right at the outset that since for Gersonides the imagination is not a receptive faculty in prophecy as such, its presence or absence is not decisive in understanding Moses' prophecy. Accordingly, Gersonides has to account for the uniqueness of Moses in another way. Moreover, since, as we have seen, Gersonides makes the Agent Intellect the direct efficient cause of prophecy, he includes Moses as subject to this general condition.[55] So if imagination is not the issue and the Agent Intellect is the immediate cause of prophecy in all the prophets, how does Moses differ from Abraham or Isaiah?

In *Wars*, Gersonides addresses this issue just once and only briefly in connection with the notion of the isolation of the intellect in prophecy. Moses differed from all other prophets in so far as he was able to isolate his intellect from all the other mental and bodily faculties to a greater extent than were the other prophets; indeed, his intellect was perfect, warranting the highest level of prophecy. Moreover, because his intellect was so isolated and perfect,

---

71; Kellner, 'Maimonides and Gersonides on Mosaic Prophecy', 65–6, 73. For the second interpretation, see Altmann, 'Maimonides and Thomas Aquinas', 16.

[53] Maimonides, *Guide*, ii. 45 (trans. Pines, 403).   [54] Ibid. ii. 37 (trans. Pines, 374).
[55] *CT*, Exod., 'Shemot', 56*a–b* (ii. 18).

it was able to dominate and subdue all his other mental powers such that he experienced no fear or trembling when he received prophecy.[56] This latter point, we have seen, was important also for Maimonides. Although this is all that Gersonides says about Moses in *Wars*, he gives us more information in his biblical commentaries.

In commenting upon Exodus 33: 11, Gersonides singles out the following features as distinguishing Moses' prophecies from those of the other prophets:

1. Moses prophesied in the waking state, a fact confirmed by God himself, as reported in Numbers 12.

2. Because his prophecies were received while he was awake his language was clear and non-metaphorical.

3. The isolation of his intellect was so great it was as if he himself was a pure intellect, totally separate from his body, a theme mentioned by Maimonides. According to Gersonides these factors are implied by the biblical statement that God spoke to Moses 'face to face'.[57] In his commentary on Numbers 12, he repeats some of these features but adds some other differentiating characteristics.

4. Because he prophesied while awake he could prophesy at will.

5. His prophecies are mostly general in nature, having to do with laws and doctrines, whereas the other prophets concern themselves for the most part with particular events.

6. Perhaps most importantly, Moses alone saw the figure of God, which Gersonides interprets as the laws of existing things (*nimus hanimtsa'ot*).[58]

7. Finally, in his commentary on the end of Deuteronomy where again Moses' uniqueness is asserted, especially in the miracles that were manifested in his presence, Gersonides remarks that these miracles were more public and lasted longer than those that occurred to the other prophets.[59] Indeed, as we have learned from his general theory of miracles, the prophet, for Gersonides, has a necessary role to play in the occurrence of miracles, a role that Maimonides tended to minimize.[60] Moses, Gersonides contends, fulfilled this function to a greater extent than did the other biblical prophets.

---

[56] *Wars*, 2.6 (ii. 56–7).   [57] *CT*, Exod., 'Ki tisa', 113*d* (ii. 429), 114*a–b* (ii. 431).

[58] *CT*, Num., 'Beha'alotekha', 184*c–d* (iv. 42).

[59] *CT*, Deut., 'Vezot haberakhah', 247*b* (v. 345–6), 248*b* (v. 351–2); Maimonides, *Guide*, ii. 35 (trans. Pines, 367–9).

[60] Maimonides, *Mishneh torah*, 'Laws of the Foundations of the Torah', 8.

The most striking and perhaps radical feature in Gersonides' account of Moses, and one that differs markedly from that of Maimonides, is his comparison between Moses and the messiah. Although Maimonides says nothing about the messiah in the *Guide*, in the *Mishneh torah* he gives a fairly detailed description of the long-awaited Davidic king.[61] One particular feature in this account is especially relevant in this context: according to Maimonides the messiah will not only not be a miracle-worker, but the messianic era will not be a time when miracles multiply. Indeed, Maimonides rejects the commonly held view that the messiah will be the one who will bring about the resurrection of the dead.[62] For Maimonides the messiah will primarily be the political leader of an ingathered Israel which will enjoy uninterrupted peace and prosperity.

Gersonides too makes no mention of the messiah in his main philosophical work. Yet in his comments on Deuteronomy he ventures into contested and dangerous territory when he compares Moses and the messiah. On the one hand, Gersonides has to be faithful to the concluding words of this last book of Moses, wherein Moses is described as the unsurpassed and unsurpassable prophet. On the other hand, he has to present a picture of the messiah that does not denigrate Moses while at the same time avoiding making him a divine being. According to Gersonides, the messiah will have some meritorious features that will distinguish him from Moses, yet lack features that made Moses special.

More faithful to Jewish tradition, Gersonides does locate the messianic period at the time of the resurrection of the dead. Moreover, and most important in this context, he makes the messiah the instrument in the performance of this miracle:

And it will be evident that his [the messiah's] miracles will be greater than those of Moses; for Moses drew only Israel to the worship of the Lord by means of the miracles that he instituted, whereas the messiah will draw all the nations to the worship of the Lord . . . And this will come about by means of a marvelous miracle that will be seen all over the earth by all the nations, and this is the resurrection of the dead.[63]

So it is not only with respect to the audience of his miracles but in regard to the most extraordinary miracle of all—the resurrection of the dead— that the messiah is a superior prophet to Moses.

[61] Maimonides, *Mishneh torah*, 'Laws of Kings and Wars', 11–12.

[62] Maimonides, *Commentary on the Mishnah*, San. 10.

[63] *CT*, Num., 'Balak', 195*b* (iv. 336–7), repeated in *CT*, Deut., 'Ha'azinu', 245*b*, fourteenth lesson (v. 331).

Nevertheless, there is one crucial fact that singles out Moses and makes him unique: he is the giver of the Torah, and the Torah is the perfect and immutable law. The messiah will not issue a new Torah, nor will he abrogate any of the laws of the Torah. Moses' nomothetic function was accomplished once and for all, not needing any modification whatsoever: 'It is said: "Never again did there arise in Israel a prophet like Moses"' (Deut. 34: 10). It is well known that from the Torah [we learn] that there has not arisen nor will arise a prophet like Moses; for no prophet will be believed . . . to modify the Torah or to change it [completely] into another law.'[64] Accordingly, even though the messiah will have a greater audience and be the instrument for the performance of the most marvellous miracle of all, he is not a nomothetic prophet. There is only one such prophet, and he was Moses.

Indeed, Gersonides even goes so far as to say that Moses' giving the Torah was itself a miracle:

> Perhaps someone might object saying: 'Why isn't it possible that some other prophet will be a giver of a Torah like Moses?' . . . The answer is that in this regard there is no equal to Moses. For his nomothetic prophecy was [itself] miraculous; this faculty [that is, to give a Torah] is not a faculty of a prophet as such, unless by way of a miracle.[65]

On this point Gersonides agrees with Maimonides: Moses' giving the Torah is an unrepeatable fact; for how could a perfect law be changed, even by a perfect law-giver? The messiah, then, is just as subject to the law of Moses as are other prophets—indeed, even more so. Gersonides' take on this question is typical of his synthesizing approach on most issues: in some respects the messiah will surpass Moses, but in one respect, at least, Moses was a superior prophet; indeed, this latter respect is the very foundation of Judaism, which the messiah is bound to obey, preserve, and promulgate.[66]

Gersonides' attempt to distinguish Moses from the messiah in the former's favour by making Moses the unique law-giving prophet raises the same question that I raised earlier in connection with Maimonides: if the giving of the Torah was a miracle involving God's will, how is this different from Maimonides' problem of invoking divine will in the withholding of prophecy? In both cases we seem to have the manifestation of an arbitrary expression of God's will.[67] Of course, one could say that in choosing Moses

---

[64] *CT*, Deut., 'Vezot haberakhah', 247*a* (v. 344), 248*a* (v. 351).
[65] Ibid. 247*a* (v. 344).
[66] *CT*, Deut., 'Va'ethanan', 209*d*–210*a*, eighth lesson (v. 27–8).
[67] Kellner, 'Gersonides on Miracles', 5–15.

God did not act arbitrarily since Moses deserved that privilege, whereas no one else did or will. But who knows? Can we be certain that in the future there will be no one who qualifies as Moses did?[68] On behalf of Gersonides we could say that, as was the case with the creation of the world, Moses' giving the Torah was a 'once and for all' example of divine intervention, truly unrepeatable, especially since the law that Moses reveals is perfect and immutable. Maimonides, however, is faced with the problem that each time God intervenes to prevent some deserving person from receiving prophecy, another miracle has to be performed. And again, why would God deprive such a person from receiving what he or she deserves? According to Gersonides there is no sufficient reason why God needs to reveal a new Torah; hence, there is no need for another nomothetic prophet. In this respect Moses' uniqueness is analogous to the indestructibility of the world. Just as there is no sufficient reason why God should destroy this world, there is no good reason why there should be another law-giving prophet.

But perhaps someone could object to the very notion of the miracle bestowed upon a particular individual named 'Moses'. Since God and the Agent Intellect do not possess knowledge of individuals as such, how is it that Moses is picked out as the one who promulgates the Torah?[69] The answer to this question is no different from Gersonides' general account of miracles. There is no real picking out of an individual as worthy of a miracle. Rather, there is in the universal plan for human history a proviso stipulating that *if* some individual satisfies certain conditions, a perfect law will be revealed through that person. Moses satisfied these conditions, and so he gave the Torah. Neither God nor the Agent Intellect had to be able to single him out. The miracle of Sinai came about because the conditions required for the giving of the Torah were de facto satisfied at that time and place by a person named 'Moses, the son of Amram'. Even if Moses' uniqueness is just contingent, it is no more problematic than the contingency of the creation of an indestructible world, which is also an expression of God's free will. In both cases divine benevolence expresses itself in an unrepeatable act. On Maimonides' theory of miracles, however, Moses' giving of the Torah was preordained, and in this sense a necessary fact of human history. In this respect Gersonides' account better preserves the uniqueness of Moses by highlighting its inherent contingency and singularity.

---

[68] Kellner, 'Maimonides and Gersonides on Mosaic Prophecy', 73.   [69] Ibid.

Are Prophets Infallible?

Throughout human history individuals have come forth proclaiming messages of divine provenance. Often these messages are predictions of some impending event of importance to the audience. Sometimes the message purportedly asserts some theoretical truth or a moral or legal prescription. But how are we to know that this individual is a genuine prophet? Are there decisive tests to determine the reliability of would-be prophets? Since in many cases biblical prophets announce miracles or are present at their occurrence, it is tempting to make the attendant miracle a test for prophetic veracity. Indeed, the Bible records instances where the would-be prophet seeks authentication by requesting a miracle, as in the cases of Moses in Exodus 4 and Gideon in Judges 6, and this seems to have been a persistent theme in the history of religions: the miracle proves the authenticity of the claimant to prophetic powers. Yet the Bible is emphatic in ruling out such a test if the message is contrary to the teachings of the Bible itself:

When a prophet or dreamer appears among you and offers you a sign or a portent and calls on you to follow other gods . . . and worship them, even if the sign or portent should come true, do not listen to the words of that prophet or that dreamer . . . That prophet or dreamer shall be put to death, for he has preached rebellion against the Lord. (Deut. 13: 1–5)

The performance of a miracle, then, is not a sufficient condition for determining the authenticity of a prophet if the message violates the teachings of the Torah. Nevertheless, Gersonides' claims that prophets must be present at the occurrence of a miracle and that they alone have the power to announce the miracle[70] do seem to provide some positive evidence for authenticating the prophetic claim *if* the prophecy involves the occurrence of a miracle. After all, most people are not capable of predicting miracles, so there must be something special about the person who correctly announces such an event. But does this mean that the occurrence of a miracle is a necessary condition for the verification of a prophet? It does not seem so, since there were biblical prophets who neither announced nor were present at any miracles—Nathan, Amos, and Micah, for example. So what seems to have been either a sufficient or a necessary condition for genuine prophecy is not really the case. Although there seems to be a close connection between miracles and prophecy, as Gersonides maintains, the connection is not strong enough to determine decisively who is or is not a genuine prophet.

[70] *Wars*, 6.2.9 (iii. 472), 6.2.10 (iii. 484).

What about the accuracy of their predictions? After all, the primary function of a prophet, according to Gersonides, is to forecast events having to do with individual providence. It would therefore seem that we could use the occurrence or non-occurrence of the predicted event as a decisive test for determining prophetic authenticity. In Deuteronomy 18: 20–2 we are told that if someone claiming to be a prophet makes a prediction that turns out to be false, such a person is not a true prophet. Moreover, if the predictions are consistently verified, the predictor would seem to be a genuine prophet, as is reported of Samuel (1 Sam. 3: 19–21). The Bible itself then seems to affirm that accuracy of prediction is a decisive test for determining prophetic authenticity.

But these biblical tests do not do the job. Take the criterion of consistent accurate forecasts, as stipulated in the case of Samuel. In Numbers 11: 24–5, we learn that the elders of Israel prophesied only once. The criterion set forth in Samuel's case is not applicable here. Nor is Deuteronomy 18: 20–2, especially in the case of predictions of doom. Suppose someone predicts, as some biblical prophets did, a catastrophe as punishment for the people's sins, but the destruction does not happen. Does this mean that the forecaster was a false prophet? Perhaps the people repented. Indeed, this seems to have been the case with several of the biblical prophets (for example, Jonah). In this type of prophecy the main point is to get the people to change their ways. If the punishment came about no matter what the people did, the prophecy would have been in vain. Indeed, the inevitability of the prediction would annul human choice. This suggests that prophecy of this type involves some kind of condition, whose fulfilment or lack thereof is relevant in determining the authenticity of the prophet. Thus, Deuteronomy 18: 20–2 cannot be understood as referring to prophecies of doom or punishment.

Here, Gersonides appeals to Jeremiah. During the Babylonian siege of Jerusalem Jeremiah's warnings of doom were challenged by another prophet, Hananiah, who claimed that Jerusalem and the Temple would not be destroyed. Aware that the purpose of his mission was to get the people to repent and obey God's will and thus avert the impending catastrophe, Jeremiah proposed that if Hananiah's predictions turned out to be true, then he, not Jeremiah, was the true prophet. As it turned out, Hananiah's forecasts were proved false (Jer. 28). The prediction of a benefit, then, would seem to serve as an adequate test for prophetic authenticity: if it materializes, the forecaster should be believed to be a prophet. This is how Deuteronomy 18: 20–2 is to be interpreted.

But there are at least two qualifying conditions in applying this test. First, this procedure provides only a necessary condition: a genuine prophet's predictions of benefits must turn out to be true. But such success is not sufficient to prove his authenticity, since diviners, dreamers, and scientists also are successful in making beneficial forecasts. Hananiah's false prediction proved that he was a false prophet; but had his beneficial predictions turned out to be true, they would not by themselves have proved his authenticity. In this sense, Jeremiah's test is a negative test: it demonstrates who is a false prophet, but cannot prove who is a genuine prophet. Secondly, if the forecast of a benefit turns out to be true, does that mean that its eventuation was inevitable, that the people's behaviour was irrelevant to its fulfilment? Many of the biblical beneficial promises and prophecies hinge upon the people's compliance with the divine commands. If we honour our parents, we will be rewarded with a long life and prosperity. Prophecy, whether beneficial or punitive, seems then to be conditional on behaviour.[71]

At this point Gersonides is confronted with a talmudic text that seems to contradict his thesis that even beneficial prophecies of individual providence are conditional. At BT *Berakhot* 7a we read: 'Every beneficial promise made by God is irrevocable even if it is conditional.' The biblical text under consideration is Exodus 32: 10, where God threatens the destruction of Israel for its worship of the golden calf, telling Moses not to interfere and promising him that he will make a great people out of him. The sages construe this beneficial prediction to Moses as unconditional: no matter whether or not he prays on behalf of Israel, he will be the father of a great nation. It would appear that Gersonides has deviated from this rabbinic principle.[72]

Gersonides resolves this apparent conflict by distinguishing between essential and non-essential conditions. In Moses' case, his prayer on behalf of Israel was a non-essential condition; hence, whatever he did, his progeny would turn out to be a great nation. And so it was: Moses did intercede for Israel, despite God's injunction not to; yet his family multiplied and was successful, as reported in 1 Chronicles 23. Had God's promise to Moses been conditional upon his interceding or not interceding, the promise would have been revocable; for in this case the condition would have been essential. To illustrate this point Gersonides gives the example of Jacob's fear of Esau despite God's beneficial promises to him (Gen. 28: 15). Jacob was fearful because he knew that these promises were conditional upon his proper behaviour, and he was worried that he might commit some sin that would annul them. Since these promises were essentially tied to his behaviour, Jacob

---

[71] *Wars*, 6.2.13 (iii. 499); Rudavsky, 'Divine Omniscience, Contingency and Prophecy in Gersonides'; id., *Time Matters*, 134–40.   [72] *Wars*, 6.2.13 (iii. 500).

was justified in fearing Esau. So beneficial promises can be conditional; it depends, however, on what kind of condition is involved.[73]

Let us now summarize this complex account of determining the authenticity of a prophet and see if it is successful. First, with respect to miracles, we have seen that, since only a true prophet can announce a miracle, if someone who satisfies the general requirements for prophetic eligibility makes such an announcement and the miracle takes place, this person is a prophet; unless of course, the message that the person transmits violates the Torah. Accordingly, this procedure is only a *qualified*, or *restricted*, sufficient condition for testing a prophet, unless it is stipulated a priori that an eligible person must not say anything that is inconsistent with the Torah. However, it is not, let us remember, a necessary condition, since some prophets are recorded as not having anything to do with miracles. Hence, we are not required, nor even is it polite, to ask a would-be prophet to announce a miracle. Moreover, although it is possible, Gersonides admits, that outstanding sages may be such that a miracle is performed in their presence or as an expression of individual providence, they are not qua sages able to announce these miracles. This ability is the singular property of prophets as such.[74] So even though a miracle is not a necessary condition for genuine prophecy, it can serve as a sufficient condition for ascertaining the authenticity of a would-be prophet as long as the message conforms to the Torah.

Second, consistent accuracy of predictions is also a relevant factor. Such success serves to rule out diviners and dreamers, whose predictions are not always accurate. But, as we have seen, the Bible recognizes 'one-time' prophets. So this test is not always applicable. Moreover, Gersonides insists, many prophecies are conditional, and there are two types of condition, essential and non-essential, that are relevant in both beneficial and punitive prophecies. So it is necessary to see what kind of condition is involved in a prediction, whether it is beneficial or punitive. If the condition is non-essential and the prediction of a benefit is not verified, then, as the sages had declared, the forecaster is not a genuine prophet. But if the condition is essential, the non-occurrence of the benefit does not falsify the forecaster. The non-fulfilment of the condition rendered the prediction inoperative. So in the case of beneficial predictions only if the condition is non-essential do we have a test.

It should be noted that, according to Gersonides, a prophet may say something that is false regarding some philosophical or scientific matter without

---

[73] *Wars*, 6.2.13 (iii. 500–2); *CT*, Gen., 'Vayishlaḥ', 40*d*–41*a* (i. 201).

[74] *Wars*, 6.2.11 (iii. 487–8); Touati, *La Pensée philosophique de Gersonide*, 465; Kreisel, *Prophecy*, 416–18.

being any less a prophet. The main business of a prophet is not to teach philosophy or science; if he does, he does so as a philosopher or scientist, not as a prophet. Gersonides considers two cases of prophetic error. The first is the prophecy given to Abraham in Genesis 15, in which he is promised that his descendants will be innumerable like the stars. Gersonides comments as follows:

'Just as the number of stars is innumerable, so will your seed be countless'. Now, in Abraham's day the [precise] number of stars was not known. Therefore, in the prophetic vision the imagination showed him the example of the number of stars as a metaphor for the extraordinary number of his progeny promised to him by God.[75]

According to Gersonides' physics, there is no such thing as an infinite number of actually existing things; moreover, the astronomy of his day has determined that the number of stars was just 1,022. So in this prophecy there was an error. But note that the error is not in the prophecy as such; it was Abraham's imagination that led him to believe that his seed would be as innumerable as the stars. That he was promised that he would be the father of many nations, both through Isaac and Ishmael, would turn out to be true; that their number would be countless was a just a metaphor contrived by Abraham's imaginative faculty.[76]

Another example of a prophet making a statement that is scientifically false is Ezekiel's description of the heavenly creatures in his visions making sounds (Ezek. 1: 24, 10: 5). Following Maimonides' lead, Gersonides interpreted these visions as referring to the heavenly bodies, and like Maimonides he denied that the heavenly bodies emitted any sounds. On this point Maimonides and Gersonides followed the teachings of Aristotle and Ptolemy. Accordingly, Gersonides maintains, Ezekiel committed an error in attributing sounds to the heavenly bodies. This false belief stemmed not from the prophecy as such, but from his own antecedent opinions that he had formulated while engaged in scientific speculation. In short, in attributing sounds to the heavenly bodies Ezekiel was not speaking as a prophet but as an ordinary astronomer, and was, like all others in that profession, subject to error.[77]

Did Gersonides succeed in his attempt to provide an adequate set of tests for determining the authenticity of a prophet? We have seen that for him the

---

[75] *CT*, Gen., 'Lekh lekha', 24*d* (i. 115).

[76] Ibid.; Touati, *La Pensée philosophique de Gersonide*, 460 esp. n. 47.

[77] Maimonides, *Guide*, ii. 8 (trans. Pines, 267); Aristotle, *On the Heavens*, 2.9.290*b*12–291*a*28; *CT*, Gen., 'Lekh lekha', 24*d* (i. 115).

announcement of a miracle (provided it is not part of a message that violates the Torah) is a sufficient condition for testing a claimant to the power of prophecy. But it is not a necessary condition, and hence is inapplicable to those accepted prophets who were not associated with any miracles at all. Moreover, why restrict the ability to announce a miracle to prophets? If, as Gersonides admits, sages can be involved in the occurrence of miracles, why can they not announce them? He does not give any argument that rules out this possibility. As Charles Touati has observed, Gersonides has not made a sharp distinction between the prophet and the sage.[78] Finally, suppose someone has a successful record in predicting catastrophes or favourable outcomes. Is he necessarily a prophet? Some political analysts and meteorologists are quite good at their trades. But we do not take them to be prophets. It has to be admitted that on this topic Gersonides has not succeeded in providing us with a foolproof procedure for determining prophetic authenticity.[79]

[78] Touati, *La Pensée philosophique de Gersonide*, 465–6.

[79] Feldman, synopsis of Book 6, pt. 2, in *The Wars of the Lord*, iii. 424–5; Kreisel, *Prophecy*, 415–19; Rudavsky, 'Divine Omniscience, Contingency and Prophecy in Gersonides'.

EIGHT

Humanity and its Destiny

Philosophical and Religious Background

ANOTHER TOPIC of common interest, both for some Greek philosophers and for believers in scriptural religions, was the question of humanity's ultimate felicity. It was assumed by adherents of both traditions that a person's mundane existence as a material entity was not the end of the matter. There had to be something more than a life of material pursuits and satisfaction. Quite early in Greek philosophy doctrines of the afterlife were developed, one of which was the notion of the immortality of the soul. This is a dominant motif in Plato. In several of his dialogues, most notably the *Phaedo*, he enunciated and argued for the doctrine that the human soul is immortal by virtue of its essential incorporeality and hence incorruptibility.[1] In some of his dialogues this core doctrine is associated with the ancillary ideas of the pre-existence of the soul and of the transmigration of souls.[2] In later Platonism, especially the philosophy of Plotinus, this basic idea is interpreted in terms of the doctrine of the ascent, or 'reversion', of the human soul to some higher entity, the World Soul, or even to the One, the ultimate reality.[3] In this supernal state the soul enjoys an existence that is vastly different from and superior to what it had experienced in its embodied state.

Aristotle had problems with Plato's psychological theory, especially its sharp distinction between soul and body. He developed an alternative theory that asserted the unity of the soul with the body, wherein the soul is the form of the body. Plato's doctrine of immortality presupposes a doctrine of psychological dualism, according to which the soul and the body are radically distinct entities, and as such are essentially separable and have different destinies. Aristotle could not accept this dualism, given his scientific, and especially biological, interests. He eventually developed a psychological theory asserting the unity of the mind and the body, wherein the soul is the form of the body. Since the form is what makes a thing what it is, it is no more separable from

---

[1] Plato, *Phaedo*, 66a–67e, 79–81d.   [2] Ibid. 70c–77a; Plato, *The Republic*, 10.
[3] Plotinus, *Enneads*, 1.6.7, 1.6.9, 6.7.34, 6.9.11.

the body than the shape of an orange is separable from the orange itself. In living things the soul, or form, is the principle of life for that thing. It would seem, then, that with the death of the body the soul perishes too.[4] However, we now come to a puzzling feature of Aristotle's philosophy. In several passages in *On the Soul*, he intimates that there may be something in or of the human soul that survives the death of the body. Speaking of the intellectual activity of the human soul, Aristotle suggests: 'But in the case of the mind and the thinking faculty nothing is yet clear; it seems to be a distinct kind of soul, and it alone admits of being separated, as the immortal from the perishable.'[5] Unfortunately, he deferred a detailed discussion of this theme to another time, which never arrived. These remarks do suggest, however, that if anything in humans is immortal, for Aristotle it is the part of the human soul that is capable of an activity that is unique to humanity: intellection. In short, if we are immortal, it is our intellect that survives.

Perhaps the most important of these 'intimations of immortality' in Aristotle is the notorious chapter 5 of Book 3 of *On the Soul*. This brief chapter may have been the most influential of Aristotle's texts, at least for the medieval philosophical treatment of human immortality. The chapter is concerned with the intellect, or thinking. Other animals have sensation and motion; some even have imagination. But humankind alone has the capacity to think. In this chapter Aristotle wants to know how this special activity takes place. He begins by applying one of his basic ideas in natural philosophy and metaphysics: the fundamental distinction between potentiality and actuality. Just as in the development of a plant or animal there is some matter that is potentially an oak tree or a butterfly and some active agents that actualize this potentiality such that an oak tree or a butterfly comes into being, something like this takes place in thinking. That is, in thinking there are two factors: one passive, or potential, the other active; that is, something that receives and something that makes or gives. Aristotle pictures the mind as a passive receptacle of information, capable of absorbing external data induced or stimulated by some agent that is productive of intellectual activity. He compares this agent to light: just as light is the catalytic agent that brings about the act of seeing, there is also a catalytic agent in the act of thinking.[6]

So far Aristotle is relatively clear. It is the remainder of this short chapter that is obscure, but despite this obscurity it is most important for our purposes. Aristotle goes on to describe the active factor of thinking in terms that

---

[4] Aristotle, *On the Soul*, 2.1–2.   [5] Ibid. 2.2.413*b*25–8; see also 1.4.408*b*18–30.
[6] Ibid. 3.5.430*a*10–17.

imply its immortality: 'Mind in this sense [that is, as active] is separable, impassive . . . it is essentially an activity . . . When isolated it is its true self and nothing more, and this alone is immortal and everlasting . . . [Whereas] mind in the passive sense [*ho pathetikos nous*] is perishable.'[7] Here Aristotle contrasts the imperishability of the catalytic agent productive of thought and the perishability of the passive aspect of the mind. That we have here a host of problems is not difficult to see. To begin with, are both the active and the passive factors in thinking internal to the mind, as some interpreters have claimed, basing their interpretation on Aristotle's opening remark: 'These distinct elements [that is, the active and passive aspects] must be present *in* the soul';[8] or, as the latter half of the chapter suggests, is the active factor an external agent separate from the passive factor, just as light is separate from the eye, as other interpreters have argued? If the latter interpretation is followed, only this transcendent active element is everlasting; if the former, the active and everlasting factor is immanent, internal to the mind, suggesting that each human intellect possesses an inherent immortality. This chapter bequeathed to Aristotle's interpreters and followers a legacy of both considerable difficulty and importance.[9]

One such commentator was Alexander of Aphrodisias (*fl.* 180–210). Although his commentary on Aristotle's *On the Soul* is not extant, his own treatise of the same title is, as well as a supplementary essay on the soul commonly referred to as the *Mantissa*.[10] One of Alexander's important contributions to the discussion was his formulation of a conceptual vocabulary for the various factors in cognition, only one of which—'the passive intellect'—was named by Aristotle. Alexander's nomenclature became the standard terminology used throughout late antiquity and the Middle Ages. In explaining the passive intellect Alexander provided equivalent terms that bring out more explicitly what Aristotle had in mind. As Aristotle himself suggested, this intellect is passive in the sense that it is literally 'in-formed', or shaped, by the cognitions that it takes on. In this sense it is like matter: just as a piece of wood can be shaped into a variety of forms, so the mind is capable of being formed by its cognitive content. Accordingly, Alexander calls the passive factor of the mind 'the material intellect' (*ho hulikos nous*).[11] Moreover, its

---

[7] Aristotle, *On the Soul*, 3.5.430*a*17–25.   [8] Ibid. 3.5.430*a*13.

[9] R. D. Hicks gives an excellent discussion of these divergent interpretations in his edition of Aristotle's *De anima*, 498–510.

[10] For a comprehensive treatment of Alexander of Aphrodisias' psychology and epistemology, see Moraux, *Alexandre d'Aphrodise*.

[11] Alexander of Aphrodisias, *De anima*, 81 (trans. Fotinus, 105).

passivity implies potentiality, its capacity to become in-formed, or cognitive; hence, it can be considered to be a 'potential intellect', or 'intellect in potentiality' (*ho dunamei nous*).[12] This capacity for cognition is, to use another Alexandrian expression, a 'disposition', or preparedness (*epitedeiotes*), to acquire knowledge, a notion that Aristotle referred to as a 'condition' (*hexis*), or habit.[13] All these terms express the idea that at the first stage of the cognitive process the human intellect is just a capacity that is itself inchoate, or empty. In this sense, Aristotle suggested, the mind is initially a blank tablet.[14]

However, Aristotle insisted that the active factor is superior to the passive factor. Alexander supplies a name for this active factor: it is the 'Agent Intellect' (*ho poetikos nous*), which we encountered in our earlier discussions of prophecy and miracles.[15] Alexander interpreted Aristotle's characterization of this intellect as 'separate, ever-active, and eternal' as referring to a transcendent active cause of cognition. Indeed, for Alexander this transcendent entity is identical with God, or the Supreme Intellect, mentioned by Aristotle in chapters 7 and 9 of Book 12 of his *Metaphysics*. This active agent is that which actualizes the potential, or material, intellect, to think and to become an intellect in act (*ho nous kat' energeian*).[16] As this intellect becomes more active, it becomes 'the intellect as habit', or a settled condition of the mind.[17] The more the human mind progresses in its intellectual journey its cognitive capital increases, eventually reaching the condition of the 'acquired intellect' (*ho nous epiktetos*), the fully mature mind.[18] Without the Agent Intellect there is no cognition; yet if there were no capacity for knowledge human beings would not be 'rational animals'.

Alexander's interpretation of chapter 5 of Book 3 of *On the Soul* was most influential: with the exception of his identification of the Agent Intellect with God, it formed the psychological framework within which many medieval philosophers developed not only their epistemological ideas but their doctrines of immortality as well. Like his mentor, Alexander left the topic underdeveloped. If the material intellect is, as Aristotle himself stated, the perishable element in cognition, then immortality seems to be a fiction, a

---

[12] Alexander of Aphrodisias, *De anima*, 81, line 23 (trans. Fotinus, 105).

[13] Ibid., line 14 (trans. Fotinus, 110); Aristotle, *Categories*, 8.8*b*26–7.

[14] Aristotle, *On the Soul*, 3.4.430*a*1–2.

[15] Alexander of Aphrodisias, *De anima*, 88–9 (trans. Fotinus, 116–20).

[16] Ibid., 82, line 6 (trans. Fotinus, 105–6).

[17] Ibid., 85, lines 26–86, line 1 (trans. Fotinus, 111).

[18] Ibid., 82, lines 1–2 (trans. Fotinus, 105).

conclusion that the Muslim philosopher Al-Farabi appears to have reached.[19] Or is there something in or about the human mind that is able to enjoy some kind of immortality by virtue of its cognitive achievements? In some passages Alexander suggests that the acquired intellect is immortal precisely because it is the mind fully in act. In this state it has been 'assimilated to', or has become similar to (*homoiosis*), the Agent Intellect. The eternity of the latter confers immortality upon the former, while the material substratum, the material intellect, perishes.[20]

Nevertheless, Alexander's allusions to immortality leave the reader with several problems. For one thing, *what* is it that becomes immortal? Alexander suggests that it is the acquired intellect. But what is the acquired intellect when it is no longer embodied? Some modern interpreters have claimed that it is just the act of thinking, or the cognitive act, the thought, which, according to Aristotle and Alexander, is identical with its object, which in this case is the Agent Intellect.[21] Assimilation is then union or identification. However, in this state of unification with the Agent Intellect there does not seem to be any basis for individuation. All the acquired intellects have become one in having the same object of knowledge and in being identified with it. Indeed, one commentator, Paul Moraux, has argued that Alexander has distorted Aristotle's own belief that it is the intellectual 'faculty', or the intellect itself, that becomes immortal.[22] On this reading of Aristotle, the immortal intellect of each person would be numerically distinct. It is, however, at least questionable if Alexander's own interpretation of Aristotle allows for such a robust account of immortality. Nevertheless, we shall see that Alexander's account of immortality influenced medieval thinkers in the Muslim and Jewish traditions, and hence opened the door for Gersonides to enter the debate.

Before we turn to Gersonides, let us consider how immortality was understood within the classical Jewish tradition. After all, Gersonides as a philosopher was faithful to the Jewish tradition as he understood it. Yet here we enter territory replete with theological obstacles. For, if the Greek thinkers worked with a small number of ideas pertaining to immortality, classical

---

[19] Al-Farabi, *Commentary on Aristotle's Nicomachean Ethics*, referred to in Averroes' *Long Commentary on Aristotle's De anima*, 433, 481, 485–6. Al-Farabi's commentary is no longer extant (Davidson, *Alfarabi, Avicenna and Averroes on Intellect*, ch. 3).

[20] Alexander of Aphrodisias, *De anima*, 89–90 (trans. Fotinus, 118–19); Reale, *A History of Ancient Philosophy*, vi. 32–3; Merlan, *Monopsychism, Mysticism, Metaconsciousness*, 18–29.   [21] Davidson, *Alfarabi, Avicenna and Averroes on Intellect*, 36–9.

[22] Moraux, *Alexandre d'Aphrodise*, 94–108.

Jewish literature is overgrown with doctrines pertaining to the afterlife: the messianic era, the Day of Judgement, the resurrection of the dead, the world to come, to mention just a few. How are these notions to be distinguished, if at all? How are they related to each other? What does each of them involve? And to make things more complicated, especially for the medieval Jewish philosophers who were familiar with the theory of the immortality of the soul, the Bible seems to be silent on the matter. If anything, the Bible's conception of the 'happy life' seems to be earthly and materialistic: a prosperous farm and a large family. Moreover, according to the doctrine of the resurrection of the dead, it is the body that is restored. How could the philosophical theory of the soul's immortality be integrated within these inherited religious beliefs? It is not surprising that someone eventually came along and undertook to provide some clarification of and system to all these ideas. Maimonides, as we would expect, was that person.

For the sake of simplicity and brevity, let us now introduce the term 'eschatology' as a general noun referring to all these ideas that have to do with the end of days.[23] Our aim here is to see whether or not these various ideas can be systematized into a coherent doctrine. That this is not just an academic exercise is proved by the fact that in one of the few expressions of theological interest found in the Mishnah it is eschatology that is singled out as a defining feature of the Jewish belief system: 'All Jews have a share in the world to come . . . But these have no share in the world to come: one who says that the resurrection of the dead is not taught in the Torah.'[24] At the outset two points need to be noted: first, the notion of the world to come is undefined and assumed to be understood; second, belief in the resurrection of the dead is also assumed to be a well-known Jewish dogma, and since it is a necessary condition for having a share in the world to come, it is distinct from the latter. This latter point was extremely important for Maimonides, as we shall now see.

In his commentary on this passage, Maimonides provides a treatise on Jewish eschatology. His main concern is to sort out the various eschatological beliefs found amongst Jews and to explain what they have to do with the world to come, which, as the Mishnah itself indicates, is the key idea. He begins by listing a number of eschatological doctrines all involving material, or corporeal, existence. Included in this group are the well-established ideas of the messianic era and the resurrection of the dead, doctrines that Maimonides himself regarded as definitive of Jewish belief. Yet these beliefs

---

[23] *Eschatos*: 'end', 'last'.   [24] Mishnah *San.* 10: 1.

are 'this-worldly': when they occur, they will take place in the world in which we live. Maimonides insists that nature will run its course, except in the case of the resurrection itself, which will of course be a miracle. Otherwise, nothing will occur that would constitute a real and permanent change in nature. Indeed, even those who are resurrected will eat and drink, and eventually die after a long second life. It is obvious then that, like the messianic age, the resurrection is literally a mundane affair.[25]

In sharp contrast to these ideas Maimonides singles out the main concept in this context, the 'world to come'. This state has nothing to do with this world. It is literally 'the other world', one that has nothing in common with our material needs and interests. Indeed, our life in this other world is utterly incorporeal; it is a spiritual existence. It is the *telos* of what it is to be human. To support this claim Maimonides quotes a passage from BT *Berakhot* 17b: 'In the world to come there is no eating, drinking, washing, anointing or sexual intercourse; but the righteous sit with their crowns on their heads enjoying the radiance of the Divine Presence.' The first clause of this sentence makes it clear that those who attain the world to come no longer have a corporeal existence and that their pleasures will not be physical. The second clause explicitly states that they enjoy a spiritual delight that is everlasting. In explaining this last point Maimonides emphasizes that this delight is purely intellectual, that it consists in the knowledge of God, which is acquired after continuous and deep study, especially of metaphysics. The term 'crown' in this rabbinic passage connotes 'the immortality of the soul being in firm possession of the Idea which is God the creator'.[26] In short, the ultimate goal for humans is immortality of the soul, which consists in knowledge of God. In his *Treatise on Resurrection*, Maimonides is again explicit that the world to come is immortality of the soul, not the resurrection of the dead or the messianic era.[27] It is clear that in these texts Maimonides subscribes to the Platonic doctrines that distinguish sharply between soul and body and that assert the soul's ultimate destiny is separation from the body. This is a state that those who attain it can enjoy as soon as their souls are emancipated from their bodies.

Although Maimonides is clear in these texts, in the *Guide* he is more evasive. In contrast to his full discussions of creation, divine attributes, prophecy, and providence, Maimonides is miserly on the immortality of the soul, confining himself to a few undeveloped hints. Since what he does say is

---

[25] Maimonides, *Commentary on the Mishnah, San.* 10; id., *Treatise on Resurrection*, 219–22; Gillman, *The Death of Death*, ch. 6.

[26] Maimonides, *Commentary on the Mishnah, San.* 10: 1 (trans. Twersky, 412).

[27] Maimonides, *Treatise on Resurrection*, 220.

relevant for our understanding of Gersonides' own theory of immortality, it is important that we try to tease out from these scattered remarks their philosophical underpinnings and implications. In the *Guide*, Maimonides is still faithful to the spiritual conception of immortality. If anything, he is more insistent on its intellectual character. In these few passages what is said to be immortal is no longer the whole soul, but only the intellectual part of it. In the concluding chapter of the *Guide*, Maimonides discusses four types of perfection, the last of which is 'the true human perfection', intellectual perfection: 'The fourth species is the true human perfection; it consists in the acquisition of the rational virtues . . . which teach true opinions concerning the divine things. This is in true reality the ultimate end; this is what gives the individual true perfection . . . and it gives him *permanent endurance*; through it man is man.'[28] The human soul is a complex entity, consisting of several disparate parts, or functions, some of which are intimately connected to the body, such as motion or sense perception. All those psychological phenomena are rooted in or deriving from the body and perish along with it. The only thing that remains is the intellect; for it is the intellect, or rational part of the soul, that truly constitutes human nature. Here Maimonides echoes Aristotle's remark that if anything about humanity survives bodily decomposition it would be the intellect.

So far Maimonides has put forth a fairly consistent account of human immortality based upon philosophical doctrines originally developed by Plato and Aristotle and expanded upon by later Greek and Muslim philosophers. However, there are two passages in the *Guide* that are troublesome. In commenting upon a midrashic text that mentions 'the souls of the righteous' as being 'in heaven', Maimonides attempts to explain this phrase as follows:

For the *souls* that remain after death are not the *soul* that comes into being in man at the time he is generated. For that which comes into being at the time a man is generated is merely a faculty consisting in preparedness, whereas the thing that after death is separate from matter is the thing that has become actual . . . What is separate is . . . one thing only.[29]

Maimonides also refers to a doctrine that he attributes to the 'later philosophers', among whom he mentions in particular the Muslim philosopher Ibn Bajja (d. 1139):

[28] Maimonides, *Guide*, iii. 54 (trans. Pines, 635); Aristotle, *On the Soul*, 1.3.407*b*2–6, 1.4.408*b*19–20, 1.4.408*b*29–30.

[29] Maimonides, *Guide*, i. 70 (trans. Pines, 173–4).

Now you know that regarding the things separate from matter—I mean those that are neither bodies nor forces in bodies, but intellects—there can be no thought of multiplicity of any mode whatever . . . Consequently all are one in number, as Abu Bakr Ibn al-Sa'igh [Ibn Bajja] and others who were drawn into speaking of these obscure matters have made clear.[30]

These passages have led some of Maimonides' medieval and modern commentators to claim that he himself subscribed to this view of immortality. Indeed, in his note to the latter passage, the modern translator of the *Guide* into English, Shlomo Pines, comments: 'Ibn Bajja's doctrine of the Unity of the Intellect accordingly seems to be accepted by Maimonides.' Pines' inference has been accepted by some commentators, although it is challenged by others.[31] For the present we can ignore this particular debate; what is important for us is that this view will be discussed and eventually rejected by Gersonides.

Gersonides' Theory of the Intellect

Right at the very beginning of Book 1 of *Wars*, Gersonides makes explicit his philosophical orientation and programme. Although the title of this book is 'Immortality of the Soul', it is immediately clear that Gersonides' focus is on something more specific:

Since the intellect is the most fitting of all the parts of the soul for immortality— the other parts are obviously perishable together with the corruption of the body . . . it is necessary that we inquire into the essence of the human intellect before we investigate whether it is immortal or not, and whether if it is immortal, in what way it is immortal.[32]

This passage resonates with Aristotelian and Alexandrian overtones. Nevertheless, unlike his predecessor, Maimonides, whom he does not mention at all in this discussion, Gersonides provides a virtual history of the problem from Aristotle to Averroes. As he makes clear, the primary theme here will be the nature of the human, or material, intellect: what its nature is, how it functions, and whether and in what way it becomes immortal.

After a detailed and critical exposition of the views and arguments of some of the Greek and Muslim commentators on Aristotle, Gersonides reaches his

---

[30] Maimonides, *Guide*, i. 74, seventh method (trans. Pines, 221).

[31] Ivry accepts Pines' interpretation in his 'Conjunction in and of Maimonides and Averroës'. Altmann attempts to salvage a more individualist account of immortality in 'Maimonides on the Intellect', 85–91.   [32] *Wars*, 1.1 (i. 109).

own conclusions about the human, or material, intellect. Concerning the ontological status of the material intellect Gersonides insists that it is not a substance, an entity essentially capable of independent existence, as the Platonists and Themistius, a fourth-century commentator on Aristotle, had claimed.[33] Nor is it a mere accidental property of the body, as some had argued.[34] It is, as Alexander maintained, a disposition, or capacity, for cognition, a potentiality, which needs some active agent to stimulate its activity. Dispositions, however, have no independent existence; they need to inhere, or belong, to some subject, or substratum. For Gersonides, as it was for Alexander, this ontological support for the disposition is the body or some part of the body, most likely the imagination. When under certain conditions this disposition is actualized, that is, when it is actually knowing, it is then an intellect 'in act'. So far Gersonides is faithful to Aristotle's cognitive psychology, as it was interpreted by Alexander.[35]

As a human being advances in the acquisition of knowledge the intellect is progressively 'substantialized', in the sense that its cognitions have endowed it with more than just potential existence. Its knowledge has made it an 'actual intellect'. In its most complete, or perfect, state this intellect is, as Alexander had affirmed, the 'acquired intellect'. However, it is important to realize that for Gersonides both material intellects and acquired intellects are individuated; they are *of* particular human beings. Nevertheless, whereas the material intellects are individuated by material factors, such as particular sensations and imaginations, the acquired intellects are individuated by their respective intellectual contents. Although the human intellect is at the outset a disposition of a corporeal substance, a person, it progressively becomes dematerialized as it increases its intellectual achievements. Let us see how this comes about.

For the Aristotelian philosopher, all knowledge is ultimately based upon sensation. The mind is a kind of cognitive sponge that absorbs data from external sources. At first these data consist of sensory images of particular objects. But for the Aristotelian such images qua particulars do not constitute knowledge, since genuine knowledge consists in universal truths.[36]

---

[33] *Wars*, 1.1 (i. 110, 112–19, 123–9). Like his knowledge of Alexander of Aphrodisias, Gersonides' acquaintance with the ideas of Themistius' psychology derives from Averroes. On Themistius, see Hamelin, *La Théorie de l'intellect*, 38–43.

[34] This view appears in some Kalam literature. See Sa'adiah Gaon, *The Book of Beliefs and Opinions*, treatise 6, ch. 1, first theory (trans. Rosenblatt, 236).

[35] *Wars*, 1.2 (i. 111–15), 1.5 (i. 144–5).

[36] Aristotle, *Posterior Analytics*, 1.24.86a3–10, 2.19.100b17.

Accordingly, our fund of particular sense data has to be transformed into something having universal validity. To accomplish this we have to strip away all the idiosyncratic features of the sense data that particularize them and form a common idea, or concept (*tsiyur*). This process is one of *abstraction*.[37] Since, in Aristotle's philosophy, the principle of individuation, or particularity, is matter—for the material features of a thing are what makes that thing a particular item and differentiate it from other items of the same type— abstraction, or conceptualization, requires that we dematerialize in thought the sensory images that we have of the sense object. For example, I have many visual, auditory, or olfactory images of individual dogs. These images are all particular, individuated by the material features of the various dogs that I have perceived. From these diverse images I can disregard what individuates each of these dogs and construct a concept of what it is to be a dog in general, or the form, or essence, of dog. In this activity the linguistic environment plays an important role. When I hear others referring to the dogs that I see or hear by the same term 'dog', even though these are different from each other, or if I hear that the term 'dog' is used to refer to dogs that I have not perceived, my concept is reinforced and made to conform to the conceptual and linguistic system in which I live. These concepts are the building blocks of my cognitive scheme and serve to enable me to form judgements and hypotheses (*imut*). The epistemic direction here is from the particular to the universal, from the material individuating factors of a thing to its general form.

But how do we know that our concepts and judgements are true, that they adequately represent the world? Aristotle and his disciples were not overly worried by this question. Aristotle's 'epistemological faith' rests upon a metaphysical belief that natural phenomena fall into groups, or types, whose individual specimens exhibit a common form, or essence. For all the different dogs we encounter there is just one dog-form, or essence. Our concept of 'dog' has to conform to this essence if it is to be usable, not only in zoology but also in our everyday life. This assumption of natural kinds, or types, is the guiding principle of Aristotle's biological classification system of genera and species.[38] In short, an adequate concept and the

---

[37] Aristotle, *Posterior Analytics*, 1.18.81*b*3–7; Gersonides, *Commentary on the Five Scrolls*, S. of S., 10*c* (*Commentary on the Song of Songs*, trans. Kellner, 38); see also Kellner, 'Gersonides on the Role of the Active Intellect in Human Cognition'; Davidson, 'Gersonides on the Material and Active Intellects'.

[38] Aristotle, *Parts of Animals*, 1.1.639*a*16–*b*4, 1.1.641*a*15–17; id., *History of Animals*, 1.1.486*a*15–25, 1.1.487*a*10–13; see also Furth, *Substance and Form*, 51–4, 70–5; Gotthelf and Lennox (eds.), *Philosophical Issues*, especially Lennox, 'Kinds, Forms of Kinds'.

judgements based upon it must conform to the formal structure of the natural world.

At this point one may want to object: 'Isn't this talk of forms and types a regression back to Plato, whose theory of the forms Aristotle spent a lot of energy refuting?' Yes and no. Yes, in so far as it is assumed here that there is an objective order that exemplifies genuine natural types and that this order can be known. In this sense there are forms; but they are 'in things'. No, if by these forms we mean the incorporeal forms of Plato's ontology that have independent existence yet are somehow 'present in and participated in by' sensible particulars. It is this Platonic thesis that Aristotle rejected. But Aristotle's victory over Plato was partial and short-lived. Gradually elements of Plato's theory infiltrated some of the doctrines of the later ancient Greek philosophers, as well as many of the theories of medieval thinkers. The later Platonists wondered, as Plato himself occasionally did, whether or not the forms have location. Some of them postulated that they do: they are located in a transcendent intellect. For some this intellect is God, or the divine mind; for others it is some supernal being subordinate to God.[39] Accordingly, if our concepts are adequate, they reflect or represent some form immanent in the natural world, but whose ultimate origin is transcendent. Human knowledge is, then, an activity in which we come to know the formal nature of our world through sense perception by means of abstraction; yet this structure has its foundation in some transcendent being. Aristotle's empiricism is now linked to Plato's doctrine of the divine craftsman who creates the world according to the forms.[40]

Since the medieval philosophers had limited first-hand knowledge of Plato's works, they understood this epistemological–metaphysical idea in Aristotelian terms, and again the doctrine of the Agent Intellect makes its appearance, albeit in Platonic garb. Whereas Aristotle and Alexander's Agent Intellect is primarily an efficient cause of or catalyst for human cognitive activity, for some of the medieval philosophers, it is also the locus and imme-diate efficient cause of the formal structure of reality. In Gersonides' language it is 'the law, order, and rightness' of the sublunar world: 'Since it is clear from the nature of the material intellect that it has potentially the knowledge of the *plan and order* of the sublunary world, it is necessary that this order be known in some sense actually by the Agent Intellect.'[41]

---

[39] Seneca, *Moral Epistles*, 65.7; Philo, *On the Creation of the World*, 16–17, 24–9; id., *Allegorical Interpretation*, 3.96; Dillon, *The Middle Platonists*, 138, 158–61.

[40] Plato, *Timaeus*, 28c–29c, 30c–31a; *Wars*, 1.6 (i. 146). [41] *Wars*, 1.6 (i. 151–2).

In explaining this idea Gersonides used the following metaphor: the Agent Intellect is like a human artisan who makes an object according to some plan in his mind. However, as is often the case, the plan in the mind of the creator is more perfect than the plan as realized in the physical object. In the case of the Agent Intellect this is always true, as Plato had maintained. The superiority of the plan in the Agent Intellect relative to the embodied plan in the world and the conceived plan in our minds lies in its unitary character. For unlike the human intellect, whose cognitive achievements are cumulative, unsystematic, and incomplete, the Agent Intellect knows the entire natural order as a coherent and unified system of laws. In this sense it is analogous to Philo's Logos or Plotinus' Nous.[42]

The Agent Intellect is also the immediate cause of the natural world being what it is; it is, to use a common medieval term, 'the giver of forms' (*donor formarum, noten hatsurot*).[43] The 'map of the world' that we draw represents, if it is accurate, the contents of the Agent Intellect that have been translated into physical form in nature. The Agent Intellect is, then, not only an efficient cause of human cognition; it is also the efficient agent of the way the world is, the immediate cause of its formal structure:

The agent responsible for the existence of the things in the sublunar world is the Agent Intellect, whose existence has been proven in *On the Soul* . . . [Also], it has been shown in chapter 16 of the *Book of Animals* that there is an agent at work in the [generation of] plants and animals and that this agent is an intellect. Aristotle calls it 'the soul that emanates from the heavenly bodies', which, he says, is a divine power, and an intellect. Many of the modern philosophers have called it 'the Agent Intellect'.[44]

Again the analogy of the artisan is at work here: the Agent Intellect is the supreme architect and builder of the sublunar world. It brings about an ordered and structured world because it itself manifests and represents this order. Now in the physical world the forms, according to which the world is fashioned, are embodied in material objects; in the Agent Intellect, however, they are abstracted from matter. In the former the forms are 'materialized', and hence appear along with idiosyncratic properties; in the latter they exist 'pure and neat', utterly universal and unified. To the extent that our concepts

[42] Feldman, 'Platonic Themes in Gersonides' Doctrine of the Agent Intellect'.

[43] *Wars*, 5.3.1 (iii. 81–2); H. Goldstein, 'Dator Formarum'.

[44] *Wars*, 1.6 (i. 152). Gersonides' reference to Aristotle is actually to his *Generation of Animals*, 2.3.736*b*28–9. In the medieval canon of Aristotle's writings this treatise was part of a comprehensive zoological work known as *The Book of Animals*.

are a true map of the world they also represent the formal order of our world as it is present in the Agent Intellect. Human knowledge is, then, the product of the activity of the Agent Intellect upon our intellect, whose cognitive base is our empirical experience of the natural world.[45]

Gersonides' theory of the intellect is thus a blend of Platonic and Aristotelian elements. It adopts Plato's ideas of form and of the divine crafts-man who creates the physical world according to a plan, but fits these ideas into an Aristotelian framework involving the Agent Intellect. We have here a synthesis of Plato's *Timaeus* and Aristotle's *On the Soul*. But before I move on to consider how Gersonides develops his doctrine of intellectual immor-tality, I must note that his theory of the intellect needs to be supplemented by bringing God into the story. Remember that the 'law and order' of the sublunar world ensconced in the Agent Intellect is precisely just that: it is the plan for the world in which we humans live. It is not the plan of the whole universe. The Agent Intellect is not the ultimate reality or cause of the entire universe: God is. It is God who has created both the physical and the spiritual worlds, the world of bodies and the world of separate intellects, including the Agent Intellect. The latter, as we have seen, is the 'giver of forms' for our world. It has no influence or efficacy over the heavenly bodies. The 'plan and order' of the whole universe is, however, in God's mind. It is according to this plan that the entire universe has been created by God. We have here an ascending hierarchy of orders: the formal order of the physical world as apprehended and understood in our minds; the order itself as it is embodied in nature; this order as represented in the Agent Intellect; and finally, the law of the whole universe in God.[46] As the summit and zenith of this 'ladder of being' God knows everything, that is, all the laws governing the entire uni-verse; at the lowest position in this scale we know only fragments of this order. Nevertheless, this partial knowledge will turn out to be sufficient for attaining human perfection, as we shall see.

The Immortality of the Intellect

What does my knowing mathematics, physics, or metaphysics have to do with my having a share in the world to come? Indeed, what is it about knowledge that confers immortality? And is this knowledge both necessary and sufficient for my enjoying this share of immortality? In answering these questions we need to see how Gersonides connects the doctrine of immortality with his

[45] Feldman, 'Platonic Themes in Gersonides' Doctrine of the Agent Intellect', 255–78.
[46] *Wars*, 5.3.5 (iii. 137); Touati, *La Pensée philosophique de Gersonide*, 349–52.

general theory of cognition. To do this we first have to recall Aristotle's principle that, in the act of knowing, the cognitive act and the object of knowledge become one. Some of the medieval thinkers, such as Al-Farabi, introduced a third element to this relationship, the intellect itself: 'Thus the meaning [of] it is "thinking in actuality," "intellect in actuality," and "intelligible in actuality" is one and the same meaning.'[47] Maimonides quotes this formula as a well-known principle of Aristotelian epistemology: 'Thus, in us too, the intellectually cognizing subject, the intellect and the intellectually cognized object are one and the same thing wherever we have an intellect in actu.'[48] In the very act of thought, then, there is, to use Altmann's felicitous phrase, a 'triunity of *intellectus*', the numerical identity of the knower, the intellect, and the object known.[49] Gersonides too focuses upon the identity of the thinker and the object of thought in the act of thinking. However, whereas for Alexander of Aphrodisias and others the object of thought with which the intellect is identified is the Agent Intellect, for Gersonides it is the abstracted concept, or intelligible form, or the proposition constituted by these concepts that is the proper object of thought.

For Gersonides the key idea in this context is the 'general nature' (*hateva hakolel*). The knowledge we acquire through the mechanisms of sense perception and abstraction are ultimately based upon the existence of generic and species natures, which in turn exist in pristine form in the Agent Intellect. Although this nature as an embodied, or material, form does perish along with the death of the particular that instantiates it, the form as represented in the Agent Intellect is everlasting and immutable. Moreover, and most important, in so far as we have accumulated knowledge of these general natures, our knowledge, or our acquired intellects, partake, to use a Platonic expression, of the original stable and permanent character of these natures: 'Knowledge is conserved and indestructible; for it is of a perpetual thing that is not destructible, i.e., it is of common natures.'[50] Since in the act of knowing the intellect becomes one with the object of knowledge, the material intellect in its mature actualization, that is the acquired intellect, has become one with its cognitions and shares their stability and perpetuity.

Gersonides expresses this idea nicely in his interpretation of Genesis 25: 8, which in reporting the death of Abraham says: 'and he was gathered to his peoples'. Gersonides comments on this passage as follows:

[47] Al-Farabi, *Letter Concerning the Intellect* (trans. Hyman, 216).
[48] Maimonides, *Guide*, i. 68 (trans. Pines, 165–6).
[49] Altmann, 'Maimonides on the Intellect', 74.
[50] Gersonides, *Commentary on the Five Scrolls*, Eccles., 30*d* (my translation).

It is possible to interpret this passage as [meaning] that he was gathered to the objects of knowledge that he acquired during his lifetime . . . After death the intellect is gathered to these cognitions . . . Scripture calls these cognitions 'peoples' because they are the general order [*hasidur hakolel*] that exists in each and every species, which the object of knowledge designates.[51]

Since the term 'people' connotes generality or commonality, the 'gathering of Abraham's soul' to his peoples means for Gersonides the identification of Abraham's intellect with the universal truths that he acquired while his intellect was embodied. In Abraham's being gathered to his peoples, these truths have been shorn of all particularity: their sensory-imaginative roots and origins have been nullified in the process of abstraction. In this sense the object of knowledge to which the intellect has been gathered is a universal, an immutable element in the 'law, order, and rightness' of the sublunar world contained in the Agent Intellect: 'Accordingly, it is evident that the acquired intellect itself is the order obtaining in the sublunar world that is inherent in the Agent Intellect.'[52] Thus the 'intellect that remains' is the sum total of one's knowledge, one's intellectual capital, accumulated through the pursuit of intellectual perfection, our true happiness.[53]

This set of universal cognitions can be said to be immaterial in so far as with their loss of particularity they have also lost all their materiality, which is the cause and source of corruption and decay. An apple rots because of the decomposition of its matter, not the destruction of its essence, or nature. The latter is a constant, an immutable component of the overall order in nature, which is a physical replica of the incorporeal plan in the Agent Intellect. Accordingly, Gersonides concludes with the following syllogism: 'The acquired intellect is immaterial, and an immaterial substance does not have the conditions requisite for corruption; and whatever lacks these conditions is incorruptible.'[54] The intellect has achieved immortality in so far as it has literally *become* its knowledge, whose perpetuity is grounded in the immutable plan in the Agent Intellect. Plato's doctrine of the immortality of the soul by virtue of its inherent incorporeality has been transformed by Gersonides into a theory of the immortality of the intellect, wherein the intellect acquires immateriality, and hence immortality. Immortality is thus not something that is inherited at birth but an achievement earned through intellectual effort and accomplishment.

Herein lies Gersonides' response to Alexander and Maimonides' apparent denial of individual immortality. Each acquired intellect is individuated by

---

51 *CT*, Gen., 'Ḥayei sarah', 33*a* (i. 158).   52 *Wars*, i.ii (ii. 213).
53 *CT*, Gen., 'Bereshit', 14*a–c* (i. 51–2).   54 *Wars*, i.ii (i. 213).

its own intellectual contents: what Abraham knows is not identical with what Isaac knows. The intellect of Einstein is not identical with the intellect of Bohr. Even though these intellects are all immaterial, they can be individuated by the specificity of their intellectual content. The differences can be qualitative or quantitative. To be sure, here matter is no longer the principle of individuation, as it is in material substances; the principle of individuation is formal: the cognitions of the forms of things achieved by each intellect. Just as the separate intellects governing the heavenly bodies are individuated by what they know of their corresponding bodies,[55] so each acquired intellect knows what it has individually understood of 'the law, order, rightness' of the sublunar world. In both instances the intellect is individuated by what it knows.[56]

It should be noted, however, that this achievement is static and terminal: upon becoming immortal the acquired intellect cannot increase its intellectual capital. Since it no longer has the sensory and imaginative apparatus to receive additional sensory inputs from which it can abstract concepts, it can no longer acquire information about the physical world. It must remain content with what it already knows.[57] Gersonides agrees with Maimonides in construing immortality as an achievement gained through intellectual perfection, yet he disagrees with him in insisting upon its individual character. But if the acquired intellect qua immortal is unable to increase its knowledge, what advantage does immortality confer upon it? The answer is that it is now able to contemplate its intellectual achievements without any hindrances supervening upon it from the body. It can now understand simultaneously what it has formally known in the step-by-step manner by which this knowledge was accumulated during the corporeal career of this intellect: 'All the knowledge that we have acquired in life will be continuously contemplated and all the things in our minds will be apprehended simultaneously, since after death the obstacle that prevents this [kind of cognition], i.e., matter, will have disappeared.'[58] For Gersonides, continuous and simultaneous understanding implies, or at least makes possible, a systematic grasp of the whole body of knowledge that one has acquired. It is for this reason that the wise do not fear death: they anticipate a more perfect and unimpeded comprehension of their knowledge.[59]

[55] *Wars*, 5.3.8 (iii. 156–63).
[56] Ibid. 1.13 (i. 224); *CT*, Num., 'Naso', 182*a* (iv. 21); see Rudavsky, 'The Jewish Tradition', 82; Manekin, 'Conservative Tendencies in Gersonides' Religious Philosophy', 306–10.   [57] *Wars*, 1.13 (i. 225); *CT*, Num., 'Ḥukat', 194*a* (iv. 109).
[58] *Wars*, 1.13 (i. 224).   [59] *CT*, Lev., 'Aḥarei mot', 158*a* (iii. 275).

In *Berakhot* 17*a*, quoted by Maimonides as support for his understanding of immortality, there is the notion that the immortals enjoy their state of immortality. They reflect upon their intellectual achievement and take pleasure in it. Gersonides agrees: 'Each man who has attained this perfection enjoys the happiness resulting from his knowledge after death . . . This pleasure is not comparable to the other pleasures and has no relation to them at all.'[60] But to enjoy or to take pleasure in something is to be aware of the object or source of the pleasure. This implies that the acquired intellect is conscious not only of its intellectual achievement but also of its immortality. Moreover, in contrast to our consciousness of our present experiences, for the most part induced by or mediated through the body, the self-consciousness experienced by the immortal acquired intellect is completely detached from and independent of the body. It does not suffer from interruptions or distractions. It is 'pure'.

Gersonides' Critique of Immortality as Conjunction with the Agent Intellect

As we noted in our discussion of Alexander, some medieval philosophers, especially in the Muslim world, developed his idea of intellectual immortality as some kind of cognitive relation with the Agent Intellect into a theory wherein Alexander's notion of 'assimilation', or 'likening', to the Agent Intellect was now interpreted as 'conjunction' or 'unification'. Immortality is construed as an intimate attachment to the Agent Intellect achieved by the acquired intellect at its most perfect stage of cognitive development resulting in union. Although the terms 'conjunction' and 'unification' have different connotations—the latter is stronger than the former—in many of the thinkers espousing this doctrine they are used interchangeably, and this is how Gersonides understands the theory.[61] He treats the tradition from Alexander to Averroes as advocating a view of immortality that implies union and hence identity with the Agent Intellect. Nevertheless, as we shall see, there are some relevant differences amongst the advocates of this doctrine, and Gersonides will focus especially upon the dissimilarities between Averroes and Alexander.

Following Gersonides' own procedure I shall first consider his exposition and critique of Averroes' position, which, Gersonides says, 'has been thought to be the most adequate explanation of the material intellect'.[62] However, I

---

[60] *Wars*, 1.13 (i. 224–5).
[61] Altmann, 'Ibn Bajja on Man's Ultimate Felicity', 53, 63–4, 78–9.
[62] *Wars*, 1.4 (i. 130).

need to note that, in his discussion of Averroes' theory, Gersonides makes no reference to Averroes' *Long Commentary on Aristotle's On the Soul*, which was translated into Hebrew only after Gersonides' death.[63] Gersonides' analysis, then, relies upon Averroes' *Epitome of Aristotle's On the Soul* and the *Middle Commentary on Aristotle's On the Soul* and several short treatises composed by Averroes dealing with conjunction. The chronological and conceptual relations between the long and middle commentaries are currently topics of scholarly debate.[64] However, I shall not enter into that discussion, since the focus here is on how Gersonides understood Averroes and those philosophers discussed by the Cordoban 'Commentator'.

Gersonides' debate with Averroes assumes that Averroes accepted Themistius' thesis that the material intellect is a separable, and hence incorruptible, substance, not a mere disposition, as Alexander had claimed. Moreover, Averroes had explicitly concluded from this thesis that the material intellect is really the Agent Intellect embodied in different humans; or conversely, the Agent Intellect is 'accidentally' the material intellect and differentiated in humans only by the particular sensory images acquired by individual perceivers. Ultimately, there is only *one* intellect, which in its receiving, or passive and potential, aspect can be regarded as the material intellect, but which in its active aspect is the Agent Intellect. In this sense the material intellect is a composite of the disposition, according to Alexander, and the separable substance, the Agent Intellect, according to Themistius and Averroes. Alfred Ivry aptly expresses this point as follows: 'It is clear that Averroes . . . believes that the different phases of intellection are all essentially part of the universal agent intellect, which despite its name, is responsible for both the creating and receiving of intelligible [that is, the objects of knowledge].'[65] The dispositional dimension of knowing is inherent in the sense data accumulated in the imagination; these data are transformed into knowledge through the activity of the Agent Intellect that is 'attached' to us. The human intellect is 'material' in the sense that it, like matter in its physical character as the recipient of form, is the potential repository of knowledge if and when it is activated by the Agent Intellect.

[63] Averroes' *Long Commentary on Aristotle's De anima* was translated into Hebrew after Gersonides' death, probably in the fifteenth century (see Steinschneider, *Hebraeische Uebersetzungen*, §73; Ivry, 'Gersonides and Averroes on the Intellect', 240).

[64] Ivry, introduction to Averroes, *Middle Commentary on Aristotle's De anima*, pp. xiii–xxix; id., 'Averroes' Three Commentaries on *De Anima*'; Davidson, *Alfarabi, Avicenna and Averroes on Intellect*, 282–99.

[65] Ivry, 'Averroes on Intellect and Conjunction', 78.

The Agent Intellect is, then, both the form and the efficient cause of the material intellect's becoming an actual intellect: 'It is clear, from the nature of this intellect [the Agent Intellect]—which, in one respect, is form for us and, in another, is the agent for the intelligible—that it is separable and neither generable nor corruptible.'[66] In this passage Averroes implies that the material intellect, by virtue of its ontological identity with the Agent Intellect, is a separable substance, and thus immortal. In its 'accidental' embodiment in individual intellects, the Agent Intellect is literally temporarily located in and differentiated according to the sensory collections of each human mind. But with the death of the human body, the accumulation of sensory images also disappears, and there is no longer any principle of individuation that differentiates one human mind from another; that is, the Agent Intellect absorbs into itself all the material intellects such that the latter all become one in the Agent Intellect. The Agent Intellect's non-essential immanent career as a knower of mundane objects and their forms is now over, and its inherent transcendent character as a self-knower has now been restored or revealed.[67] The unicity of the Agent Intellect, a thesis admitted by all the participants in this debate, is now 'inherited' by the material intellect as it returns to its source. We can now speak of the 'unicity of the material intellect', a thesis that was deemed so dangerous that it was condemned by the bishop of Paris in 1277 and provoked Thomas Aquinas to write his polemical treatise *On There Being Only One Intellect.*[68] The Aristotelian analysis of human cognition has become the basis for a 'rational mysticism' that makes Aristotle a forerunner of Plotinus.[69]

Averroes makes no effort to conceal or gloss over the fairly obvious corollary to his monopsychism: in the union of all human intellects in the Agent Intellect there is no longer any differentiation. In short, there is no individual immortality. On this major question the two great Cordoban Aristotelian philosophers—Averroes and Maimonides—appear to agree.[70] This conclusion leads Gersonides to confront Averroes head-on and results in a detailed refutation of the latter's doctrine. His critique of Averroes comprises several arguments that can be divided into three groups, or categories: theological (or religious), epistemological, and metaphysical. It should be noted,

[66] Averroes, *Middle Commentary on Aristotle's De anima*, 116.

[67] Ivry, 'Averroes on Intellect and Conjunction', 83; id., 'Gersonides and Averroes on the Intellect', 248–9.

[68] Tempier, *Condemnation of 219 Propositions*, proposition 117.

[69] Merlan, *Monopsychism, Mysticism, Metaconsciousness*, 98–113.

[70] Ivry, 'Conjunction in and of Maimonides and Averroës'.

however, that the theological arguments are not appeals to religious texts; they are, on the contrary, philosophical arguments defending the traditional theological belief in individual immortality, which, as we have seen, is itself formulated by Gersonides within the framework of Aristotelian psychology.

Suppose there is just one intellect for all humans and that immortality is purchased at the price of obliterating all individuality. After all, if immortality is the human perfection *par excellence*, what does it matter if we all acquire

it after corporeal death and without distinction? To Gersonides it matters a great deal. He mounts a barrage of *reductio ad absurdum* arguments showing that Averroes' theory is false. It is agreed by all that the pursuit of wisdom is an essential component in the good life, which is supposed to warrant immortality. But if immortality automatically accrues to every material intellect without distinction upon death, what point is there in engaging in the long and arduous enterprise of living the good life? On Averroes' view, 'learning in the theoretical sciences whose goal is not action would be pointless. For if they have no effect on human perfection, i.e., immortality of the intellect, it is clear that they have no utility at all.'[71] Gersonides believes that the human intellect, especially its theoretical, or speculative, capacity, is not a fortuitous accident of human nature. We have it because it has a goal or function, which if not realized results in the frustration of a natural end. Moreover, we have a natural desire to acquire knowledge, as Aristotle insists in the opening paragraph of his *Metaphysics*.[72] If this desire has no point, then a natural human capacity and disposition has no terminus or goal. This violates Aristotle's dictum that nature does not do anything in vain.[73] Accordingly, the pursuit of wisdom would be otiose if 'the unification with the Agent Intellect . . . be achieved upon death, by any man, be he fool or sage'.[74] The contemplative life, glorified by Aristotle, Averroes, and Maimonides, would have no essential connection with human perfection as immortality, if it is achieved by anyone just by dying.

If someone is unconvinced by this teleological defence of a theological belief in individual immortality and claims that there is no essential connection between the pursuit of wisdom and immortality, the former being worthy in itself regardless of any of its possible consequences,[75] Gersonides now introduces several metaphysical arguments that undermine the Averroist

---

[71] *Wars*, 1.4 (i. 130).   [72] Aristotle, *Metaphysics*, 1.1.980a20.

[73] Aristotle, *Physics*, 2.7.198b4–5; *Parts of Animals*, 1.1.641b12; Gersonides, *Commentary on the Five Scrolls*, S. of S., 6b–c (*Commentary on the Song of Songs*, trans. Kellner, 20).   [74] *Wars*, 1.4 (i. 131).

[75] As suggested by Ivry in 'Gersonides and Averroes on the Intellect', 247–51.

doctrine. As we have already seen, for the Aristotelian the human intellect needs to be stimulated and assisted in its actualization and maturation. Now if the material intellect and the Agent Intellect are really one, as Averroes maintains, then one and the same entity is both the actualizer and that which is actualized, which violates Aristotle's principle that nothing can actualize itself. According to the medieval Aristotelians we come to know a scientific law through the agency of the Agent Intellect, which itself knows this law and either transmits it to us or aids us in abstracting it from data. However, if the material intellect and Agent Intellect are really just the same thing, then one and the same thing would be both knowing this law and not knowing it at the same time. This is, Gersonides claims, clearly absurd.[76]

Moreover, if two things are really identical, then if one has the property F, the other should have it too. Now, if the material intellect and Agent Intellect are one entity, their properties should be identical. But they are not. Indeed, their very definitions are radically different. The material intellect is defined in terms of its potentiality for knowledge and by the domain of its cognitive activity, namely the natural world; the Agent Intellect is defined as intrinsically actual and as primarily a self-knower: 'But if we were to claim that the two are identical, then two things of different natures would be numerically identical, which is absolutely absurd. For it is impossible for them to be one in species [that is, by definition]; all the more so is it impossible for them to be numerically identical.'[77] The Themistian–Averroist attempt to bring the Agent Intellect 'down to earth' or to elevate the material intellect to the incorporeal world of the separate intellects results in a metaphysical morass. A thing is what it is and not another thing. A thing whose nature is to know the world outside itself is one thing; something whose nature is to know itself is quite a different thing.[78]

Indeed, there is a gap in Averroes' doctrine of the materialization of the Agent Intellect. How does that which is intrinsically incorporeal and transcendent become embodied and immanent? If we say that it transforms itself into the latter condition by some self-induced change, it thereby loses its status as an immutable, incorporeal substance. If we claim that it is transformed by some other agent, what or who is this external agent that has the power to change that which is essentially incorporeal and transcendent into something that is corporeal and immanent? And how would it accomplish this extraordinary, if not miraculous, deed?[79]

---

[76] *Wars*, 1.4 (i. 132).   [77] Ibid. 1.4 (i. 133–4).
[78] Ibid.   [79] Ibid. 1.4 (i. 134, 137).

Moreover, how does something that is essentially one become accidentally many? Here we are confronted with a serious problem raised by Plato in his dialogue *Parmenides*. If a unique, simple, separate, and incorporeal form is present in and participated in by many corporeal particulars, how can these essential properties of the form be preserved intact?[80] Averroes, Gersonides argues, has the same problem. According to Aristotle's philosophy, matter is the principle of individuation, as we have seen. If the immanence, or presence, of the Agent Intellect in a plurality of minds is effected by its being particularized by the sensory forms that each such mind has accumulated, then the Agent Intellect has ceased to be a separate intellect. It has been divided up into a plurality of material intellects, losing its original and inherent status as a separate, incorporeal intellect. What was initially one has now become many; what was intrinsically incorporeal and simple has now become corporeal and divisible. This is unacceptable.[81]

Now let us consider some of the epistemological difficulties that beset Averroes' doctrine. If two individuals A and B have the same intellect, then what A knows B should know. Obviously this is not always the case.[82] Averroes would reply that the requisite sensory information is available to A but not to B, and it is in this sense that we can say that their respective intellects differ.[83] But, Gersonides would retort, why can we not say that the sensory data that enable A to know some empirical fact are sufficient for B's knowing this same fact, even though B lacks these data? 'For when it is assumed that this intellect requires the senses in what it knows, it is evident that what is sensed by one man alone would be sufficient for [the presence] of the conception of what is sensed in *all* men. But this is absurd.'[84] In this counter-argument Gersonides believes that if A and B have the same material intellect, the relevant sensory data for knowing some proposition need not be present in both A and B. Their common intellect would use just one set of sense data to affirm the truth of the proposition in question. If A possesses the required sensory information and asserts the truth of that proposition, then B, having the same intellect, should also affirm that proposition. Since affirmation, or judgement, is one of the activities of the intellect, once the common intellect has affirmed the truth of a proposition on the basis of empirical data, everyone would make the same judgement. This is of course not the case.

---

[80] Plato, *Parmenides*, 130a–135c.
[81] *Wars*, 1.4 (i. 138).   [82] Ibid. 1.4 (i. 138, 141).
[83] Averroes, *Long Commentary on Aristotle's De anima*, 329, 333–4.
[84] *Wars*, 1.4 (i. 138).

Moreover, what about instances where either A and B have the same sense data or where sensory information is irrelevant, as in mathematics, yet they make different judgements? In the first case, looking at a figure, A says that it is a duck; B, looking at the same figure, says that it is a rabbit. Each knows what ducks and rabbits are like; but one and the same figure leads to different judgements, despite A and B having the same intellect. In mathematics, where sensory information plays no significant role, different mathematicians may infer different conclusions from the same set of premises. If they have the same intellect, this should not be possible. In sum, Averroes' attempt to salvage his unicity of the material intellect thesis while at the same time acknowledging individual differences in cognition fails. It proves either too much or too little.

Having disposed of Averroes' doctrine of the intellect and its corollary of non-individual immortality, Gersonides now returns to the alternative version of conjunction, suggested by Alexander and advocated by several of his medieval followers, such as Ibn Bajja and perhaps Maimonides: assimilation with, or attachment to, the Agent Intellect. Here, let us remember, we are not talking about an original ontological identity between the material intellect and the Agent Intellect, as in the case of Averroes, but about a supervenient and/or acquired epistemic relation between an intellect and the object of its knowledge.[85] The assimilation or conjunction is a state that is 'earned' by the human intellect by virtue of its cognitive efforts and achievements. This is the significance of the term 'acquired' in the concept of the acquired intellect. In the ideal case this epistemological relation results in union with the Agent Intellect, which is sufficient to confer immortality upon the human intellect. The fundamental assumption of this theory is the Aristotelian epistemological principle that, in knowing, the knower and the object of knowledge become identical. Accordingly, if the knower has acquired complete knowledge of the eternal Agent Intellect, then it has achieved the desired conjunction or union, which confers immortality. Expressed in spatial terms, the relation can be considered as cognitive congruence: the mental contents of the human knower are congruent with the contents of the Agent Intellect. Now in the medieval context we have to ignore Alexander's unique identification of the Agent Intellect with God and consider the Agent Intellect alone as the relevant object of knowledge. To achieve immortality then is for our intellects to become congruent with the contents of the Agent Intellect.[86]

[85] Merlan, *Monopsychism, Mysticism, Metaconsciousness*, 18–29.

[86] Davidson, *Alfarabi, Avicenna and Averroes on Intellect*, 34–9; Reale, *A History of Ancient Philosophy*, iv. 28–33.

Despite his adherence to Alexander's psychology, and in particular to the latter's understanding of the material intellect as a disposition, Gersonides rejects his concept of intellectual immortality as conjunction with the Agent Intellect. As we have already noted, the cognitive apparatus and procedures of the human intellect differ considerably from those of the Agent Intellect, resulting in a kind of cognitive dissonance or distance that prevents complete conjunction. In the first place, the human intellect requires sensory inputs as the bases for its knowledge, and thus needs a body; the Agent Intellect dispenses with such requirements. Indeed, it does not acquire knowledge; it possesses it *ab initio*. Secondly, the human intellect acquires its knowledge cumulatively over time, often intermittently, and occasionally falling into error. In the Agent Intellect the objects of knowledge are simultaneously and perfectly present. Thirdly, we often accumulate knowledge haphazardly, not realizing or pursuing the systematic relationships between different cognitions or ideas. The Agent Intellect's knowledge is a unified system, the complete 'law, order, and rightness' of the sublunar world.[87]

Finally, in addition to the differences in the modes of cognition, the human intellect and the Agent Intellect can never be cognitively congruent. No matter how great or how accurate our knowledge is it can never be as complete as the knowledge in the Agent Intellect. What we know is just a subset of the cognitive content inherent in the Agent Intellect. Even the most prominent physicist or economist is just that: he or she has attained excellence in these fields only, whereas the Agent Intellect represents the whole body of laws governing our world. All of these differences make conjunction or union with the Agent Intellect impossible for us: 'It is impossible for man to apprehend completely the Agent Intellect . . . In this some of the recent philosophers have erred, thinking that man could apprehend completely the Agent Intellect and become numerically one with it, and that herein lies human happiness . . . and immortality.'[88] Cognitive disparity between the human intellect and its ultimate cognitive goal is therefore an ineluctable and permanent fact of the human condition.

In one of the few places in Book 1 of *Wars* where Gersonides cites biblical or rabbinic material, he discusses a debate between two sages concerning the world to come. According to Gersonides' own understanding of the debate, Rabbi Judah bar Simon interpreted the biblical passage 'And God saw that the light was good' (Gen. 1: 4), as referring to the intellectual illumination of the separate intellects which is reserved only for God, according to the

---

[87] *Wars*, 1.6 (i. 147–8, 151).   [88] *CT*, Exod., 'Shemot', 56*b*, eighth lesson (ii. 19).

statement 'The light dwells with him' (Dan. 2: 22). Other sages, however, interpreted the passage from Genesis as implying that the light is given to the righteous of the world, according to the passage 'Light is sown for the righteous' (Ps. 97: 11). Gersonides reads this rabbinic *midrash* as anticipating his debate with Alexander. He sides with Rabbi Judah bar Simon in denying that humans can attain complete cognitive congruence with the Agent Intellect. Nevertheless, he agrees with the other sages in allowing for a more limited form of epistemic conjunction with the Agent Intellect that enables us to acquire knowledge and become immortal by virtue of this knowledge.[89]

In concluding Book 1 of *Wars* Gersonides reverts to the mishnaic formula 'All Israel has a portion in the world to come' and interprets it in the light of his own philosophical understanding of immortality. How can we say that someone who has not studied and mastered philosophy and the sciences has achieved immortality? Gersonides' rigorous construal of immortality as intellectual perfection would seem to rule out most Israelites. However, let us not despair: as Gersonides is quick to point out, the Torah is a rich source of information concerning the truths that will perfect us. Some will understand these truths more than others; yet in so far as all Israelites believe that God has created the world and that he is provident, to take just two fundamental theoretical truths, they have acquired some at least of the truths requisite for intellectual perfection, and thus immortality. As we shall see in the following chapter, Gersonides believed that the Torah is an extremely valuable guide in leading us to our ultimate destiny and happiness.[90]

[89] *Wars*, 1.12 (i. 222).   [90] Ibid. 1.13 (i. 225).

NINE

The Torah

Do We Need the Torah?

IF OUR ULTIMATE DESTINY is defined in terms of intellectual perfection, which involves knowledge of the sciences and metaphysics, and if such knowledge is attainable through human reason, as Gersonides firmly believed, then one could well wonder why a divine revelation, in particular the Torah, was given. Gersonides' whole enterprise of showing the philosophical provability of the fundamental truths of metaphysics, as they pertain to our true happiness, reveals his complete confidence in the powers of reason. Was Gersonides, then, a 'pure philosopher', one who, like Spinoza, believed in the absolute autonomy and sufficiency of philosophy? Was his adherence to Judaism just a formal, or nominal, expression of familial and ethnic loyalty, which afforded him a safe place in an acknowledged tradition? After all, in the Middle Ages one could not just write 'non-affiliated' on one's identification papers.

These questions resonate with the venerable problem of the contrast and perhaps conflict between human reason and divine revelation. Already in the Talmud some of the sages warn us of keeping our speculations within definite limits, and in particular of refraining from enquiring into deep and lofty questions pertaining to cosmology.[1] The famous story of the four sages who entered Paradise, only one of whom returned whole, is another expression of the rabbinic reluctance to engage in metaphysical and cosmological speculations, which in one case at least led to heresy.[2] Similar reservations were expressed by early Christian thinkers, even those who were philosophically trained. Tertullian, for example, enunciated the loaded question: 'What does Athens have to do with Jerusalem?', implying that philosophy and revelation have nothing to do with each other.[3] A little later Augustine recorded his tortuous journey from Neoplatonic philosophy to Christianity, which began with a confession of his dissatisfaction with philosophy and his ultimate salvation through faith in divine revelation.[4]

---

[1] BT *Ḥag.* 11*b*, 13*a*.　　　　　　　　　[2] BT *Ḥag.* 14*b*.
[3] Tertullian, *Prescription Against the Heretics*, 7.　　　　[4] Augustine, *Confessions*.

However, with the gradual and ultimately successful assimilation of Greek philosophy and science, first in the Arabic-speaking world and then later in the Latin West, it was no longer possible to dismiss philosophy as dangerous, irrelevant, and superfluous. An honest reading of Plato, Aristotle, or Plotinus revealed that the Greeks too were interested in some of the same questions as the theologians and that their answers could not be rejected out of hand. Thus, a dialogue between philosophy and theology ensued, and, in the course of this conversation, the respective boundaries of these disciplines were discussed by many important thinkers in the Christian, Jewish, and Muslim traditions.[5]

One of the earliest Jewish theologians to confront this issue head-on was Sa'adiah Gaon. In the introduction to his treatise *The Book of Beliefs and Opinions*, he asks: 'Inasmuch as all matters of religious belief, as imparted to us by our Master, can be attained by means of research and correct speculation, what was the reason that prompted [divine] wisdom to transmit them to us by way of prophecy . . . and miracles rather than intellectual demonstrations?'[6] Sa'adiah himself was quite confident in his own rational powers and throughout his book engaged in philosophical argument to show that Judaism was a religion wholly compatible with human reason, albeit revealed through prophecy. With respect to many of the fundamental Jewish dogmas Sa'adiah attempted to prove them philosophically or to show that they were not philosophically unacceptable. Divine revelation for Sa'adiah seems to fulfil two main purposes: (1) it is addressed to all Jews, not just the philosophically literate, and (2) it provides supplementary information, especially in legal matters, that helps us apply the general teachings of the Torah to the specific circumstances of everyday life.[7] His younger Muslim contemporary, the philosopher Al-Farabi, reached a similar conclusion with respect to Islam, but formulated the difference between philosophy and religion in a way that was more radical and subversive in its implications for Islam. For Al-Farabi, religion was addressed to the ordinary believer, philosophy to the properly educated believer. In the former the basic truths are conveyed in a language comprehensible to anyone. This language is a poetic rendition or translation of the abstract truths reached through logic in philosophy. Indeed, Al-Farabi dares to say that religion is an imaginative representation of philosophical truths directed to the masses.[8] A third view, radically opposed to the opinions

---

[5] Gilson, *Reason and Revelation.*

[6] Sa'adiah Gaon, *The Book of Beliefs and Opinions,* introductory treatise, ch. 6 (trans. Rosenblatt, 31).   [7] Ibid., treatise 3, ch. 3 (trans Rosenblatt, 145–7).

[8] Al-Farabi, *The Political Regime,* 41.

of Sa'adiah and Al-Farabi, was expressed by Al-Ghazali in Islam and Judah Halevi in Judaism: that philosophy and prophecy are two radically different modes of cognition and that the latter is vastly superior to the former.[9]

Neither Averroes nor Maimonides could accept Al-Ghazali and Halevi's solution, as it severely limited philosophy's role and scope. Each in his own way attempted to assign human reason an essential role in religion without sacrificing either domain. Both believed that revealed Scripture is *au fond* a philosophical book *when properly understood*. And the key to understanding Scripture is philosophy. But not everyone is capable of using this key to open up the true meaning of the holy book. Only those who are capable are entrusted with the key, whose use must be exercised with caution.[10] The philosophically illiterate, including the theologians and jurists, are not to engage in theoretical speculations; like the ordinary believers, they too must accept divine revelation *as written*, except where the literal meaning of the text requires interpretation, which task is given over to the philosophers. In some cases the correct interpretation is revealed to all; in other cases it must be hidden, lest it be misunderstood, and heresy result.[11]

There is, however, an important difference between Gersonides' two philosophical predecessors: whereas Averroes had complete faith in the harmony between Aristotelian philosophy and religion, Maimonides did not. Since, for both thinkers, Aristotle was the philosopher *par excellence*, adherence to his philosophy was the affirmation not only of the legitimacy of philosophy but also of the power of reason to know what is essential for human happiness. So, for example, on the question of whether the world was created or is eternal, Averroes accepted without question Aristotle's thesis that the universe is eternal and believed that it can be proved philosophically. Maimonides did not. And in showing first the incompatibility of Aristotle's eternity thesis with biblical revelation and secondly the invalidity of the arguments in its favour, Maimonides advocated a certain philosophical modesty, implying that human reason has its limits, especially in cosmology and metaphysics.[12] Indeed, for Maimonides, Aristotelian philosophy fails to provide

[9] Al-Ghazali, *Deliverance from Error*, 3.2; Halevi, *Kuzari*, iv. 3–10, 41–5.

[10] Averroes, *The Decisive Treatise*, 302–11; Maimonides, *Guide*, 'Introduction' (trans. Pines, 5–10).

[11] Averroes, *The Decisive Treatise*, 311–16; Maimonides, *Guide*, 'Introduction' (trans. Pines, 5–10).

[12] Maimonides, *Guide*, i. 33–5 (trans. Pines, 70–81), ii. 13 (trans. Pines, 281–2), ii. 15 (trans. Pines, 289–90), ii. 16 (trans. Pines, 293–4). Maimonides' 'real view' on creation and his pre-Kantian doctrine of the limits of human reason are matters of considerable

definitive or even adequate answers to a number of crucial questions, whose solutions need to be revealed through prophecy. Philosophy, then, is not sufficient. Moses was not just Aristotle for the masses; indeed, he is the teacher for the philosopher as well as for the butcher.

Gersonides forged a different path, one that led him to diverge from both his philosophical predecessors. As we have seen, like Maimonides, he could not accept Aristotle and Averroes' doctrine of the eternity of the world. But, unlike Maimonides, Gersonides believed that the beginning of the universe could be philosophically proved and that the doctrine of creation *ex nihilo* is demonstrably false. Nevertheless, in spite of his differences with Aristotle and Averroes, Gersonides had the utmost confidence in the power of human reason and its employment in the attainment of human perfection and felicity. Moreover, he believed that there is no ineluctable conflict between correct philosophy and the Torah. It is just that Aristotle and Averroes failed to supply the correct philosophy. But if, for Gersonides, philosophy retains its power, why was the Torah revealed? Is it, as the Quran was for Al-Farabi, just philosophy made palatable and comprehensible to the masses?

At very beginning of his *Commentary on the Torah*, Gersonides announces that the goal of the Torah is identical with that of philosophy: 'the divine Torah, is a law by means of which its followers can attain perfectly true happiness'.[13] As we saw in the previous chapter, humanity's ultimate happiness consists in the immortality of the intellect, which is achieved through intellectual perfection. The latter is itself attained by means of cognitive achievements in the sciences and in philosophy. In principle human reason employed at the highest level is competent to achieve human happiness. Thus, both the Torah and philosophy lead to the same goal. Yet even though philosophy and the Torah have the same purpose, the Torah has a special role, which is not just a watered-down version of philosophy. The Torah actually, and perhaps even necessarily, serves as a guide (*haysharah*) in our pursuit of the truth. Some at least of the fundamental metaphysical and cosmological truths are extremely difficult, requiring intensive study and preparation. True, reason will ultimately triumph; but along the way there will be many traps and pitfalls, some of which may have disastrous consequences. In his love for mankind God gives us a push towards the right road, which if followed will

current debate. For our purposes, however, we can ignore these controversies. We shall be concerned here only with how Gersonides understood Maimonides. His reading of the *Guide* led him to believe that Maimonides accepted the traditional belief in creation *ex nihilo* but that this belief could not be philosophically demonstrated.

[13] *CT*, Gen., 'Bereshit', 2*a* (i. 1).

reach the desired goal. With regard to the question of creation, for example, the Torah actually begins with this doctrine, difficult and controversial as it is, to assist us in attaining the truth on this matter: 'For this reason the Torah begins with the story of the creation of the world, which is one of the more difficult questions, such that the attainment of truth on it is extremely unlikely for a wise person using reason [alone] unless it is established for him what the Torah *guides* him toward.'[14] The Torah, then, is a guidebook on our journey towards human perfection, one that supplements philosophy by pointing the way, especially when the going gets tough. Perhaps one could reach the same goal by using philosophy alone; but it would be more arduous and dangerous. Nevertheless, in no way should we abandon philosophy; for, as both Averroes and Maimonides taught, philosophy provides us with the true meaning of sacred Scripture. Revelation and reason, then, are two complementary means of achieving the same truth.

Gersonides' use of this concept of divine guidance should not be construed as a confession of philosophical impotence in the face of transcendent, perhaps mysterious, paradoxes or secrets. Unlike Maimonides, Gersonides is not suggesting that some basic truths are essentially hidden from us or that they are philosophically undecidable, in fact or in principle, such as the creation of the world. For Gersonides even the most difficult questions are, at least in principle, amenable to philosophical discussion and proof. Indeed, this was the very motivation behind the composition of *Wars*: to take up the most disputed questions and to resolve them once and for all by means of philosophy. Nor is his book just another Kalam-style philosophical defence of antecedently held theological dogmas, as was Sa'adiah's treatise:

> The reader should not think it is the Torah that has stimulated us to verify what shall be verified in this book, [whereas in reality] the truth itself is something different . . . Accordingly, it is our practice in these discussions to begin with an exhaustive philosophical inquiry into the question at hand, and then to show that what we have philosophically discovered concerning the question is compatible with the Torah.[15]

Even though Gersonides has told us that the Torah serves as a guide, in this passage the autonomy and sufficiency of reason are affirmed.

There seems to be, however, one important exception to this thesis. In his explanation of the Tree of Knowledge of Good and Evil, he remarks that although this tree does afford humanly attainable knowledge of moral

---

[14]	*CT*, Gen., 'Bereshit', 9*a*–*b* (i. 20), my emphasis.
[15]	*Wars*, 'Introductory Remarks' (i. 91–8).

concepts, such information is not the primary knowledge that God really intended humanity to have.[16] Human perfection lies elsewhere, as we saw in the previous chapter. Here Gersonides seems to be echoing Maimonides' distinction between moral cognition and the theoretical knowledge found in mathematics, the sciences, and to a limited extent in metaphysics.[17] The latter is signified by the Tree of Life. It is this latter knowledge that affords us immortality. A little later Gersonides expands upon this theme. He goes on to say that moral concepts suffer from their intrinsic a posteriori status, their lack of specificity, and a surfeit of diversity.[18]

In the first place, the moral domain is one of variety and change; space, time, and circumstances are all too relevant in moral reasoning and decision-making. Even if one can rationally construct useful moral principles, they could not be necessary a priori truths having the same validity as the principles of mathematics and of the natural sciences, a point that Aristotle himself admitted:

We must be content in speaking of such subjects and premises [that is, ethics and politics] to indicate the truth roughly and in outline, and in speaking about things which are only for the most part true and with premises of the same kind to reach conclusions that are no better . . . for it is the mark of an educated man to look for precision in each class of things just so far as the subject admits.[19]

Gersonides echoes this general principle: 'The philosophers have already affirmed that this subject [moral and political philosophy] doesn't allow for complete confirmation; rather, in it commonly held premises [*hakdamot mefursamot*] are in evidence. These premises allow for contraries, as is explained in [Aristotle's] *Topics*.'[20] Commonly held propositions in Aristotelian logic are statements whose contradictories are logically possible. Hence an argument based upon them is not strictly demonstrative; their conclusions are not necessarily true, and thus the propositions of such a science are only contingently true. Gersonides thus clearly subordinates moral philosophy to the theoretical sciences. Despite its importance as a preliminary to intellectual perfection, it cannot be the ultimate goal of our

---

[16] *CT*, 'Introduction', 2*a*–*b* (i. 1–2); Gen., 'Bereshit', 14*d* (i. 52).

[17] Maimonides, *Guide*, i. 2 (trans. Pines, 23–6); Gersonides, *Commentary on the Five Scrolls*, Eccles., 25*d*–26*a*.

[18] *CT*, 'Introduction', 2*a*–*b* (i. 1–2); Gen., 'Bereshit', 16*c* (i. 65–6); *Commentary on the Five Scrolls*, Eccles., 25*a*–*b*.   [19] Aristotle, *Nicomachean Ethics*, 1.3.1094*b*19–27.

[20] Gersonides, *Commentary on the Five Scrolls*, Eccles., 25*a*. Gersonides seems to be referring to Aristotle's *Topics*, 1.1.100*b*22–3.

intellectual efforts, since moral principles do not possess the logical weight and epistemic value exhibited in mathematics and the sciences. Indeed, the reason why King Solomon entitled his book *Kohelet* (Ecclesiastes) is that this word derives from the root *khl* which means 'gather'. The first thing that one does in an enquiry dealing with commonly held opinions about a subject is to gather all the available positions about the topic and then proceed to analyse them, ultimately arriving at propositions that seem to be the most probable or reasonable. This is what takes place in moral and political philosophy.

Another problem with moral philosophy is its intrinsic generality or abstractness.[21] Even if everyone agrees that murder is wrong, people disagree about what kinds of killing constitute murder. Is killing murder if done in war? Is killing in self-defence murder? Similar questions can be asked regarding other moral rules. For example, suppose we all agree that charity is a moral virtue. How much should I give to a specific fund or person? After all, I have children or grandchildren to consider. Moreover, to whom should I give my money? I cannot give to all who ask me. Here the Torah, especially in its subsequent development and interpretation, is most helpful. It provides guidance in the specifics of charity-giving. Consider the biblical laws governing the harvesting of one's fields. When harvesting one has to a leave a corner for the poor; when loading the wagons with the harvest, sheaves or clusters that fall are to be left for the poor (Lev. 19: 9–10, 23: 22; Deut. 24: 19–21). From these laws we can infer by means of specific principles of legal reasoning other laws that are applicable to other kinds of charity-giving.

Unlike mathematics and the natural sciences, moral and political principles are various and diverse. Whereas the laws of physics pretty much command the assent of all competent scientists, opinions about morals often contradict each other. Since human beings are material entities composed of diverse physical elements in different proportions, their judgements vary. What I consider to be good, someone else judges to be bad. Commenting upon Proverbs 29: 18, 'Where there is no prophecy, the people are unrestrained', Gersonides remarks: 'Because of the differences in their biological mixtures [of elements] men differ considerably in their [mental] characteristics. As a result their social life is disordered.' Here Gersonides claims that human nature is such that we make moral and political judgements primarily on the basis of our emotions, which are rooted in our individual biological make-up. There is therefore an ineluctable diversity in our moral beliefs. Moral

---

[21] *CT*, 'Introduction', 2*a*–*b* (i. 1–2); Touati, *La Pensée philosophique de Gersonide*, 514.

relativism seems to be a necessary feature of human existence. However, God is good, and, knowing what human nature is like and having given human beings the choice to become 'a little lower than the angels' (Ps. 8: 5 (Eng.), 8: 6 (Heb.)), he also sends prophets to them to teach the moral and political rules whereby they can live in peace with each other: 'Prophecy guides [men] in the acquisition of morals and the right leadership, both in the house and in the social order. There is no way to achieve the [right] moral guidance in the political order without prophecy.'[22] The Torah therefore eliminates the inevitable conflicts that arise in moral and political discourse and practice. It unites the variety of individuals into one community by revealing a specific and uniform set of moral and legal principles.

Gersonides' defence of the necessity of a divine law seems to be similar to the claim of those who argue for the need and primacy of an authoritative law imposed by some external law-giver, divine or human. Such a law would be final in the sense that there would be no other criterion or authority that acts as its rationale or judge. It would appear that Gersonides is taking up the position defended by the naive Euthyphro in Plato's dialogue of that title, or one similar to the concept of absolute sovereignty later advocated by Hobbes in *Leviathan*. As if to ward off such a suggestion, Gersonides frequently enunciates a theme that pervades his biblical commentaries: the Torah is not an alien law imposed upon us by an arbitrary law-giver. Rather, the Torah by its very nature commands the respect and obedience of its followers. In his explanation of a passage wherein the Israelites are commanded to obey the laws of the Torah, Gersonides comments: 'Do not think that the words of my laws, which I command you, are burdensome and govern you [resulting in your] humiliation and loss of respect. [On the contrary], I shall not burden you with harsh servitude; but I shall make you free and honored . . . and not like other nations who are corrupted by despicable actions.'[23] Gersonides is insistent that the Torah is not a law that compels its subjects; just the contrary, it makes its followers free in the sense that its precepts liberate them from laws that violate sound morality and are contrary to human nature: 'The Torah is not a law that makes compliance compulsory; but it is a law that by its very nature is utterly beautiful and perfect, so that it is proper for man to follow it of his own accord.'[24]

In other passages he describes the laws of the Torah as inherently 'wise', and as such eliciting compliance by their very rationality. In commenting on

---

[22] Gersonides, *Commentary on Proverbs*, 29: 18.
[23] *CT*, Exod., 'Yitro', 74*b* (ii. 139).   [24] *CT*, Exod., 'Ki tisa', 113*c–d* (ii. 428).

Deuteronomy 4: 6, 'You shall observe and do [the commandments], for they are your wisdom and your understanding in the eyes of the nations, who upon hearing all these laws will say, "Indeed, this is a wise and understanding people"', Gersonides remarks:

In general, our Torah is unique among the laws of the other nations; for our Torah does not contain anything that equity and reason do not decree. Therefore, our divine law attracts man by its very nature so that they follow it. However, the laws of the other nations are not like this; for they are not ordered according to equity and wisdom. They are laws foreign to human nature and men follow them under compulsion out of fear . . . not because of the [laws'] own nature.[25]

Here Gersonides may be alluding to the Christian practice and praise of celibacy and virginity, as well as extreme exculpatory practices such as self-flagellation and morbid asceticism found in some Christian and Muslim sects.[26] Later in this chapter we shall see how Gersonides illustrates the inherent rationality of the commandments of the Torah.

These comments seem to suggest that, even though the Torah is a divine law revealed to humanity, it is also 'natural' in the sense that its very rationality commands respect and compliance. According to some medieval philosophers and theologians, natural law is a set of moral principles based on reason, and hence naturally knowable to humanity; yet, although it is consistent with divine law, it is independent of revelation.[27] This is not, however, Gersonides' position. If the Torah is a natural law, why was it revealed? As we have seen, the Torah was revealed because there was a need for it. Here Gersonides appeals to an analogy with the crafts to illustrate his contention that the divine law perfects nature:

Now, the Torah is not like a natural phenomenon; rather it perfects us, just as many crafts administer to and perfect nature, such as agriculture and other similar crafts. And so it is with the Torah. Man has the natural capacity to attain human perfection, which [capacity] is actualized by means of the divine law in those who choose to follow it perfectly, just as the crafts that minister to nature are voluntary.[28]

Even the best ethical system based upon reason suffers from shortcomings, as we have seen; it needs to be supplemented with additional information to remedy these defects. It is true that, in so far as humans are endowed with reason and choice, they are essentially moral agents; unlike the rest of the

---

[25] *CT*, Deut., 'Va'ethanan', 210*b* (v. 30).

[26] *CT*, Deut., 'Ekev', 216*b*, lesson 17 (v. 80), 'Re'eh', 219*a* (v. 102), 220a, lesson 1 (v. 112–13).   [27] Aquinas, *Summa Theologiae*, I q. 91 art. 2, I q. 94.

[28] *CT*, Lev., 'Emor', 171*a* (iii. 356).

animal world, humans have rights and responsibilities, which they have the natural potential to fulfil. But this natural capacity by itself cannot be easily realized or perfected; it requires some catalytic agent to actualize and bring it to perfection. Here the Torah is like the Agent Intellect in that it stimulates and assists us in the cognitive activities that are natural to us and enable us to achieve our true perfection. To use a typical Gersonidean expression, from one point of view the Torah is not natural, since it is divine and is revealed miraculously through one prophet, Moses; yet from another aspect, the Torah is not unnatural, since there is nothing in it that goes against sound reason and our own human nature. As it is said, 'its ways are ways of pleasantness' (Prov. 3: 17).[29]

Does this mean that Gersonides has no moral theory, as some have claimed?[30] True, he does not advocate, as did David Hume and J. S. Mill, a utilitarian moral theory, although many of his moral lessons are utilitarian in nature. Nor did he attempt to formulate and defend, as Immanuel Kant did, a general moral law, or imperative, although some of his moral maxims are expressed in categorical terms. Nevertheless, his argument for the ethical and political necessity of divine revelation can be considered an *ethical meta-theory*: a theory about the general nature of moral beliefs and principles, their logical status and their epistemological limits. In the terminology of current moral theory, his position seems close to what is called 'the divine command theory'.[31] But unlike those versions of this theory wherein moral imperatives depend solely upon divine will, and hence are not subject to any further appeal or independent criteria, Gersonides insists upon the inherent wisdom and rationality of these imperatives. Whereas the strict advocate of the divine command theory (for example, Euthyphro) holds that whatever the gods command is by definition right and good, Gersonides maintains that whatever God commands is right and good because God is himself just and good. This is why Abraham could challenge God's willingness to destroy all of Sodom and Gomorrah; for there might be some righteous people there, and it would not be just for them to be punished along with the sinners.

---

[29] Touati, *La Pensée philosophique de Gersonide*, 481. Several modern scholars have debated whether or not Judaism recognizes a natural law. See Schwarzschild, 'Do Noachites Have to Believe in Revelation?'; Bleich, 'Judaism and Natural Law', 11; Fox, 'Maimonides and Aquinas on Natural Law' (Heb.); Melamed, 'The Law of Nature in Jewish Political Thought' (Heb.).

[30] Touati, *La Pensée philosophique de Gersonide*, 517; id., 'Théorie et praxis'.

[31] Quinn, 'Moral Obligation'; Rachels, 'God and Goodness'.

How Should We Read the Bible?

The Torah is obviously a text that needs to be read and studied. How do we go about doing this? It is not a simple matter. For one thing Scripture comprises many books of different literary genres and styles. One cannot read the book of Genesis as one reads the book of Job. In these diverse books different linguistic modes are employed: prose, poetry, laws, and many others. In some cases it is not easy to know whether or not a passage is to be construed literally or metaphorically. Moreover, as Maimonides has insisted, much of biblical language is equivocal, 'crying out for interpretation'. But how far can we take our interpretations? Are there limits to the exegetical project?

Throughout Jewish biblical study there have been different exegetical styles. One of the earliest is the rabbinic aggadic midrash, imaginative expansions of biblical narratives, which often fill in the details or supply the context for what the biblical text relates sparsely. Thus, according to the sages, when Abraham leaves his father Terah in Haran at God's command, he was really fleeing Terah, as he had destroyed his father's idols.[32] This was the method favoured by Rabbi Solomon ben Isaac of Troyes (Rashi, 1040–1105), the most widely studied Jewish commentator. A very different hermeneutical mode was adopted by another medieval Jewish scholar, Abraham ibn Ezra (1089–1164), who preferred and practised a more philological approach to the biblical text. Although occasionally he allowed himself some exegetical liberty, for the most part Ibn Ezra attempted to get to the exact meaning of the word or phrase and generally avoided rabbinic midrash.

In the opening remarks of his *Commentary on the Torah*, Gersonides makes plain his refusal to employ aggadic midrash in his biblical commentaries, a principle that he adheres to quite consistently: 'We have not consented to bring in this commentary what our revered rabbis have said in their explanations by means of *derash*. Even if they are good in their own right, they are not explanations of the verses of the Torah . . . We intend, however, to explain the words of the Torah according to their own meanings.'[33] Gersonides concedes that rabbinic *midrash* has its merits as edifying discourse and moral instruction; but it does not reveal the real meaning of the biblical text. Nor does the strict philological method of Ibn Ezra succeed in conveying this meaning, despite its attempt to stick to the literal connotation of the words. Although Gersonides himself usually begins his commentaries with an

---

[32] *Genesis Rabbah* 38: 13.   [33] *CT*, Gen., 'Bereshit', 2c (i. 3).

explanation of the key words or phrases and then proceeds to give a running commentary on the narrative, he maintains that the meaning of the word is really constituted by the overall meaning of the section of the chapter in which it appears. The unit of meaning is not the single word or phrase but the conceptual context in which it is situated. In his introduction to his *Commentary on Job*, Gersonides formulates this hermeneutical principle as follows:

We have not found among our predecessors . . . anyone who has explained the intention [or meaning], of the [book]; rather, their goal was to explain the meaning of the words, and hence they were far from the right [path] in [their] commentary. It is proper for a commentator to comment upon the words according to the contextual meanings intended by the authors, [especially] since the words are ambiguous . . . And if [the commentator] does not first understand the meaning of the conceptual context, he will not be able to explain the meanings of the words, except accidentally.[34]

Ibn Ezra would seem to be a good example of the philological commentator criticized in this passage. Although Gersonides does not mention anyone in particular among his predecessors, whom he has 'studied in his youth', he does say that their strict philological method has hindered his comprehension of the book. It was only after some time that he finally realized that to understand individual words he would have to get a grip on the whole meaning of the book or specific chapters thereof.[35]

But if neither the midrashic nor the strict philological methods are appropriate, how is one to understand the biblical text? As early as Philo of Alexandria a different interpretative mode emerged—the philosophical. The Torah is read as a philosophical book, full of philosophical teachings that constitute the real meaning of the text. To get at this teaching we often have to read the text as an allegory. Philo employed this method in his writings, most of which were commentaries on various books or sections of the Bible.[36] Maimonides also assumed that the Torah speaks in different styles and is addressed to different audiences, one of which is the philosophically adept reader who can decipher the text to penetrate its hidden meanings.

---

[34] Gersonides, *Commentary on Job*, 'Introduction' (trans. Lassen, 4–5).

[35] Eisen, *The Book of Job in Medieval Jewish Philosophy*, 147–8. Gersonides' biblical hermeneutics are discussed by Touati ('Les Idées philosophiques', 337–40), and Feldman (appendix to *The Wars of the Lord*, ii. 230–38); see also Klein-Braslavy, 'Les Commentaires bibliques'; Sirat, 'La Méthode d'exégèse'; Freudenthal, 'Gersonide, génie solitaire'.

[36] Philo, *Allegorical Interpretation*, 1–3.

Gersonides too can be placed in this school of philosophical biblical exegesis. But his philosophical hermeneutics differ from those of Philo, of whose very existence he and medieval Jewry were ignorant, and Maimonides.

Whereas Philo and Maimonides could read a biblical book or narrative as an extended allegory where the literal meaning is relegated to the background or completely ignored, for the most part Gersonides avoids this approach. In several places in his biblical commentaries he explicitly rejects the attempt to allegorize certain passages, especially those that seem, at least to some readers, to beg for a non-literal interpretation. Consider, for example, the begetting of Cain and Abel by Adam and Eve: 'In the case of Eve, there is no reason that requires [that we interpret the story] as an allegory . . . Nor should what follows concerning her giving birth to Cain and Abel be understood allegorically.'[37] Contrary to Philo and the medieval Jewish allegorists, including Maimonides, whom Gersonides singles out here, Gersonides takes the story of Adam and Eve's producing children as historical fact, although other parts of the story he does not, as we shall see. Another example is the book of Job. Unlike some of the sages and perhaps Maimonides, Gersonides believes in the factuality of the story: Job was a real person and he actually suffered the evils that befell him.[38]

It will be useful here to examine more precisely the term 'allegory'. Gersonides uses two terms in this context—*mashal* and *ḥikuy*—for the most part interchangeably.[39] In some of their uses these terms are equivalent to the word 'metaphor', as in Deuteronomy 4: 24, 'God is a devouring fire'. Obviously, God is not fire; but in certain contexts the biblical writer believed it useful to depict God in this way. This is not the use that is especially relevant here, however, since we are concerned with prose narratives that are not obviously metaphorical, yet must be construed, at least in part, non-literally. As we have just seen, some parts of the Garden of Eden story are to be taken as historical fact, but others are not. The latter have some non-literal meaning that annuls or replaces the surface, or plain, meaning. For example, snakes cannot speak, so we have to understand this part of the narrative differently. For Gersonides, the snake is a 'symbolic representation' of the seductive powers of the imagination, which frequently leads us not only into empirical error but also into moral sin.[40]

---

[37] *CT*, Gen., 'Bereshit', 16*c–d* (i. 66).
[38] BT *BB* 15*a*; Maimonides, *Guide*, iii. 22 (trans. Pines, 486); Gersonides, *Commentary on Job*, 'Introduction', 1 (trans. Lassen, 6–7). [39] *Wars*, 2.6 (ii. 54–6).
[40] *CT*, Gen., 'Bereshit', 14*d* (i. 52), 15*d* (i. 56–7), 16*c* (i. 65–6).

However, there is one book that Gersonides believes must be read allegorically, the Song of Songs. Indeed, the allegory that he seems to be imposing on the text is for him *the real meaning*. Unlike other classical commentators, Jewish and Christian, Gersonides does not recognize a level of significance in this book that is prior to and independent of its philosophical meaning. In this instance the philosophical understanding of the text is the *peshat*, or the plain meaning, even though it is difficult and hence cannot be divulged to the masses.[41]

In some cases, however, the biblical text is so rich that in addition to its plain or literal meaning it also possesses an allegorical meaning that does not replace the former but enhances it. Consider, for example, Jacob's dream of a ladder with angels going up and down it (Gen. 28: 10–16). A literal reading of the passage does not present any deep problems. We all have dreams. Moreover, the text itself reveals the plain meaning of the dream: God tells Jacob that he and his progeny will inherit the land of Canaan. Nevertheless, this is not all that the story signifies. What is the significance of the ladder and the angels? They do not seem to have any role in the dream. According to Gersonides, in addition to revealing to Jacob the Israelite inheritance of the land of Canaan, the dream instructed Jacob, and us as well, that the universe has an ordered and hierarchical structure. The rungs of the ladder represent the various levels of reality in descending order. On the highest rung stands God; the lower rungs, representing the lower levels of reality, descend, or emanate, from God. Each such level or rung is occupied by angels, that is, the separate forms, or intelligences. Looking at the ladder in its upward direction we recognize that God is the first form, as well as the first efficient cause of all the lower forms. In short, the dream teaches Jacob something about the cosmological structure of existence as well as about the future of his family.[42]

Accordingly, not everything we read in the Torah should be taken just literally; nor should we be too quick to dismiss the plain meaning and let our imagination run riot. The crucial question is: do we have a criterion whereby we can tell that a passage must be understood non-literally? As the example of the snake illustrates, we have to read that story in the light of what we know from biology and our ordinary experience of snakes. As we have already indicated, the Torah does not command us to believe in the

---

[41] Gersonides, *Commentary on the Five Scrolls*, S. of S., 'Introduction'; see Kellner's introduction to his translation of Gersonides' *Commentary on the Song of Songs*.

[42] *CT*, Gen., 'Vayetse', 36*d* (i. 178).

irrational. Gersonides' analysis of miracles shows that he was most reluctant to resort to miraculous interventions, and when the latter do occur, they happen through natural causes that involve the least disturbance to the ordinary course of nature. In the story of the snake and elsewhere in the Bible we have to supply the interpretation of the text that makes the most sense in the light of both reason and Scripture. A faithful reader of the Torah does not have to be a gullible fool. Like Sa'adiah Gaon and Maimonides, Gersonides adheres to the literal meaning of the text unless that meaning violates what science and philosophy have taught.[43]

Yet there is a fundamental difference between Maimonides' and Gersonides' uses of non-literal interpretations. It is not just that the former was more liberal in his employment of allegorical exegesis; rather, it is Maimonides' reluctance to reveal such readings to the masses that contrasts with Gersonides' willingness to share his understandings with the general public. For Maimonides, both the Bible and the *Guide* are written in such a way that their real meaning can be understood by some but not by others. Gersonides, however, is not, with the exception of his comments on the Song of Songs, an esotericist. His biblical commentaries are replete with philosophical and scientific teachings that he believes are fundamental and essential for the attainment of human perfection, and hence need to be divulged to all. In earlier chapters of this volume Gersonides' biblical commentaries have been employed not only to illustrate how, in his understanding, the Torah and true philosophy are consistent with each other, but also to show how the former often guides us in learning what the latter teaches. Indeed, we need guidance from the Torah right at the outset of our journey towards human perfection; for in some cases the Torah teaches things, especially in the sciences and metaphysics, that are extremely difficult to understand even with special preparation and education. In his tripartite division of the teachings of the Torah into commandments, moral and political maxims, and 'the science of existent things', the third class, 'ideas' (*de'ot*), are the scientific and philosophical truths about the nature of reality, which need to be taught to everyone.[44] Let us consider an example of how the Torah provides explicit guidance in the attainment of knowledge of such truths.

In part 2 of Book 6 of *Wars*, Gersonides' stated purpose is to show that not only are his philosophical and scientific theories in part 1 consistent with the Torah, but that the latter actually teaches the former. Modelled to some

---

[43] *CT*, 'Introduction', 2*c* (i. 3); Sa'adiah Gaon, *The Book of Beliefs and Opinions*, treatise 7, ch. 2 (trans. Rosenblatt, 265–6); Maimonides, *Guide*, ii. 25 (trans. Pines, 327–30).

[44] *CT*, Gen., 'Introduction', 2*b* (i. 2).

extent on Maimonides' own attempt to interpret Genesis 1 in the light of his preceding philosophical discussion of creation,[45] Gersonides' philosophical exegesis of the biblical story of creation offers the reader an 'up-to-date', scientific understanding that meets the standards of both reason and faith. In this undertaking Gersonides refuses to take the easy road later followed by those, such as Galileo, who dismissed the scientific content of the opening chapter of the Bible.[46] Since the Torah is our guide towards human perfection and happiness, it has to teach us the important truths about the universe, especially how and why it came into being. For from these truths about nature we come to know truths about God and the 'secrets of existence'.[47]

One problem that has often puzzled readers of the biblical account of creation is the notion of the 'six days of creation'. Is this to be understood literally as involving six temporal acts or intervals? Are these distinct and discrete acts of making? If so, it seems that God is subject to change and time. The sages faced these questions and came up with the thesis that everything was created at once, a cosmological claim seconded by Maimonides.[48] But if this so, why describe the creative act as taking place in 'six days', a phrase that connotes temporal priority? For both Maimonides and Gersonides the sequence of days does not imply any temporal 'before' and 'after'. The priority here is non-temporal.[49] As Aristotle had shown, the notions of priority and of causality have several meanings. Although some types of priority imply the temporal priority of the cause over its effect, not all notions of priority and causality involve temporality. Consider, for example, the relationship between the premises of a valid argument and its conclusion: the premises are prior to the conclusion in the sense that they cause, or produce, the conclusion; yet there is no temporal relation between the premises and the conclusion. This is also true of some other types of causal relationships where the cause is not temporally prior to the effect, but is necessary and sufficient for the existence of the effect, as is the case, according to Aristotle and Gersonides, with the heavenly bodies and their movers.[50]

Light was created on the first day (Gen. 1: 4). Since the Torah begins the story of creation by having us imagine a pre-existent scene of darkness, it is most reasonable for the first act to be the production of light. With the

---

[45] Maimonides, *Guide*, ii. 30 (trans. Pines, 348–59).
[46] Galileo, 'Letter to the Grand Duchess Christina'.
[47] *CT*, Gen., 'Introduction', 2*a*–*b* (i. 1-2).
[48] BT Ḥag. 12*a*; Maimonides, *Guide*, ii. 30 (trans. Pines, 350).
[49] *Wars*, 6.2.2 (iii. 431), 6.2.8 (iii. 446–7); *CT*, Gen., 'Bereshit', 9*b* (i. 21).
[50] Aristotle, *Metaphysics*, 5.1–2, esp. 1013*a*32–5.

creation of light we are now able to recognize the emergence of the natural world from its initial state of confusion and obscurity. But for Gersonides there is more to the story than this simple transition from darkness to light. In the first place, and most importantly, the light referred to here is not the physical phenomenon that enables us to see. In fact, it is not physical at all. Here the light refers to the domain of the separate intellects, of which some are the movers of the heavenly bodies. Since as their movers and causes they are prior to them, these intellects are created first. Lest this interpretation throw his readers into a state of confusion, Gersonides introduces this idea gradually by first saying that these creatures are the angels, entities with which his readers were already familiar: ' "Let there be light". This light is the world of the angels, which is the true light . . . This light is not the visible light. It is according to the Rabbis the light of the intellect.'[51] When a little later Gersonides describes the creation of the heavenly bodies, he explicitly identifies the world of the angels with the world of the separate intellects:

Behold, God put the creation of the spheres at the second level of generation and did not include them with the creation of the angels; for the latter are the form for the former, indicating that these forms, i.e., the separate intellects, do not inhere in them like the material forms inhere in matter. Rather, their forms are separate [from matter]. Hence, the Torah attributes their creation to the first day, whereas the creation of the spheres is ascribed to the second day.[52]

Gersonides introduces his cosmological theory into the opening of his biblical commentary, believing that his readers will not be surprised, puzzled, or offended. He is confident that his readers are already familiar with this idea, since he finds it alluded to in Daniel 2: 22 and adumbrated in a rabbinic debate in *Midrash Psalms* on Psalm 27. Daniel 2: 22 reads: 'The light is with him.' Since God is an incorporeal substance, the light referred to here cannot be corporeal light; it must be the world of the separate intellects. This reading is confirmed, Gersonides believes, by the rabbinic discussion of light, which he used in his discussion of conjunction with the Agent Intellect. The sages understood the opening phrase of Psalm 27, 'The Lord is my light and salvation', as referring to the world of the intellect, access to which, if access is possible, is reserved only for the righteous, who by virtue of their intellectual perfection have a kind of epistemological, but not ontological, conjunction with the Agent Intellect, as we saw in the previous chapter. So on both scientific and textual grounds Gersonides feels entitled to

[51] *Wars*, 6.2.5 (iii. 438–9); *CT*, Gen., 'Bereshit', 10*a* (i. 26).
[52] *CT*, Gen., 'Bereshit', 10*c–d* (i. 27).

read the story of the creation of light as describing the creation of the angels, or separate intellects.[53]

Gersonides' interpretation of the first day of creation as the creation of the angels has the merit not only of anticipating and answering a question that a percipient reader of Genesis 1 would be likely to raise—'When were the angels created?', an event not mentioned in the biblical text—but also of resolving a rabbinic debate on this question. The sages were puzzled by the fact that Genesis does not mention the creation of the angels. A discussion ensued wherein some sages opted for the second day, whereas others chose the fifth day.[54] Gersonides maintains that they were created first, not first in time, but prior in causality and substance. In their role as movers of the spheres or as the agent of cognition and prophecy, the angels, or separate intellects, are next to God in their level of substantiality and causality. Without them the heavenly bodies do not move; without the Agent Intellect not only is there no human cognition and prophecy, there is also no generation of living things on earth. We need to be told, then, at the very outset of our religious and philosophical education that there are such creatures. This is the meaning of 'day one'.[55]

Here too a feature of Platonic cosmology can be seen in Gersonides' understanding of the first day of creation. In *Timaeus* 28*a*—29*b*, Plato suggested that the divine craftsman created the physical world according to a plan, a 'paradigm', presumably the world of the forms, which, like the craftsman, is eternal. Nevertheless, in Book 6 of the *Republic*, Plato advances the theory that the forms are subordinate to a 'super-form', the form of the Good, which is in some sense the cause of the other forms.[56] This inconsistency, or at least ambiguity, was to vex the later Platonists, who attempted in various ways to reconcile Plato's statements concerning the cosmological status of the paradigm or forms.[57] Philo, for example, developed his theory of the Logos, one aspect of which captured Plato's notion of the paradigm. In creating the world God used the Logos as his blueprint. The physical world, as Plato suggested, is a copy of the immaterial Logos. However, unlike Plato, Philo is quite explicit in claiming that the Logos is itself created; it is not on the same ontological level as is the divine creator. The paradigm is then an effect of God, its cause.[58] Thus, the path was prepared for Plotinus to

---

[53] *Midrash Psalms*, Ps. 27; *Wars*, 1.12 (i. 222); *CT*, Gen., 'Bereshit', 9*d*–10*a* (i. 26).

[54] *Genesis Rabbah* 1: 3, 3: 8; Moore, *Judaism*, i, ch. 3; Ginzberg, *Legends of the Jews*, v. 20–1 n. 61.　　　　[55] *Wars*, 6.2.5 (iii. 438–9); *CT*, Gen., 'Bereshit', 9*d*–10*a* (i. 26).

[56] Plato, *Republic*, 6.505a–509a.　　　　[57] Dillon, *The Middle Platonists*, 155–60.

[58] Philo, *On the Creation of the World*, 4.16–7.29; id., *On the Cherubim*, 35.127.

develop his theory of the three hypostases, the fundamental ontological units that, for him, define reality: the One, Nous or Intellect, and Soul.[59] Nous corresponds to Philo's Logos: it too is the paradigm, the world of the forms.[60] Yet, like Philo's Logos, Nous is secondary to the One, its source. In Plotinus' language it 'flows', or emanates, from the One, a notion that was quite influential in medieval philosophy.[61] It turns out then that although Gersonides' philosophical framework is basically Aristotelian, his understanding of the cosmological role of the Agent Intellect is Platonic. Like Philo's Logos and Plotinus' Intellect it too is the paradigm according to which the material world is fashioned. And like Philo's Logos and Plotinus' Nous it too is ontologically derivative from the ultimate source of reality, God or the One.[62] Gersonides' reading, then, of 'day one' of creation can be seen as a variation on this Platonic theme.

The Commandments

The Torah is also a book of law, containing specific commandments (*mitsvot*) that constitute the foundation stones of Jewish religious practice. Unlike Maimonides, Gersonides did not devote himself to composing a detailed commentary on the Mishnah or to compiling a comprehensive code of Jewish law. In fact, hardly any legal works of his have come down to us. In his comments on Deuteronomy, he mentions a commentary that he wrote on the Babylonian Talmud tractate *Berakhot*, which is, however, not extant; two legal responsa are also attributable to him.[63] From this slender list one could easily and reasonably conclude that law was not a major concern for Gersonides. This would be a most fallacious conclusion. Even a cursory look at the legal portions of his *Commentary on the Torah* clearly reveals a deep mastery of rabbinic literature and a sophisticated juridical mind. Gersonides is not just content to discuss biblical laws as particular commandments; he is interested in showing how these precepts can be derived directly from the biblical text according to a new set of juridical hermeneutical principles he had composed. Moreover, whenever he is about to discuss a group of commandments concerned with a specific legal topic, he attempts to reduce these rules to a small set of 'roots' (*shorashim*), fundamental legal principles that

---

[59] Plotinus, *Enneads*, 5.1.　　　　　　　　　　　　　　　[60] Ibid. 3.2.1–2, 5.9.6.

[61] Ibid. 5.1.5–8, 5.4.1–2; Rist, *Plotinus*, ch. 6; Maimonides, *Guide*, ii. 12 (trans. Pines, 279–80).

[62] Feldman, 'Platonic Themes in Gersonides' Doctrine of the Agent Intellect'.

[63] *CT*, Deut., 'Devarim', 207*b* (v. 10); Touati, *La Pensée philosophique de Gersonide*, 60–1.

are the bases of these commandments. This aspect of his scholarship is beyond the scope of this book and the powers of its author. Nevertheless, it is a subject that sorely needs to be studied.[64] My concern will be instead with the philosophical or theological dimensions that Gersonides finds in the commandments.

Here again Gersonides finds himself in the tradition of Philo and Maimonides, both of whom were very concerned to rationalize the commandments, especially those that seem to be most resistant to rationalization. Already in rabbinic literature it was recognized that many biblical laws have no apparent reason; they are just statutes (*ḥukim*) that are to be followed simply because God has commanded them. If they have some reason or purpose, it eludes our understanding; nevertheless, they are still obligatory. In Kalam literature, Jewish and Muslim, a distinction was made between 'rational commandments' and 'commandments by way of revelation': the former are such that natural reason would dictate them to us, whereas the latter are binding only because God revealed them.[65] Like Maimonides, Gersonides has no use for this latter distinction; indeed, he does not even acknowledge it.[66] All the commandments have a reason or purpose; they are not the capricious whims of an arbitrary law-giver. After all, God is wise and good, and his Torah is wise, making its devotees wise as well.

Now there are several ways one could rationalize the commandments, especially the *ḥukim*. One could show that a specific ritual law is rational by pointing to the pragmatic advantages of its observance. Let us call this the 'first-order' meaning of the precept. In the face of Greek and Roman criticism of the sabbath as a type of laziness or economic disutility, one could say that, on the contrary, the sabbath affords rest from physical labour and thus enables workers to perform their work more efficiently.[67] In the case of the dietary laws, Maimonides pointed to their hygienic benefits.[68] Another method of demonstrating the value of the *ḥukim* would be to indicate some 'second-order' meaning that the law implies. In addition to its practical, or first-order, purpose, the precept in question hints at or symbolizes some

---

[64] Touati, *La Pensée philosophique de Gersonide*, 506–13.

[65] Sa'adiah Gaon, *The Book of Beliefs and Opinions*, treatise 3, chs. 1–2 (trans. Rosenblatt, 138–45). Sa'adiah himself attempts to rationalize some of the *ḥukim*.

[66] Maimonides, *Guide*, iii. 26 (trans. Pines, 506–7); Touati, *La Pensée philosophique de Gersonide*, 492–3.

[67] Tacitus, *Histories*, 5.4; Sa'adiah Gaon, *The Book of Beliefs and Opinions*, treatise 3, ch. 2 (trans. Rosenblatt, 143); Maimonides, *Guide*, iii. 43 (trans. Pines, 570).

[68] Maimonides, *Guide*, iii. 48 (trans. Pines, 598–9).

higher meaning. The sabbath, for example, also teaches us about the creation of the world and divine providence. Some laws may have no practical purpose at all; for example, the particular details involved in building the Tabernacle. Whereas the purpose of the Tabernacle is stated explicitly, its particular arrangement and decoration seem to be arbitrary. Maimonides himself did not explain some of these items, explicitly admitting that he did not know the reason for the table of the shewbread.[69] But if a particular commandment lacks a first-order, or practical, significance, it does not preclude its having a second-order meaning. Gersonides' explanation of the architecture of the Tabernacle is indicative of how he finds in a seemingly unimportant and arbitrary decorative detail some significance of deep philosophical import.

Gersonides recognizes in all the rules for building the Tabernacle a mini-lesson in metaphysics. The main theme in this lesson is a principle that is necessary for the achievement of human happiness: the primacy of form over matter.

We lay down here a general premise that in some sense encompasses all the things concerning the Holy Sanctuary. It is well-known to anyone familiar with the doctrine of the ancient [philosophers], according to what Aristotle reports, that in the days of Moses (May he rest in peace!) philosophy was most imperfect, such that they were ignorant of all the [types of] causes, except the material cause; they were especially ignorant of the formal cause, and this accounted for their not recognizing the efficient and telic causes . . . [Ultimately] this led to the ignorance of the wisdom in existent things, the knowledge of which is the happiness of the soul.[70]

Gersonides singles out Epicurus as the primary guilty party. In denying that the natural world exhibits any formal and teleological order, the materialist eventually rejects its having any ultimate efficient cause. As we saw in Gersonides' theory of creation, knowledge of natural science, especially its formal and teleological structure, leads directly to knowledge of God. Hence, knowledge of the formal structure of the world is most important. And the structure of the Tabernacle gives us some of this information.

Just consider what seems like a small and insignificant piece of decorative detail: the figures of two *keruvim* (cherubs) on the top of the Ark of the Covenant. Why cherubs? Why not lions? According to Gersonides, the Ark contains the Torah, the book of instruction. To study and understand this book, one must obviously use the mind. The Ark directly and explicitly tells

---

[69] Exod. 25: 23–30; Maimonides, *Guide*, iii. 45 (trans. Pines, 578).
[70] *CT*, Exod., 'Terumah', 104*b* (ii. 362).

us that the ultimate happiness afforded by the Torah consists in intellectual perfection, which is physically represented by the two cherubs. Each of these is a form, one of them symbolizing the human intellect and the other the Agent Intellect. They are placed facing each other, signifying that there is an intimate relationship between them, ultimately leading to the immortality of the human intellect.[71]

Another group of commandments also seems to be pointless, especially to a modern reader: the laws of purity and impurity. Why should menstrual blood or a seminal emission be impure, requiring rigorous rules of purification? Speaking in general about the laws of purity Gersonides remarks:

> It is appropriate here that we explain what the Torah mentions with respect to the laws of purity and impurity . . . The Torah wisely established for us the truths of existence, as far as possible, for this is the [ultimate] purpose of man . . . And since the most important root in this matter is that we believe in the *existence of forms* . . . the Torah guided us . . . in the matter of the Holy Temple and the sacrifices.[72]

Here too we see in Gersonides' philosophy a pervasive contrast and tension between form and matter. All imperfections are ultimately traceable to matter, whose resistance to form leads to corruption and decay. Many of the ritual laws of the Torah are instituted to inculcate in us this lesson. In the impurity laws, the paradigmatic case is the human corpse, which the sages termed 'the father of impurity'.[73] According to Gersonides, a human cadaver is most impure precisely because a living human exhibits the most perfect form found in the animal kingdom: 'The more noble an animal is the more impure is its impurity, indicating that the form in it is noble . . . Accordingly, since the human form is the most noble by far in the animal kingdom, it is appropriate that the impurity of a dead human be the most severe.'[74] What makes the dead human body impure, Gersonides explains, is the absence of its original form. All that remains is the corruptible cadaver; for the body is now formless, and soon decays:

> Since in the dead person the human form is missing and hence because of the lack [of form] the person is dead, the Torah makes it completely impure. [It does so] in order that we become aware that the virtue and glory that accrues to man over all other composite substances is not in his matter but is because of his form. The dead person has all its limbs; what it lacks is its form . . . This teaches us that the matter is quite inferior to the form.[75]

[71] Ibid. 104*c* (ii. 362–3).   [72] *CT*, Lev., 'Shemini', 137*c* (iii. 144).
[73] Mishnah *Kel.* 1: 4.   [74] *CT*, Num., 'Zot ḥukat', 193*d* (iv. 107).
[75] *CT*, Lev., 'Shemini', 137*d* (iii. 146–7).

Whether or not the purity laws have any practical, or first-order, meaning or value, for Gersonides they convey an important, indeed a basic, truth about the structure of reality, especially the fundamental nature of form.[76]

This principle is also evident in the precepts prohibiting the mixing of plants or animals (Lev. 19: 19). They teach us that the formal structure of nature is not to be tampered with. Each plant or animal species has a definite form that is essential to it and thus should not be changed or modified. We might call this 'Gersonides' law of the conservation of form'.[77] Unlike Maimonides, who explained these laws in historical and sociological terms as measures preventing the Israelites from adopting the practices of the idolatrous nations,[78] Gersonides provides a metaphysical explanation. What matters for him is the philosophical meaning that these prohibitions convey. Recognition of the formal structure in the earthly realm eventually leads us to see all of reality as exhibiting form, ultimately terminating in the first form, God. Hybridization of plants or animals ignores form in favour of matter: the coupling of two animal bodies of different species or the mixing of the seeds from two different kinds of plants is an attempt to eliminate this formal structure. Besides being an affront to God, it is an obstacle to our pursuit of intellectual perfection, which consists in the knowledge of the forms of substances, both natural and supernatural. In sum, the Torah through its commandments frees us from the domination of matter and enables the intellect, our form, to achieve its proper goal, knowledge of the first form, God.[79]

Many of the ritual commandments are often linked to the notion of holiness (*kedushah*). The performance of these commandments renders one holy and thus enables the performer to be 'like' God, the most Holy One.[80] Now, what is it to be holy? The biblical term itself implies that something is holy if it is in some sense 'separate', set off from everything else. God is holy because he is completely differentiated from everything in the universe. Israel is holy in so far as it keeps itself separated from the nations, especially from their laws.[81] For Gersonides, however, this idea of separateness is intimately connected to the notion of form: 'As we mentioned earlier, the holy is from the form; and whatever is more cleansed from matter is its holiness greater. And

---

[76] Touati, 'Les Idées philosophiques', 346–51.

[77] *CT*, Lev., 'Kedoshim', 162*a* (iii. 299), 162*c* (iii. 302–3); Feldman, appendix to *The Wars of the Lord*, ii. 242–5.　　[78] Maimonides, *Guide*, iii. 37 (trans. Pines, 540–50).

[79] *CT*, Lev., 'Shemini', 137*c–d* (iii. 146–7), 'Kedoshim', 162*c* (iii. 302–3).

[80] Lev. 19: 2; *CT*, Lev., 'Kedoshim', 160*d* (iii. 292).

[81] Exod. 19: 5–6; Lev. 18: 1–5; Deut. 18: 9.

it is for this reason that with reference to the separate forms [the Torah] calls them "holy of holies".'[82] Again Gersonides' Platonism is quite evident. This sharp distinction between form and matter is for Gersonides expressive of a profound metaphysical distinction between the material and transcendental domains. Like Plato and Philo he sees matter as essentially imperfect and corrupting, whereas form is perfect and preservative. To the extent that we cultivate our form, we endure; complete actualization of our form results in immortality. Expressed in theological language, form is sanctifying; matter is profane. Through form we become holy. The command to imitate God's holiness is therefore the command to realize to the maximum our innate form. Indeed, the whole idea of holiness, especially as it is embodied in the commandments, becomes identical with the principle of the primacy of form. The holiness of Israel is a function of its performance of the commandments, which in their second-order, or symbolic, meaning inculcate the significance of form over matter. The commandments enable each Israelite to achieve the actualization of his proper form, the intellect, and thus attain human perfection and happiness.

Is the Torah Immutable?

Last, but not least, there is the question of the Torah's inherent perfection and validity over time. Can it be changed? Could it be replaced by another law or no law at all? These are more than just academic questions. They were vehemently and sometimes violently debated issues throughout antiquity and the Middle Ages. Within Judaism, especially during the Second Temple period, different Jewish groups had diverse views concerning the Torah's status. One sect, the Sadducees, claimed that the Torah as edited by Ezra and his disciples was a fixed document, allowing for no additions or subtractions. Indeed, this is exactly what is written in Deuteronomy 4: 2: 'You must not add anything to the words that I have commanded you nor subtract from them.' Other groups, notably the Pharisees, had a more flexible approach to the Torah and the Jewish canon, permitting interpretation and supplementation. In the early Christian church, especially in its Pauline version, the whole question of the validity of the Torah and its applicability to the non-Jewish converts was a major issue. The ultimate solution was that the legal content of the Torah was not obligatory for non-Jewish converts nor even for Jewish converts; indeed, the Torah was the 'old testament' now superseded by the 'new testament'. Jesus' death made the observance of the commandments

---

[82] *CT*, Lev., 'Kedoshim', 163*d* (iii. 310).

not only obsolete but superfluous as well. When Islam entered the picture, both testaments were abrogated by the new prophetic dispensation, the Quran and its prophet, Muhammad. The medieval Jewish theologian had his hands full. It had to be shown that the Torah needs no additions nor is to be diminished and that it is everlastingly valid. There can be no new Torah.

In the various and many polemical debates between Jews and Christians and Jews and Muslims, Jewish scholars often appealed to the Torah, which Christian scholars accepted as valid for a certain time and Muslim scholars respected as genuinely prophetic but wrongly interpreted or handed down. Passages from the Torah were cited as supporting its immutability and ever-lasting validity. The passage from Deuteronomy 4 quoted above was funda-mental. It was supported by another passage in the same chapter: 'What great nation is there whose statutes and laws are just, as is all this law which I am setting before you today?' (Deut. 4: 8). Against both Christians and Muslims, Sa'adiah Gaon quoted the passage from Jeremiah in which the Torah is stated to be imperishable, like the heavenly bodies (Jer. 31: 35–6). Maimonides also made the immutability and everlasting validity of the Torah a basic dogma of the Jewish religion; it is the ninth of his Thirteen Principles of the Jewish religion. His argument for this thesis derives from his firm belief in the uniqueness of Moses' prophecy: if Moses was the most perfect prophet and not to be surpassed by any other human in his proximity and access to God, then the law he revealed inherits these qualities.[83]

But for the philosophically minded Jewish theologian or philosopher, quoting the Torah was not enough. After all, the Christians and the Muslims had emancipated themselves from it. Purely philosophical arguments had to be adduced to defend the Torah's authority. In this debate Sa'adiah cleverly used the Muslim argument of abrogation against the claim that the Quran superseded the Torah: if the Quran abrogated the Torah and the Gospels, why cannot the Quran itself be abrogated? Indeed, the possibility of abroga-tion could go on indefinitely. So what is the point of laying down a law in the first place? A legislator proposes a law because it is believed to be a good law. If a law-giver thinks that the law is of only temporary value and validity, why did he not propose at the outset a better and more perfect law that would not have to be modified or completely abrogated?[84]

Gersonides, as we have seen, insisted upon the inherent perfection of the

---

[83] Sa'adiah Gaon, *The Book of Beliefs and Opinions*, treatise 3, ch. 7 (trans. Rosenblatt, 157–63); Maimonides, *Commentary on the Mishnah*, San. 10.

[84] Sa'adiah Gaon, *The Book of Beliefs and Opinions*, treatise 3, ch. 7 (trans. Rosenblatt, 160).

Torah: it contains all the truths, moral and intellectual, that a person needs to attain human perfection. Moreover, it teaches these truths in plain language, accessible to all, not just the philosopher or the Jew. Indeed, it teaches some truths more clearly and easily than philosophy does.[85] So there is no need at all for a new law. Moreover, if God were to change or annul the Torah, this would involve a change in God, and this is impossible. Commenting on Deuteronomy 5: 29, where the Israelites are told to teach the commandments to their children throughout the generations, Gersonides remarks:

> This entire passage shows that the Torah was given to the following generations without end. And this is one of the fundamental cornerstones of the Torah. Moreover, reason itself implies this principle. For it is not possible to attribute to God a change in will . . . Indeed, the prophet has said: 'I am the Lord; I do not change' [Mal. 3: 6].[86]

There is here an interesting parallel with Gersonides' argument for the indestructibility of the world. In Chapter 2, I noted his argument against the world's corruptibility: if God could destroy the world, he would have to have a reason for doing so. But no reason can be given that would warrant his destroying what he voluntarily made as perfect as possible. The same is true for the Torah: it too is perfect; there is, then, no need for another law. For God to amend or abolish the Torah would be to put him on the level of a human law-maker; but God is not human.

The Christian or Muslim would likely object that, with the coming of the messiah, Jesus, or the 'seal of the prophets', Muhammad, a new law had been revealed. At the conclusion of his *Commentary on the Torah*, where he discusses the messiah and the differences between the messiah and Moses, Gersonides makes it very clear that, however great the messiah will be, he will not issue a new law, that the Torah revealed by Moses is unique; indeed, like the miraculous nature of Moses' prophecy, it too is a miracle: '[When it is said,] "there will never arise a prophet in Israel like Moses", it is obvious from the words of the Torah itself that there will never be another law-giving prophet . . . or one who will change the Torah for another.'[87] Although the messiah will be the agent by whom the miracle of resurrection of the dead will be performed, he will not issue a new or different law. Just the contrary, he will obey and promulgate the Torah, as every Jew is obliged to do.[88] Indeed, this was admitted by Jesus himself when he said: 'I have come not to annul the law but to fulfil it' (Matt. 5: 17–19).

---

[85] *CT*, Deut., 'Va'ethanan', 211*a–b* (v. 36).   [86] Ibid. 211*c*, lesson 4 (v. 38).
[87] Ibid., 'Vezot haberakhah', 247*a* (v. 344).   [88] Ibid. 247*a*, 248*a–b* (v. 344–5, 351).

TEN

Conclusion

TOWARDS THE END of his life the German philosopher Immanuel Kant wrote a treatise entitled *Religion Within the Limits of Reason Alone*. In it he defended the thesis of the autonomy of philosophical ethics and the inherent rationality of the laws of morality. On the basis of this principle he concluded that if religion is to be admitted as a legitimate mode of thought and practice it would have to be measured by reason. In particular, revealed, or historical, faiths, such as Judaism, Christianity, and Islam, containing dogmas, mysteries, and ceremonial laws, would have to be judged by whether or not they are compatible with and conducive to the promotion of 'pure religion', the religion of morality based upon reason. Using this principle Kant further concluded that of the three historical faiths only Christianity in its Protestant form came close to satisfying the rational and moral conditions that reason and morality prescribe. Perhaps influenced by Spinoza,[1] Kant maintained that Judaism was more a national polity primarily focused upon ceremonial law and having no intrinsic relevance to the moral law; hence it possessed no application or validity to all mankind. Islam fares no better: according to Kant it is simply a religion of conquest and subjugation, in which moral autonomy and reason are despised.[2] Only a religion purified of irrational and compulsory dogma and mystery, containing minimal ritual law, could, according to Kant, attain the status of a 'religion within the limits of reason alone'.

A little over a century later the Jewish neo-Kantian philosopher Hermann Cohen accepted for the most part Kant's general conception of a religion of reason but rejected his judgement concerning Judaism. In his last important work, *The Religion of Reason out of the Sources of Judaism*, Cohen attempted to show the essential rationality of Judaism and its foundation in the moral law. Having adopted the common Christian view of Judaism as a legalistic religion, Cohen argued, Kant intentionally glossed over the moral teachings

---

[1] Guttmann, 'Mendelssohn's Jerusalem and Spinoza's Theological-Political Treatise' (Heb.); Yovel, *Spinoza and Other Heretics*, 9.

[2] Kant, *Religion Within the Limits of Reason Alone*, preface, Book 4, pt. 1.

of the prophets and was totally ignorant of the doctrines of the sages and the medieval Jewish philosophers and moralists. Cohen's work was an attempt to correct Kant as well as an argument for the thesis that Judaism is a religion of reason. Nevertheless, for Cohen, no less than for Kant, the guiding principle is that reason is the ultimate authority in religion.[3]

It will be useful here to employ the notion of a 'control belief' introduced by the American philosopher Nicholas Wolterstorff. A control belief, or a specific set of such beliefs, serves to determine which other beliefs can be admitted into the whole corpus of beliefs held by a person. Not all our beliefs function in the same way or have the same status; some are more privileged than others. Someone's belief in the theory of evolution, for example, makes it impossible for that person to accept literally the biblical account of the origin of species; in this case evolutionary theory controls all other views about biology. Inversely, someone who adheres to a literal reading of the story of the sun standing still in Joshua 10 would have to deny modern astronomy. When there is an incompatibility between one's control beliefs and some other belief or theory, one may argue that the incompatibility is only apparent. A suitable interpretation or revision of either belief would eliminate the apparent inconsistency. For some people the tenets of philosophy or science constitute their controlling beliefs, and hence whatever religious views they may hold have to be interpreted or revised according to the dictates of philosophical or scientific theory. For others it is just the reverse: the scientific theory has to be interpreted or revised in such a way that it is made compatible with the set of religious beliefs. Some contemporary religious thinkers, for example, have been able to admit modern evolutionary theory by interpreting it in such a way as to allow for 'intelligent design', thus making an opening for theistic religion. Yet others would interpret the Bible liberally, relegating biblical biology to the status of an archaic myth. In either case a specific set of beliefs is taken as controlling all other beliefs, and by appropriate interpretation or even rejection the entire set of beliefs is made consistent. This approach can be called 'compatibilism'.[4]

But one could claim that such an apparent conflict in belief is indicative of a genuine incompatibility between the control belief and some other belief. One should honestly affirm this inconsistency and make no attempt to reinterpret or revise either belief. Instead, one has to choose between them. In the early history of Christianity the Church Father Tertullian (d. *c.*220) sharply formulated this crisis in belief by his rhetorical question: 'What does

---

[3] Cohen, *The Religion of Reason*, 4–11.
[4] Wolterstorff, *Reason within the Bounds of Religion*, chs. 1–2.

Athens have to do with Jerusalem, the Academy with the Church?'[5] Although learned in ancient Greek philosophy, Tertullian came to believe that there was a fundamental and ineliminable incompatibility between philosophy and Christianity, between reason and faith. His other famous dictum expresses this either/or predicament in an even more radical fashion: 'I believe precisely because it is absurd.'[6] Candidly admitting that some Christian theological dogmas are from the standpoint of philosophy irrational, Tertullian opted for faith over reason: Christian revelation always trumps Athenian philosophy. In the nineteenth century the Danish theologian Søren Kierkegaard expressed similar views.[7]

The Tertullian antithesis between Athens and Jerusalem was used to reach a set of different conclusions by the twentieth-century Jewish historian of philosophy and political philosopher, Leo Strauss. In several of his studies, Strauss accepted the essential contrast between reason and revelation, insisting that neither can impugn the methods and contents of the other, since each is fundamentally independent of the other.[8] Strauss himself, somewhat ambivalently, opted for Athens, while expressing deep appreciation for Jerusalem, a choice not available to most medieval philosophers. Since they were members of religious communities whose authority they did not question, divine revelation was for them just as much a datum as it was for the non-philosophical believer. Accordingly, Strauss claimed, it was obligatory for these philosophers to show that philosophy is not only compatible with revelation but also that it is permitted by and relevant to it. This was especially urgent for Jewish and Muslim philosophers because of the dominant role that the study of the law plays in these two traditions. Hence, before one begins to philosophize, one has to 'justify philosophy before the Law'. To this end Averroes, for example, wrote an essay entitled *The Decisive Treatise Determining the Nature of the Connection between Religion and Philosophy*. The introduction to Maimonides' *Guide* also deals with this general issue. Both thinkers were sensitive to the earlier controversies concerning the alleged corrosive influence of philosophy and wanted to show that philosophy was not only safe but permissible, indeed necessary for sound religious belief.[9]

There is a rabbinic *midrash* that exemplifies this principle, although Strauss does not appeal to it. On the passage, 'May God enlarge Japheth and let him

---

[5] Tertullian, *Prescription Against Heretics*, 7; Chadwick, *Early Christian Thought*, ch. 1.

[6] Tertullian, *On the Flesh of Christ*, 5, as cited in Chadwick, *Early Christian Thought*, 2.

[7] Kierkegaard, *Concluding Unscientific Postscript*, 30–5, 384, 505–7.

[8] Strauss, 'Jerusalem and Athens'.   [9] Strauss, *Philosophy and Law*, ch. 2.

dwell in the tents of Shem' (Gen. 9: 27), the *midrash* interprets this verse as follows: 'May the words of Japheth be in the tents of Shem'. The rabbis suggest here that some of the cultural achievements of the Greeks, who in traditional Jewish anthropology are descended from Japheth, can be safely assimilated by the Jews, the descendants of Shem, so long as the former are or can be made compatible with the Torah.[10] Greek wisdom is made 'kosher' by suitable interpretation or modification. Athens is domesticated by Jerusalem through a critical and selective evaluation of what the former can contribute to the fortification and glorification of the latter. In bringing Japheth into the tents of Shem medieval Jewish philosophers were relocating Athens in Jerusalem;[11] or, as Wolterstorff entitled his book, in opposition to Kant, 'reason [is to be] within the bounds of religion'.[12]

In chapter 2 of his *Philosophy and Law*, entitled 'The Legal Grounding of Philosophy', Strauss included Gersonides with Averroes and Maimonides as writers who attempted to show the legal legitimacy of philosophy: '[The] primacy of the Law is just as secure for Levi as for Maimonides and Averroes.'[13] There is no doubt that for Gersonides the Torah was divinely revealed and hence true. In this sense the Torah is primary, at least chronologically and pedagogically. Yet, as Strauss himself indicated, there are some important differences between Gersonides, on the one hand, and Averroes and Maimonides, on the other. Among the differences between Gersonides and Maimonides, Strauss lists their disagreements concerning the creation of the world and their differing attitude towards 'the freedom of public communication of philosophical truths'.[14] In his discussion of the former issue Strauss correctly points to Gersonides' firm belief that this topic is capable of philosophical resolution. As we saw in Chapter 2, Gersonides was convinced that he had succeeded in proving that the world had a temporal beginning and was created by God. In emphasizing Gersonides' more generous approach to the dissemination of the results of his philosophical and scientific research, Strauss rightly claims that for Gersonides reason has a greater potency than it has for Maimonides. Indeed, it is precisely because reason is competent that the philosopher and the scientist ought to divulge the results of their research. The truths that these modes of enquiry yield are capable and deserving of being publicly revealed to all those prepared and willing to receive them. They are God's gift to humanity, just as the Torah is. Maimonides' reluctance to divulge the 'secrets of the Torah', which his *Guide* discloses, albeit in an enigmatic

[10] BT *Meg.* 9*b*.   [11] Shavit, *Athens in Jerusalem*, esp. chs. 4, 9–11.
[12] Wolterstorff, *Reason within the Bounds of Religion*, 7–8.
[13] Strauss, *Philosophy and Law*, 78.   [14] Ibid. 74.

manner, to the select few, seems to reflect or express a certain intellectual hesitancy or self-doubt, which some recent scholars have interpreted as scepticism.[15] By contrast, Gersonides generally manifests no such worries. Admittedly, no human being can know everything and there may be some questions for which definitive answers may not be forthcoming. But that does not mean we should abandon philosophy or science. The pursuit of knowledge is an ongoing endeavour, in which many participate. In many cases what one generation has failed to discover or solve another generation succeeds in doing. This intellectual optimism entails that one's philosophical and scientific speculations and their results be made available to other participants in this enterprise. The pursuit of knowledge is, then, a co-operative and public activity. Maimonides' intellectual pessimism and esotericism are not compatible with scientific and philosophical progress.

But the differences between Gersonides and Maimonides are more far-reaching, so much so that one may wonder whether for Gersonides philosophy and science need to be 'justified before the Law', as Strauss claims. Consider Strauss's point concerning the provability of creation. Gersonides not only differed from Maimonides in his belief that he had shown the provability of this doctrine, but in addition he rejected the traditional teaching of creation *ex nihilo*, which Maimonides had accepted as the Torah's theory of creation. Indeed, its falsity can be philosophically and scientifically demonstrated. The true theory of creation is creation *ex aliquo*, creation out of some primordial, shapeless body. Here, reason provides the correct interpretation of what the Torah teaches. That Gersonides defies centuries of traditional Jewish teaching concerning creation is of no importance. Biblical cosmology must be 'within the limits of reason'.

Strauss also claims that, for Gersonides, 'one must rely on Scripture in regard to the teaching of miracles'.[16] This is true in so far as biblical miracles were empirical facts observed by our forefathers, whose testimony we regard as reliable. But the more interesting question is, *how* are these facts to be understood? As I have shown in Chapter 6, Gersonides consistently explains these phenomena in naturalistic and scientific terms. The supernatural element virtually disappears. This is most blatant in Gersonides' treatment of what appears to be the most extraordinary of the biblical wonders: the stopping of the solar and lunar motions, described in Joshua 10. In his discussion of this miracle Gersonides preserved the natural motions of the heavenly bodies, insisting that the laws of celestial motion cannot be violated.

[15] Pines, 'The Limitations of Human Knowledge'; Stern, 'Maimonides on the Growth of Knowledge'.   [16] Strauss, *Philosophy and Law*, 75.

Whatever the ordinary believer thinks, the miracle must lie elsewhere. Again, science limits revelation in so far as it controls what we can believe about this event and how this miracle is to be understood. Moreover, as we have learned, God himself was not the direct cause of the miracle, which is not what the literal meaning of the story might imply. The proximate cause of the miracle was the Agent Intellect. Although Gersonides' naturalistic accounts of miracles have offended traditional believers, medieval and modern, he was not afraid to use science to explain these phenomena.

Perhaps the most radical and controversial of all of Gersonides' doctrines is his theory of divine omniscience. It has certainly been abhorred and criticized throughout the generations. Nevertheless, although he realized that his theory was not traditional, Gersonides did not shy away from drawing the logical conclusions from what he considered to be true philosophical premises. The conventional belief, supported throughout the Torah, that God knows individual human beings and that he reveals himself to them as individuals, is simply not true. And this means that God does not know the truth-status of propositions about future contingent events. As we have argued, Gersonides pretty much adopted the view of the philosophers on this issue and rejected Maimonides' defence of the traditional doctrine of strong omniscience.[17] This required him to read the Torah in a non-conventional way, as his account of Abraham's sacrificing Isaac illustrates. Before Abraham actually lifted up the axe to kill Isaac, his obedience to God's command was not yet known, even to God.

Strauss also notes that Gersonides rejected Averroes' doctrine of human immortality as conjunction with the Agent Intellect, citing Gersonides' argument from 'the insufficiency of the human intellect' to know what the Agent Intellect knows. No matter how much any individual knows, this information will never match the whole system of knowledge about terrestrial affairs possessed by the Agent Intellect.[18] Nevertheless, Gersonides does not bemoan this shortcoming as fatal to the belief in human immortality or to philosophy's competence to prove it. Epistemic finitude is not an argument against immortality. Instead, he proposes a different account of human immortality, one that is not defeated by the obvious fact of human intellectual limitations. Yet Gersonides' theory of immortality is not the traditional one believed by most Jews. From Aristotle, Averroes, and Maimonides he learned that immortality is of the intellect, that it is acquired through intellectual activity and perfection. One's immortality consists in

---

[17] See Chapter 4 above.   [18] Strauss, *Philosophy and Law*, 76.

what one knows. Moreover, in the world to come there will be no remembering of what we did in this world nor any additional learning in the 'heavenly yeshiva', since the psycho-physical faculties needed for memory and learning—imagination and sense perception—are no longer available to us. Accordingly, many of the traditional rabbinic ideas about immortality, still held today by many Jews, are wrong.

The claim advanced by several modern commentators that Gersonides' account of immortality manifests a conservative tendency or conciliatory agenda is therefore not entirely correct.[19] It is true that, compared with the views of Averroes and some other Muslim philosophers, and perhaps also in contrast to Maimonides, Gersonides did not accept the conjunction theory of immortality. This theory did imply the loss of individual immortality, an idea essential to the conventional belief in immortality. But Gersonides' own view was by no means more easily squared with traditional themes, such as remembering one's loved ones or regularly learning a new page of the Talmud. True, Gersonides did reject the conjunction theory, but his arguments were for the most part philosophical; nor did they lead to epistemological scepticism, as Strauss suggests. Gersonides did defend individual immortality, but his understanding of this belief was a radical departure from the traditional accounts of this doctrine. Here again, a philosophical theory determines how a religious belief is to be understood. If we are to retain Strauss's thesis, we should reformulate it in Gersonides' case as 'justifying philosophy before the Law *as philosophy understands the Law*'; that is, Athens is the interpreter when Jerusalem speaks.

A reader of chapter 14 of Book 1 of *Wars* might object: 'Doesn't Gersonides say in this chapter that if his philosophical conclusions are incompatible with religious convictions, the latter are to be affirmed and the former rejected? Doesn't this statement imply that revelation "controls" reason?' Yes, but the apparent inconsistency between this statement and some of the conclusions reached in the treatise is not fatal to Gersonides' philosophical enterprise; it is just a sop to the faithful, which should be taken with the proverbial grain of salt. Conscious that some of his ideas may be offensive to more traditional readers, Gersonides feels the need to mollify his audience and express his fidelity to tradition. But note how he concludes this chapter: 'The incompatibility is to be attributed to our shortcomings.' That is, there is no real incompatibility; any inconsistency is to be explained as the result of

---

[19] Manekin, 'Conservative Tendencies in Gersonides' Religious Philosophy', 306–10; Ivry, 'Gersonides and Averroes on the Intellect', 236.

human error. Sooner or later a more adequate philosophical or scientific theory or a deeper understanding of the religious belief will reveal that it is compatible with true philosophy. And of course the true understanding of religious belief is provided by philosophy.

The heterodox nature of Gersonides' interpretation of several fundamental doctrines of Judaism was clearly perceived by some of his medieval critics, most notably Hasdai Crescas and Isaac Abravanel. Although they recognized his vast and deep learning in both sacred and secular studies, they could not accept his radical conclusions concerning creation, miracles, omniscience, and immortality. They rejected his theory of creation out of a formless body; indeed, Abravanel called it a form of dualism, a doctrine explicitly condemned by the sages.[20] They were also repelled by his supernaturalistic explanations of miracles. Indeed, they were prepared to read Joshua 10 literally and accept that God can change all the celestial motions in such a way that no terrestrial catastrophes result.[21] Gersonides' theory of omniscience fared no better in their hands. It was an affront to God to say that he cannot know individuals as such and that he is ignorant of future contingent events. Indeed, it is a complete misreading of the Torah.[22] Finally, how can Gersonides maintain that immortality is achieved only through intellectual perfection? What about the person who has not studied science and philosophy? Are not *talmud torah* and performance of the commandments sufficient?[23] For these critics, Gersonides, along with Maimonides and the other medieval Jewish philosophers, was an intellectual elitist, restricting divine providence and reward only to those like themselves. To make themselves philosophically respectable they went too far in the direction of the philosophers, whose principles they adopted, explicitly or esoterically, even to the point of subverting traditional Jewish belief. To his critics Gersonides' *Wars of the Lord* was not a defence of God and his Torah but a war *against* God and the Torah.[24]

It appears, then, that Gersonides cannot be categorized by the formulae of Tertullian or those of the rabbis and Strauss. He certainly did not believe that philosophy and revelation are completely at odds with each other and

---

[20] Crescas, *Or adonai*, 3.1.3; Abravanel, *The Deeds of God*, 2.5. Touati provides a survey of Gersonides' reception in Jewish literature (*La Pensée philosophique de Gersonide*, 541–59).   [21] Feldman, ' "Sun Stand Still" ', 78–80.

[22] Crescas, *Or adonai*, 2.1.3.

[23] Ibid. 3; Feldman, *Philosophy in a Time of Crisis*, ch. 9.

[24] Shem Tov ibn Shem Tov (1390–*c*.1440), cited in Touati, *La Pensée philosophique de Gersonide*, 545.

that the latter must be kept pure and untainted by the former. Nor did he really believe that philosophy needs to justify itself before revelation if this means that the latter controls what philosophical and scientific beliefs are admissible. His basic assumption was that reason and revelation are consistent because the source of both is God himself. But it is the task of philosophy to demonstrate their mutual compatibility. Whatever revelation teaches must be consistent with true philosophy, and traditional religious beliefs must be justifiable in terms of philosophy and science. If they are not, they are to be discarded or radically revised. In short, the tents of Shem have to be brought within the boundaries of Japheth.

But how far can this relocation or transposition be carried out? Was Gersonides naive in thinking that Shem and Japheth could cohabit in everlasting harmony? In one sense this ecumenism was easier for Gersonides to believe in than it is for us. We are the heirs of Spinoza, who taught us that the 'Word of God' is not necessarily found in a book and that whatever book we read and regard as canonical must be read contextually as a document written in a specific cultural environment.[25] Accordingly, for many modern religious Jews the Bible is no longer believed to be the actual Word of God. Nor are the 'gates of interpretation' so wide that we can read into it anything we want. Unlike Maimonides and Gersonides, we cannot assume that whatever the Torah teaches, especially about science, is true if properly understood. If we are to take the Bible 'as it is', we have to admit that some of its teachings are false. For those who accept the traditional teachings of the Torah the situation is in one sense simpler: they may either reject philosophy and science altogether or persist in the attempt to reconcile biblical teachings with modern thought by means of an expansive exegesis.[26] But for many these alternatives are not adequate: science cannot be so easily dismissed, and the Torah cannot be interpreted *ad libitum*. What, then, are they to do?

Does this mean that, for the modern Jew, Gersonides is at best just a historical curiosity, of interest only to the scholar of medieval thought? Is there

[25] Spinoza, *The Theological-Political Treatise*, chs. 7, 12.

[26] Consider again the theory of evolution. Some Orthodox Jews and fundamentalist Christians reject it outright. Others accept it and attempt to make it compatible with the book of Genesis by interpretation. For example, in the widely used *Pentateuch and the Haftorahs*, the editor, Rabbi Dr J. H. Hertz, although an Orthodox Jew, is open to the theory of evolution and seeks to show its compatibility with Judaism ('Additional Notes to Genesis', 193–202). More recently Gerald Schroeder, an Orthodox Jewish scientist, has also advanced this thesis in his *The Science of God*. Roman Catholicism has adopted a similar approach.

anything to be learned from him? In raising this question we have to be cautious. We should not look to Gersonides for anticipations of space travel or twist what he says beyond recognition so as to accommodate our ideas or interests. Yet, as many modern historians of philosophy and science have shown, there is something to be gained by reading ancient and medieval texts from a contemporary perspective.[27] In the first place, we can learn to avoid their errors. Secondly, and more importantly, we can discover things in them that illuminate our own problems. In Gersonides' case we cannot, to be sure, accept his science, and modern philosophy has advanced beyond Aristotle. In some instances we shall have to reject his conclusions. The whole doctrine of the Agent Intellect, for example, and the uses that Gersonides makes of it, no longer have a place in our philosophy and science. Nevertheless, Gersonides' attempt to make prophecy and miracles understandable in terms of some commonly held philosophical or scientific theory is paradigmatic of a religion that is not afraid of reason. Prophecy and miracles are in this sense rational, not mysterious. As he was fond of saying, the Torah does not compel us to believe in it; it persuades by its inherent rationality.

Gersonides' general principle that reason should function as a control of what we believe has some interesting and important implications for the modern reader. It may indeed turn out that we have to declare certain traditional religious beliefs untenable; reason and interpretative integrity do not allow us to accept some doctrines. We saw how he rejected the popular belief, shared even by some rabbinic scholars, in demons. In some cases it may be that Gersonides' philosophical account of some religious beliefs is more reasonable than the traditional understanding of them. His doctrine of divine omniscience, for example, may be the most plausible solution to the venerable dilemma of the apparent conflict between divine omniscience and human freedom, as some contemporary philosophers have argued.[28] If we believe in free will, this concept should be robust enough to be meaningful. Choices are genuine when we have real options in whatever situation we may find ourselves. In this sense, as Gersonides has argued, the future must be 'open'. The traditional belief in divine omniscience 'closes' the future. We can still

---

[27] In his magisterial study of Plato, Paul Friedlaender devotes a chapter to Plato's physics in the light of contemporary science (Friedlaender, *Plato*, vol. i, ch. 14). Recent studies of the late ancient Greek commentator and critic of Aristotle, John Philoponus, have pointed out several interesting anticipations of Newtonian ideas concerning inertia and space (Sorabji (ed.), *Philoponus and the Rejection of Aristotelian Science*, 12, 22–4, 217).

[28] Lucas, *The Freedom of the Will*, ch. 14; Swinburne, *The Coherence of Theism*, ch. 10.

maintain that God is omniscient so long as we understand correctly what this theological belief means: God is omniscient in so far as he knows whatever is knowable. However, future contingent events, by their inherent openness, are not knowable. Gersonides' account of divine providence too seems to offer a better explanation of natural evils than many of the traditional doctrines. That earthquakes and diseases result from natural forces and causes independent of divine control is a more credible explanation than those that vainly attempt to fit these phenomena into some kind of divine plan or purpose. Try telling parents that their child's suffering from a painful and terminal disease is God's will and is for the best. Here Gersonides' doctrine of the shapeless primordial body out of which the world was created offers a more believable account of the various imperfections of nature that cause suffering.

Gersonides came to write *The Wars of the Lord* because of his belief that the dogma of creation was crucial to Judaism. It turned out that this topic required the longest book in the entire treatise. Gersonides' discussion of this subject is problematic, but in an interesting way. Like most medieval thinkers he believed that the world had a beginning and that it was created by God.[29] The claim that the universe had a temporal beginning is now part of contemporary cosmology. Aristotle's eternity theory, defended by Gersonides' predecessor Averroes, has been discarded.[30] Nevertheless, to claim further, as Gersonides does, that the world has been created by God is to go beyond what contemporary cosmology allows. This latter thesis is metaphysical or theological, as Gersonides' arguments for it illustrate. But it is noteworthy that his basic argument here—the teleological argument[31]— is one favoured by many contemporary thinkers who attempt to incorporate modern science into their religious belief system. The world may be millions of years old and have evolved according to Darwinian laws; yet it betrays evidence of the 'finger of God'. This is the doctrine of 'intelligent design'.

---

[29] Although these ideas are frequently used interchangeably, they should be kept distinct. The world's having a temporal beginning is simply the claim that past time is finite, for which thesis Gersonides gives a distinct set of arguments. That the world was created by God is about *how* and perhaps *why* the world came into existence. On this point Gersonides gives a different set of arguments. The two theses are logically independent of each other. Most contemporary cosmologists accept the first but are neutral with respect to the second; one medieval philosopher, at least, accepted the second but not necessarily the first claim: Hasdai Crescas (Feldman, 'The Theory of Eternal Creation').

[30] Hawking, 'The Origin of the Universe'; Schroeder, *Genesis and the Big Bang*, ch. 4.

[31] See Chapter 2 above.

Admittedly, this theory has had a mixed reception in spite of its popularity, and here we may have to depart from Gersonides and the modern proponents of this doctrine. Yet what is most important is that Gersonides was not afraid to make religious beliefs philosophically and scientifically credible. One could say that for him there is an 'ethics of belief': one is not entitled to believe in just anything one wants.[32] There are constraints on what is believable, especially in religion. In this respect Gersonides was a precursor of Kant and Hermann Cohen: Judaism is, or should be, a religion within the limits of reason.

[32] Clifford, *The Ethics of Belief*, 71–96.

Bibliography

Works by Gersonides

Menachem Kellner has published three excellent annotated bibliographical essays on Gersonides that ought to be consulted: 'Rabbi Levi ben Gerson: A Bibliographical Essay', *Studies in Bibliography and Booklore*, 12 (1979), 13–23; 'Bibliographia Gersonideana: An Annotated List of Writings by and about R. Levi ben Gershom', in Gad Freudenthal (ed.), *Studies on Gersonides: A Fourteenth-Century Jewish Philosopher-Scientist* (Leiden, 1992), 367–414; and 'Bibliographia Gersonideana, 1992–2002', *Aleph*, 3 (2003), 345–74. Two additional bibliographies can be found in the third volume of *The Wars of the Lord*, trans. Feldman (Philadelphia, 1999), 520–32; and in Sirat, Klein-Braslavy, and Weijers (eds.), *Les Méthodes de travail de Gersonide et le maniement du savoir chez les scolastiques* (Paris, 2003), 357–76.

Commentary on the Five Scrolls [Perush al ḥamesh megilot] (Koenigsburg, 1860).

Commentary on the Former Prophets [Perush al nevi'im rishonim] (Leiria, 1494).

Commentary on Job [Perush al iyov] (Ferrara, 1477); English translation by Abraham Lassen (New York, 1946).

Commentary on Proverbs [Perush al mishlei] (in *Mikra'ot al ketuvim*) (Leiria, 1492).

Commentary on the Song of Songs [Perush shir hashirim], in *Commentary on the Five Scrolls*; English translation by Menachem Kellner (New Haven, 1998).

Commentary on the Torah [Perush haralbag al hatorah] (Venice, 1547); 5 vols. (Jerusalem, 1992, 1994, 1997, 1998, 2000).

Supercommentary on Averroes' Commentary on Aristotle's On Interpretation [Be'ur sefer hamelitsah], Bodleian MS Hebrew 1361; Michael MS 347.

The Wars of the Lord [Milḥamot hashem] (Leipzig, 1866); English translation by Seymour Feldman, with introduction and notes, 3 vols. (Philadelphia, 1984, 1988, 1999); French translation by Charles Touati, with notes, *Les Guerres du Seigneur: Livres III et IV* (Paris, 1968).

Primary Sources

ABRAVANEL, ISAAC, *Commentary on the Torah* [Perush al hatorah] (New York, 1959).

—— *The Deeds of God* [Mifalot elohim] (Lemberg, 1863; Jerusalem, 1988).

ALEXANDER OF APHRODISIAS, *De anima*, ed. I. Bruns, in *Supplementum Aristotelicum*, ii (Berlin, 1887); trans. into English by A. Fotinus as *The De Anima of Alexander of Aphrodisias* (Washington, DC, 1974).

—— *The Mantissa*, trans. Robert Sharples as *Supplement to 'On the Soul'* (Ithaca, NY, 2004).

—— *On Fate*, trans. and commentary R. Sharples (London, 1983).

AL-FARABI, *The Attainment of Happiness* [Tahsil al-sa'ada], trans. Muhsin Mahdi; excerpted in Ralph Lerner and Muhsin Mahdi, *Medieval Political Philosophy: A Sourcebook* (New York, 1063), 58–82.

—— *Letter concerning the Intellect* [Risala fi al-'aql], trans. Arthur Hyman, excerpted in Arthur Hyman and James Walsh (eds.), *Philosophy in the Middle Ages* (Indianapolis, 1987), 215–21.

—— *On the Perfect State* [Mabadi ara ahl-madina al fadila], trans. Richard Walzer (Oxford, 1985).

—— *The Political Regime* [al-siyasa al-madaniyya], trans. F. Najjar; excerpted in R. Lerner and M. Mahdi (eds.), *Medieval Political Philosophy: A Sourcebook* (New York, 1963), 31–57.

AL-GHAZALI, *Deliverance from Error* [al-munqidh min al-dalal], trans. W. Watt as *The Faith and Practice of Al-Ghazali* (London, 1951); excerpted in Arthur Hyman and James Walsh (eds.), *Philosophy in the Middle Ages* (Indianapolis, 1987), 267–83.

—— *The Incoherence of the Philosophers* [Tahafut al-falasifa], trans. Arthur Hyman, excerpted in Arthur Hyman and James Walsh (eds.), *Philosophy in the Middle Ages* (Indianapolis, 1987), 283–291.

ANSELM OF CANTERBURY, *Proslogium*, in *Saint Anselm's Basic Writings*, trans. S. W. Deane, 2nd edn. (LaSalle, Ill., 1962).

AQUINAS, THOMAS, *On There Being Only One Intellect*, trans. R. McInery (West Lafayette, Ind., 1993).

—— *Summa Contra Gentiles*, trans. Anton Pegis as *On the Truth of the Catholic Faith* (New York, 1955).

—— *Summa Theologiae*, ed. Anton Pegis (New York, 1948).

ARAMA, ISAAC, *The Binding of Isaac* [Akedat yitshak] (Pressburg, 1849).

AUGUSTINE OF HIPPO, *The Confessions*, trans. R. S. Pine-Coffin (New York, 1961).

—— *On the Free Choice of the Will* (Indianapolis, 1964).

AVERROES [IBN RUSHD], *The Decisive Treatise Determining the Nature of the Connection between Religion and Philosophy* [Kitab fasl al-maqal], trans. G. F. Hourani as *Averroes on the Harmony of Religion and Philosophy* (London, 1961); excerpted in Arthur Hyman and James Walsh (eds.), *Philosophy in the Middle Ages* (Indianapolis, 1987), 297–316.

—— *Epitome of the Parva Naturalia* [Talkhis kitab al-hiss wa'al-mahsus], trans. A. Blumberg (Cambridge, Mass., 1961).

—— *Long Commentary on Aristotle's De anima* [Averrois Cordubensis commentarium magnum in Aristotelis 'De anima' libros], ed. F. S. Crawford (Cambridge Mass., 1953); trans. Arthur Hyman; excerpted in Arthur Hyman and James Walsh (eds.), *Philosophy in the Middle Ages* (Indianapolis, 1987), 324–34.

—— *Long Commentary on Aristotle's Metaphysics*, trans. Charles Genequand as *Ibn Rushd's Metaphysics: A Translation with Introduction of Ibn Rushd's Commentary on Aristotle's 'Metaphysics', Book Lām* (Leiden, 1984).

—— *Middle Commentary on Aristotle's De anima* [Talkhis kitab al-nafs], trans., with notes and introduction, Alfred Ivry (Provo, Utah, 2002).

—— *Tahafut al-tahafut* [lit. 'The Incoherence of the Incoherence'; a critique of al-Ghazali's *Incoherence of the Philosophers*], trans. Simon van den Bergh, 2 vols. (London, 1954).

BOETHIUS, *The Consolation of Philosophy*, trans. V. E. Watts (Baltimore, 1969).

CELSUS, *On the True Doctrine*, trans. R. J. Hoffmann (New York, 1987).

CRESCAS, HASDAI, *Or adonai* [The Light of the Lord], ed. Shlomo Fisher (Jerusalem, 1990).

GALILEO GALILEI, 'Letter to the Grand Duchess Christina', trans. and excerpted in S. Drake, *Discoveries and Opinions of Galileo* (New York, 1957), 179–87.

HALEVI, JUDAH, *The Book of the Kuzari* [Sefer hakuzari], Hebrew trans. Joseph Kafi (Kiryat Ono, 1997); French trans. Charles Touati, *Le Kuzari: Apologie de la religion méprisée* (Louvain and Paris, 1994).

HUME, DAVID, *An Inquiry Concerning Human Understanding*, ed. Charles Hendel (New York, 1955).

—— *A Treatise on Human Nature*, ed. L. A. Selby-Bigge (Oxford, 1958).

IBN EZRA, ABRAHAM, *Commentary on the Torah* in the rabbinic Pentateuch [Mikra'ot gedolot] (New York, 1950).

KANT, IMMANUEL, *The Critique of Pure Reason*, trans. Norman Kemp Smith (London, 1956).

KANT, IMMANUEL, *Religion Within the Limits of Reason Alone*, trans. Theodore Greene and Hoyt Hudson (New York, 1960).

KIERKEGAARD, SØREN, *Concluding Unscientific Postscript*, trans. D. Swenson and W. Lowrie (Princeton, 1974).

LOCKE, JOHN, *An Essay On Human Understanding*, ed. Alexander Fraser, 2 vols. (New York, 1959).

MAIMONIDES, MOSES, *Commentary on the Mishnah* [Mishnah im perush rabenu mosheh ben maimon] (New York, 1954).

—— *Eight Chapters* [Shemonah perakim], trans. Raymond Weiss in Raymond Weiss and Charles Butterworth, *The Ethical Writings of Maimonides* (New York, 1975).

—— *The Guide of the Perplexed* [Arabic: Dalalat al-ḥa'irin; Hebrew: trans. Samuel ibn Tibbon, Moreh nevukhim]; English trans. S. Pines (Chicago, 1963).

—— *The Medical Aphorisms of Moses Maimonides*, trans. Fred Rosner and Suessman Muntner, 2 vols., Studies in Judaica (New York, 1971).

—— *Mishneh torah. The Book of Knowledge* [Sefer hamada], trans. Moses Hyamson (Jerusalem, 1962).

—— *Treatise on Resurrection*, trans. A. Halkin, in D. Hartman (ed.), *Epistles of Maimonides: Crisis and Leadership* (Philadelphia, 1985), 209–33.

NEWTON, ISAAC, *Correspondence of Isaac Newton*, vol. iii, ed. H. W. Turnbull (Cambridge, 1961).

OBADIAH OF BERTINORO, *Commentary on the Mishnah.* [Perush al hamish-nah], included in Maimonides' *Commentary on the Mishnah* (New York, 1954).

PHILOPONUS, JOHN, *Against Aristotle*, trans. C. Wildberg (Ithaca, NY, 1987).

—— *On the Eternity of the World: Against Proclus*, ed. H. Rabe (Leipzig, 1899); trans. Michael Share and James Wilberding, 3 vols. (Ithaca, NY, 2005, 2006).

PROCLUS, *The Elements of Theology*, trans. E. Dodds (Oxford, 1992).

—— *Ten Doubts Against Providence*, trans. Carlos Steel, in *On Providence* (Ithaca, NY, 2007).

SA'ADIAH GAON, *The Book of Beliefs and Opinions*, trans. S. Rosenblatt, Yale Judaica series (New Haven, 1989).

SPINOZA, BARUCH, *The Ethics*, trans. Samuel Shirley (Indianapolis, 1992).

—— *The Theological-Political Treatise*, trans. Samuel Shirley, 2nd edn. (Indianapolis, 1998).

TEMPIER, ETIENNE, *Condemnation of 219 Propositions*, trans. E. Fortin and P. O'Neill in R. Lerner and M. Mahdi (eds.), *Medieval Political Philosophy: A Sourcebook* (Ithaca, NY, 1963), 335–54.

TERTULLIAN, *Prescription against the Heretics*, trans. S. Tewall, in J. Saunders (ed.), *Greek and Roman Philosophy after Aristotle* (New York, 1966), 343–51.

THEMISTIUS, *Commentary on Aristotle's De anima*, trans. R. B. Todd (Ithaca, NY, 1996).

Secondary Sources

ALTMANN, ALEXANDER, 'Gersonides' Commentary on Averroes' Epitome of the *Parva Naturalia*', *Proceedings of the American Academy for Jewish Research, Jubilee Volume*, pt. 1 (1980), 1–31.

——'Ibn Bajja on Man's Ultimate Felicity', *Harry Austryn Wolfson: Jubilee Volume*, English section, vol. i (Jerusalem, 1965), 47–88.

——'Maimonides on the Intellect and the Scope of Metaphysics', in id., *Von der mittelalterlichen zur modernen Aufklaerung* (Tübingen, 1987), 60–129.

——'Maimonides and Thomas Aquinas: Natural or Divine Prophecy', *AJS Review*, 3 (1978), 1–20.

BLEICH, J. DAVID, 'Judaism and Natural Law', *Proceedings of the Eighth World Congress of Jewish Studies*, Division C (1982), 7–11.

BURTT, EDWIN, ARTHUR, *The Metaphysical Foundations of Modern Science* (New York, 1954).

CHADWICK, HENRY, *Early Christian Thought and the Classical Tradition* (Oxford, 1984).

CLIFFORD, WILLIAM KINGDOM, *The Ethics of Belief and Other Essays* (Amherst, NY, 1999).

COHEN, HERMANN, *The Religion of Reason: Out of the Sources of Judaism*, trans. S. Kaplan (New York, 1972).

CRAIG, WILLIAM, LANE, *The Problem of Divine Foreknowledge and Future Contingents from Aristotle to Suarez* (Leiden, 1988).

DAVIDSON, HERBERT, *Alfarabi, Avicenna and Averroes on Intellect* (New York and Oxford, 1992).

—— 'Averroes on the Active Intellect as a Cause of Existence', *Viator*, 18 (1987), 191–225.

—— 'Gersonides on the Material and Active Intellects', in Gad Freudenthal (ed.), *Studies on Gersonides: A Fourteenth-Century Jewish Philosopher-Scientist* (Leiden, 1992), 195–265.

—— *Moses Maimonides: The Man and his Works* (Oxford, 2005).

—— *Proofs for Eternity, Creation and the Existence of God in Medieval Islamic and Jewish Philosophy* (New York and Oxford, 1987).

DILLON, JOHN, *The Middle Platonists* (Ithaca, NY, 1996).

DUHEM, PIERRE, *Medieval Cosmology: Theories of Infinity, Place, Void and the Plurality of Worlds* (Chicago, 1987).

EISEN, ROBERT, *The Book of Job in Medieval Jewish Philosophy* (Oxford, 2004).

—— *Gersonides on Providence, Covenant and the Chosen People* (Albany, NY, 1995).

FACKENHEIM, EMIL, 'The Possibility of the Universe in Al-Farabi, Ibn Sina and Maimonides', *Proceedings of the American Academy for Jewish Research*, 16 (1946–7), 39–70.

FELDMAN, SEYMOUR, 'The Binding of Isaac: A Test-Case of Divine Foreknowledge', in T. Rudavsky (ed.), *Divine Omniscience and Omnipotence in Medieval Philosophy: Islamic, Jewish and Christian Perspectives* (Dordrecht, 1985), 105–33.

—— 'The End of the Universe in Medieval Jewish Philosophy', *AJS Review*, 11 (1986), 53–77.

—— 'Gersonides on the Possibility of Conjunction with the Agent Intellect', *AJS Review*, 3 (1978), 99–120.

—— 'Gersonides' Proofs for Creation of the Universe', *Proceedings of the American Academy for Jewish Research*, 35 (1967), 30–70.

—— *Philosophy in a Time of Crisis: Don Isaac Abravanel—Defender of the Faith* (London, 2003).

—— 'Platonic Themes in Gersonides' Cosmology', in Saul Lieberman and Arthur Hyman (eds.), *Salo W. Baron Jubilee Volume*, 3 vols. (Jerusalem, 1975), i. 383–405.

—— 'Platonic Themes in Gersonides' Doctrine of the Agent Intellect', in L. Goodman (ed.), *Neoplatonism and Jewish Thought* (Albany, NY, 1992), 255–78.

—— 'A Scholastic Misinterpretation of Maimonides' Doctrine of Divine Attributes', *Journal of Jewish Studies*, 19 (1968), 23–39.

—— ' "Sun Stand Still"—A Philosophical—Astronomical Midrash', *Proceedings of the Ninth World Congress of Jewish Studies*, Division C (Jerusalem, 1986), 77–84.

—— 'The Theory of Eternal Creation in Hasdai Crescas and Some of his Predecessors', *Viator*, 11 (1980), 289–320.

FISCHEL, HENRY, *Rabbinic Literature and Greco-Roman Philosophy* (Leiden, 1973).

FOX, MARVIN, 'Maimonides and Aquinas on Natural Law' (Heb.), *Dinei yisra'el*, 3 (1972), 5–46.

FREDE, MICHAEL, 'The Original Notion of Cause', in M. Schofield, M. Burnyeat, and J. Barnes (eds.), *Doubt and Dogmatism* (Oxford, 1980), 217–49.

FREUDENTHAL, GAD, 'Cosmogonie et physique chez Gersonide', *Revue des Etudes Juives*, 145 (1986), 295–314.

——'Epistemologie, astronomie et astrologie chez Gersonide', *Revue des Etudes Juives*, 146 (1987), 357–65.

——'Gersonide, génie solitaire', in C. Sirat, S, Klein-Braslavy, and O. Weijers (eds.), *Les Méthodes de travail de Gersonide et le maniement du savoir chez les scolastiques* (Paris, 2003), 291–316.

——'Human Felicity and Astronomy: Gersonides' Revolt Against Ptolemy' (Heb.), *Da'at*, 22 (1989), 55–72.

——'Les Sciences dans les communautés juives médiévales de Provence: Leur appropriation, leur rôle', *Revue des Etudes Juives*, 153 (1993), 29–136.

——(ed.), *Studies on Gersonides: A Fourteenth-Century Jewish Philosopher-Scientist* (Leiden, 1992).

FRIEDLAENDER, PAUL, *Plato*, 3 vols. (New York, 1958).

FURTH, MONTGOMERY, *Substance and Form: An Aristotelian Metaphysics* (Cambridge, 1988).

GILLMAN, N., *The Death of Death: Resurrection and Immortality in Jewish Thought* (Woodstock, Vt., 1997).

GILSON, ETIENNE, *Reason and Revelation in the Middle Ages* (New York, 1938).

GINZBERG, LOUIS, *Legends of the Jews*, 7 vols. (Philadelphia, 1909–38).

GLASNER, RUTH, 'The Early Stages in the Evolution of Gersonides' *The Wars of the Lord*', *Jewish Quarterly Review*, 87 (1996), 1–47.

——'Gersonides' Lost Commentary on the *Metaphysics*', *Medieval Encounters*, 4 (1998), 130–57.

——'Gersonides on Simple and Composite Motions', *Studies in the History and Philosophy of Science*, 28 (1997), 545–84.

——'Gersonides' Theory of Natural Motion', *Early Science and Medicine*, 1 (1996), 151–203.

——'Knowledge of Arabic among Jewish Scholars in Fourteenth Century Provence: Levi ben Gershom (Gersonides)', *Aleph*, 2 (2002), 235–57.

——'Levi ben Gershom and the Study of ibn Rushd in the 14th Century', *Jewish Quarterly Review*, 86 (1995), 51–90.

——'On the Question of Gersonides' Acquaintance with Scholastic Philosophy', in C. Sirat, S. Klein-Braslavy, and O. Weijers (eds.), *Les Méthodes de travail de Gersonide et le maniement du savoir chez les scolastiques* (Paris, 2003), 281–7.

GOLDSTEIN, BERNARD, *The Astronomy of Levi ben Gerson (1288–1344)* (Berlin, 1985).

GOLDSTEIN, BERNARD, 'Levi ben Gerson's Theory of Planetary Distances', *Centaurus*, 29 (1986), 272–313.

—— 'The Physical Astronomy of Levi ben Gerson', *Perspectives in Science*, 5 (1997), 1–30.

—— 'Preliminary Remarks Concerning Levi ben Gerson's Contributions to Astronomy', *Proceedings of the Israel Academy of Sciences and Humanities*, 3 (1969), 174–85.

GOLDSTEIN, HELEN T., 'Dator Formarum: Ibn Rushd, Levi ben Gerson and Moses ben Joshua of Narbonne', in I. al-Faruqi and A. Nassif (eds.), *Essays in Islamic and Comparative Studies* (Washington, DC, 1982), 107–21.

GOTTHELF, A., and J. LENNOX (eds.), *Philosophical Issues in Aristotle's Biology* (Cambridge, 1987).

GRANT, EDWARD, *God and Reason in the Middle Ages* (Cambridge, 2001).

—— *Planets, Stars, and Orbs: The Medieval Cosmos, 1200–1687* (Cambridge, 1994).

GUTTMANN, JULIUS, 'Levi ben Gerson's Theory of the Concept' (Heb.), in S. Bergmann and N. Rotenstreich (eds.), *Religion and Knowledge* [Dat umada] (Jerusalem, 1955), 136–48.

—— 'Mendelssohn's Jerusalem and Spinoza's Theological-Political Treatise' (Heb.), in Samuel Bergmann and Natan Rotenstreich (eds.), *Religion and Knowledge* [Dat umada] (Jerusalem, 1955), 192–217.

—— *Philosophies of Judaism*, trans. David W. Silverman (New York, 1973).

HADOT, PIERRE, *What Is Ancient Philosophy?*, trans. M. Chase (Cambridge, Mass., 2002).

HALLAMISH, MOSHE, and AVI RAVITSKY (eds.), *The Land of Israel in Medieval Jewish Thought* [Erets yisra'el bahagut hayehudit biyemei habeinayim] (Jerusalem, 1991).

HAMELIN, OCTAVE, *La Théorie de l'intellect d'après Aristote et ses commenteurs* (Paris, 1953).

HAWKING, STEPHEN, 'The Origin of the Universe', in id., *Black Holes and Baby Universes* (London, 1993), 85–100.

HERTZ, J. H., *The Pentateuch and Haftorahs* (London, 1960).

HICKS, ROBERT (ed.), *Aristotle: De Anima* (Cambridge, 1907).

HUSIK, ISAAC, *A History of Medieval Jewish Philosophy* (Philadelphia, 1948).

HYMAN, ARTHUR, and JAMES WALSH (eds.), *Philosophy in the Middle Ages* (Indianapolis, 1987).

IVRY, ALFRED, 'Averroes on Intellect and Conjunction', *Journal of the American Oriental Society*, 86/2 (1966), 76–85.

—— 'Averroes' Three Commentaries on *De Anima*', in G. Endress and J. Aertsen (eds.), *Averroes and the Aristotelian Tradition* (Leiden, 1999), 199–216.

—— 'Conjunction in and of Maimonides and Averroës', in J.-B. Brenet (ed.), *Averroës et les averroïsmes juif et latin* (Brepols, 2005), 231–47.

—— 'Gersonides and Averroes on the Intellect: The Evidence of the Supercommentary on the *De anima*', in G. Dahan (ed.), *Gersonide et son temps* (Louvain and Paris, 1991), 235–51.

KAUFMANN, DAVID, *Geschichte der Attributenlehre in der juedischen Religionsphilosophie des Mittelalters von Saadja bis Maimuni* (Gotha, 1877).

KELLNER, MENACHEM, 'Gersonides and his Cultured Despisers: Arama and Abravanel', *Journal of Medieval and Renaissance Studies*, 6 (1976), 269–96.

—— 'Gersonides on Miracles, the Messiah and Resurrection' (Heb.), *Da'at*, 4 (1980), 5–34.

—— 'Gersonides, Providence and the Rabbinic Tradition', *Journal of the American Academy of Religion*, 42 (1974), 673–85.

—— 'Gersonides on the Role of the Active Intellect in Human Cognition', *Hebrew Union College Annual*, 65 (1994), 233–59.

—— 'Maimonides and Gersonides on Mosaic Prophecy', *Speculum*, 52 (1977), 62–79.

—— *Maimonides on Judaism and the Jewish People* (Albany, NY, 1991).

KENNY, ANTHONY, 'Divine Foreknowledge and Human Freedom', in id. (ed.), *Aquinas: A Collection of Critical Essays* (New York, 1969), 255–72.

KLEIN-BRASLAVY, SARA, 'Les Commentaires bibliques: Les Introductions', in C. Sirat, S. Klein-Braslavy, and O. Weijers (eds.), *Les Méthodes de travail de Gersonide et le maniement du savoir chez les scolastiques* (Paris, 2003), 193–215.

—— 'Gersonides on Determinism, Possibility, Choice and Foreknowledge' (Heb.), *Da'at*, 22 (1989), 5–53.

—— 'Gersonides on the Mode of Communicating Knowledge of the Future to the Dreamer and the Clairvoyant', in A. Ivry, E. Wolfson, and A. Arkush (eds.), *Perspectives on Jewish Thought and Mysticism* (Amsterdam, 1998), 171–200.

—— 'Gersonides' Use of the *Meteorology* in his Accounts of Miracles', *Aleph* (forthcoming).

—— 'Les Méthodes diaporematiques de Gersonides dans les *Guerres de Seigneur*', in C. Sirat, S. Klein-Braslavy, and O. Weijers (eds.), *Les Méthodes de Gersonide et le maniement du savoir chez les scolastiques* (Paris, 2003), 105–34.

—— 'Prophecy, Clairvoyance and Dreams and the Concept of "Isolation" in Gersonides' Thought' (Heb.), *Da'at*, 39 (1997), 23–68.

KNEALE, WILLIAM, and MARTHA KNEALE, *The Development of Logic* (Oxford, 1962).

KREISEL, HOWARD, 'The Land of Israel and Prophecy in Medieval Jewish Philosophy' (Heb.), in M. Hallamish and A. Ravitsky (eds.), *The Land of Israel in Medieval Jewish Thought* [Erets yisra'el bahagut hayehudit biyemei habeinayim] (Jerusalem, 1991), 40-51.

—— 'Miracles in Medieval Jewish Philosophy', *Jewish Quarterly Review*, 75 (1984), 99–133.

—— *Prophecy: The History of an Idea in Medieval Jewish Philosophy* (Dordrecht, 2001).

—— 'Verificatory Dreams and Prophecy in Gersonides' (Heb.), *Da'at*, 22 (1989), 73–84.

LANGERMANN, TZVI, 'Gersonides and Astrology', in *The Wars of the Lord*, trans. Seymour Feldman, vol. iii (Philadelphia, 1999), 506–19.

LEAMAN, OLIVER, *Evil and Suffering in Jewish Philosophy* (Cambridge, 1995).

—— *Introduction to Classical Islamic Philosophy* (Cambridge, 2002).

LENNOX, JAMES, 'Kinds, Forms of Kinds', in A. Gotthelf and J. Lennox (eds.), *Philosophical Issues in Aristotle's Biology* (Cambridge, 1987), 341–59.

LERNER, R., and M. MAHDI, *Medieval Political Philosophy: A Sourcebook* (New York, 1963).

LEVY, TONY, 'Gersonide commentateur d'Euclide: Traduction annotée de ses glosses sur les *Eléments*', in Gad Freudenthal (ed.), *Studies on Gersonides: A Fourteenth-Century Jewish Philosopher-Scientist* (Leiden, 1992), 83–147.

LUCAS, JOHN, *The Freedom of the Will* (Oxford, 1970).

MANCHA, JOSE-LUIS, 'Gersonides' Astronomical Work: Chronology and Christian Context', in C. Sirat, S. Klein-Braslavy, and O. Weijers (eds.), *Les Méthodes de Gersonide et le maniement du savoir chez les scolastiques* (Paris, 2003), 39–58.

MANEKIN, CHARLES, 'Conservative Tendencies in Gersonides' Religious Philosophy', in D. Frank and O. Leaman (eds.), *The Cambridge Companion to Medieval Jewish Philosophy* (Cambridge, 2003), 304–44.

—— *The Logic of Gersonides* (Dordrecht, 1992).

—— 'On the Limited-Omniscience Interpretation of Gersonides' Theory of Divine Knowledge', in A. Ivry, E. Wolfson, and A. Arkush (eds.), *Perspectives in Jewish Thought and Mysticism* (Amsterdam, 1998), 135–70.

MARMURA, MICHAEL, 'Some Aspects of Avicenna's Theory of God's Foreknowledge of Particulars', *Journal of the Association of Oriental Studies*, 82 (1962), 299–312.

MELAMED, ABRAHAM, 'The Land of Israel and the Theory of Climates in Jewish Thought' (Heb.), in M. Hallamish and A. Ravitsky (eds.), *The Land of Israel in Medieval Jewish Thought* [Erets yisra'el bahagut hayehudit biyemei habeinayim] (Jerusalem, 1991), 52–78.

—— 'The Law of Nature in Jewish Political Thought in the Middle Ages and the Renaissance' (Heb.), *Da'at*, 17 (1986), 49–66.

MERLAN, PHILIP, *Monopsychism, Mysticism, Metaconsciousness* (The Hague, 1963).

MOODY, ERNEST, *The Logic of William of Ockham* (New York, 1965).

MOORE, GEORGE F., *Judaism*, 2 vols. (Cambridge, Mass., 1954).

MORAUX, PAUL, *Alexandre d'Aphrodise* (Paris, 1942).

PETERS, FRANCIS E., *Jerusalem: The Holy City in the Eyes of Chroniclers, Visitors, Pilgrims and Prophets from the Days of Abraham to the Beginnings of Modern Times* (Princeton, 1985).

PIKE, NELSON, 'Divine Omniscience and Voluntary Action', *Philosophical Review*, 74 (1965), 27–46.

—— *God and Timelessness* (London, 1970).

PINES, SHLOMO, 'The Limitations of Human Knowledge According to Al-Farabi, Ibn Bajja and Maimonides', in I. Twersky (ed.), *Studies in Medieval Jewish History and Literature*, vol. i (Cambridge, Mass., 1979), 82–109.

—— 'Scholasticism after Thomas Aquinas and the Teachings of Hasdai Crescas and his Predecessors', *Proceedings of the Israel Academy of Sciences and Humanities*, 10 (1967), 1–101.

PRIOR, ARTHUR, *Formal Logic* (Oxford, 1962).

—— *Past, Present and Future* (Oxford, 1967).

QUINN, PHILIP, 'Moral Obligation, Religious Demand and Practical Conflict', in R. Audi and W. Wainwright (eds.), *Rationality, Religious Belief and Moral Commitment* (Ithaca, NY, 1986), 195–212.

RACHELS, JAMES, 'God and Goodness', in S. Cahn (ed.), *Exploring Philosophy of Religion* (New York, 2009), 5–7.

RAVITSKY, AVI, 'The Anthropological Theory of Miracles' (Heb.), *Jerusalem Studies in Jewish Thought*, 2 (1983), 323–61.

REALE, GIOVANNI, *A History of Ancient Philosophy: The Schools of the Imperial Age*, iv (Albany, NY, 1990).

RIST, JOHN, *Plotinus: The Road to Reality* (Cambridge, 1967).

ROSENTHAL, ERWIN I., *Averroes' Commentary on Plato's Republic* (Cambridge, 1956).

ROSENTHAL, ERWIN I., 'The Place of Politics in the Philosophy of ibn Rushd', *British Society of Oriental and African Studies*, 15 (1953), 258–63.

—— *Political Thought in Medieval Islam* (Cambridge, 1958).

RUDAVSKY, TAMAR, 'Divine Omniscience, Contingency and Prophecy in Gersonides', in T. Rudavsky (ed.), *Divine Omniscience and Omnipotence in Medieval Philosophy* (Dordrecht, 1984), 161–81.

—— 'Divine Omniscience and Future Contingencies in Gersonides', *Journal of the History of Philosophy*, 21 (1983), 513–36.

—— 'The Jewish Tradition: Maimonides, Gersonides and Bedersi', in J. J. E. Gracia (ed.), *Individuation in Scholasticism: The Later Middle Ages and the Counter-Reformation, 1150–1650* (Albany, NY, 1994), 69–96.

—— *Time Matters* (Albany, NY, 2000).

SAMBURSKY, SAMUEL, *The Physical World of the Greeks* (Princeton, 1962).

SAMUELSON, NORBERT, 'Gersonides' Account of God's Knowledge of Particulars', *Journal of the History of Philosophy*, 10 (1972), 399–416.

SCHABEL, CHRIS, 'Philosophy and Theology across Cultures: Gersonides and Auriol on Divine Foreknowledge', *Speculum*, 81 (2006), 1092–1117.

SCHROEDER, GERALD, *Genesis and the Big Bang* (New York, 1991).

—— *The Science of God: The Convergence of Scientific and Biblical Wisdom* (New York, 1998).

SCHWARZSCHILD, STEVEN, 'Do Noachites Have to Believe in Revelation?', *Jewish Quarterly Review*, 52 (1962), 297–308; 53 (1963), 330–65.

SEESKIN, KENNETH, *Maimonides on the Origin of the World* (Cambridge, 2005).

SERMONETTA, JOSEPH, 'La dottrina dell'intelletto e la "fede filosofia" de Jehudah e Immanuel Romano', *Studi Medievali*, 3rd ser., 6/2 (1965), 3–78.

SHATZMILLER, JOSEPH, 'Gersonide et la société juive de son temps', in G. Dahan (ed.), *Gersonide en son temps* (Paris, 1991), 33–43.

—— 'Gersonides and the Jewish Community of Orange', *Studies in the History of the Jewish People and the Land of Israel*, 2 (1972), 111–26.

SHAVIT, YAACOV, *Athens in Jerusalem: Classical Antiquity and Hellenism in the Making of the Modern Secular Jew* (London, 1997).

SILVERMAN, DAVID WOLF, 'Some Remarks of Gersonides concerning Prophecy', in A. Chiel (ed.), *Perspectives on Jews and Judaism: Essays in Honor of Wolfe Kelman* (New York, 1978), 395–408.

SIRAT, COLETTE, *A History of Jewish Philosophy in the Middle Ages* (Cambridge, 1990).

——'La Méthode d'exégèse suivie d'une brève analyse de l'exégèse de deux péricopes de la Torah', in C. Sirat, S. Klein-Braslavy, and O. Weijers (eds.), *Les Méthodes de travail de Gersonide et le maniement du savoir chez les scolastiques* (Paris, 2003), 215–58.

——'Le Problème posé par les rapports entre Gersonide et le milieu ambiant', in C. Sirat, S. Klein-Braslavy, and O. Weijers (eds.), *Les Méthodes de travail de Gersonide et le maniement du savoir chez les scolastiques* (Paris, 2003), 9–32.

—— *Les Théories des visions surnaturelles* (Leiden, 1969).

——SARA KLEIN-BRASLAVY, and OLGA WEIJERS (eds.), *Les Méthodes de travail de Gersonide et le maniement du savoir chez les scolastiques* (Paris, 2003).

SORABJI, RICHARD (ed.), *Philoponus and the Rejection of Aristotelian Science* (Ithaca, NY, 1987).

—— *Time, Creation and the Continuum* (Ithaca, NY, 1983).

STAUB, JACOB, *The Creation of the World According to Gersonides* (Chico, Calif., 1982).

STEINSCHNEIDER, MORITZ, *Die hebraeischen Uebersetzungen des Mittelalters und die Juden als Dolmetscher* (Berlin, 1893; repr. Graz, 1956).

STERN, JOSEF, 'Maimonides on the Growth of Knowledge and the Limitations of the Intellect', in T. Levy and R. Rashed (eds.), *Maimonide: Philosophe et savant* (Louvain, 2004), 143–91.

STRAUSS, LEO, 'Jerusalem and Athens: Some Introductory Reflections', in id., *Studies in Platonic Political Philosophy* (Chicago, 1983), 147–73.

—— *Persecution and the Art of Writing* (Glencoe, Ill., 1952).

—— *Philosophy and Law: Essays Toward the Understanding of Maimonides and his Predecessors* (Philadelphia, 1987).

SWINBURNE, RICHARD, *The Coherence of Theism* (Oxford, 1977).

TESTER, S. JAMES, *A History of Western Astrology* (Wolfeboro, NH, 1987).

TOUATI, CHARLES, 'Les Idées philosophiques et théologiques de Gersonide dans ses commentaires bibliques', *Revue des Sciences Religieuses*, 28 (1954), 335–67.

—— *La Pensée philosophique et théologique de Gersonide* (Paris, 1973).

——'Les Problèmes de la génération et le rôle de l'intellect agent chez Averroës', in J. Jolivet (ed.), *Multiple Averroës* (Paris, 1978), 157–65.

——'Théorie et praxis', in G. Dahan (ed.), *Gersonide en son temps* (Paris, 1991), 151–8.

TWERSKY, ISADORE, 'The Land of Israel and Exile in the Teaching of Maimonides' (Heb.), in Moshe Hallamish and Avi Ravitsky (eds.), *The Land of Israel in Medieval Jewish Thought* [Erets yisra'el bahagut hayehudit biyemei habeinayim] (Jerusalem, 1991), 90–122.

VLASTOS, GREGORY, 'Creation in the *Timaeus*. Is It a Fiction?', in R. Allen (ed.), *Studies in Plato's Metaphysics* (London, 1965), 401–19.

—— 'The Disorderly Motion in the *Timaeus*', in R. Allen (ed.), *Studies in Plato's Metaphysics* (London, 1965), 379–99.

WEIJERS, OLGA, ' Le Cursus des études et le cadre institutionel et intellectuel juif et chrétien', in C. Sirat, S. Klein-Braslavy, and O. Weijers (eds.), *Les Méthodes de travail de Gersonide et le maniement du savoir chez les scolastiques* (Paris, 2003), 18–31.

WOLFSON, HARRY A., 'Hallevi and Maimonides on Prophecy', in I. Twersky and G. H. Williams (eds.), *Studies in the History and Philosophy of Religion*, ii (Cambridge, Mass., 1977), 60–119.

—— 'Maimonides and Gersonides on Divine Attributes as Ambiguous Terms', in *Mordecai M. Kaplan Jubilee Volume* (New York, 1953), 515–30.

—— 'Maimonides on Negative Attributes', in *Louis Ginzberg Jubilee Volume* (New York, 1945), 411–46.

—— 'Notes on the Proofs of the Existence of God in Jewish Philosophy', *Hebrew Union College Annual*, I (1924), 575–96, repr. in id., *Studies in the History of Philosophy and Religion*, i (Cambridge, Mass., 1973), 561–82.

—— *The Philosophy of the Kalam* (Cambridge, Mass., 1976).

—— 'Plato's Pre-Existent Matter in Patristic Philosophy', in id., *Studies in the History of Philosophy and Religion*, i (Cambridge, Mass., 1973), 170–81.

WOLTERSTORFF NICHOLAS, *Reason within the Bounds of Religion* (Grand Rapids, Mich., 1976).

YOVEL, YIRMIYAHU, *Spinoza and Other Heretics: The Adventures of Immanence*, vol. ii (Princeton, 1989).

Index

A

Abraham ibn Ezra 8, 57, 97–9, 127, 141, 208–9
Abravanel, Isaac 53, 94, 144 n. 41, 231
abstraction 182, 186
Agent Intellect:
  cause of dreams, divination, and prophecy 112–14, 147–57, 161
  cause of miracles 140–3
  cause of reproduction 64–7, 183–5
  'giver forms' 64, 183–4
  relationship to God and the other separate intellects 67, 185
  role in human cognition 173–5, 183–5, 189–96, 219
  role in immortality 175–6
  role in providence 118–20
Akiva, Rabbi 81–4, 95–6, 106
Alexander of Aphrodisias 12, 82, 174–6, 181, 186, 189, 195
Al-Farabi 35, 146–7, 175–6, 186, 199–200
Al-Ghazali 139 n. 26, 200
allegory 2, 209–12
Altmann, Alexander 186
angels 64, 214–15
  role in prophecy 160–1
  see also intellect: separate
Anselm's ontological argument 60
Aquinas, Thomas 8, 13–14, 59–60, 102, 191
Arama, Isaac 94, 144 n. 41
Aristotle:
  creation vs. eternity of the universe 10, 28, 32, 38–44
  foreknowledge 82, 86, 88–9, 93–4
  immortality 12, 172–4
  prophecy 146–7
  providence 105, 122–3
astrology 90–1 n. 28, 108–11, 152
astronomy 5, 18, 23, 26

Augustine of Hippo 83, 198
Auriol, Peter 103
Averroes (ibn Rushd):
  on the cause of reproduction 64–7
  commentaries on Aristotle 4–5, 7–8;
    Epitome of the Parva Naturalia 148–50; *Long Commentary on Aristotle's Metaphysics* 66; *Long Commentary on Aristotle's On the Soul* 190; *Middle Commentary on Aristotle's Metaphysics* 4; *Middle Commentary on Aristotle's On the Soul* 190
  on conjunction with the Agent Intellect 189–95
  on dreams, divination, and prophecy 146–55
  on human intellect 189–92
  On the Harmony of Religion and Philosophy (*Kitab fasl al-maqal*; *The Decisive Treatise*) 226
  on reason and revelation 13–14, 200, 226–7, 229
Avicenna (ibn Sina) 35, 64, 69, 83

B

biblical exegesis 6–7, 19–21, 55–7, 95, 99–100, 208–16
body:
  'the body that doesn't preserve its shape' 51–5, 57, 234
  celestial bodies 10, 45–7, 62
Boethius 83, 104–5

C

Cantor, Georg 44
choice (free will) 81–3, 88, 91–2, 97–8, 100–1
Christian scholasticism 2, 8–9, 101–3

cognition:
  divine 83–6, 90–3, 96–7, 100, 229; *see also* foreknowledge
  human 173–6, 181–7; *see also* intellect: acquired
Cohen, Hermann 224–5, 235
contingency 81–2, 86, 88–92, 94, 100, 102–3
cosmology, Aristotle's 10, 55–7, 211
creation of the world:
  Aristotle's arguments against, *see* Aristotle: creation vs. eternity of the universe
  biblical account 48–51
  from matter (*ex aliquo*) 29–30, 51–5, 123–4
  from nothing (*ex nihilo*) 11, 28, 48–51, 56, 123–4
  Gersonides' proofs 31–44
  Maimonides, *see* Maimonides
  Philoponus (John the Grammarian), *see* Philoponus, John
  Plato, *see* Plato, on creation
Crescas, Hasdai 94, 131, 231

D
determinism, *see* contingency
Deuteronomy:
  Gersonides' commentary on 7, 129–30, 162, 205–6, 223
divination 108–11, 148–50, 152
dreams 110–11, 146, 148–50
Duns Scotus, John 103
Duran, Profiat (Efodi) 84 n. 12

E
Ecclesiastes:
  Gersonides' commentary on 6, 204
Elisha ben Abuya 106, 122
emanation 35–6, 49, 62–3
empiricism 23, 26–7
Epicurus 24, 82, 104, 106, 218
eschatology 176–7
eternity of the universe:
  Gersonides' critique 31–44
  see also Aristotle: creation vs. eternity of the universe

ethics 202–7
Euclid:
  Gersonides' commentary on the *Elements* 5–6, 23
evil, causes, *see* matter: source of evil and imperfection
Ezekiel 32

F
falasifa (Muslim philosophy) 35
foreknowledge 81–103, 229
  divine, *see* cognition: divine
form vs. matter 62, 64–8, 181–3, 219–21

G
'general natures' 186–7
  see also universals
Glasner, Ruth 9
God:
  attributes 69–80
  Gersonides' critique of Maimonides' doctrine of negative attributes 72–80
  not the mover of a celestial sphere 69
  proofs of the existence 59–63, 65, 68

H
hesed (loving kindness) 15
hitbodedut (isolation) 155–7
holiness 220–1
human happiness 18, 172–80, 188–9
  see also immortality
Hume, David 1, 135, 207
Husik, Isaac 99

I
Ibn Bajja 179–80, 195
Ibn Tibbon, Samuel 8, 98
imagination 113–14, 149–57, 161, 187
immortality 15–16, 121, 172–97
  conjunction of the human intellect with the Agent Intellect 176, 189–97
  individual 176, 179–80, 187–9, 191–2, 229
indestructibility of the universe 44–8
intellect:
  acquired intellect 175–6, 181, 187–9
  Agent Intellect, *see* Agent Intellect

divine intellect, *see* cognition: divine
human (material) intellect 174–5,
  180–7, 219
separate intellects 61, 63–4, 66–8, 188,
  214
see also cognition: human
Israel:
  land 125–30
  people 16, 124–30, 220–1
Ivry, Alfred 190

J
Job 15, 107, 115–20, 209
Judah Halevi 11, 127, 200

K
Kalam (Muslim theology) 37–8, 65, 83,
  107–8, 115, 202, 217
Kant, Immanuel 1, 65, 85, 207, 224, 235
Kaufmann, David 70
Kellner, Menachem 237
Kenny, Anthony 100 n. 48
Kierkegaard, Søren 226

L
Latin Averroists 8
logic, Gersonides' writings on 3–4, 9

M
Maimonides, Moses:
  biblical exegesis 19–21, 209–13, 227–8
  on the commandments 217–18, 220
  on creation 10–11, 21, 28–30, 35, 50–1
  on divine attributes 69–75
  on divine cognition, or foreknowledge
    83–5, 87–8, 98–9, 229
  on immortality 13, 177–80, 186–9, 230
  on the messiah 163
  on miracles 133–4, 136–8
  on prophecy 145–8, 152–5, 157–62, 164,
    170
  on providence 107–8, 115, 120–2
  on reason and revelation 200–2, 226–8,
    232
  on resurrection 134, 178
  on sacrifices 158
matter:
  role in creation 48–55, 57

source of evil and imperfection 117,
  123–4, 219–21
messiah, the 163–4, 223
metaphysics 23–4
methodology, of Gersonides 20–7
Mill, J. S. 207
miracles 56, 131–44, 228–9
  agent 135–6, 140–4
  domain 136–40
  'law of miracles' 139–44
  role of prophet 140–4
Moses Narboni 8

N
natural law 206–7
Neoplatonism 7, 39, 104
  see also Plotinus; Proclus
Newton, Isaac 35

O
Obadiah of Bertinoro 133
omnipotence, *see* miracles
omniscience, *see* foreknowledge
Origen 53

P
Philo of Alexandria:
  biblical exegesis 209–10
  on the commandments 221
  on creation and matter 52–3
  On the Creation of the World 132
  on the Logos and the Agent Intellect
    113, 184, 215–16
  on miracles 131–2
  on providence 105
Philoponus, John 4, 7, 42, 46, 233 n. 27
Pike, Nelson 100 n. 48
Pines, Shlomo 8, 98, 101–3, 180
Plato:
  on creation 11, 28 n. 1 30, 38, 45, 48–55
  on forms 67, 183, 185, 194
  on immortality 172
  on knowledge and belief 91
  on matter and evil 221
  on prophecy 145–7
  on providence 104
  on the soul 172, 187

Plotinus:
  on emanation 29
  on immortality 172, 191
  and Neoplatonism 7
  on the Nous (Intellect) 67, 113, 181,
    215–16
  on providence 104
  on separate intellects 10, 61
Prior, Arthur 100 n. 48
Proclus 46, 104
proofs of creation 42, 46
prophecy:
  general theory 145–7
  Gersonides' theory 147–59
  and miracles 140–4, 162, 164–5
  Moses' prophecies 159–65
  role of music and sacrifices in 157–9
  testing of the prophet 166–71
providence 104–30
  general 104–5
  individual 104–15, 128
  and Israel 124–30
Psalms 15
Ptolemy 5
  and astrology 108–11, 170

R
Rashi (Rabbi Solomon ben Isaac of
    Troyes) 208
reason and revelation 18, 21–2, 198–202,
  230–5
resurrection of the dead 163

S
Sa'adiah Gaon:
  biblical exegesis 8, 212
  Book of Beliefs and Opinions 8, 199
  on the commandments 217 n. 65
  on creation from matter 53
  on creation from nothing 48–9
  on foreknowledge 84 n. 12
  on the immutability of the Torah 222
  on miracles 133, 136
  on reason and revelation 199, 202

sacrifices 158
Schabel, Chris 103
Sermonetta, Joseph 8
Shatzmiller, Joseph 2
Sirat, Colette 99
Song of Songs:
  Gersonides' commentary on 6, 68,
    211
soul, *see* immortality
Spinoza 1, 35, 76, 154, 198, 224, 232
Strauss, Leo 226–7
sufferings of the righteous 115–24

T
teleology 32, 65
  and creation 32–6
Tempier, Stephen 9
Tertullian 198, 225–6
Thales 114
Themistius 7, 12, 64, 181, 190
time:
  and creation 38–42
  future 42–3, 82, 86, 88–90
Torah 198–223
  commandments 19, 216–21
  Gersonides' commentary on 6, 14–16,
    19, 25
  immutability of 221–3
  and philosophy 198–208
Touati, Charles 171

U
universals 17, 108 n. 16
  role in immortality, *see* immortality
  see also abstraction; 'general natures'

V
vacuum 10, 50

W
William of Ockham 9, 103
Wolfson, Harry 70
Wolterstorff, Nicholas 225, 227

Printed and bound by CPI Group (UK) Ltd, Croydon, CR0 4YY

13/04/2025